Teaching
Against Islamophobia

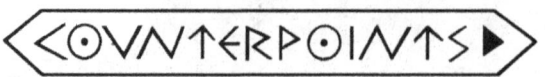

Studies in the
Postmodern Theory of Education

Shirley R. Steinberg
General Editor

Vol. 346

PETER LANG
New York • Washington, D.C./Baltimore • Bern
Frankfurt • Berlin • Brussels • Vienna • Oxford

Teaching Against Islamophobia

EDITED BY Joe L. Kincheloe, Shirley R. Steinberg, Christopher D. Stonebanks

PETER LANG
New York • Washington, D.C./Baltimore • Bern
Frankfurt • Berlin • Brussels • Vienna • Oxford

Library of Congress Cataloging-in-Publication Data

Teaching against Islamophobia / edited by Joe L. Kincheloe,
Shirley R. Steinberg, Christopher D. Stonebanks.
p. cm. — (Counterpoints: studies in the postmodern theory of education; 346)
Includes bibliographical references.
1. Islam—Study and teaching—United States. 2. Islamophobia—United States.
3. Muslims—Public opinion. 4. United States—Public opinion.
I. Kincheloe, Joe L. II. Steinberg, Shirley R. III. Stonebanks, Christopher Darius.
BP43.U5T43   297.2'9—dc22   2010011436
ISBN 978-1-4331-0808-2 (hardcover)
ISBN 978-1-4331-0336-0 (paperback)
ISSN 1058-1634

Bibliographic information published by Die Deutsche Nationalbibliothek.
Die Deutsche Nationalbibliothek lists this publication in the "Deutsche
Nationalbibliografie"; detailed bibliographic data is available
on the Internet at http://dnb.d-nb.de/.

Cover art by Daniel Luna

The paper in this book meets the guidelines for permanence and durability
of the Committee on Production Guidelines for Book Longevity
of the Council of Library Resources.

© 2010 Peter Lang Publishing, Inc., New York
29 Broadway, 18th floor, New York, NY 10006
www.peterlang.com

All rights reserved.
Reprint or reproduction, even partially, in all forms such as microfilm,
xerography, microfiche, microcard, and offset strictly prohibited.

Printed in the United States of America

This book is dedicated to all of my Muslim relatives, friends, students and colleagues who, unlike many non-Muslim counterparts, have never asked where my religious allegiance lies or tried to convince me that I am, or am not, Muslim

— Christopher D. Stonebanks

To our kids, in a hope that they will continue to celebrate their Jewishness by embracing social justice and equity for all Semitic peoples

—Shirley R. Steinberg and Joe L. Kincheloe

Contents

Foreword
 Re-educating against Miseducation ix

Part One: There Is No One "Muslim World"

One
 Why Teach against Islamophobia: Striking the Empire Back........... 3
  Joe L. Kincheloe and Shirley R. Steinberg
Two
 The Inescapable Presence of 'Non-existent' Islamophobia........... 29
  Christopher D. Stonebanks
Three
 Islam: The Fundamentals Every Teacher Should Know 49
  Khurrum Mirza and Naved Bakali
Four
 What Is Islam? A Conversation with the Magisterial
  Intellectuals of the Past 65
  Hassan Ahmad Mian

Part Two: Reading Islamophobia

Five
 Islamophobia: The Viewed and the Viewers...................... 79
  Shirley R. Steinberg
Six
 Holy Islamophobia, Batman! Demonization of Muslims and
  Arabs in Mainstream American Comic Books 99
  Jehanzeb Dar
Seven
 "Mad Man Hassan Will Buy Your Carpets!": The Bearded
  Curricula of Evil Muslims 111
  Özlem Sensoy
Eight
 Barack Obama, Islamophobia, and the
  2008 U.S. Presidential Election Media Spectacle................. 135
  Michael D. Giardina

Part Three: Categories on the Board — "Muslims You Never Knew"

Nine
The Undercover Muslim: An African American Perspective on Transitions of Muslim Identity..................161
Preacher Moss

Ten
Faith or Fight: Islam in the African American Community 169
Samaa Abdurraqib

Eleven
The Dialectics of Islamophobia and Homophobia in the Lives of Gay Muslims in the United States.....................187
Younes Mourchid

Twelve
"Yes, My Name is Ibrahim and I Am an Atheist!" Confessing Asrar: Atheism, Arts, Answerability, Imagination and the Muslim You Have Never Known 205
Awad Ibrahim

Thirteen
Know the Ledge but Don't Hit the Edge: Building with the God Jahmega Allah..215
Habib Siam

Fourteen
Pieces of Iman: The Pilgrimage Home.........................227
Yassin Alsalman

Part Four: Teaching Against Islamophobia

Fifteen
Common Sense, Uncommon Knowledge and Fighting Words.......239
Carolyne Ali-Khan

Sixteen
Footnotes on Reflective Practice..............................269
Anastasia Kamanos Gamelin

Seventeen
A Frank Intercourse: Combating Islamophobia in Sex Education 281
Fida Sanjakdar

Eighteen
A *Bifocal* Lens on Islamophobia: Using Young Adult Fiction as a Teaching Tool..................297
Krista Riley

Nineteen
Teaching Islamic Themes at the College Level....................309
Sevak Manjikian

Twenty
"How Do You Expect Me to Teach This without Any Resources?"...321
Melanie Stonebanks

Contributors..331

Foreword

Re-educating against Miseducation

This is a book for teachers, a way to open a discussion about the racism and fear that has been created through what we call Islamophobia. Naturally, we are aware that there are many racisms and that Islamic and Arabic peoples are not the exclusive victims of hatred. However, this book will specifically address issues which apply to those who are Muslim or who come from largely Muslim countries. We use the term Islamophobia to isolate instances which have been applied to Islamic peoples or those who appear to be Muslim…naturally, all Muslims are not Arabs, and not all Arabs are Muslims, but in an Islamophobicly constructed 21st century, those who perpetuate crimes of hatred and discrimination don't ask for nuanced identities.

Islam has become a target of discrimination and bigotry and has often been misconstrued in the media, vilified by news pundits, religious leaders, and politicians, and is a subject of miseducation in schools. We categorize these acts as Islamophobic. A short but current list delineates some global incidents:

- The 2005 youth riots in France which blamed Muslims for their inability to integrate and assimilate
- The Danish *Jyllands-Posten's* publication of unfavorable cartoons of the Prophet Mohammed

- The suggestion that Muslim women wearing *hijabs* was anti-feminist (by non-Muslim women)
- The refusal of Muslim prayer space in universities
- The continued detainment of and accusations surrounding "home-grown" terror plots of countless Muslims in North America
- Suspicion of terrorist sympathies in Muslim youth born in Western countries

Muslims have been defined inaccurately by media and politicians, perpetuating a misinformation "trickledown" in communities and schools. Muslims and Arabic peoples often live under a political climate and an education system that has continued to create Islamophobic perceptions in many citizens.

The term, "Islamophobia" creates controversy, with notable authors, such as Rushdie and Manji (2009), writing that they "… refuse to renounce our critical spirit out of fear of being accused of 'Islamophobia,' a wretched concept that confuses criticism of Islam as a religion and stigmatisation of those who believe in it." Adding to the confusion between Islam and the variances of those who call themselves "Muslim" is the use of the term "phobia," which alludes to some kind of mental illness, an involuntary revulsion of sorts when confronted with the Qur'an, prayer rugs, or Muslims in general as opposed to a learned bias.

Although we recognize the limitations of the term Islamophobia, we understand that it defines experiences of discrimination, dehumanization, and misrepresentations of Muslims, those of Muslim heritage, and a systemic miseducation about Islam itself. Islamophobic bias has targeted a large mosaic of people associated with the religion and amalgamated them as one. The *Ummah*, the global Muslim community and collective consciousness including those Muslims living in diaspora, has been in a continued state of varying assault. From the physical violence at such places as Bosnia, Iraq, and Afghanistan to assault on identity, as can be seen in the overwhelming portrayal of Muslims and people associated with "Islamic countries," Islamophobia has played a hand in the overt and tacit acceptance of the majority in the West to these horrific and disturbing actions.

In this sense, we recognize that current aggressive actions against Muslims in the East and the West stem from the historic Islamophobic views of the East and, as a consequence, we frame our theoretical approach of this manuscript in a "de-colonizing" or "anti-colonial," critical pedagogy, acknowledging that Islamophobia reflects the ongoing experience of colonialism and imperialism. It is important to note that colonialism is not a "thing of the past," but an ongoing reality for much of the world. If educators are committed to breaking the cycle of prejudice and bias against Muslims and Arabs, then the historic context to the Western–Eastern relations needs to be understood beyond Osama Bin Laden and 9/11. For instance, 9/11 was not the direct result of disapproving public responses to such issues as women wearing the *hijab* to vote, or the manner in which the printed media, in particular, frame Muslim images. These types of perceptions existed in the West long before 9/11 changed the world. Scholars like Jack Shaheen and Edward Said have discussed the deeply seeded racist fears sown through Islamophobia.

Although visible Muslims (women and men who dress in traditional religious manner) receive great amount of prejudice, people who are connected to Islam in less obvious manners are also the targets of intolerance. This book discusses both religiously recognizable Muslim experience and less researched groups, such as second and third North American generation students with Muslim or Arabic backgrounds. How does the child of Muslim grandparents navigate through an education system's systemic set of public *truths* that consistently portray Islam and Muslims in a negative manner? Is the option for this child to denounce his or her heritage, ways of knowing and loved family members to successfully navigate through schools? This practice is not unlike other minority experiences in our schools in which defence of their heritage, ancestors, and ways of knowing must be set aside to conform to Western sets of *acceptable* facts and knowledge (Stonebanks, 2008).

Our hope is for educators to move toward an inclusive classroom which creates personal and classroom spaces of learning based on research and personal discovery, so that they may become active participants in their world (Steinberg, 2009; Steinberg & Kincheloe, 1998). However, we do recognize that information regarding Islam has not been made readily accessible to teachers, administrators, policy makers, and the public. We hope that the content of this book will assist teachers and students to move toward the emancipatory educational path of critically considering reasons for Islamophobia and popular perceptions toward Islam, Muslims, and Arabic peoples. This book should not be considered a panacea for Islamophobia, but we will provide pedagogical considerations. We will discuss the historical context of Islam, the diversity of the Muslim experience, Muslim contributions to civilization, the manner in which media and schools shape Western understanding of Islam and Muslims, and, educational resources. Our hope is that educators consider this collection of writings as the first step to research within their own classrooms and that progress against Islamophobia stems from their own and their students' efforts.

Our intent is to provide educators and students an accessible understanding of some of the current struggles of members of the greater Muslim community. We will discuss the context from which these struggles derive, the manner in which formal and non-formal locations of learning have reproduced misconceptions and strategies to develop a just classroom. A major incentive for developing this manuscript comes not only from our own research and prior publications but also from our extended conversations in developing this book with Joe Kincheloe, whose deep commitment to recognizing that individual beliefs, familiarity, "ways of knowing," and connections to Islam through personal experience had to counter the prevalent distorted perspectives of Islam "taught" by both non-formal and formal locations of education. It is Joe's pedagogy, his spirit of indignation, against Islamophobia we hope to emulate in creating a socially just curriculum.

We have organized the book into four parts. In Part One: *There Is No One "Muslim World,"* the authors establish a historical and ideological framework for teaching against Islamophobia. In Part Two: *Reading Islamophobia,* each chapter engages in a content analysis of Islamophobic texts. Part Three: *Categories on the Board—"Muslims You Never Knew,"* speaks on the politics of identity and autobiographical narrative. We complete the book with Part Four: *Teaching against Islamophobia* in which the authors give specific examples of anti-Islamophobic teaching in schools. This book can begin to name Islamophobia, and to create a dialogue. We have created a forum on our website, freireproject.org, and invite you to participate in this endeavor to engage in the conversation about critical pedagogical attempts to change and redefine educational discourse.

References

Rushdie, S. and Manji, I. (July 25, 2009) Honor and Shame Within Islam and Freedom of Expression. http://tundratabloid.blogspot.com/2009/07/irshad-manji-and-salman-rushdie-discuss.html. Date of last recovery: March 28, 2010.

Steinberg, S. R. (2009). *Diversity and multiculturalism: A reader.* New York: Peter Lang.

Steinberg, S. R. and Kincheloe, J. L. (1998). *Students as researchers: Creating classrooms that matter.* London: Falmer Press.

Stonebanks, C. D. (2008). From politicized knowledge to standardized knowing. In N. D. Giardina (Ed.), *Qualitative inquiry and the politics of evidence* (pp. 250–269). Walnut Creek, CA: Left Coast Press.

Part One

There Is No One "Muslim World"

One

Why Teach against Islamophobia? Striking the Empire Back

Joe L. Kincheloe and Shirley R. Steinberg

In the Western tradition of teaching about, writing about, researching, and representing Islam, Europeans have consistently positioned Muslims as the irrational, fanatic, sexually enticing, and despotic others. In this book, we argue that this portrayal has been as much about Western anxieties, fears, and self-doubts as it has about Islam. As educators, we are concerned about these representations in light of the events of the early 21st century. After September 11, 2001, and the wars in Afghanistan and Iraq, the ways images of Islam have been embedded in the Western and especially the American consciousness become extremely important to everyday life. With these concerns in mind, the editors and authors attempt to re-write within current curricula to contextualize and construct a liberatory framework to teach against Islamophobia. In this context, this chapter discusses the role of miseducation within Western and global views of Islam. In order to teach against a traditional paradigm, we contend that we must first historicize how it began.

The Empir(ical) Creation of Islamophobia

Central to any description, Islamophobia is the West's effort—especially after the Scientific Revolution of the 17th and 18th centuries—to depict its own superiority. In the first decade of the 21st century, it is high time to clean up the historical distortions developed centuries ago and passed down across the generations. If the United States is to become a great nation guided by a moral compass, it can do so only by way of its relationships with other nations and cultures. Nations like individuals develop a self-image in their interaction with others. Christopher Stonebanks's work offers compelling insight into this issue (Stonebanks, 2004). Through a respectful interaction with those different from ourselves, we come to new modes of consciousness. We gain a chance to see ourselves as the others see us; indeed, our familiarity with ourselves is made strange. Only when a nation gains this view of itself can it move toward maturity (Koechler, 2002). Such a view in no way dictates a particular response to an atrocity such as the 9/11 attacks, but it does help a nation reflect on larger social, cultural, and historical dimensions as to why groups such as radical Islamists might hold the United States in contempt. In its maturity the nation acquires the disposition to learn from tragedy.

The mature culture/nation is dedicated to learning from difference. In such a nation's schools, for example, citizens come to understand that schools are contested public spaces shaped by diverse forces of power. Learning from difference means that teachers are aware of the histories and struggles of colonized groups and oppressed peoples. Such teachers would understand the complicity of educational institutions themselves in such oppression. Many scholars maintain that the classroom is a central site for the legitimization of myths and silences about non-Western and often non-Christian peoples. If educators who value the power of difference were to teach about the history of Islam, they would have to rethink the canonical history of the West. Indeed, when school texts distort the history of Islam, they concurrently distort all history. Teachers and educational leaders who act on the power of difference forge such recognition into a politically transformative mode of education. Such pedagogy understands Western societies as collectivities of difference, where the potential exists for everyone to be edified by interaction with the other and the ways of knowing he or she brings to an encounter. Of course, in contemporary America, such respect for difference is viewed by many as an anti-American position.

Because of its transformative power, difference in contemporary America must not only be tolerated but also cultivated as a spark to human solidarity and creativity. This is what this book attempts to do: to think about the power of difference in relation to Western–Islamic interactions and their portrayal in educational institutions. Any description of a rigorous education needs to include an understanding of the power of difference that nurtures a critical sense of empathy. Cornel West (1993) contends that empathy involves the ability to appreciate the anxieties and frustrations of others, never to lose sight of the humanity of the marginalized no matter how wretched their condition—and we would add, no matter how much some of them may express their hatred for us. The point emerging here involves the pedagogical, ethical, and cognitive benefits derived from the confrontation with difference and the diverse vantage points it provides us for viewing the everyday world. Educators who value difference often begin their analysis of a phenomenon by listening to those who have suffered most as a result of its existence. These different ways of seeing allow educators and other individuals access to the new modes of cognition—a cognition of empathy. Such a perspective allows individuals access to tacit modes of racism, cultural bias, and religious intolerance that operate to structure worldviews.

There is little doubt that this valuing of difference or understanding of the miseducation of the West would not end the terrorist activities of groups such as Al-Qaeda. But such understandings, put into action over the long term, will operate to change the nature of the United States' relationship with most of the Islamic world. Given the dominant political consciousness of the Bush Administration, and its diplomatic and educational operatives, such views of difference are being challenged and discredited at every opportunity. The examination of right-wing educator Chester Finn's Fordham Foundation's epistle to America's teachers "September 11: What Our Children Need to Know" (2002), is essential in understanding how post-9/11 curriculum discourse has been formed. This report pushes this discreditation of difference in the educational realm in profoundly disturbing ways. As Finn puts it, he had to act because so much "nonsense" was being put out by the educational establishment. What Finn describes as nonsense can be read as scholarship attempting to provide perspective on the long history of Western–Islamic relations. Finn's use of "so much" in relation to this nonsense is crass exaggeration. Most materials published about 9/11 for educators were rather innocuous pleas for helping children deal with the anxiety produced by the attacks. Little elementary or secondary school material devoted to historicizing or contextualizing the Islamic world and its relation with the West appeared in the first two years after the tragic events of 9/11.

Reflecting the viewpoints of the former G. W. Bush Administration on how to properly educate Americans about the Islamic world, the Fordham report illustrates the traditional Western tendency to promote its own moral, political, and cultural superiority whenever it has to deal with Muslim societies. As Victor Davis Hanson (2002) puts it in one of the essays included in the collection:

> Not all cultures are equal in their moral sensibilities; few dictators, theocrats, tribal leaders or communists welcome the introspection and self-criticism that are necessary for moral improvement. So before we seek guidance from others abroad or adjust our policies to an apparent international consensus Americans must first ask of other nations in the world: do their people vote, do they respect women, do they enjoy freedom, and can they express themselves without audit or censorship?

Other authors in the Fordham collection write about "teaching nonsense" and "foolishness" in a way that many would interpret as references to pedagogies that question American superiority and infallibility. Are we promoting foolishness when we argue that it is necessary for Americans in this era to study how individuals from Islamic nations understand the world, themselves, their histories and cultures, and the West? Teaching such understandings is not foolishness; it is an effort to understand the peoples of the world, so we can interact with them in more culturally sensitive and equitable ways. In the case of the diverse peoples of the Islamic world, Westerners, Americans in particular, need to contemplate why so many of them are angry about both the historical and contemporary relationships between the Islamic World and the West (Sarder, 1999).

Again, the Fordham Foundation's opposition to such types of understanding manifests itself. Finn writes that educators take values such as "tolerance and multiculturalism" and carry them "to extremes." These nebulous educators (we think we are the types Finn and the other Fordham authors are referencing) are totally unconcerned with history and civics. The world is rather black and white, Finn suggests, and there is no need to understand diverse points of view. In the post-9/11 world, our children need to clearly understand the difference between "heroes and villains," "freedom and repression," "hatred and nobility," "democracy and theocracy," and "civic virtue and vice" (Finn, 2002). Such pronouncements remove Americans from history, while in their lack of specificity vilify the Islamic other. "They" were after all the ones that attacked us—"they" referencing Islam as a whole. In the name of teaching "true history," Finn and his fellow Fordham authors move America to a historiographical Disneyland where all of our intentions are good. American history becomes the happiest history on Earth. It is understanding the underpinnings of policy and curriculum construction by organizations/government documents like Fordham, that we understand where we find ourselves in the second decade of a new millennium.

The propaganda-like teaching of American history, signaled by the Fordham report, connotes more than merely a jingoistic response to 9/11. It represents a return to a 1954 view of America as the bearer of the democratic torch to the anti-democratic forces of the world. Concurrently, and more importantly, it signifies a larger effort to use 9/11 as the referent for an American empire freed from the need to understand the rest of the world in any way outside imperial military necessities. A critical education must counter such tendencies and work to conceptualize 9/11 in a variety of contexts (Hesse & Sayyid, 2001). Without this critical challenge, the effort to simply appreciate the perspectives of individuals from other cultures, other social systems, and other religious heritages can be dismissed as irrational, anti-

American, and even anti-Christian. Historically contextualizing, the Moors in Europe, for instance, illustrates a specific effort to dismiss the contributions of Islam to Western civilization. Shirley recounts this incident: "while touring the Alhambra this year, I asked a guide to describe to me his account of the 'Arab occupation of Spain.' He understood the nuance of my question and admitted that his tour presentation implied that the Moors, and African Muslims who came up the Iberian Peninsula did not *occupy* as he had stated, but instead, *inhabited*."

In the context many educators, a work such as *The Miseducation of the West* (Kincheloe & Steinberg, 2004) is socially unacceptable knowledge. Many educational policies are ideologically complicit with advancing the power of the new American Empire, and in this role must avoid humanizing "the enemy." In this context, disinformation becomes the rule of the day, as generalizations about the monolithic Islamic world proliferate. The power of difference in this ideological frame is dead. As is stated numerous times in Fordham's "September 11: What Our Children Need to Know," such forms of understanding and celebrating difference are dangerous to the future of America.

Tacit Ops by the Empire

In many ways 9/11 was a profound shock to millions of Americans who obtain their news and world views from the mainstream, corporate-owned media, and their understanding of American international relations from what is taught in most secondary schools, and in many colleges and universities. Such individuals are heard frequently on call-in talk radio and TV shows expressing the belief that America is loved internationally because it is richer, more moral, and more magnanimous than other nations. In this mind-set those who resist the United States hate our freedom for reasons never quite specified—jealousy maybe. These Americans, the primary victims of the miseducation, have not been informed by their news sources of the societies that have been undermined by covert U.S. military operations and U.S. economic policies (Parenti, 2002). Many do not believe, for example, the description of the human effects of American sanctions on Iraq between the First and Second Gulf Wars. Indeed, the hurtful activities of the American Empire are invisible to many of the empire's subjects.

The complexity of the relationship between the West (the United States in particular) and Islam demands that we be very careful in laying out the subtle arguments we are making about the miseducation. The activities of the American Empire have not been the only forces at work creating an Islamist extremism that violently defies the sacred teaching of the religion. American misdeeds have also played an important role in the process. A new critical education, based on an appreciation of difference, can help the United States redress some of its past and present policies toward the diverse Islamic world. While these policies have been invisible to many Americans they are visible to the rest of the world—the Islamic world in particular. Ignoring the history of the empire, Kenneth Weinstein (2002), writes that the Left "admits" that differences do exist between cultures.

> but paradoxically downplays their violent basis through relativism and multiculturalism. It views cultural diversity and national differences as matters of taste arguing that the greatest crime of all is judgmentalism.

Weinstein concludes this paragraph by arguing that Americans are just too nice and as such are naïve to the threats posed by many groups around the world.

Weinstein sets up a classic straw man argument in this context. The Left, as portrayed by them, equates difference with a moral relativism that is unable to condemn the inhumane activities of particular groups. Implicit throughout, "9/11: What Our Children Need to Know" is the notion that this fictional American Left does not condemn Al-Qaeda and their crimes against humanity. This type of misrepresentation is an egregious form of miseducation. It is the type of distortion that equated opposition to the Second Gulf War with support for Saddam Hussein's Iraqi regime. "How can these malcontents oppose America?" authors ask. Their America is a new empire that constantly denies its imperial dimensions. The new empire is not like empires in the previous historical eras that overtly boasted of conquest and annexing of colonies. The 21st century is the era of the postmodern empire that speaks of its moral duty to unselfishly liberate nations and return power to the people. Empire leaders speak of free markets, the rights of the people, and the domino theory of democracy. It is an empire whose public relations people portray it as the purveyor of freedom around the world. When its acts of liberation and restoration of democracy elicit protest and retaliation, its leaders express shock and disbelief that such benevolent actions could arouse such irrational responses.

With all of their concern for teaching history, right-wing perspectives often ignore the warnings of past American leaders, such as George Washington, against the temptations of empire building. As President John Quincy Adams put it in the 1820s: "If America were tempted to become the dictatress of the world, she would be no longer the ruler of her own spirit" (Ignatieff, 2003, p. 24). As the American Empire spends massive sums of money on its foreign excursions, it finds it more and more difficult to designate money for democratic essentials at home such as infrastructural needs and education. The costs of the empire consistently undermine the promise of domestic democracy and economic justice.

It is important to consider the inability of American leaders to understand the impact of empire building in the Persian Gulf on the psyches of those personally affected by such activities when teaching and discussing issues involving Iran. In the case of Iraq in the Second Gulf War, American leaders simply disregarded the views of nations around the world, the Muslim world in particular, as they expressed their opposition to the American invasion. History was erased as Saddam Hussein was viewed in a psychological context as a madman. References to times when the United States supported the madman were deleted from memory. The empire, thus, could do whatever it wanted, regardless of its impact on the Iraqi people or the perceptions of others (irrational others) around the world.

An epistemological naiveté—the belief that dominant American ways of seeing both itself and the world are rational and objective and that differing perspectives are irrational—permeates the Fordham report. As John Agresto (2002) writes:

> It is not very helpful to understand other cultures and outlooks and not understand our own country and what it has tried to achieve. What is it that has brought tens of millions of immigrants to America, not to bomb it, but to better its future and their own? What is it about the promise of liberty and equal treatment, of labor that benefits you and your neighbor, of an open field for your enterprise, ambition, determination and pluck? Try not to look at America through the lens of your own ideology or political preference but see it as it really is. Try, perhaps, to see the America most Americans see. That can be a fine antidote to smugness and academic self-righteousness.

Studying the Fordham Foundation's ways of looking at and teaching about America, with its erasures of history deployed in the very name of a call to teach history, we are disturbed. When this is combined with an analysis of media representations of the nation's war against terrorism and the Second Gulf War, we gain some sobering insights into America's future. The inability or refusal of many Americans, especially those in power, to see the problematic activities of the "invisible" empire does not portend peace in the world in the coming years. The Fordham Foundation's work has paved the road for future decades and its significance can't be ignored. The way knowledge is produced and transmitted in the United States by corporatized media and an increasingly corporatized/privatized educational system is one of the central political issues of our time. Yet, in the mainstream political and educational conversations it is not even on the radar.

Understanding the Politics of Knowledge to Teach against Islamophobia

North Americans—as well, of course, as other peoples around the planet—are victimized by the new American Empire's politics of knowledge. In the contemporary electronic world saturated by the information of corporate knowledge producers, many Americans simply are unaware of knowledges constructed by diverse groups and individuals. I (Joe) spoke with several Americans who sought diverse information sources in the relation to the Second Gulf War. Other than the Pacifica Radio Network and programs such as Free Speech Network News and Democracy Now, it was very difficult to find alternative news of the war. Such alternative news attempted to transcend the outlawing of the history of U.S.–Muslim relations promoted by mainstream information sources. Such historical erasure is central to the miseducation of the U.S. public, as it subverts the democratic process. Without the benefits of historical context the society is depoliticized, for all political positions involve particular historical interpretations. Combined with the confusion caused by the cacophony of hyperreal information saturation, dehistoricization produces depoliticization and its telltale characteristics: nihilism, cynicism, apathy, and escapism (Ali, 2002; Parenti, 2002).

In the Fordham report's contribution to this oppressive politics of knowledge any historical study of Western–Islamic or U.S.–Islamic relationships is off limits. The history that needs to be studied, Fordham authors Lynne Cheney (2002) and Gloria Sesso and John Pyne (2002) insist, are patriotic documents such as Thomas Paine's *Common Sense, The Declaration of Independence, Letters from an American Farmer*, the Gettysburg Address, Franklin Roosevelt's "Four Freedoms" speech, and Reagan's statement to the country after the *Challenger* explosion. While we would not question the value of any of these documents, the call to study them in lieu of histories of Islam and Western/U.S. relations with Islam in this context is perplexing. The message of Lynne Cheney in her short piece in the Fordham report and in her chilling American Council of Trustees and Alumni's "Defending Civilization: How Our Universities Are Failing America" is that any historical study of Islam or American relations with Islam is anti-American. Why anti-American? Because it implies that the United States did something to incite the attacks of 9/11.

To historicize and contextualize, the right-wing story goes, is to fail to condemn the terrorist acts of 9/11. Such scholars, Former Secretary of Education William Bennett (2002) argues in the Fordham report, are the "fools" who have argued "that there is no such thing as evil." Thus, understanding complexity in foreign affairs and international relations is viewed as a form of irredeemable relativism. The issue of U.S.–Islamic relations in this right-wing politics of knowledge is quite simple and requires little analysis: the United States has played a passive, innocent, and benevolent role in the Muslim world and then without warning was hit with an inexplicable attack (Husseini, 2001). To argue that this is a crass oversimplification of a complex story is not to justify on any level the acts of the 9/11 terrorists. What the right-wing positions delineated here actually do is shut down democratic conversation about the new world situation in which the United States finds itself.

The right-wing story about the contemporary world situation conveniently omits the last 500 years of European colonialism, the anti-colonial movements around the world beginning in the post-World War II era and their impact on the U.S. civil rights movement, the women's movement, the anti-war movement in Vietnam, Native American liberation struggles, the gay rights movement, and other emancipatory movements. In other work, we have labeled the reaction to these anti-colonial movements that have set the tone and content of much of American political, social, and educational experience over the last three decades (Gresson, 1995, 2003; Kincheloe & Steinberg, 1997; Kincheloe, Steinberg, Rodriguez, & Chennault, 1998; Rodriguez & Villaverde, 2000).

Using Aaron Gresson's concept "the recovery of white supremacy," which refers to what was perceived to have been lost in the liberation movements, one can study dominant cultural groups' attempts to reclaim cultural and intellectual supremacy by positioning themselves as victims of the so-called "oppressed" (Rose & Kincheloe, 2003). The attacks of 9/11 fit quite well into this discursive construction of white/European victimization. In the years following the attacks much has been made of alleged Muslim persecution of Christians in Islamic countries from Iran to Palestine (Husseini, 2001). In the same context persecution of Muslims by Europeans and Chinese has been virtually ignored. In the post-9/11 context it is obvious who the innocent victims are in the racial and cultural conflicts around the world in the discourse of victimization: white, European, Christians. The American Empire has no choice—it must discipline these barbaric forces.

How is it in a free society that such a politics of knowledge can go unchallenged? The answer to this question is extremely complex. And while it is one of the key issues this book addresses, it is far broader and more complicated than this work can do justice (for insight into the question, see Hammer & Kellner, 2009; Macedo & Steinberg, 2007; Chomsky, 2001; Herman & Chomsky, 1988). For the most part such a politics of information is not imposed by the U.S. government but is more of a self-censorship by the media. Over the last several centuries knowledge about the Islamic world in the West has been produced with conquest and control as objectives. If such a politics of knowledge remains unchallenged, as Edward Said accurately predicted in *Covering Islam* (1981):

> we will face protracted tension and perhaps even war, but we will offer the Muslim world, its various societies and states, the prospect of many wars, unimaginable

suffering, and disastrous upheavals, not the least of which would be the birth of an "Islam" fully ready to play the role prepared for it by reaction, orthodoxy, and desperation. (p. 164)

How the Right Wing Constructs the Barbarian Other

The right-wing politics of knowledge intersecting with the political-economic dimensions of globalization and geo-political needs of the American Empire have rendered Said's words eerily prescient. This politics of knowledge with its American assumptions makes for a world where reality is perceived across a great chasm of misconstruction (Sarder, 1999). Distorted pictures of an irrational and barbaric people shape decision-making in areas of foreign policy, economics, and education. Scientific ways of seeing in the cultural sphere while claiming neutrality are profoundly shaped by discursive, ideological, linguistic, social, cultural, political, economic, and historical contexts. Islam has been seen and continues to be viewed on a certain horizon and within particular contexts. In the Second Gulf War, reporters for the major TV networks denied that their coverage was framed by a particular American perspective toward the war. U.S. TV was objective and fair while Qatar's Al-Jazeera was biased and characterized by low journalistic standards.

One of the lessons scholars around the world learned in the last three decades of the 20th century was that no knowledge is disinterested. All information is produced by individuals operating at a particular place and a specific time—they see the world and employ methods for viewing the world from a particular point in the complex web of reality. Understanding, for example, a speech by an Islamic cleric about his revulsion in relation to American culture's influence in his nation or region involves a different type of contextualized and historicized analysis than a mathematician solving an obstinate mathematical problem. Those from the West who study and examine the words of the Islamic cleric must

- understand the unique interpretive circumstances of a Western student engaging with an Islamic text.
- be sensitive to the power relationships between the interpreter's culture and the culture of the cleric.
- be aware of the purposes for which the interpretation will be used.

Thus, a key dimension of the miseducation of the West assumes that Western knowledge of Islam and the Islamic world is objective and disinterested. The West's distorted view of Islam, labeled by Said as Orientalism, has reemerged in the last couple of decades of the twentieth and the first decade of the twenty-first centuries in a new and more dangerous version. Postmodern Orientalism is now promoted by TV news, film (see Shirley Steinberg's chapter on Islam and Hollywood), edutainment CD-ROMs, and video games. A distorted, demonized view of the Islamic world is passed along by a pedagogy much more powerful than traditional academic scholarship. The new cultural pedagogy colonizes consciousness via the pleasure of the entertainment media. No matter how horrible the Second Gulf War may have been, it was damn good entertainment for many back home. As a colleague described a conversation between himself and two of his male university students before the outbreak of the war:

> Professor: So you understand the reasons many people oppose the war in Iraq?
>
> Student 1: Yeah, the arguments make a lot of sense but still, you know, uh, uh…
>
> Student 2: What we're saying is that it's going to be so much fun to watch on TV. We can hardly wait.

Such a powerful politics of knowledge wins the consent of individuals to dominant American power along an axis of pleasure even when their logical faculties might resist. Despite its new attire and high-tech modes of transmission, postmodern Orientalism still relies on traditional Orientalism's medieval images of Islam as a barbaric and derivative theology of sodomites. Some of the comments of fundamentalist Christian theologians such as Jerry Falwell and Franklin Graham in the post-9/11 years have echoed such medieval images with a vengeance. Recent CD-ROMs that cover Islam include *Microsoft Bookshelf*, *Microsoft Encarta*, the *Compton Interactive Encyclopedia*, *Hutchinson History Library*, and Dorling Kindersley's *History of the World*.

In all of these multimedia works, Islam—and the rest of the world for that matter—is seen through the geo-political interests of the American Empire. America becomes the barometer for all human civilization with the alumni of the Harvard Business School occupying the highest link of the civilizational food chain. Muhammad is a minor character in world history here; the *Microsoft Bookshelf*, for example, grants him a less than a paragraph: "Islam has enshrouded Muhammad's life in a mass of legends and traditions" (Sardar, 1999, p. 109). Civilization and human accomplishment in these contemporary sources are exclusively European phenomena and the contemporary world is viewed through a U.S. Cold War and post-Cold War national interest perspective. In the post-Cold War framework, the icon of the Muslim terrorist represents the general Islamic threat to U.S. global dominance. After the fall of the "evil empire" of the Communist bloc, the Islamic threat fills the enemy vacuum quite effectively. From these and countless other Western sources on Islam, one would learn that not only did Islam promote ignorance but there was no role for Islam in a grand universal history of mankind (Sardar, 1999).

So when educators with a critical consciousness of the consequences of colonialism and the distortions of the right-wing politics of knowledge began to construct pictures of Islam that considered different ways of seeing the world, right-wing scholars were angered. Although such representations rarely find their way into elementary and secondary curricula, right-wing scholars—especially after 9/11—asserted that they did and attempted to scare their constituencies with allegations that these perspectives were taking over the field. Teacher educators, Chester Finn (2002) asserted, were especially guilty of such un-American offenses:

> The second chapter of this unhappy story was written by education experts who have opined in scholarly journals about the "educational meanings of September 11th." The good news is that few firing-line educators read such journals. The bad news is that the people who write in them are also, characteristically, the men and women who prepare future teachers in our colleges of education.

The antidote to this distortion of the facts, the contributors to the Fordham report argue, is readily available. Teachers, they contend, should simply quit teaching lies and instead teach factual knowledge about America. There is nothing complicated about social, cultural, political, historical, philosophical, and economic data about the world. Everyone knows what is right. Teachers must simply start telling the truth about America. Researchers writing about the miseducation of the West would not need to discuss such simple-mindedness in regard to the complexity of the knowledge of the social sciences and humanities except for the realization that in the political/educational world of the 21st century; this is the argument being made by right-wing groups such as the Fordham Foundation and the American Council of Trustees and Alumni. Scholars or analysts such as ourselves cross the ideological line in the sand when:

- we question the benevolence of the use of American military power.
- we connect a people's contemporary anger with their colonized or historically colonized status.
- we maintain that U.S textbooks and media representations possess an American bias that blinds Americans to the reasons many people around the world criticize the United States so vociferously.

In this right-wing context Douglas Kellner's assertion that the American media after 9/11 "performed disastrously, whipping up war hysteria, while failing to provide a coherent account of what happened, [and] why it happened" is not the type of analysis necessary in a media-dominated, electronic democratic society (Kellner, 2004). The Finns, Bennetts, and Lynne Cheneys of the contemporary landscape view such critique as inappropriate and anti-American. Such a right-wing perspective does not respect democratic discourse.

Mistrusting the American Discourse

One dimension of the story we are telling in this book involves the reasons for the hatred and mistrust of the United States in the Islamic world. It is true that not all Muslims around the world in their cultural, political, social, and theological diversity hate the United States. But why is it that so many do? One answer to this complex question is directly related to the miseducation delineated here: so many people in the Islamic world hate the United States because many Americans have no idea why they should harbor such feelings. Many Muslims around the world express shock at widespread ignorance among Americans about the U.S. role in the world and in Islamic history. When Chester Finn (2002) writes that 9/11 presents a chance for Americans "to teach our daughters and sons about heroes and villains, about freedom and repression, about hatred and nobility, democracy and theocracy, about civic virtue and vice" the American blindness to colonial and neo-colonial atrocities around the world is revealed. Also, there is a degree of cowardice in Finn's Manichaean binaries for he never simply states that Muslims are the villains, repressors, haters, theocrats, and purveyors of vice—he simply implies it over and over against in order to maintain plausible deniability of racism.

Finn and Fordham, Bush and the Cheneys, and other purveyors of the right-wing politics of knowledge simply refused to recognize that 9/11 in part reflected the rage toward the U.S. pulsing through the veins of many Muslims. The indifference displayed by many U.S. policymakers toward the suffering of everyday people around the Islamic world fanned the flames of this anti-American fury. In Iraq, for example, the indifference of American leaders to the effects of the post-First Gulf War sanctions put into place in 1991, angered millions of Muslims around the world as well as the Iraqi people (Sudetic, 2002). This is one of many reasons that when U.S. and British forces invaded the country in March of 2003, they were not met with the flowers and kisses of a grateful people that George W. Bush promised Americans. Most Iraqis obviously did not see the Second Gulf War as the War of Iraqi Liberation despite their disdain for Saddam Hussein. Moroccan scholar Loubna Skalli captures the nuance of these Islamic sentiments so well:

> Fundamentalists...are a generation of Muslim youth in revolt. They are in revolt against the imposed colonial projects of modernization in their countries and the

unfulfilled promises of their post-colonial political regimes and national elite. They are in revolt against the unequal distribution of wealth and resources within and among nations; against their won socio-economic and political exclusions, as well as against the widening circle of the disenfranchised classes from which most of them come. They are in revolt against their own sense of powerlessness in the face of all the global forces that threaten their religious and cultural identity.

More important perhaps, fundamentalists are in revolt against the traumatic legacy of Western colonialism that continues to destabilize the core of their social and cultural fabric—a process kept alive, if not exacerbated by American hegemony, and its perceived homogenizing materialistic values. (Skalli, 2004)

Compare Fordham author John Agresto's (2002) view of these same Islamic fundamentalists with Skalli's:

> The anniversary of September 11th gives us the opportunity not to preach the usual pap about diversity—that different cultures see the world in different but equally valid ways. Rather, we now have the opportunity to show that there are people and cultures with ideas radically and fundamentally different from our own. Different even on the most basic givens we take for granted as the basis of civilized life—that, for example, the ends do not justify the means, that innocents are to be treated with respect, that people should not be exploited as means to ideological or religious ends, that the subjugation of women is an affront to human dignity, indeed that there is such a thing as human dignity. Consider with your students how, despite the fact that human nature may be everywhere the same, political, religious or economic ideologies might so affect people's outlook that even the deepest principles of civilized society are, to some easily rejected.

Agresto makes no effort to humanize "the enemy," to understand the forces—many constructed by Western and U.S. colonialism—that shape the fanaticism of some Muslims. Just as importantly, he fails to distinguish the fanatic from the angry but reasonable majority. The uses of the word "civilized" denotes an absence of civilization in Islamic culture that can only be corrected by learning from the rational West. Skalli's description differs from Agresto's in that while she may not agree with many of the beliefs and actions of the young Islamic fundamentalists, she understands many of the forces that have helped create them. Agresto's black and white portrait seems, in its own way, to illustrate a cultural fundamentalism similar to the absolutism of any religious fundamentalist group, Christian, Judaic, Hindu, or Islamic.

The fundamentalism of the right-wing politics of knowledge is central to our understanding of the hatred and mistrust of the West, the United States in particular. Fundamentalism as used in this context is defined as the belief in the inerrancy of Americana, the American political philosophy in particular as well as the Western scientific creed and its methods for producing objective knowledge. The Fordham report well illustrates this fundamentalism albeit in a manner that avoids unambiguous statement of its position. The ideology and rhetoric of the report make it a document well worth extended analysis.

The Fordham report assumes from the beginning that this Americana and American political philosophy are monolithic expressions of one culture's social and political values. The United States is not now nor has it ever been monocultural and of one political mind. The effort to construct the assumption that America has a common culture and politics is an attempt to position particular ethnicities and specific political points of view as existing outside the boundaries of true Americanism. When educators focus on diversity, the right-wing logic posits, they are misleading their students and pushing a relativistic agenda where nothing is right or wrong. The epistemological naivete of such assertions is blatant, as Fordham authors ignore an entire body of social theoretical work that moves far beyond the polar extremes of pure objectivity on one end of the continuum and relativism on the other (Gadamer, 1975; Kincheloe, 2001; Madison, 1988; van Manen, 1991; Thayer-Bacon, 2003).

Finn asked the 23 authors of the report to answer the question: "What civic lessons are the most imperative for U.S. K–12 teachers to teach their pupils, as the 'anniversary' of the September 11th attacks draws near, about the United States and what it means to be an American?" In his introduction, Finn (2002) actually asserts that the Fordham Foundation sought a wide range of responses to the question:

> but we did not seek people who would repeat the conventional wisdom of the education profession—there's already plenty of that for anyone who wants it. Nor did we seek people who would psychologize the topic or whose reverence for tolerance dwarfs their appreciation of other compelling civic values. Above all, we sought people who take history and civics seriously, people who take America seriously.

There is something profoundly disingenuous in this quotation. First, Finn and the Fordham Foundation did not seek a wide range of responses—they sought individuals who for the most part offered the same viewpoints about American culture, politics, and education as Finn himself. It's fine to offer a generally homogeneous view. In the name of intellectual honesty, however, it is important to admit that one is doing so. Second, there is no monolithic conventional wisdom of the educational profession. There is as much diversity of belief among teachers and teacher educators as there is in America writ large. Again, there is a level of duplicity at work here. Finn and many of his ideological brothers and sisters have for years been painting the education profession and teacher education in particular as radical, incompetent enemies of true Americanism. The unstated purpose here is to continue to discredit such professionals in order to eventually end public schooling and teacher education as they now exist. Thirdly, tolerance is positioned in a false binarism with civic values. It is simply absurd to assert that promoting the value of tolerance is at odds with the larger notion of civic values. And finally, the continuing efforts of Finn and his ideological companions to equate disagreement with their perspectives are examples of not taking history and civics seriously and not taking America seriously. The implication here moves us back to equating dissent against this right-wing politics of knowledge with anti-Americanism.

In his introduction, Finn also argues that there are teachers who are patriots, who "love our country and the ideals for which it stands." Because of their love of country, Finn asserts, these teachers "need no advice whatsoever." They will know what to teach, Finn tells his readers, because of their love of America. The anti-intellectualism and even anti-scientific pursuit of knowledge in this assertion tells us that what to teach about 9/11 is an affair of the heart not the mind. Thus, there is no reason to study the history of Afghanistan and its relations with Europe, especially the Soviet Union and recently with the United States. There is no reason to explore the colonial history of Iraq and the nation's relationship with the United States over the last 30 years. There is no reason to trace the recent history of Iran. Even the best teachers, Finn contends, "may find their resolve shaken, their ideas challenged, their lesson plans disputed, when they encounter materials from their peers, associations, professors, [and] journals." Alas, what a problematic situation—an open *democratic* debate might break out around the issues raised here.

The fundamentalism of Finn and the right-wing leaders of the United States in the first decade of the 21st century frightens the world in ways that many Americans are only beginning to understand. People around the world are baffled that such scholars seem to believe that there is only one objective history of the world and such a chronicle is constructed from an American point of view. "Do they not understand the arrogance and ethnocentrism of such a perspective?"—scholars from Spain, Germany, Brazil, Turkey, Mexico and many other countries ask us as we travel around the world. When Lynne Cheney (2002) argues in her chapter in the Fordham report that in response to 9/11 American teachers need to teach about traditional documents and great speeches of American history—all of which should be in the social studies curriculum, we all agree—she misses some important dimensions of such a pedagogy.

While it is necessary to teach about the historical ideals of the United States, it is also important to study the struggles to enact such principles. The devil is in the details of these struggles, endeavors marked by profound successes and profound failures. Contrary to the party line of Finn and his compatriots, the study of the failures is not anti-American but a celebration of one of the central ideals of American democracy. As has been argued by many since the emergence of democratic impulses in a variety of cultures around the world, a society is democratic to the degree that it allows for self-criticism. Self-critique does not seem to occupy a very high rung on the Fordham ladder of democratic values. It is indoctrination that seems at odds with such democratic principles.

Thus, legitimate disagreements about the politics of information around U.S. relations with Islamic nations and about the meaning of 9/11 and the ways we teach about it are squashed by Finn, Cheney, Bennett, and their supporters. The assertion that it is too simplistic to argue that religious fanaticism was the only cause of 9/11 was met with accusation of treason, siding with the terrorists, and "blaming America first" by purveyors of the dominant politics of knowledge in government and the media (Parenti, 2002). Indeed, only enemies ask the United States to consider its past in terms of studying its history in relation to other nations and cultures. The erasure of history takes place in the name of history, as we have seen with the Fordham report. As Lynne Cheney (2002) argues, it was not our lack of understanding of Islam that led to the 9/11 attacks.

On one level it is trite to argue that Americans need to know more about the world. But in the context of the right-wing politics of knowledge, progressives must insist on more sophisticated understandings of the perspectives of other cultures, especially the role of the United States in the world. We must demand higher media news standards—TV and radio coverage that provides multiple perspectives and viewpoints from around the world. U.S. media must get beyond representing the United States as victim in international relations and provide insight into America's role in the complex system of world events. In this complex context, understanding and addressing the genesis of terrorism and anti-American sentiments in the world should not constitute a controversial act.

Historicizing Islamophobia

When educators struggle to place the events of the late twentieth and early twenty-first centuries in historical context, do they discern historical continuity connecting the intersection of Western (or Christian) cultures and Islam? Is it a misappropriation of history to trace Western–Islamic relations from the rise of Islam in the 7th century through Charles Martel's victory at the Battle of Tours in the 8th century, the Crusades, the Ottoman Empire, and the rise of other Islam societies, European colonialism to the Islamophobia of the present? Obviously, human beings make selective uses of the past to make sense of and rationalize particular dimensions of the present (Runnymede Trust, 1997). To some extent all political positions are historical interpretations. These are important questions that must be kept in mind by educators and policy makers as they attempt to understand contemporary Western and Islamic relations.

Despite the contemporary stereotypes of Muslims as intolerant and prone to terrorism and violence, historical scholarship teaches a very different picture. For example, in Spain from the 8th century to the 14th century, Abukhattala argues, the Muslim empire was one of the most tolerant in history. Jews, Christians, and Muslims lived and worked together in harmony for 800 years. From the First Crusade at the end of the 11th century onward, Muslims in the Middle East experienced European entry into Islamic lands as an assault. As the British and French moved into the Muslim world in the 18th century, the assault from the Islamic perspective continued and intensified (Abukhattala, 2004).

From the Crusades and colonialism the Europeans "learned' that Muslims were barbaric, ugly, zealous, and ignorant. Such perceptions allowed a moral justification to the European colonial project around the world. With the coming of European modernity in the 17th and 18th centuries, there emerged a new articulation of European superiority that positioned the Muslims and other peoples around the world as profoundly incompetent and inferior. Viewing these "inferior" peoples played a central role in shaping European self-consciousness. In the medieval period, Europeans had been intimidated by what they knew was the superior learning of the Muslim civilization. After the Scientific Revolution and the birth of modernity Europe was seen by Europeans as most definitely superior. This notion of European superiority became the foundation for the miseducation of the West.

At the very least, we begin to learn from these historical insights that the Islamophobic depictions of Western–Islamic relations are more complex than the right-wing politics of education would have us believe. While there are no disinterested selections of historical events, we can conclude, at the very least, that there exist many versions of this story. The story told in mainstream media and education cannot be separated from the influence of historical and contemporary Islamophobia. What is interesting here is that these historical and contemporary versions of Islamophobia intersect in what we call the miseducation of the West. The barbaric images of Islam developed during the Crusades and colonialism lay in wait, ready to be deployed when the political climate needed them—as during the oil embargo of 1973 or the First Gulf War of 1991. When most post-Enlightenment Western scholars researched Islam through the conceptual lenses of Western modernity employing its assumptions about knowledge production, the ways human societies should develop, the nature of civilization, and the writing of history, they found—not surprisingly—Islamic culture(s) to be inferior.

Islamic law in these studies was not real jurisprudence and Islamic ways of making meaning not real rationality. Soon a canon of Islamic studies developed and these ethnocentric assumptions became sanctified as the findings of the old masters of the field. Scholars of the tradition maintain that it became quite authoritarian and aggressively resisted criticism, both from within and outside the discipline. Samuel P. Huntington's *The Clash of Civilizations: Remaking of World Order* (1996) is the most popular contemporary articulation of this scholarly tradition. The thesis is by no means original—violence and barbarism are central traits of Muslims—but in Huntington's hands they are turned into a broader ideology. The ideology that there is an inevitable clash of civilizations between the Western Christian nations and the Eastern Islamic and Confucian societies is injected into the discourse of U.S. foreign policy. If the United States does not act decisively, the ideology asserts, bloody Islam will continue its warring tradition against the West. The idea that Muslims have often been victims of Western violence is conveniently omitted from Huntington's thesis (Hippler, 1995; Lueg, 1995; Sardar, 1999).

With the inauguration of the George W. Bush Administration, the ideology of civilizational clashes quickly became a basic concept in U.S. foreign policy. With the 9/11 attacks, the concept was sanctified and wars against Afghanistan and Iraq quickly followed. This clash of civilizations ideology reinvigorates American colonial impulses with its concept of cultural superiority under attack. Islam is represented as posing a threat against civilization itself with its inferior ways of seeing and being and its alien values. In this context add Bernard Lewis's best-selling *What Went Wrong: Western Impact and Middle Eastern Response* (2002) and we begin to get the idea that Islamophobic scholarship is thriving in the 21st century. Lewis continues Huntington's miseducation, arguing Muslim inferiority, barbarism, and failure as a culture. Having first coined the term "clash of civilizations" in a 1990 article in *Atlantic Monthly*, Lewis argues that contemporary Muslims want someone to blame for their failures and have irrationally chosen the guiltless United States—an America that has never done anything to harm the Islamic world. We now have no alternative to war, Lewis concludes. The United States must fight the Islamic world and establish control over it.

The contemporary Islamophobic miseducation of the West is guided by this inevitable cultural conflict model. The notion that the United States exercises new forms of economic and cultural colonialism or that the United States has intervened in the internal affairs of different nations to help install governments favorable to U.S. economic and geo-political interests is forbidden knowledge in these models. The idea that U.S. oil companies might have engaged in corporate practices that were not fair to oil-producing Muslim nations is also erased. The racism toward Muslims sanctioned by such models can be heard in countless media productions. The following is an excerpt from Bob Grant's syndicated radio show on WABC in New York the day after the Oklahoma City bombing—the most listened-to radio station in the country at that time.

> Grant: Tommy from Brooklyn, hello.
>
> Caller: Well, I'd like to say that it's very amazing that both, as far as the O. J. Simpson trial and this awful tragedy that happened yesterday, people are saying that O. J. is guilty and nobody ever saw nothing. And now they're talking about Muslims and Mr. Salameh and all this, this is what you're saying, and no one ever saw anything. That's just as worse.
>
> Grant: Now—yeah—we did see a lot of things. We saw the Simpson case—Nicole with the throat slashed.... In the Oklahoma case, you klutz, in the Oklahoma City case, we don't know how many more dead people we need to convince you that somebody did that. And the indications are that those people who did it were some Muslim terrorists. But, a skunk like you, what I'd like to do is put you up against the wall with the rest of them, and mow you down along with them. Execute you with them. Because you obviously have a great hatred for America, otherwise you wouldn't talk the way you talk, you imbecile. (quoted in Husseini, 2001)

To avoid misunderstanding, let us pause for a moment to review the argument being made here. The miseducation of the West emerges from a long history of distorted Western knowledge about Islam. In the contemporary post-Cold War era we witness a new period of Islamophobia fanned by numerous scholars and the media. What the editors and authors of this book are not arguing is that Islamic nations have no responsibility for intolerance, fundamentalist zealotry, and inhuman terrorism. What we are maintaining is that all of these traits can be found in all cultures and religions, and that Western scholarship and education have often painted a Eurocentric black and white picture of who is "civilized" and who is not. For example, the anti-Jewish sentiment expressed in many parts of the Islamic world is racist and frightening. Of course, anti-Jewish sentiment and actions are not the exclusive province of Muslims. None of our arguments for a more reasoned, balanced, and contextualized view of the Islamic world should be connected to the anti-Jewish sentiment to be found in particular Muslim locales. The Israeli-Palestinian question is profoundly complex. While we do not support many of the policies of Israeli governments over the last decades, this disagreement should in no way be viewed as an anti-Jewish sentiment. We are vehemently opposed to anti-Semitism of both an anti-Jewish and Islamophobic variety.

Diversity Is Islam...Islam Is Diverse

A key point that we have already alluded to involves the understanding that there is no essentialized, unified Islamic world about which we can make uncomplicated generalizations. Of course, one of the failings of Finn, Lynne Cheney, Huntington, and Lewis and many others involves their depiction of a monolithic Islamic world. The portraits of Islam delineated by Orientalists both old and new never existed and do not exist in the first decade of the 21st century. The perception of Islam as the "enemy" is a social construction of Westerners, especially Americans. As argued previously, rejecting this enemy status does not mean that we should affirm all actions of Islamic peoples and societies (Lueg, 1995). When, however, a secondary school textbook such as Petrovich, Roberts, and Roberts's *World Cultures* chooses a picture of Muslim men praying with their guns beside them out of the millions of photographs of Muslim men praying, a critical education of Islam "calls out" such fear-mongering (MESA, 1994).

Obviously, some elements of the Islamic world, specifically some individuals often referred to as Islamic fundamentalists, have made violence a central duty of true believers. These individuals often allude to traditional Western/U.S. colonialism and its new economic and cultural varieties as *al-Salibiyyah*—the Crusade. This new Crusade while less violent has exerted a more powerful impact on the Islamic world than did the medieval invasions by Christian warriors. In the new Crusade of economic and cultural colonialism, the Muslim world has been positioned as dependent on the United States, and major cultural displacements have resulted from modernization and economic development programs. In the Muslim world, as well as in the societies populated by other religions, individuals have been taken aback by the secular dimensions of the new colonialism. In response they have turned to a literal and insular fundamentalist version of their faiths. As they fight back against those they perceive as the infidels, they replace the central values of generosity, love, and justice with more and more strident forms of intolerance and hatred (Armstrong, 2002). The Western/U.S. retaliation for the violent acts that come out of this fundamentalist intolerance increases the cycle of hatred and violence.

Recognition of this complexity and diversity in the Islamic world and the one-dimensional representations of the politics of knowledge, we are referring to here as the miseducation, demands a pedagogical revolution. Such a revolution would involve:

- understanding the United States from the perspectives of diverse groups around the world.
- gaining a historical awareness of the relationship between the United States and the rest of the world.
- appreciating the reasons many individuals around the world claim that the U.S. population is historically and politically uninformed.

Without these insights and understanding of the nature of the way U.S. power operates in the world, America is entering into a dangerous period where wars with perceived threats to the American Empire will be the order of the day. We do not believe that the United States, like many militarily overextended empires before it, will survive such a future. As a result of the miseducation, the United States encounters every new international circumstance as if it were a totally new situation, completely unrelated to colonial histories and global political and economic issues—a veritable *Groundhog Day* of context.

A complex and rigorous education ignores the right-wing call to dispose of multiculturalism and diversity in our schools (Finn, 2002). A rigorous and critical education analyzes the United States and the world as well as the U.S. relationship to the world. Teachers, students, and citizens must understand how knowledge is produced about these subjects, the ways that power shapes the types of knowledge to which we have access. The questions of where do we get our knowledge, how is it produced, and whose interests does it serve grant us access to one of the most important concerns of our time—the politics of knowledge in an age of electronic media. When we are openly discouraged by the advocates of a right-wing politics of knowledge from exploring diverse knowledges and perspectives, our political crap detectors should detonate. Such a policy is not compatible with a democratic society, not to mention a democratic education. A key dimension of a democratic education involves a literacy of power that enables an individual to explore the relation between power and knowledge, to expose the imprint of power on the knowledge that confronts us. "Inevitable civilizational conflicts" has a Fascist ring to it, as it forces us into direct conflict with Islamic others. If the conflict is inevitable then we might as well go ahead and take their oil fields, because they are just going to use the oil money to attack us anyway. We suggest a preemptive strike; we have no choices. We actively teach against Islamophobia, we name it, we historicize it, and we debunk it.

Anti-Islamophobic Education

A literacy of power helps us understand that the United States has entered a new phase in its national development. The American Empire in the 2nd decade of the 21st century stands ready to use military action to defend its economic and geo-political interests whenever necessary. Under the rhetorical cover of fighting for democracy and liberation, the United States seeks a new form of global domination. Most of the time it will avoid directly ruling a nation, opting instead for installing friendly governments that allow the U.S. economic and cultural domination. These friendly governments face few restrictions around issues of democracy or human rights as long as they create friendly business climates for American corporations. In these good business climates the nation's land, labor, markets, and natural resources are open to exploitation by transnational corporations (Parenti, 2002).

In the name of democracy, the United States has supported dictators and tyrants in the Islamic world including Saddam Hussein before the First Gulf War and Osama bin Laden in the Afghan fight against the Soviets. Wrapped in the flag of freedom the United States has insisted that Muslim governments silence the voices that criticize American policies in the region (Hesse & Sayyid, 2001). Such contradictions are repressed in the mainstream media and in the right-wing politics of knowledge in general. As William Damon (2002) writes in his chapter in the Fordham report:

> To understand that freedom and democracy must be defended, young people need to know three things: 1) What life is like in places that honor these ideals and in places that don't; 2) How these ideals have come to prevail in some places and not in others; and 3) Why some people hate these ideals and what we must do about that.

If it were only that simple and free from contradictions, Damon's first two points reference the simplistic binarism contrasting those (the United States) that support freedom and democracy and those (the despotic Muslims) who don't. His third point deals with the mission of the 21st century empire. Those who hate these ideals must be dealt with so that the empire can function more efficiently.

Despite the power of the U.S. corporate media to produce an information environment that refuses to refer to the American Empire or give credence to alternative views of U.S. relations with the Islamic world, many Americans still protested the Second Gulf War with Iraq. In speeches Shirley and I delivered after 9/11 explaining some of the reasons for the anger many Muslims have felt toward the United States, even politically conservative audiences were interested by the alternative information and perspectives we were providing. Members of the audience wisely asked why they had not heard the information we were providing. We live in an era of depoliticization, where public discourse around political questions slowly fades away in a world of ideologically charged entertainment. In such a cosmos, a literacy of power becomes more and more important as we struggle to counter the miseducation that continues to shape American views of the world.

References

Abukhattala, I. (2004). The new bogeyman under the bed: Image formation of Islam in the Western school curriculum and media. In J. Kincheloe & S. Steinberg (Eds.), *The miseducation of the West: How schools and the media distort our understanding of the Islamic world.* Westport, CT: Praeger.

Agresto, J. (2002). Lessons of the preamble. In Thomas B. Fordham Foundation. *September 11: What our children need to know.* Retrieved from http://www.edexcellence.net/sept11/september11.pdf

Ali, T. (2002). *The clash of fundamentalisms: Crusades, jihads and modernity*. New York: Verso.
Armstrong, K. (2002). *Islam agonistes: The arrival of the West*. Retrieved from http://dhushara.com/book/upd3/2002a/histis.htm
Bennett, W. (2002). Seizing this teachable moment. In Thomas B. Fordham Foundation. *September 11: What our children need to know*. Retrieved from http://www.edexcellence.net/sept11/september11.pdf
Cheney, L. (2002). Protecting our precious liberty. In Thomas B. Fordham Foundation. *September 11: What our children need to know*. Retrieved from http://www.edexcellence.net/sept11/september11.pdf
Chomsky, N. (2001). *9-11*. New York: Seven Stories Press.
Damon, W. (2002). Teaching students to count their blessings. In Thomas B. Fordham Foundation. *September 11: What our children need to know*. Retrieved from http://www.edexcellence.net/sept11/september11.pdf
Finn, C. (2002). Introduction. In Thomas B. Fordham Foundation. *September 11: What our children need to know*. Retrieved from http://www.edexcellence.net/sept11/september11.pdf
Thomas, B. Fordham Foundation (2002). *September 11: What our children need to know*. Retrieved from http://www.edexcellence.net/sept11/september11.pdf
Gadamer, H. (1975). *Truth and method*. G. Barden & J. Cumming (Trans. and Eds.), New York: Seabury Press.
Gresson, A. (1995). *The recovery of race in America*. Minneapolis, MN: University of Minnesota Press.
Gresson, A. (2003). *America's atonement*. New York: Peter Lang.
Hammer, R., and Kellner, D. (eds) (2009). *Media/cultural studies: Critical approaches*. New York: Peter Lang.
Hanson, V. (2002). Preserving America, man's greatest hope. In Thomas B. Fordham Foundation. *September 11: What our children need to know*. Retrieved from http://www.edexcellence.net/sept11/september11.pdf
Herman, E., & Chomsky, N. (1988). *Manufacturing consent: The political economy of mass media*. New York: Pantheon Books.
Hesse, B., & Sayyid, S. (2001). *A war against politics?* Retrieved from http://opendemocracy.net/forum/document
Hippler, J. (1995). The Islamic threat and Western foreign policy. In J. Hippler & A. Lueg (Eds.), *The next threat: Western perceptions of Islam*. London: Pluto Press.
Huntington, S. (1996). *The clash of civilizations: Remaking of world order*. New York: Touchstone.
Husseini, S. (2001). A media crusade. *Globalspin*. Retrieved from http://www.globalspin.org/media_crusade.html
Ignatieff, M. (2003). The burden. *New York Times Magazine*. (January 5). pp. 22–27, 50–54.
Kellner, D. (2004). September 11, terror war, and blowback. In J. Kincheloe & S. Steinberg (Eds.), *The miseducation of the West: How schools and the media distort our understanding of the Islamic world*. Westport, CT: Praeger.
Kellner, D. (1995). *Media culture: Cultural studies, identity, and politics between the modern and postmodern*. New York: Routledge.
Kincheloe, J. L. (2001). *Getting beyond the facts: Teaching Social Studies/Social Sciences in the twenty-first century*. New York: Peter Lang.
Kincheloe, J. L. & Steinberg, S. R. (1997). *Changing multiculturalism*. London: Open University Press.
Kincheloe, J. L., Steinberg, S. R., Rodriguez, N., & Chennault, R. (1998). *White reign: Deploying whiteness in America*. New York: St. Martin's Press.
Koechler, H. (2002). *After September 11: Clash of civilizations or dialogue*. Retrieved from http://www.up.edu/ph/forum/2002/Mar02/wept.11.html
Lewis, B. (2002). *What went wrong? Western impact and Middle Eastern response*. New York: Oxford University Press.
Lueg, A. (1995). The perception of Islam in Western debate. In J. Hippler & A. Lueg (Eds.), *The next threat: Western perceptions of Islam*. London: Pluto Press.

McLaren, P., Hammer, R., Reilly, S., & Sholle, D. (1995). *Rethinking media literacy: A critical pedagogy of representation.* New York: Peter Lang.
Macedo, D. (1994). *Literacies of power: What Americans are not allowed to know.* Boulder, CO: Westview.
Macedo, D. and Steinberg, S. R. (eds) (2007) *Media literacy: A reader.* New York: Peter Lang.
Madison, G. (1988). *The hermeneutics of postmodernity: Figures and themes.* Bloomington, IN: University of Indiana Press.
Middle East Studies Association (MESA) (1994). *Evaluation of secondary-level textbooks for coverage of Middle East and North Africa.* Retrieved from http://www.umich.edu/~iinet/cmenas/textbooks/reviews/summarya.html
Parenti, M. (2002). *The terrorism trap: September 11 and beyond.* San Francisco, CA: City Lights Books.
Rodriguez, N., & Villaverde, L. (2000). *Dismantling white privilege.* New York: Peter Lang.
Rose, K., & Kincheloe, J. L. (2003). *Art, culture, and education: Artful teaching in a fractured landscape.* New York: Peter Lang.
Runnymede Trust (1997). *The nature of Islamophobia.* Retrieved from http://www.runnymedetrust.org.meb/islamophobia/nature.html
Said, E. (1979). *Orientalism.* London: Vintage.
Said, E. (1981). *Covering Islam: How the media and the experts determine how we see the rest of the world.* New York: Pantheon.
Sudetic, C. (2002). The betrayal of Basra. *Utne Reader,* 110, 45–49.
Sesso, G., & Pyne J. (2002). Defining the American identity. In Thomas B. Fordham Foundation. *After September 11: Clash of civilizations or dialogue.* Retrieved from http://www.edexcellence.net/sept11/september11.pdf
Skalli, L. (2004) Loving Muslim women with a vengeance: The West, women, and fundamentalism. In J. L. Kincheloe, & S. R. Steinberg (Eds.), *The miseducation of the West: How schools and the media distort our understanding of the Islamic world.* Westport, CT: Praeger.
Steinberg, S. R. (2009). (ed.) *Diversity and multiculturalism: A reader.* New York: Peter Lang.
Stonebanks, C. (2004). Consequences of perceived ethnic identities. In J. L. Kincheloe & S. R. Steinberg (Eds.), *The miseducation of the West: How schools and the media distort our understanding of the Islamic world.* Westport, CT: Greenwood Press: Praeger.
Thayer-Bacon, B. (2003). *Relational "(e)pistemologies."* New York: Peter Lang.
Van Manen, M. (1991). *Researching lived experience.* Albany, NY: State University of New York Press.
Weinstein, K. (2002). Fighting complacency. In Thomas B. Fordham Foundation. *After September 11: Clash of civilizations or dialogue.* Retrieved from http://www.edexcellence.net/sept11/september11.pdf
West, C. (1993). *Race Matters.* Boston: Beacon Press.

Two

The Inescapable Presence of "Non-existent" Islamophobia

Christopher D. Stonebanks

It doesn't exist, yet it is inescapable. A return KLM flight from Lilongwe, Malawi, gives me a chance to decompress from a month and a half of work away from home and an opportunity to anticipate seeing my wife and our three children. The viewing control screen fixed to the back of the seat in front of me (and two inches from my face) provides a distraction from my clock-watching, counting the seconds, minutes, and hours to seeing my family again that feels like it's still days, weeks, and months away. Pressing the touch screen, I roll over the options: maps, music, television, film. Rotating through some of the film choices I note: *Underworld: Rise of the Lycans* (2009), *Paul Blart: Mall Cop* (2009), and *Taken* (2009). *Taken* stirs memories of the commercials on television: frightening, frantic images of a daughter being kidnapped and a father (Liam Neeson) desperately, heroically fighting to save her. The commercial, so effective, would cause a good deal of anxiety for my two elder children, with my youngest usually being warned to cover her eyes. My children would ask if I would fight with equal desperation to get them back if they would ever be kidnapped. What would I be willing to do to "save" them? Of course, I tell them I would do anything for my children. *Taken* is my emotional choice as it stirs protective, patriarchal instincts in me, so I watch the film.

Taken progresses with all the usual "action movie" formulas of the Hollywood blockbuster, and reference to it in a chapter on Islamophobia obviously gives something about my analysis of the film. In the film, Neeson's character, Bryan Mills, a retired paramilitary operative (the CIA), is struggling with an increasingly distanced relationship with his daughter, Kim, due to his ex-wife's marriage to her wealthy husband. Bryan's modest economic existence compared to his daughter's lifestyle leaves him on the periphery of her privileged world, but he refuses to stop keeping a watchful eye, because, as he is quick to point out, he *knows* the world. Despite his protests, Kim and her friend venture to France with plans to follow the band U2 during their European tour. In short time upon arrival in Paris, Kim is kidnapped, "taken" for the sex slave trade and, we soon find out, that what Bryan *knows* about the world and his "particular set of skills" become vital if his daughter is to be saved. Bryan's search for his daughter unravels the web of the horrific sex slavery and, as he has promised, he kills each person involved as he works his way to the top of his daughter's threat pyramid. At the base of the pyramid is a young, attractive, seemingly reluctant, white Frenchman who seduces the young girls into the trap. His superior, a "scary black man" (falling closely into Bogle's (1995) categorization of the "big, black, buck") pulls the young Frenchman's strings for his own Albanian Mafia masters. The Albanian Mafia members sport tattoos of the crescent and star associated with Islam, small ones on their hands that warrant close-ups, just so you do not confuse them with the Christian half of Albania. The Albanians sell Kim to an elaborate sex-slave auction room, where an Arab henchman/villain (Shaheen, 2001) purchases the virgin (being a 17-year-old white virgin increases her value) for his Arab sheikh (Shaheen, 2001) master. The Arab henchman provides some physical challenge for Bryan, but he is quickly killed. The Arab sheikh, fat and weak, begs for his life, offers money, and is summarily executed as well. Am I surprised that at the top of the pyramid is the stereotypical, unattractive, sexually voracious but sexually inept, morally vulgar, sloth-like, slovenly, and rich with, as is the case with all income related to Arab sheikhs, an unearned oil wealth? Not in the slightest. I am a person of mixed Iranian/European descent, a half/half (O'Hearn, 1998), who grew up in Canada on American media and have seen this "act" my whole life. What does continue to surprise me is that for something that does not exist, it truly does seem so inescapable to me. Perhaps a true test of the need to examine a "supposed" prejudice is if it is either and/or both casually ignored or so vehemently denied.

Intent

In the mid-1980s and in my early teens, I remember sitting in the stereotypical basement of a suburban house (imagine the basement of television's *That 70s Show*, but with patches of pink fibreglass exposed on the walls to protect us from winter) when I first heard the song "Killing an Arab" I recall straining to listen to The Cure's lead singer, Robert Smith's, whiny, squeaky singing style to confirm if he had just said "killing an Arab." In short time, when one of my high school peers pointed at me during the chorus and screamed, while laughing, "Killing an Arab!", the words were confirmed. Communication in the 1980s not being what it is today, it took a decade before I discovered that the song was a tribute to Albert Camus' 1943 novel *The Stranger* (L'Étranger), but I somehow doubt whether the song's acknowledgment of Camus' literary skills was fully (if at all) understood by my high school chum. Fast forward to 2009 and a quick poll of whether my pre-service teachers ever heard the song and I discover that it is still part of the Goth music canon, and, no, they have no idea what the song is about, besides "killing an Arab." Consumed, but not questioned, a song like "Killing an Arab" would make a powerful teaching tool. Not only for the obvious connections to Camus' book (brought back to popular media attention in 2006, since it was U.S. President George W. Bush's summer vacation reading), but also for its unexamined message.

It is not the intent of this chapter to point to specifics and state, "this is discrimination, this is racism, this is Islamophobia." Rather, it is hoped that by connecting definitions and characterizations for or against Islamophobia with the often overlooked but pervasive popular culture, the reader may begin to examine whether the call to "Teach against Islamophobia" is one worthy of attention. What, for instance, can we make of the Charlie Daniels Band song, *This Ain't No Rag, It's a Flag*? Even as a member of Canadian society, I cannot ignore the song's impact on those around me and, if my parents had made the choice to immigrate to the United States, the words of the song would have even greater weight. I can easily imagine this song being consumed by students passively or actively, perhaps a purposeful download on iTunes or background music played over scratchy speakers on a schoolbus ride home. Whichever the case, its success as a song, therefore its media rotation and mass appeal, cannot be denied and, if this is so, should it be analyzed in our schools? Accordingly, based on our inclusion or exclusion of this analysis, what does that have to say about what we learn about Islam, Muslims, and our acceptance or denial about Islamophobia in schools?

I make references to popular culture as either an example of what has been viewed as Islamophobic or comments from artists who have commented on Islamophobia. Do not be confused if you observe a balance in the two and interpret it as my own attempt at neutrality. My own life experience, teaching, and research have left me with the fairly strong conclusion that the portrayal of Muslims in the media has been overwhelmingly negative. My inclusion of artists is in recognition that there are people who have recognized discrimination and are trying to teach against it. The lyrics from Rage

Against the Machine's *Wake Up!* (1992) echo in my head: "Ya know they murdered X, And tried to blame it on Islam."

A Very Special Episode

> That's another thing America really needs to think about is our racism. Racism that comes from the United States towards Muslim people and towards Arabic people and that's something that has to stop and the United States has to start respecting people from the Middle East in order to find a solution to the problem that's been building up over many years. I thank everyone for your patience in letting me speak my mind on that. (Adam Yauch, Beastie Boys, MTV Video Awards, 1998)

Perhaps I missed ABC's *After School Special*, or that primetime episode of NBC's *Blossom* or CBC's *Beachcombers* that dealt with "Paki Bashing" (although I am fairly certain a show like CBC's *Degrassi High* had a "Muslim girl" episode). As a kid, I waited for some kind of recognition of the Middle Eastern/West Asian experience from television or film, but we were non-existent. When we did appear on the screen, we certainly were not portrayed with any kind of depth or nuance; we were mostly either victims of our own background or villains. Watching films like *Raiders of the Lost Ark* (1981) was not the same for me as it was for my friends. Although not an Arab, I squirmed at the caricatures of the Middle Eastern people, knowing that further confirmation of the all encompassing Orientalist Other's (Said, 1985) inferiority was, yet again, established.

> I maintain that if pedagogy involves issues of knowledge production and transmission, the shaping of values, and construction of subjectivity, then popular culture is the most powerful pedagogical force in contemporary America. (Steinberg, 2004, p. 173)

Popular media (film, television, music, print, etc.) have had, and continue to have, a profound impact on the manner in which Islam and the Muslim people are viewed. Whatever doubt exists of its power and the scope of the message it delivers should have been obvious to all of us after the first Gulf War. Marketed to us through the provocative image conjuring of the public relations firm Hill and Knowlton, false narratives of Arab soldiers killing babies (MacArthur, 2004) seemed completely ready for consumption after decades of the villainous Muslim. Post-9/11, little has changed as the repeated media message of Iraq's imminent danger given their, still yet to be discovered, weapons of mass destruction paved the way to acceptance of a second Gulf War and countless more innocent Iraqi deaths. So, when I hear cautions of placing too much importance on the media that surrounds us and too little respect for individuals' ability to be critical thinkers and construct their own knowledge, I wonder what the dead of Iraq or Afghanistan would think of this assessment. I maintain that the literalness that many take from the media has not really been challenged in our schools in the manner in which pre-service teachers and teachers believe it has. In the social commentary comedy of the late and great George Carlin, he angrily reflects on the First Gulf War and his country's fascination with war and their new target: "brown people."

> Especially if your country is full of brown people. Oh, we like that, don't we? That's our hobby now. But it's also our new job in the world: bombing brown people. Iraq, Panama, Grenada, Libya. You got some brown people in your country? Tell 'em to watch the fuck out, or we'll goddamn bomb them! (…) Now you folks might've noticed, I don't feel about that Gulf War the way we were instructed to feel about it by the United States government. My mind doesn't work that way. You see, I've got this real moron thing I do; it's called 'Thinking.' And I guess I'm not a very good American, because I like to form my own opinions; I don't just roll over when I'm told. Most Americans roll over on command. (George Carlin, 2005)

Certainly, Carlin also questions his fellow citizenry's ability to think critically and their ability to analyze the message they receive. From his "Life is Worth Losing" tour, taped in 2005 for HBO, Carlin rages on why "education sucks" and why it will never be fixed. Placing the blame clearly on "big business" he concludes that "… they don't want a population of citizens capable of critical thinking. They don't want well informed, well educated people capable of critical thinking. They're not interested in that. That doesn't help them. That's against their interest." Big business, media, interest, and lack of critical thought are all connected with discrimination, and what we learn through the powerful media makes me question if Islamophobia meets such resistance because the media "informs" them that it does not exist. Where, I wonder, are all the examples of critical reflection that are bandied as hallmarks of my field of education when so many examples clearly point to discrimination against Muslims and Islam? Returning to Carlin, I am reminded that the ultimate goal of big business is that "(t)hey want obedient workers, obedient workers. People who are just smart enough to run the machines and do the paperwork and just dumb enough to passively accept…." To what extent are we in the field of education simply passively accepting what is and is not taught in our schools regarding discrimination? Have we become just smart enough to run the machines?

> A regressive politics of knowledge helps produce a technicist education that is more concerned with "how to" than "why" questions. (…) Imagining what could be—a central goal of any critical pedagogy—has no place in such regressive schools. (Kincheloe, 2008, p. 4)

In more polite moments, some education students, these wonderful prospective teachers, may simply plead that they have had enough reading, hearing, and discussion about critical thinking, multicultural teaching, considerations of such things as Islamophobia and the practice of reflection about, amongst other things, what makes up or does not make up their curriculum. In less polite moments, these same wonderful pre-service teachers can roll their eyes and let out exasperated groans that they are, once again, being asked to contemplate a topic or concept critically and spend some of their time considering meaning or outcome regarding curriculum. My favorite reaction came from a student whose lengthy response included, "think critically, multiculturalism: we get it" and "we've been 'reflected' to death" when she surmised that a required course assignment included reference to these notions. The responses are never, or perhaps I should say never intentionally, rude or impolite, but I have experienced a palpable opinion that these are not so much concepts that need to be considered in depth, as they are often viewed as somewhat inherent truisms to the practice of teaching; a one-time directive, reinforced by societal norms that does not require repeat exercise of thought, due consideration and multiple viewpoints. It is this very standardized comprehension or comfort with a formulaic process of learning that leads to the all too common grade question, "Sir, what exactly do we have to do to get an 'A'?" This all too familiar step-by-step mantra, from many of these otherwise bright and eager pre-service teachers, demonstrates that even though it has been over two decades since *Education Under Siege* (Aronowitz & Giroux, 1985) was published, we, the teaching profession and field of study of education, are still very much "…enslaved to the concrete" (p. 49).

In 1985, my first year of college and two years before my own entry to university, Aronowitz and Giroux wrote about the "… gradual but relentless growth of anti-intellectualism" (p. 48) in the general American culture and in higher education in particular. Problematic for educational locations that claim critical thinking, they warn of "… a tendency towards literalness in thought" in students wrought through mass culture and the education system itself that did little to foster the kind of individual thinking that they often profess to encourage. Much like the inclusion of multiculturalism in schools and teacher education programs, where very few would stray from stating that they are proponents of promoting diversity, social justice, and equity (Stonebanks & Stonebanks, 2009), in the field of education, very few would claim that they were against critical thinking. Moreover, even the students that asked for a formula to get their "A" would state that their future teaching would reflect an anti-banking knowledge approach and utilize a critical constructivist teaching method that would make Paulo Freire delighted.

Because using Aronowitz and Giroux's work from 1985 represents my own generation of learners, this somewhat alleviates my students' resentment to the idea that production and acquisition of knowledge are potentially superficial, controlled through the acquiescence of a society and mass culture that would rather "not know." Still, as we discuss that although their intellectual capacity to comprehend some of these concepts, such as Islamophobia, is not being questioned, rather it is our collective commitment to truly engage in some of the ideas we profess to be a part of our profession, they are in part relieved that this has been an ongoing struggle not confined to their generation. However, what sets our two generations apart is that for the current "Generation Me" (Twenge, 2006) demographic presently making their way through university and into the schools, a generation defined by individualism and diversity, coming to terms with what are essentially discussions of revealing the hegemonic nature of schooling and society, and accepted racism seems ridiculous. After all, if they are defined by individualism and diversity, which they then associate with critical thought and tolerance, so, why should they be concerned about hegemony of their perceptions toward discrimination? What becomes hard to reflect on for this current generation is what it means to be raised in an era where mega-corporations like Disney and just plain big corporations like Coca-Cola and Pepsi sell individualism and diversity through absurd "everybody buy this product and be unique!" advertisement campaigns. In this context, the gradual but relentless growth of anti-intellectualism and literalness Aronowitz and Giroux cautioned about becomes increasingly problematic as the influences for acquiescence to dominant culture becomes highly corporatized and efficient. For those of us who attempt to forward critical thinking, anti-discrimination, and social justice into the classrooms beyond what currently exists in mission and vision statements, espousing these concepts in a manner that rarely moves beyond the text, our task is certainly a challenge. In this continued and pervasive learning environment, Islam and Muslims are either framed as a problem for the West or, if any suffering of a Muslim is acknowledged, it is portrayed as self-inflicted (Bayoumi, 2008). Overwhelmingly, we are taught that teaching against Islamophobia is not worthy of consideration.

Recognizing the Need to "Teach against Islamophobia"

> We should invade their countries, kill their leaders and convert them to Christianity. We weren't punctilious about locating and punishing only Hitler and his top officers. We carpet-bombed German cities; we killed civilians. That's war. And this is war.
> (Coulter, 2001, p. 18)

To "Teach against" a prejudice requires that the person engaged in the teaching acknowledges that the discriminatory practice in question actually exists and, if so, is worth teaching against. As I have argued elsewhere (Stonebanks, 2004), in the case of Islamophobia in Canada and the United States, it is not recognized as a prejudice that receives grand dissuasion from macro society and therefore receives similar treatment in the micro society of the classroom as well. It is entirely different, for example, for a pre-service teacher to listen to a lecture on the overwhelmingly negative experience of Indigenous Peoples in Canada's residential schools or an educator watching a documentary film on the United States' desegregation struggle of schools in the 1950s and think they would have been in solidarity fighting against the injustice and actually being one of the first to stand up and teach against these discriminations at the time. Teachers who are told of the possibility of the classroom being a location of social justice and transformative learning, often make the mistake of perceiving that this can happen in the absence of deep reflection, accountability (in this meaning, quite apart from standardization accountability), research, and (understandably), the most frightening of all, risk (Shor & Freire, 1987). After all, those educators who did stand up and teach against Islamophobia, did so at a risk (Stonebanks, 2008). In the post-9/11 environment, political television pundits can advocate racial profiling with a "good old, plain common sense" approach, without any apprehension of their comments being racist or discriminatory. For media pundits like Ann Coulter, however repugnant some may find her comments, she certainly cannot be considered as a pariah for her suggestions that Muslim civilians be carpet bombed. Why are comments like those made by Coulter so passively accepted in our society? Perhaps, as Coulter would be proud to point out, her opinions are shared by many within her society.

> The latest nationwide survey by the Pew Research Center for the People and the Press and the Pew Forum on Religion and Public Life, released in the summer of 2005 indicates, 'About a third of Americans (36%) say the Islamic religion is more likely to encourage violence among its followers' (The Pew Research Center, 2005). A *Washington Post*–ABC News Poll released in the spring of 2006 further documents the increase in the negative perception of Islam in the US. According to the poll, 'nearly half of Americans—46 percent—have a negative view of Islam, seven percentage points higher than in the tense months after Sept. 11, 2001.' A report released in September 2006 by the Council on American–Islamic Relations (CAIR) reported that anti-Muslim incidents in the US increased almost 30% from the previous year. Another recent survey conducted by CAIR Research Center (2006) asked people to respond to the open-ended question 'When you hear the word Muslim, what is the first thought that comes to your mind?' Out of 1000 interviews conducted during this survey, 26% of respondents made negative comments, including 'violence,' 'hatred,' 'terrorists,' 'war,' 'guns' and 'towel-head.' (Ramarajan & Runell, 2007, p. 88)

Putting aside the narratives and experiences of Muslims in regard to the discrimination they may encounter, according to the statistics given by non-Muslims toward Islam and Muslims, it is clear that a negative perception is widespread. In defining what Islamophobia means, Mohideen and Mohideen (2008) conclude that it "...may be defined as the practice of prejudice against Islam and the demonisation and dehumanisation of Muslims. This is generally manifested in negative attitudes, discrimination, physical harassment and vilification in the media" (p. 73). Turning to the influential report by the British Runnymede Trust, an anti-racism think-tank, Mohideen and Mohideen cite their analysis of the major causes for prejudice against Muslim and Islam. Islamophobia occurs when:

1. Islam is seen as a monolithic bloc, static and unresponsive to change.
2. Islam is seen as separate and "other." It does not have values in common with other cultures, is not affected by them, and does not influence them.
3. Islam is seen as inferior to the West. It is seen as barbaric, irrational, primitive, and sexist.
4. Islam is seen as violent, aggressive, threatening, supportive of terrorism, and engaged in a "clash of civilisations."
5. Islam is seen as a political ideology and is used for political or military advantage.
6. Criticisms made of the West by Islam are rejected out of hand.
7. Hostility towards Islam is used to justify discriminatory practices towards Muslims and exclusion of Muslims from mainstream society.
8. Anti-Muslim hostility is seen as natural or normal. (Runnymede Trust, 1997, p. 4)

These major causes fall closely with the four "myths" about Islam and Muslims laid out by scholar Seyyed Hossein Nasr that lead to Islamophobia. They are: (1) that Islam was a monolithic whole; (2) that Islam wanted to rule the Western World; (3) that Islam was anti-Western; and (4) that Islam was against modernity and democracy (United Nations, 2004, p. 30). Speaking at the same United Nations "Unlearning Intolerance" seminar, as Seyyed, Professor John L. Esposito noted that "like anti Semitism and other forms of intolerance, Islamophohia could not be eradicated without the participation of religious and political leaders, as well as the media and educators" (United Nations, 2004, p. 31). Including all the above-mentioned characteristics of Islamophobia, Abu Sway (2005) adds "...verbal abuse...vandalizing of property...discrimination in employment...discrimination in the provision of health services, exclusion from managerial positions and jobs of high responsibility and exclusion from political and governmental posts. Ultimately, Islamophobia also comprises prejudice in the media, literature, and everyday conversation" (p. 15). In all examples of defining Islamaphobia and combating it, scholars note that education, both the personal process of learning about Islam beyond the stereotypes perpetuated in the media and teaching of others, is essential. Returning to the prevalence of anti-intellectualism in the media and literalness of understanding for the consumers of the media, we briefly turn to the critics of the existence of Islamophobia and the ultimate impact they have on the acceptance of prejudice.

Critics of the Term and Existence of Islamophobia

If it walks like a duck and quacks like a duck ...
—(Anonymous)

So shave that dadgum moustache off, so you're not so conspicuous, so you look like maybe an Italian. Or somethin' (...) As far as from people lookin' at ya. I see a lot of people and I think "there's a dadgum Muslim, I wonder what kind of bomb he's got strapped to him".
—(Borat, 2006)

As stated in the foreword of this book, I completely understand the limitations of a word like "Islamophobia." Any kind of "phobia" descriptor brings to mind some kind of clinical phobias that involve an involuntary medical/psychological reaction to prayer rugs, hijabs, and kufis as opposed to a learned social prejudice. Gottschalk and Greenberg (2008) write, "Islamophobia: anxiety of Islam? Can this really be compared to individual psychological traumas, such as acrophobia, arachnophobia, or xenophobia?" (p. 5). Perpetuated by mainstream media and popular culture, Gottschalk and Greenberg believe that "Islamophobia" accurately reflects a *social* anxiety toward Islam and Muslim cultures. With a comprehension of the shortcomings, the overall popular culture and media critiques of Islamophobia do not seem to focus on its limitations of capturing the human suffering that is a result of prejudice toward Muslims and the religion of Islam, rather its intent appears to devalue the lived experience of those who have faced discrimination. For instance, in critiquing the term Islamophobia, academics like Dr. Kamal Aboulmagd state "... that he preferred the term 'anti-Islamism' because, similar to anti Semitism, it focussed on the agony of the victims while 'Islamophobia' reflected the state of mind of those who felt threatened" (United Nations, 2004, p. 31). This assessment focusses on finding a term that accurately reflects the recognition of human suffering and the promotion of ending it. Looking for a term that is more accurate than Islamophobia does not deny that pain has been inflicted on Muslims due to hateful discrimination.

Measuring the influence intellectuals and academics have had on the contribution to the debate regarding Islamophobia in the United Kingdom, Allen (2006) notes there are "very few" (p. 83), and similar conclusions can be drawn from Canada and the United States. Media, Allen notes, are "...the primary source for which knowledge and information about Muslims and Islam in the West is gleaned" (p. 75). Some public intellectuals, forwarding their thoughts in the supposed open spaces of media, such as the United Kingdom's John Gross, regard Islamophobia as something that can be scoffed at. In his article "Phobia of Phobias" (2004) it is difficult to ignore the ridicule he acertains in the concept, in comparison to other prejudice he places on a higher scale—almost as if he has developed a ranking of worthiness. To put the following quote in context, Gross is deriding Ken Livingston's (who at the time was the Mayor of London) interactions with controversial (BBC, 2004) cleric Dr. Yusuf al-Qaradawi.

> The only conclusion one can draw is that for the time being he regards homophobia and the maltreatment of women as secondary issues. They have been overshadowed in his mind by a greater menace—the phobia of phobias, Islamophobia. He is hardly alone in this. The idea that Islamophobia is the most dangerous of current social evils had taken root within a few days, perhaps even hours, of 9/11, and since then it has become widely accepted wisdom. We are constantly warned to be on guard against prejudice toward Muslims. We have inevitably been instructed that British society is "institutionally Islamophobic." Islamophobia is a word which means a number of different things, and the confusion which can result suits many of those who use it very well. (p. 34)

Although the statement "phobia of phobias" is somewhat meant to mock Islamophobia in Gross' numerical order of prejudice importance, it does not completely devalue the experience of Muslims in the United Kingdom. Notice, however, the statement that "…Islamophobia is a word which means a number of different things, and the confusion which can result suits many of those who use it very well" (ibid.). This idea that those who "claim" to experience discrimination do so to further advance their advantage has been a fairly common objection amongst the powerbloc" (Kincheloe & Steinberg, 1997); their earned privilege being stolen in a politically correct, multicultural environment that unfairly benefits "minorities" to the detriment of the deserved. American television pundit and radio talk show host, Denis Prager, repeats the same sentiment, asserting "(w)hoever coined the term 'Islamophobia' was quite shrewd. Notice the intellectual sleight of hand here." (Prager, 2007) "Suits them," "sleight of hand" conjure up images of the manipulative, dishonest, and scheming "Ay-rab" that fill our television and movie screens. Prager's take on Muslims in the United States and their "sleight of hand" ways became apparent when Congressman Keith Ellison became the first Muslim elected to the United States Congress and asked to be sworn in using the Qur'an.

> Devotees of multiculturalism and political correctness who do not see how damaging to the fabric of American civilization it is to allow Ellison to choose his own book need only imagine a racist elected to Congress. Would they allow him to choose Hitler's "Mein Kampf," the Nazis' bible, for his oath? And if not, why not?

On what grounds will those defending" Ellison's right to choose his favorite book deny that same right to a racist who is elected to public office? (Prager, 2006)

In Prager's comment on a Muslim Congressman's right to use the Qur'an in his swearing-in ceremony, Hitler's *Mein Kampf* is used as an end result of the use of the Qur'an. If not used as a tactic to instil in the reader's mind a comparison between the Qur'an and *Mein Kampf*, it can, at the very least, be assumed that the Qur'an is some kind of "gateway" hate literature leading to the Nazi handbook. Sleight of hand, indeed!

> Sut Jhally: Orientalism tries to answer the question of why, when we think of the Middle East for example, we have a preconceived notion of what kind of people live there, what they believe, how they act. Even though we may never have been there, or indeed even met anyone from there. More generally Orientalism asks, how do we come to understand people, strangers, who look different to us by virtue of the color of their skin? The central argument of Orientalism is that the way that we acquire this knowledge is not innocent or objective but the end result of a process that reflects certain interests. That is, it is highly motivated. (MEF, 2005, p. 2)

Perhaps what the sleight of hand media authors like Prager are cautioning us against is, if it walks like a duck and quacks like a duck, it's probably a terrorist dressed up like a duck! What are the motivations behind the various media sources that devalue Islamophobia as a term to stand for discrimination against Muslims? Even The British Runnymede Trust notes that "(t)he term is not, admittedly, ideal. Critics of it consider that its use panders to what they call political correctness, that it stifles legitimate criticism of Islam, and that it demonises and stigmatises anyone who wishes to engage in such criticism" (p. 4). But, a general review of these critics reveals a decidedly ideological/political objective; often couching the denial of the word within an anti-political-correctness, a down-to-earth sensibility, and/or a hyperrationality (Kincheloe, 1999) that seems to be more concerned with the semantics of the expression rather than the morals of dismissing it. So, when Abdel Majri, the president of the League of Swiss Muslims, responds to the November 2009 vote in Switzerland to ban minarets on mosques, stating "We were a bit shocked, we hadn't expected this result.... This is another step toward Islamophobia in Switzerland and Europe in general," from the perspective of the "sleight of hand" gang, we should not take at face value that he is really interested in the freedom of Muslims to have places of worship that reflect their aesthetic and religious beliefs, rather, we should be aware of their ulterior motives. With this in mind, perhaps, I wonder if Majri himself owns a minaret construction company.

As an educator that tries to be committed to an anti-discrimination school environment, these arguments seem as pointless to me as analyzing the validity of using the term "anti-Semitism" in the face of responding to a

Holocaust denier, questioning the breadth of who should be included in the term "Semite." Or, being bogged down in questioning whether or not homophobia is really a medical phobia when, for instance, a lesbian youth is being physically threatened in a school hallway. Not to suggest by any stretch of the imagination anti-Semitism and homophobia have been solved in schools, but, in most Canadian educational contexts there would be fewer educators who denied their existence than (to varying degrees) a few short decades ago. We can debate whether society or the media were first to acknowledge discriminations like anti-Semitism and homophobia, but I can be fairly certain that our schools followed suit only when such perspectives became "acceptable." Although the concept that classrooms are locations of societal reproduction is not a shock to those who study schools through a sociological lens, to a great many pre-service teachers and teachers who enter the profession with the noblest of intentions, the idea that they could reproduce any kind of bias related to race, ethnicity, religion, gender, etc...seems a repugnant thought. But, as I point out in my courses, one must critically engage taken for granted assumptions to uncover discrimination. Islamophobia continues to fall into the category of an unexamined prejudice.

> Day after day...I witnessed classic expressions of petty racism. An Arab man would come in to declare the birth of a son. As was (and still is) customary, the office workers would shake hands, usually twice (when he arrived and departed). The interview was invariably polite and formal. But as soon as the man left, the comments would begin. The person who had shaken the Arab's hand would rush to wash his own, making a fuss about how dirty "those people" were. The office staff would ridicule the name of the child ("they're always called Nasser or Mohammed"), and they'd recount horror stories about the dysfunctional lives of the infidels. I usually listened quietly, until one day I was drawn into the conversation. This happened because of the news from America. Riots were exploding in Newark and Detroit (and over a hundred smaller cities) that summer, and my host wanted to know how it was that such terrible racism existed where I came from. In France, they told me, no such prejudice existed; no such riots would ever occur. (Scott, 2007, p. 43)

Gottschalk and Greenberg challenge, "(i)f you are sceptical about the notion of 'Islamophobia,' get a piece of paper and brainstorm. Write down, with as little thought and as much honesty as possible, all of the words that come to mind when you think of the words 'Islam' or 'Muslim'" (p. 3). This is a difficult task for anyone to accomplish in a public space, especially in the field of education when terms like "celebrating diversity" are regularly bandied about. No one wants to admit discrimination. In some of my classes, like a multiculturalism classroom, I ask students to take a private moment and write down everything that comes into their head when they hear the word "Iran" (Stonebanks, 2008a).

> Dilios: The enemy outnumber us a paltry three to one, good odds for any Greek. This day we rescue a world from mysticism and tyranny and usher in a future brighter than anything we can imagine. (*300*, 2006)

When I ask my students to think about what comes into their head when they hear the word "Iran," do they think of something positive or negative, something drawn from personal experience or from the media? Only they know the truth. Peruse the newspaper, television, radio, movies, comic books, or even video games in any given day. How many images and messages are you bombarded with every day that *tell* you about Muslims, the religion of Islam and people from the Middle East to West Asia. How much are you able to filter without it becoming a stereotype, with that stereotype leading to a passive reaction to discrimination. When asked what inspired him to write the book *Orientalism*, Edward Said noted that one of the reasons was "…the constant sort of disparity I felt between what my experience of being an Arab was, and the representations of that that one saw in art" (MEF, 2005, p. 2). Like many of the authors of this book who are Muslim or of Muslim heritage, or allies of "teaching against Islamophobia," we have all experienced the great divide between what we see in the media and the people who we are or who we know. The media narratives we consume teach us that Islamophobia is prevalent, but there are counter-narratives as well (Sensoy & Stonebanks, 2009; Stonebanks, 2008a).

Islamophobia Narrative and Counter-narrative

How much is the dehumanization of Islam a part of our schools? When my wife who is of English European descent announced in her staffroom that she was engaged to marry me, she received some congratulations but also overwhelming gasps that many of them had seen the film *Not Without My Daughter* and would never let their daughters marry an Iranian. Can anyone imagine the same response to a young teacher saying she's marrying someone of Irish descent? Would they warn her about *Angela's Ashes*? Of course not, because this is one perspective of the rich mosaic of voices we hear from people of Irish descent. A humanizing narrative mosaic that is lost to Islam in the West.

> Often in the West Islam is depicted as a monolith, and little attention is paid to the rich diversity within both the religion and civilization of Islam. (Nasr, 2004, p. 57)

Is it possible that Islam, and the cultures associated with it, are the monolith extremes that are portrayed by popular pundits, the media in general or even the extreme fundamentalist Muslim voices that are given consistent "air-time"? Often, the answer to the question is right in front of us, but somehow does not penetrate our collective imagery. Teachers must begin to ask themselves, how do these experts and the research they have done to gain the title of expert benefit the people they have studied? The common narrative about Muslims and Islam is clear, but we just do not want to admit it is a prejudice.

> "This is way too smart for Iranian scientists"
> —(*The Transformers*, 2007)

Oftentimes, like in the film *The Transformers*, it is a message that comes in "just under the radar." We know that we just heard someone say, "This is way too smart for Iranian scientists," but we do not want to analyze what a loaded, scripted, and edited statement like that means. What does it mean? Nothing? Something? Anything? Again, if we changed "Iranian" for another ethnicity, would the meaning change? Would it seem bigoted? Why does it or does it not seem bigoted when we use the word "Iranian"? I wonder if the writers of *The Transformers* could have spoken with President George W. Bush in regard to his statement, "Look, Iran was dangerous, Iran is dangerous, and will be dangerous if they have the knowledge necessary to make a nuclear weapon" (Denzin & Giardina, 2008, p. 10) and tell him, "relax, this is way too smart for Iranian scientists." Of course, joking aside, the narrative on this matter is clear: Iranians are just, *just*, smart enough to have this dangerous knowledge and this knowledge must not be allowed to get into their hands (or heads), because of *who* they are.

> And then allegations are made that the Iranian state is peopled by crazy people. The argument is—it's a frankly racist argument—that you're dealing with madmen here, and therefore they may not be allowed to get nuclear weapons. (…) I mean, I'm against proliferation myself. I think it's better that fewer countries that have these things, the better off the whole world is. But the Iranian state hasn't invaded aggressively another country for 200 years. It hasn't demonstrated itself to be peopled by wild men. (Cole, "Democracy Now!," 2006)

In agreement with Cole's position that I am also against nuclear proliferation and (again) as an educator that tries to live a social justice, anti-racist curriculum, I do have serious criticisms of my motherland, but, the Western narrative of Iran is a bizarre one. Do the research yourself: look up how many nuclear weapons (we do not call Western weapons "Weapons of Mass Destruction" for another bizarre reason) the United States is in possession of, then compare the military spending of the United States versus Iran and finally look up Cole's statement that Iran has not attacked another country in 200 years. Draw your own conclusions and then contrast that to the Western grand narrative on Iran. What would the counter-narrative be to this bizarre situation?

Maya: What could you possibly know about comedy anyway? There are no comedians in Iran?
Majeed: I was the funniest one in school ... and the funniest one in explosives training!
—(*Looking for Comedy in the Muslim World*, 2006)

"No comedians in Iran," fits the stereotype of the humorless Muslim (Shaheen, 2008) quite well. Iranian American comedian, Maz Jobrani, observed regarding the portrayal of people of the Middle-East, "Just once show us baking cookies or something. Cause I've been to Iran, we bake cookies. Never gonna happen, though. Even if they did that, they'd follow it up with, 'This just in, a cookie bomb just exploded' (New City Stage, 2009)." Through humor, Jobrani's counter-narrative is powerful, insightful, and enticing. So, here is my counter-narrative endeavor through humor; a comedic skit for your imagination to counter the grand narrative about Iran and President Bush's insistence that they not be allowed to have knowledge. Let us imagine, *they agreed with his logic.* Also, just for our visual imagery, let us cast British Iranian Omid Djalili as the Komiteh Member (moral standards police) and Maz Jobrani as civilian, Ali Samani.

(Fade in to a man dressed in a bureaucratic manner knocking on a door, up a short flight of stairs, inside a courtyard that houses numerous apartments early on a Tuesday morning. A man, obviously just woken up, opens the door dressed in pyjama bottoms and a t-shirt.)

Komiteh Member: Ali Samani?

Ali Samani: Yes?

KM: The same Ali Samani who attended Ryerson University in Ontario, Canada between 1985 and 1989?

Ali: Yes.

KM: Sir, I'm a Komiteh member. What did you study?

Ali: I was in the department of arts, I studied graphics and communication ... what is this all about?

KM: Sir, as you may already know, President Bush of the United States of America has declared a ruling that Iran, I quote here now, "Look, Iran was dangerous, Iran is dangerous, and will be dangerous if they have the knowledge necessary to make a nuclear weapon."

Ali: He is so eloquent when he speaks.

KM: Yes, and apparently even more poetic when it is spoken in his native English language. But, please do not interrupt.

Ali: Sorry.

KM: Yes, okay. Well, based on his declaration that has received wide support around the world, the revolutionary government has decided to comply and has asked the Komiteh, in accordance with our obligation to ensure

Iranian morality, to go to each citizen of Iran and ensure that no one has any knowledge that may lead to the development of a nuclear weapon.

(long pause, Ali stands blinking for a while)

Ali: ... Yes?

KM: Sir, do you have any knowledge that may lead to the development of a nuclear weapon or what may be referred to an "Islamic Bomb"? (begins to take notes)

Ali: What? I'm a graphic designer!

KM: Okay, well I have a number of questions, picked randomly of course, that have been generated for you, Mr. Ali Samani. Please remember that time is an important factor in determining the honesty of your response, so please answer as quickly as possible. Have you ever seen the movie "Back to the Future"?

Ali: No.

KM: Are you sure, the film that made Michael J. Fox the darling of America in the mid-80s?

Ali: No, I missed that one.

KM: Did you ever see *True Lies*?

Ali: (nervously) ...yes.

KM: Thank you sir; that was a trick question to test your honesty. You see, whereas in "Back to the Future" the Islamic terrorists were trying to build a bomb, thereby demonstrating that they had knowledge of nuclear technology, in *True Lies* the Islamic terrorists had bought the bomb, so they probably did not know how to build it. Do you see?

Ali: I guess.

KM: There is a difference, don't you agree?

Ali: ... I guess.

KM: Okay, moving from the Arts into your education ... uhhh ... when you were in Canada, did you take any courses relating to nuclear technology?

Ali: I'm a graphic designer, remember?

KM: Oh, yes. That's right; you couldn't get into the sciences ... your parents must be disappointed.

Ali: Hey!

KM: Let's then continue to literature. Did you ever read a biography, auto, unauthorized or otherwise on Oppenheimer or Einstein?

Ali: No (but now joking) but, but I did have a poster of Einstein up in my dorm room!

KM: (seriously) The black and white kind?

Ali: (now nervously again) ... yes.

KM: The one with his tongue sticking out?

Ali: ... yes.

KM: Mr Ali Samani, I must now inform you that you must return with me to the Komiteh headquarters for further questions. (grabs Ali off the porch and starts escorting him down the stairs into the courtyard)

Ali: (protesting) But, I also had Nagel posters in my dorm room too, everyone was doing it ... it was the 80s.

KM: Sir, you are not helping your cause.

(Fade out)

I cannot really talk to the Bryan Mills' fictional character from *Taken*, but if I did have the opportunity to speak to the movie's writers, Luc Besson and/or Robert Mark Kamen, I would like to tell them, "I know the world too, sweetie, and it's a lot different than yours."

References

Allen, C. (2006). *Securitization and religious divides in Europe: Islamophobia in the United Kingdom*. Paris: European Commission on Security Issues in Europe.

Aronowitz, S, & Giroux, H. (1985). *Education under siege*. New York: Bergin & Garvey.

Bayoumi, M. (2008). *How does it feel to be a problem?* Toronto: Penguin Press.

BBC. (2004, July 7). *Controversial preacher with 'star status'*. Retrieved April 6, 2008, from BBC News: http://news.bbc.co.uk/2/hi/uk_news/3874893.stm

Bogle, D. (1995). *Toms, coons, mulattoes, mammies & bucks: An interpretive history of blacks in American films*. New York: Continuum International Publishing Group.

Camus, A. (1943). *The stranger*. Paris: Éditions Gallimard.

Coulter, A. (2001, September 12). *This is war: We should invade their countries*. Retrieved March 2, 2007, from National Review Online: http://www.nationalreview.com/coulter/coulter.shtml

Democracy Now! (2006, September 25). *Juan Cole on Civil War in Iraq, the hyping of WMD Intel on Iran, and how the Lebanon War has weakened Israel*. Retrieved February 3, 2008, from Democracy Now! The War and Peace Report: http://www.democracynow.org/2006/9/25/juan_cole_on_civil_war_in

Denzin, N. & Giardina, M. (2008). *Qualitative inquiry and the politics of evidence*. Walnut Creek, CA: Left Coast Press.

Gottschalk, P, & Greenberg, G. (2008). *Islamophobia: Making Muslims the Enemy*. Lanham, MD: Rowman & Littlefield Publishers, Inc.

Gross, J. (2004, September). The phobia of phobias. *The New Criterion*, 33–35.

Jhally, S. (Director). (2005). Edward Said on Orientalism. MEF.

Kincheloe, J. (1999). *The post-formal reader: Cognition and education*. J. L. Kincheloe & S. R. Steinberg (Eds.), New York: Falmer Press.

Kincheloe, J. L. (2008). *Critical pedagogy* (2nd ed.). New York: Peter Lang.

Kincheloe, J. L. & Steinberg, S. R. (Eds.). (1997). *Changing multiculturalism: New times, new curriculum*. London: Open University Press.

Kincheloe, J., L. & Steinberg, S. R. (Eds.). (2004). *The miseducation of the West: How schools and the media distort our understanding of the Islamic world*. Westport, CT: Praeger Press.

MacArthur, J. R. (c2004). *Second front: Censorship and propaganda in the 1991 Gulf War*. Berkeley, CA: University of California Press.

Mohideen, H., & Mohideen, S. (2008). The language of Islamophobia in Internet. *Intellectual Discourse*, 16(1), 73–87.

Nasr, S. H. (2004). *The heart of Islam: Enduring values for humanity*. New York: HarperCollins.

New City Stage. (2009, February). *New city stage*. Retrieved June 1, 2009, from Preview: Maz Jobrani: http://newcitystage.com/2009/02/09/preview-maz-jobranilakeshore-theater/
O'Hearn, C. C. (1998). *Half and half: Writers on growing up biracial and bicultural.* New York: Pantheon.
Prager, D. (2006, November 26). *America, not Keith Ellison, decides what book a congressman takes his oath on.* Retrieved May 23, 2008, from Townhall: http://townhall.com/columnists/DennisPrager/2006/11/28/america,_not_keith_ellison,_decides_what_book_a_congressman_takes_his_oath_on?page=full
Prager, D. (2007, July 31). *Why 'Islamophobia' is a brilliant term.* Retrieved May 6, 2008, from Real Clear Politics: http://www.realclearpolitics.com/articles/2007/07/why_islamophobia_is_a_brillian.html
Ramarajan, D. & Runell, M. (2007). Confronting Islamophobia in education. *Intercultural Education,* 18(2), 87–97.
Runnymede Trust (1997). Islamophobia: a challenge for us all. Commissioned by Straw, J. London: British Commission on Muslims Publication.
Said, E. (c1985). *Orientalism.* Harmondsworth, UK: Penguin.
Scott, J. W. (2007). *The politics of the veil.* Princeton, NJ: Princeton University Press.
Sensoy, Ö. & Stonebanks, C. D. (2009). *Muslim voices in schools: Narratives of identity and pluralism.* Rotterdam, The Netherlands: Sense Publishing.
Shaheen, J. G. (2001). *Reel bad Arabs.* New York: Olive Branch Press.
Shaheen, J. (2008). *Guilty: Hollywood's verdict on Arabs after 9/11.* Northampton, NY: Olive Branch Press.
Shor, I., & Freire, P. (1987). *A pedagogy for liberation: Dialogues on transforming education.* Westport, CT: Bergin & Garvey.
Steinberg, S. R. (2004). Desert Minstrels: Hollywood's Curriculum of Arabs and Muslims. In Kincheloe, J. L. and Steinberg, S. R. (Eds.), *The miseducation of the West: How schools and the media distort our understanding of the Islamic world.* Westport, CT: Praeger.
Stonebanks, C. D. (2004). Consequences of perceived ethnic identities. In Kincheloe, J. L. and Steinberg, S. R. (Eds.), *The miseducation of the West: How schools and the media distort our understanding of the Islamic world,* (pp. 87–102). Westport, CT: Praeger.
Stonebanks, C. D. (2008a). From politicized knowledge to standardized knowing. In N. D. Giardina (Ed.), *Qualitative inquiry and the politics of evidence* (pp. 250–269). Walnut Creek, CA: Left Coast Press.
Stonebanks, C. D. (2008b). Spartan superhunks and Persian monsters: Responding to truth and identity as determined by Hollywood. *Studies in Symbolic Interaction,* 31, 207–221.
Stonebanks, C. D., & Stonebanks, M. (2009). Religion and diversity in our classrooms. In Shirley R. Steinberg (Ed.), *Diversity: A reader.* New York: Peter Lang.
Sway, A. M. (2005). Islamophobia: Meaning, manifestations, causes. *Palestine-Israel Journal of Politics, Economics & Culture,* 12(2/3), 15–23.
Twenge, J. (2006). *Generation me.* New York: Free Press.
United Nations. (2004). Confronting Islamophobia. *UN Chronicle,* 4, 30–31.

Media References (Film)

Bay, M. (Director). (2007). *The transformers* [Motion Picture]. United States: Hasbro, Marvel Productions, Sunbow Productions, Toei Animation.
Brooks, A. (Director). (2006). *Looking for comedy in the Muslim World* [Motion Picture]. United States: Warner Bros..
Carr, S. (Director). (2009). *Paul Blart: mall cop* [Motion Picture]. United States.: Relativity Media, Happy Madison.
Charles, L. (Director). (2009). *Borat* [Motion Picture].
Morel, P. (Director). (2009). *Taken* [Motion Picture]. France: EuropaCorp
Snyder, Z. (Director). (2006). *300* [Motion Picture]. United States: Legendary Pictures, Virtual Studios, Atmosphere Pictures, Hollywood Gang.

Spielberg, S. (Director). (1981). *Raiders of the lost ark* [Motion Picture]. United States: Lucasfilm Limited.

Tatopoulos, P. (Director). (2009). *Underworld: Rise of the Lycans* [Motion Picture]. United States: Screen Gems.

Media References (Television)

Carlin, G. (June 19, 2005). George Carlin on Bush War. www.georgecarlin.com. Date of last retrieval, March 29, 2010.

Mandabach, C. (Executive Producer). (1998–2006). *That 70s show (television series)*. US: FOX Broadcasting Company.

Reo, D. (Executive Producer). (1991–1995). *Blossom (television series)*. US: NBC Broadcasting Company.

Schuyler, C., & Hood, K. (Creators). (1989–1991). *Degrassi high (television series)*. Canada: Canadian Broadcasting Company.

Strange, M., & Strange, L. (Creators). (1998–2006). *Beachcombers (television series)*. Canada: Canadian Broadcasting Company.

Media References (Music)

Charlie Daniels Band. (2001) *This ain't no rag, it's a flag* [CD], US: Capitol.

de la Rocha, Z. (1992). *Wake up!* [CD], US: Epic Records.

Smith, R. (1978). *Killing an Arab*. On *Boys don't cry*. [CD], UK: Small Wonder.

Three

Islam: The Fundamentals Every Teacher Should Know

Khurrum Mirza and Naved Bakali

Whether one is teaching in a secondary or an elementary school, in a public or a private institution, in a highly multicultural school or an entirely homogenous milieu, today's teacher cannot escape a discussion on Islam and Muslims. Since the events of 9/11 and the subsequent war on terror, the faith and its followers have been placed in the spotlight. It is virtually impossible to sit down to watch the nightly news and not come across at least one story involving Muslims. In a recent survey, 32% of Canadians admitted to having a thorough understanding of Islam (Green, 2009). Where should we as teachers of the 21st century fit? In order to properly present Islam and Muslims to our students, whether as part of a planned lesson or in response to a question raised in class, it is imperative that today's educators have a basic understanding of the religion, the main tenets of the faith, and contemporary points of interest. Furthermore, both teachers and administrators need to be aware of the needs of their Muslim students and how to best respond to issues such as prayer space, the *hijab*, fasting, and other relevant points of interest.

As practicing Sunni Muslims who were born and raised in North America, we are cognizant of the growing sense of Islamophobia in the West. Furthermore, as individuals associated with public schools in Canada, first as students and presently as teachers, we feel that we have a unique perspective of the issues faced by Muslim students (both practicing and non-practicing)—the way Islam is perceived by the general student body, and the role of the school in meeting these challenges. It is our hope that this chapter addresses these issues and leaves the educators with the tools needed to properly address Islam in the classroom as well as gain a better understanding of their Muslim students.

Brief History of Islam and Muhammad (Peace Be upon Him)[1]

No discussion on Islam can take place without a close look at its Prophet, and no discussion on Islam or Muhammad (pbuh) can be complete without first examining its connection with the earlier faiths of Christianity and Judaism. When reading on Islam, many non-Muslims are surprised with the number of common characters and events shared between the faiths of Judaism, Christianity, and Islam. This has to do with the fact that Islam teaches that God has sent a long line of messengers to mankind starting from Adam, and running through a list of men including Noah, Abraham, Moses, Jesus, and concludes with Muhammad (peace be upon them). Aside from Muhammad (pbuh), these are names that are familiar to anyone who has read the Bible. Regarding Jesus (pbuh), specifically, Islam views him as a great prophet of God and not the son of God. He left behind scripture and the example of righteous conduct for his followers. The consensus amongst the various Muslim groups is that the message of Jesus (pbuh) was not preserved and over time it was altered by the hand of man, and therefore strayed from its original meaning. According to Islamic theology each of the 25 prophets mentioned in the Qur'an, as well as the thousands of others whose names are not known,[2] were sent to their people with the message to worship the one true God while enjoining good and forbidding evil (Al-Ashqar, 1999). If one is successful, the believer would have the ultimate reward in the afterlife of peace and comfort in heaven.

While Muslims believe the overall message delivered was common to all prophets, the rituals associated with acts, worship, and the specific laws given to a people have varied over time. Therefore, even though Moses, Jesus, and Muhammad (pbut) have each received revelation from the same God, the specific details of how to pray, the days of fasting, what is forbidden, what is permitted, etc. may have varied. Muslims believe Muhammad (pbuh) to be the last messenger sent to mankind with the laws and practices brought down in his prophethood bearing the seal of revelation.

Muhammad (pbuh) was born in the year 571 CE in the city of Mecca located in present day Saudi Arabia. This city represents the center of the Islamic world, as it is the direction toward which Muslims make their daily prayers. His father died before his birth and his mother passed away when he was six years old. Although he was taken care of by his grandfather and then his uncle, his personal experience as an orphan instilled in him the need to take care of the weak and helpless in society. He worked as a merchant during his adult years and was viewed as an honourable and upright individual among his people long before his prophethood, but all this changed once the revelation started. At the age of 40 he received his first visit from the Archangel Gabriel, the angel of revelation sent by God to all his prophets (Sarwar, 2002).

Muhammad's (pbuh) prophethood lasted 23 years in total and can be divided in two parts. The first 13 years were spent in Mecca. In the early days of Islam the message placed emphasis on the oneness of God, reminded people of their purpose in this life, and warned them of a Day of Judgment where all of God's creatures would be held accountable for their actions. Islam grew slowly at first as Muhammad (pbuh) preached privately to those close to him. The message resonated most with the poor among Meccan society. Once the command from God was issued to preach openly Muhammad (pbuh) faced stiff opposition from the tribal leaders and most prominent members of Meccan society. The Prophet and his followers suffered physical, emotional, and financial persecution and were eventually forced to leave Mecca and sought refuge in the city of Medina.

The Medina years mark the next phase in the life of Muhammad (pbuh) and the mission of Islam. In fact, the Islamic calendar begins not at the birth of Muhammad (pbuh) or the first revelation he received, but rather from the year of his migration to Medina. In Medina, Muhammad (pbuh) became more than a religious leader; he was now the head of state. The revelation now included more detailed references to the requirements of building a society including basic civil and criminal laws. As the years moved on, more and more people around the Arabian Peninsula began to hear the message of Muhammad (pbuh) and many embraced Islam. At the same time, tensions between the Muslims centered in Medina and the tribes of Mecca continued, with armed conflict occurring on a few occasions. Eventually, in the 8th year after his migration to Mecca, Muhammad (pbuh) and the Muslims conquered Mecca and did so with very little resistance. Muhammad (pbuh) granted amnesty to the entire Meccan community, many of who had fought him and his message from the onset. This is quite remarkable considering that blood feuds and tribal warfare were the norms of Arabia during this period of time. Muhammad (pbuh) lived out the major part of his remaining days in Medina. He passed away at the age of 63 (Lings, 1983).

In the remarkably short period of 23 years as Prophet, Muhammad (pbuh) transformed not only a small community of Arabs, but the world as a whole. In his analysis of the most influential figures of world history,

Michael H. Hart places Muhammad (pbuh) at the top of the list. The author cites Muhammad's (pbuh) functions as diplomat, merchant, legislator, orator, military leader, amongst others roles for his selection (Hart, 1992). The message of Islam spread to the different parts of the world and now embraces over 1 billion followers worldwide.

Key Terminology and Main Tenets of Islam

After studying some of the early history of Islam and a brief look at the life of Muhammad (pbuh), we can now look at the faith of Islam in more detail. Let us first examine some basic terminology. An important distinction to make is between the terms Islam and Muslim. Islam is the religion and can be translated as "submission to God"; a Muslim is someone who follows the religion of Islam and the term can be translated as "the one who submits to God." As is evident, the terms Islam and Muslim stress the monotheistic foundation of the faith. In fact, although the terms are Arabic in origin, followers of the faith whether in Japan, Senegal, Indonesia, Bangladesh, or Saudi Arabia will identify themselves using the word Muslim, and their religion as Islam. There are many names for God in the Arabic language, with most emphasising a characteristic of God. Examples include *Ar-Rahman* (The Most Merciful) or *Al-Khaliq* (The Creator); however, the name most commonly used is *Allah*. Although it can be simply translated as God, its beauty both stylistically and linguistically is difficult to convey in the English language.

Regarding the beliefs of Muslims, the six basic articles of faith in Islam are as follows:

1. *To believe in Allah*—There is no God but He and that He has no associate.
2. *To believe in His Angels*—God has an untold number of angels that do various tasks throughout the universe.
3. *To believe in the holy books*—God has sent scriptures in the past including the Torah through Moses, the Psalms of David, the Gospel of Jesus, and the Qur'an through Muhammad (pbut).
4. *To believe in His messengers*—He has sent down prophets to convey His message and as examples to follow.
5. *To believe in the afterlife*—God will raise us all once again and a Day of Judgment will occur after which each soul will be sent to heaven or hell.
6. *To believe in destiny*—Each human has the free will to choose his or her own actions; however, ultimate knowledge and control lies with God. His is the plan that is unfolding and nothing occurs in the universe except by His command.

These articles represent the main beliefs a Muslim has; however, as educators, the more practical interaction we may have with Muslim students involves the Five Pillars of Islam. These are the main actions required by a Muslim and are considered fundamental to the faith. However, it is important to keep in mind that much like any other faith group not all Muslims are observant of these practices. Nonetheless it is useful for teachers to be aware of these pillars.

Shahadah (Testimony)

The first pillar of Islam is essentially a foundational pillar, which forms the backdrop of all the other pillars of Islam. This pillar consists of two testimonies the utterance of which enters one into the fold of Islam. The first part of the testimony is *Ash-hadu alaa ilaaha ilallah* (to testify there is nothing worthy of worship except God). This testimony is an utterance of pure monotheism negating the belief in all other deities, other than God. For Muslims, the belief of God is the focal point of all the acts and rituals in their life. All the rituals in Islam are expressions and manifestations of a Muslim's obedience and servitude to God. A Muslim's understanding of God is that of a transcendent Being who is the Creator of the heavens and the earth and all that is between them. There is nothing that bears the slightest resemblance to Him, as He is the Creator but was not created, the Eternal to whom there is no equivalent.

The belief of God in Islam entails total submission to Him, which is accomplished through the second testimony, *Wa ash-hadu anna Muhammadar-rasulullah* (testifying that Muhammad is the messenger of God). This second testimony acknowledges the belief in the finality of Muhammad (pbuh) as a prophet of God who, as mentioned previously, was preceded by many prophets before him. Muslims are required to believe in these previous prophets, as denying any one of them is tantamount to denying them all. For a Muslim, belief in Muhammad (pbuh) as the final prophet and messenger of God means that the believer is to follow his example and teachings. The foundation of these teachings is embodied in the four other pillars of Islam, namely the *Salah, Zakat, Siyam,* and *Hajj.*

Salah (Prayer)

The pillar after the *Shahadah* which plays the most fundamental part of a Muslim's life is the *Salah*. These are the daily prayers offered at five different times throughout the day facing the holy city of Mecca. These ritual prayers are an expression of the centrality of God in a Muslim's life. As the believer is engaged in different activities throughout the day, they are required to take a brief break to observe these prayers. For example, the first prayer of the day is the dawn prayer offered about an hour before sunrise. Muslims are required to interrupt their sleep in order to observe this prayer. Later on in the day comes the afternoon prayer, which generally occurs at a time when people are at work or in the case of students during school hours. Thereafter comes the mid-afternoon prayer, followed by the sunset prayer, and then the final prayer, which is observed during the evening. The prayer rituals consist of two to four units of bowing, prostrating, and reciting prayers and verses from the Qur'an in Arabic. This is not meant to be a mere physical ritual in which one just moves the limbs in monotonous motions; rather, it is a personal spiritual journey in which the observer should be inwardly focused and contemplative.

Muslims are expected to observe these prayers whether they are at work, school, resting, or relaxing with their family members. This may seem a bit extreme for some; however, for Muslims it serves as a reminder of the constant connection one is to maintain with their Lord. For this reason, Muslim students often request their schools for prayer or multi-faith rooms in which they can observe these rituals during their recess or lunch break. The main requirement for a prayer room is that the room is quiet and free from impurities.

Siyam (Fasting)

Muslims are required to fast during the holy month of Ramadan, which is the 9th month of the Islamic calendar. As these months are lunar months, they are subject to moon sighting, which signifies the beginning of the month. It is for this reason that the month of Ramadan, and the Eid festival celebrated thereafter, changes from year to year, because the lunar year is 10 days shorter than the solar year.

The fasting of Ramadan requires abstinence from food, drink, and conjugal relations from dawn till sunset. However, there is also emphasis placed on increasing virtuous actions, spending generously on others, and strengthening bonds with friends and family. In other words, the holy month of Ramadan is a time for Muslims to sacrifice, reflect, and engage in spiritual renewal. Additionally, fasting engenders a sense of empathy toward the poor and hungry in society and helps develop a sense of appreciation for one's blessings. The fasts are maintained for 29–30 days consecutively from the beginning of the lunar month till the sighting of the new moon for the next month. Certain categories of people are exempt from fasting, including the sick, pregnant, elderly, and travelers, all of whom can make up the fasts if physically able to at a later time or expiate for it by feeding the hungry. Children under the age of puberty are not required to fast. The end of Ramadan is marked by the celebration of *Eid-al-Fitr*, one of the two main celebrations of the Islamic calendar. This holy day is marked by communal prayers in the morning, usually in the local mosque or a larger place of assembly followed by activities with family and friends. Muslims in the West often take these days off from work or school to celebrate the day with their loved ones.

While fasting students may display signs of fatigue in any one of their classes, special attention should be given to Physical Education. As fasting requires abstinence from food and drink, strenuous physical activity can often pose a challenge for students; therefore, some reasonable accommodation should be considered by the instructor. Perhaps some physical testing can be performed prior to or after the month of Ramadan in order to ensure that Muslim students are able to fulfill course requirements.[3]

Zakat (Alms Giving)

The next pillar to examine is *Zakat*. Zakat is a compulsory tax paid by Muslims, which is distributed among the needy in the community. In general, charity plays an incredibly important role in the Islamic code of conduct. While zakat cannot be strictly classified as an act of charity, since it is something the Muslim is commanded to do as opposed to something optional, zakat stresses to the believer the overall importance of community and helping those less fortunate. It is in fact an act of worship for the believer.

Much like our system of income tax today, there is a minimum income level one must attain in order to be required to pay zakat. Those who fall below the minimum income level are exempted from paying zakat and may in fact be eligible to receive zakat when it is distributed to the needy in the community. Zakat is a flat tax of 2.5% on the value of one's net assets held over the year. These assets can include cash on hand, bank deposits, securities, rental property, jewellery, precious metals, etc. Although this amount for most Muslims is not overly burdensome to pay, it nevertheless remains one of the pillars many followers in both Muslim lands and the West have neglected.

While there is no specific date for Muslims to pay the zakat, it is up to each individual to affix a date on the Islamic calendar to abide by. As there is no zakat collector knocking on their door when zakat is due, Muslims living in the West often give their zakat money to the local mosque. Based on their knowledge of the community and its members, the mosque is then able to distribute the funds to the needy. In other cases, Muslims may send their zakat money to the impoverished overseas through various charities and organizations.

Hajj (Pilgrimage)

The fifth pillar of Islam is the *hajj*, or sacred pilgrimage to Mecca, Saudi Arabia. It is required of adult Muslims to perform this journey at least once in their lifetime, provided they are physically and financially able to do so. The period for hajj occurs once a year and falls in the 12th month of the Islamic calendar. It is the largest annual assembly of pilgrims in the world, with an estimate of 3 million participants in 2008 (BBC News, 2008). While the hajj itself only takes 5 days to perform, Muslims often spend two weeks or more when making this journey to the holy city of Mecca. For many this will be the only chance in their lives to see the Ka'bah closely and to pray in Islam's most sacred site.

What many non-Muslims are unaware of is that the main rituals associated with the hajj are representative not of Prophet Muhammad's (pbuh) life, but rather the lives of Prophet Abraham, his wife Hagar, and their son Ishmael (pbut). Arabs consider themselves the descendants of Abraham through his son Ishmael. Together by the command of God the two built the Ka'bah and as such the Ka'bah had been a venerated site for centuries prior to Islam.

Perhaps the most evident transformation for the believer during the hajj occurs when entering into *ihram*. Ihram is a physical and spiritual state into which the pilgrim enters when beginning the hajj. For men, ihram requires the wearing of two sheets of unstitched white cloth while for women their regular clothing is acceptable provided it adheres to Islamic requirements. The simple act of physically changing one's attire has profound spiritual implications. Whether a millionaire who is arriving to Saudi Arabia by air in the luxury of first class or a simple farmer who has made the long trip on bus spending all his life savings in the process, all are united in simplicity before their Lord. Aside from the change of dress, in the state of ihram the pilgrim is forbidden to use fragrance or perfume, to kill animals (including insects), to cut one's hair or nails, or to have conjugal relations. These, amongst other regulations, are meant to invoke the sense of simplicity, mercy, and humility before God and amongst the community as a whole.

One of the more famous visual images depicted around the world during the hajj season is that of pilgrims circling around the Ka'bah, known as *tawaf* in Arabic. In addition to the tawaf, pilgrims walk between the hills of Saffa and Marwa, drink water from the well of Zamzam, spend time in the valley of Minna, pray in the plain of Arafat, and stone three monuments representing Satan. The end of the hajj is marked by the sacrifice of an animal, whose meat is distributed to the needy. After the animal sacrifice, the pilgrim can remove themselves from the state of ihram. For males this entails a shaving or clipping of the hair. At the conclusion of the hajj on the 10th day of month, Muslims celebrate *Eid-al-Adha*. This is the second of the holy days in the Islamic calendar and is celebrated by Muslims around the world, not only the ones in Mecca performing the pilgrimage. Festivities are similar to the *Eid* celebration which follows the month of Ramadan.

For anyone who has done the hajj it is truly a journey of a lifetime. Perhaps the best account of hajj and the transformation it can make on an individual is given by Malcolm X, the African American civil rights activist of the mid-20th century. During his pilgrimage and upon his return to America, he remarked on what he had experienced in Mecca and how this had challenged his previous beliefs of segregation and the incompatibility of co-existence between the races. When asked about what impressed him most, regarding the hajj, he replied, "The *brotherhood!* The people of all races, colors, from all over the world coming together as *one!* It has proved to me the power of the One God" (X, 1966, p. 338).

The Qur'an

The Qur'an is the holy book that Muslims believe to be the word of God. It is the primary authoritative text in Islam from which the commandments to perform the various pillars and rituals are derived. The details on these practices are outlined in the sayings and actions of Prophet Muhammad (pbuh). The Qur'an is an Arabic text, which was revealed to Prophet Muhammad (pbuh) over a span of 23 years starting in the year 610 CE till his death in 632 CE. The revelation of the Qur'an to Muhammad (pbuh) was through the Archangel Gabriel, who was sent by God to convey the Qur'an. Throughout the period of revelation, the companions of Muhammad (pbuh) would transcribe the verses of the Qur'an on whatever material was available to them. This was done because the Prophet himself was illiterate and unable to read or write. One of the subtle ironies of the Qur'an is that it is regarded as a literary masterpiece of the Arabic language and yet it was revealed to a man who could neither read nor write.

The Arabic text of the Qur'an has remained unchanged and true to its original form from the time of its compilation shortly after the death of Muhammad (pbuh). The Qur'an consists of 114 chapters dealing with the main themes of monotheism, morality, and religious injunctions and legislations. Millions of Muslims worldwide have committed the entire Qur'an to memory, many of whom do not even speak the Arabic language. Therefore Muslims regard the Qur'an as a miracle because it is not only preserved in the lines of books but also in the hearts of people.

During prayers a Muslim must recite the Qur'an solely in Arabic, but since many Muslims are not fluent in the language in which the Qur'an was revealed numerous translations are available. However, given the eloquence and pristine level of the Arabic language in the Qur'an, an exact word-for-word translation is unachievable. Nonetheless, a non-Arabic-speaking audience can achieve a basic understanding of the Qur'an through these translations and the accompanying commentaries that exist.

Clarifying Misconceptions of the Qur'an

As two Muslim educators, we are quite aware of the miseducation surrounding the Qur'an. For instance, some may claim that the Qur'an promotes violence and hatred toward non-Muslims. These statements could not be further from the truth. The proponents of such sentiments quote verses of the Qur'an without taking into consideration the context in which these verses were revealed. As stated earlier, the Qur'an was revealed to the Prophet Muhammad (pbuh) over a span of 23 years as various situations unfolded. Therefore, some of the verses in the Qur'an have a general import and are relevant for any circumstance, while other verses are tied to specific situations and do not carry a general meaning. For example, an often-quoted verse in the Qur'an, which is taken out of context, is from chapter 9, verse 5, which states: *"...kill the polytheists wherever you find them and capture them and besiege them and sit in wait for them at every place of ambush...."* This verse is referring to those aggressors during the life of Muhammad who oppressed the Muslim community. These people had shown open hostility toward Islam for 22 years. This verse is a license for the first Muslim community to wage war against these specific aggressors, to stop their oppression and persecution. This verse is further qualified by the verse immediately following it which states: *"And if anyone of the polytheists seeks your protection, then grant him protection...."* In other words, permission was granted to fight those who oppressed, persecuted, and killed; however, if members of the opposing side showed signs of clemency then it was binding to offer them protection (Qutb, 2003).

Similarly, other verses in the Qur'an referring to war, for the most part, are tied to specific instances and do not carry a general sentiment of aggression and violence for every occasion toward any group of non-believers. Unfortunately the misinterpretation of the Qur'an occurs all too often. Non-Muslim individuals and groups may misinterpret lines, which serve to further vilify an entire faith group in the eyes of the public while extremist Muslim groups inaccurately point to verses in order to justify their radical views. This point is essential for educators to understand because the religion of Islam that is often portrayed through the media, Hollywood, and by fringe elements of the Muslim community misrepresents the true spirit of the faith.

Clarifying Misconceptions about Women in Islam

Muslim women have been a focal point in the media over the last few years. The common discourse that we have become accustomed to hearing is that women are oppressed and mistreated in Islam. Historically this has not been the case. Islam gave women inheritance rights, rights in marriage, the choice to accept or reject marriage proposals, the right to work, the right to education and the right to own property over 1,400 years ago. Though we take these rights for granted in present times, these were practically nonexistent for women in the Western world until a few centuries ago. From the onset of Islam, women were permitted to voice their concerns and grievances directly to the head of the Muslim state. The Prophet Muhammad (pbuh) would seek the advice and counsel of women on issues affecting the Muslim community. In present times a number of Muslim countries and communities around the world illegitimately limit the rights of women. These examples should not be understood as the standard of treatment that women are entitled to in Islam.

Some people associate the *hijab* or the Islamic head veil and dress code for women as a sign of oppression. In light of these accusations, it must be clear that Islam does not condone the forceful observance of religious rituals and obligations. The Qur'an clearly states, "There shall be no compulsion in the religion" (chapter 2, verse 256). What this means is that though Muslims are required as a part of their faith to observe certain rituals and practices, no one can force an individual to do so. In regard to the *hijab*, Muslim women are required to observe the *hijab* but no one can force them to do so, it must be done from their own volition.

The dress code for both men and women in Islam seeks to promote modesty. Men are to wear loose-fitting clothing and are minimally required to cover between their knees and naval. Women are also to avoid form-fitting clothing and need to cover their entire bodies, except for their hands and face. This modest form of dress is not uncommon to other religious traditions. Christian nuns wear very similar loose-fitting clothes covering their entire bodies except their hands and faces, and many Jewish women also wear loose clothing and cover their hair. In Islam the dress code for women is not seen as a means to assert male domination over women, rather it is to recognize that women possess certain physical characteristics that differ from men. As such, the dress code for a woman is different from that of a man.

Another issue, which has received a lot of media attention, is the practice of "honor killings." Honor killings refer to the horrific act where family members kill a female because of an act which has brought "shame" to the family. Honor killings have absolutely no basis whatsoever in Islam. Often these acts of "honor" occur in tribal cultures, and while the participants may be Muslim, the acts themselves have no religious justification. Similar acts of aggression against women are prevalent in North American societies as well; however, instead of honor killings they are referred to as acts of domestic violence against women. Similarly, female genital mutilation and inaccessibility to education for young girls in certain countries is another cultural practice and not a religious injunction. The key issue to understand, especially for teachers, in this discourse is that many cultural practices are associated with the religion of Islam even when such practices have no basis and are condemned by the faith.

Your Classroom and the Muslim Student

The student populations in our schools today reflect an unprecedented level of international diversity. Both students and teachers share the hallways and classrooms with individuals representing different religions, cultures, languages, and nationalities from around the world. This presents both a challenge and opportunity for us as educators to enable an environment of understanding and respect to flourish. Muslims represent nearly 2% of the Canadian population (Statistics Canada, 2005), while in the United States figures range from 0.6% (CIA, 2007) to 2.1% (Baghby, Perl, & Froehle, 2001). As teachers, are there any assumptions we can make if a student says that they are from Egypt or that their parents emigrated from Pakistan? Much like the nations of the West, albeit perhaps not to their overall level of diversity, countries in the Muslim world represent a mix of various groups.

The terms "Arab" and "Muslim" are sometimes used interchangeably, and this is incorrect. Using the definition of an "Arab" as being someone whose native tongue is Arabic, a rule of thumb to keep in mind is the following: *most Arabs are Muslims but most Muslims are not Arabs*. From Morocco and Mauritania in the west to Oman and the Gulf States to the east, the nations where Arabic is the prime language of communication number nearly 20. In addition, seven nations in Africa and Asia include Arabic as one of their official languages. It is spoken by over 280 million people worldwide as a first language and millions more as a second language (Prochazka, 2006). Much like a native English speaker can detect the differences between the English spoken in the United States, Ireland, and Jamaica, the dialect of Arabic spoken can also vary across the region. Aside from speech, there are also unique items in dress and food that characterize the Arab world.

Most Arabs are Muslims: If we return to the first part of the rule of thumb discussed earlier, we can note that the vast majority of Arab speakers are indeed Muslim; however, non-Muslim populations are present in some Arab states. Examples include Egypt with 11% Coptic Christians and Lebanon with 39% Christian (CIA, 2007). As teachers, it is therefore important to keep in mind that while one may note that a certain student is of Arab origin, to assume that they are Muslim is another matter.

Most Muslims are not Arabs: Let us broaden the discussion and look at the second part of our statement. The global Muslim population is estimated to be in the neighbourhood of 1.5 billion, which makes it the second largest religion after Christianity. Less than a quarter of the Muslim population are native Arab speakers, so where do the rest of these Muslims live? The most populous Muslim countries in order are Indonesia, Pakistan, India, Bangladesh, and Turkey, which together account for approximately half of total Muslim population (CIA, 2007). These are countries to which Islam spread in its early years of expansion. There are significant Muslim populations in Central Asia, China, Sub-Saharan Africa, and a growing number in Europe and North America as well.

As with other religions, Islam has different groups that fall under the banner of the faith. The main division is between Sunni and Shia sects, with the former representing approximately 85% of the adherents to Islam. Iran, Iraq, and Lebanon are nations with a significant Shia population; however, Shia minorities are present in many other countries too. Interfaith violence has occurred between the two groups in parts of the Muslim world, for reasons most often not associated with theological concerns, but rather petty politics and a cycle of revenge attacks. The prime difference between the two groups dates back to a dispute over the succession of Muhammad (pbuh), although other areas of divergence exist. Other than the Sunni–Shia divide, a number of sects and denominations exist in the Islamic world with differences ranging from major to minor.

Aside from differences in place of origin and sect, Muslims are not unlike other faith groups in the fact that followers may have various levels of practice. It goes without saying that religion and spirituality are incredibly personal experiences. Two siblings who have grown up in the same Muslim household may be as different as night and day. One may pray five times a day, read the Qur'an daily, and stay clear from all the prohibitions of the faith, while the other may have little time for the rituals of the religion and openly consume alcohol. The Muslim students in our classrooms come from homes where great emphasis may or may not be placed on adhering to the pillars of Islam, and there may be varying degrees of acceptance of Western or secular customs. For example, some Muslim students may come to class dressed up for Halloween, while others will say it is against their religion. As teachers it is not only important to have a general knowledge of the religion but to also be aware that levels of practice differ.

Despite the differences that exist across the Muslim world, be it in practice, language, and geography, there exists an overriding sense of community that stretches across borders to unite Muslims in a unique way. Islam is believed to be a universal message that is meant for all people, regardless of race, language, gender, or socio-economic status. This is in fact one of the key reasons why Islam spread so quickly and gained so many followers beyond the Arab lands. Prophet Muhammad (pbuh) emphasized this spirit of brotherhood in one of his oft-quoted traditions when he mentioned that "the Muslim *ummah* (community) is like one body. If the eye is in pain then the whole body is in pain and if the head is in pain then the whole body is in pain" (Muslim, 2005). In part, this explains why in recent times when conflict has erupted in parts of the Muslim world such as Iraq, Afghanistan, Bosnia, or Palestine it is not uncommon to hear voices from other parts of the Islamic world condemning violence against Muslims. It is however imperative to note that Muslims need not simply support their brethren right or wrong, for this is contrary to the teachings of Islam. The Qur'an and the actions of Muhammad (pbuh) illustrate in numerous instances the importance of justice over attachment to creed and race.

A final point to note is how the Muslim world is portrayed in the West, specifically considering the geo-political climate of the 21st century. Part of the interaction teachers and students will have with Islam in the classroom is in addressing some areas of conflict from around the globe. No doubt there are problems and hot spots in the Muslim world; however, these challenges must not be pinned on the religion of Islam. If we look at the case of Afghanistan, it is far too simple to blame all that plagues the nation as a result of Islam or the Taliban's rise to power. Afghanistan's case goes back for decades, and Western hands are complicit in the civil war and instability that led to the rise of extremism in that country. Before talking about the Taliban, it is relevant to present a brief history of the region from the Cold War onwards. Afghanistan and the portrayal of Muslims are but one example. Often through the sound bites we are exposed through the news media we are only given a snapshot of events, the same snapshot witnessed by our students. This is why it is extremely important that we as teachers bear the responsibility, when presenting any issue, to go beyond the headlines and do justice to a topic.

Conclusion

Islamophobia is a growing concern for Muslims living in the West. A 2008 poll in Canada showed that 36% of Canadians responded that they had an unfavorable view of Muslims, a rise of 9% from the previous year (Council on American-Islamic Relations Canada, 2008). For many non-Muslim students, the only exposure they get to Islam is through the news media and the associated stories of terrorism, war, and issues regarding the violation of women's rights. While these are stories that need to be told, the classroom should be a place where we can go beyond the headlines, where a greater understanding can be fostered, and where prejudices and stereotypes can be quashed. Teachers of Social Sciences and Moral and Religious Education courses often deal directly with issues regarding the Muslim World and/or Islam; however, Islam may enter the classroom through works of literature in Language Arts, in Media Studies class, and even Mathematics when looking at some of the key historical figures in the field. As with speaking on any issue, teachers need to be responsible, respectful, and accurate when engaged in a discussion on Islam and Muslims. What we do or say can reinforce, reject, and greatly shape the opinions of our students. Hopefully this chapter has given some clarity to the faith of Islam and the people who follow it.

Endnotes

1. Islamic tradition reserves great respect for the Messengers of God. It is the practice of Muslims to recite a short prayer of blessing whenever the name of a prophet is mentioned, the meaning of which can be translated as "peace be upon him" and which will hereafter be denoted as (pbuh) or (pbut) for "peace be upon them" in plural cases.
2. According to the opinion of the majority of Islamic scholars, the total number of prophets sent to mankind is 124,000.
3. On a side note, Hakeem Olajuwon, widely considered as one of the 50 greatest NBA players of all time, claimed that fasting made him play better, "I was better during Ramadan, more focused...lighter." (Meenaghan, 2009)

References

Al-Ashqar, U. S. (1999). *Islamic creed series volume 4: The messengers and the messages*. Riyadh: International Islamic Publishing House.

Al-Mubarakpuri, S.-R. (2002). *The sealed nectar: Biography of the noble Prophet (pbuh)*. Riyadh: Darussalam.

Baghby, I., Perl, P. M., & Froehle, B. T. (2001). *The mosque in America: A national portrait*. Washington, DC: Council on American-Islamic Relations.

BBC News. (2008, December 7). *In pictures: Hajj pilgrimage* . Retrieved August 15, 2009, from http://news.bbc.co.uk/2/hi/in_pictures/7769689.stm

CIA. (2007). *CIA—The World Factbook—United States*. Retrieved August 20, 2009, from CIA—The World Factbook: https://www.cia.gov/library/publications/the-world-factbook/geos/us.html

Council on American-Islamic Relations Canada. (2008, September 20). *CAIR-CAN press releases: Poll shows islamophobia on the rise*. Retrieved August 20, 2009, from CAIR-CAN: http://www.caircan.ca/itn_more.php?id=A3003_0_2_0_M

Green, J. (2009, August 21). *Special report—Ottawa citizen*. Retrieved August 22, 2009, from Ottawa Citizen: http://www.ottawacitizen.com/news/Special+report/1913408/story.html

Hart, M. H. (1992). *The 100: A ranking of the most influential persons in history*. New York: Carol Publishing Group/Citadel Press.

Lings, M. (1983). *Muhammad: His life based on the earliest sources*. Cambridge, MA: Islamic Texts Society.

Meenaghan, G. Hakeem the dream: My life as a Muslim (2009, September 11). Retrieved October 11, 2009, from Emirates Business 24/7: http://www.business24-7.ae/Articles/2009/9/Pages/10092009/09112009_2b3d524fc308481c8c5b852a09fb0d41.aspx

Muslim, I. (2005, November). *Sahih muslim: English translation*. Retrieved October 30, 2009, from Sahih Muslim: http://www.iiu.edu.my/deed/hadith/muslim/032_smt.html

Prochazka, S. (2006). Arabic. In K. Brown (Ed.), *Encyclopedia of language and linguistics,* 2nd ed. (pp. 423–431). Oxford: Elsevier.

Qutb, S. (2003). *In the shade of the Qur'an vol. VIII.* A. Salahi, (Trans.) Leicestershire, UK: Islamic Foundation & Islamonline.net.

Sarwar, G. (2002). *Islam: Beliefs and teachings.* New Delhi: Markazi Maktaba Islami Publishers.

Statistics Canada. (2005, January 25). *Population by religion, by province and territory (2001 Census).* Retrieved August 20, 2009, from Statistics Canada: http://www40.statcan.gc.ca/l01/cst01/demo30a-eng.htm

X, Malcolm. (1966) *The Autobiography of Malcolm X.* New York: Grove Press.

Four

What Is Islam?
A Conversation with the Magisterial Intellectuals of the Past

Hassan Ahmad Mian

As a pre-service teacher, I think that it is very important for our students to know about what the voices from within Islam say about the most controversial issues that are raised today and ascribed to Islam: What about suicide? What about bombs? Jihad? Women's rights? Education? Al-Qaeda? And the list goes on. My stance in writing this chapter, however, is not a reactive one. I am not writing to defend an accused. I would rather give the message of Islam as I know it being a Muslim. I would write about experiences that pulled me from a life of dissatisfaction to one of wholeness. I would non-apologetically write about what consciousness Islam and its Holy book have given me in my daily life. I in no way claim that this consciousness has been perfected. I consider myself to be a traveller on a spiritual path, which will only be completed by Divine grace. At the time I write this piece, there is a lot of work left before this path draws near its completion.

The Quest

For the first 18 years of my life, I was raised in an affluent home in Pakistan. I attended one of the best schools in the country, where future leaders are trained. This school had an area of about 176 acres and had activities ranging from horse-riding to world-class cricket being played in its confines. We were convinced that we were the very best, and the way of the elite in a largely poor country was morally correct. Our gods were those of wealth, status, and power. We were aloof from the world of poor people around us—people who begged all day to put bread on their tables; mothers who had been forced into prostitution because tax-payer money had been embezzled by a succession of corrupt governments; young children whose innocent faces had been burnt by acid by mafias that ran begging networks so that people might take pity on these burnt faces and give them a little more money, which went directly to those mafias. Life was about achieving more than the others, and that is what gave it all its meaning. Students graduating from this high school would get top marks in the SAT (Scholastic Aptitude Test) and typically get accepted to Ivy League universities. I received a prestigious scholarship to a "top tier" school.

Leaving my country at the young age of 18 and coming to a place that I had only read about or seen in pictures put me out of my comfort zone. The protective structure of the society that I had been accustomed to was no longer around me. I tried to get satisfaction out of my life at the university; however, I felt something missing. I could not derive satisfaction and meaning from my life and this led me to a state of utter neediness and thirst. I needed to be cared for and to be loved. However, the worldly love that we know to exist was too finite to fill the need that existed in my heart. I was inspired to call upon the Divine presence to fill this vacuum, and I did see a glimpse of true love and care. The words of the Holy Prophet Muhammad (May Allah bless him and give him peace) made experiential sense to me.

> .... Be mindful of Allah, and Allah will protect you. Be mindful of Allah, and you will find Him in front of you. If you ask then ask Allah; and if you seek help, seek help from Allah. Know that even if people were to gather together to benefit you with something, they would not benefit you with anything except that which Allah has already destined for your benefit, and that if they gather together to harm you with something, they would not be able to harm you with anything except that which Allah has destined against you. The pens have been lifted and the pages have dried. (Tirmidhi & Mahfuz, 2003)[1]

The first step of seeking the Divine had to come from within me and what gushed back was the Divine solicitude that solaced me in the midst of the many storms of life. That experience of the Divine presence has pushed me to seek it more. I call this experience true and unconditional love. The spiritual gnostics within the Muslim tradition have termed this as necessary love, out of which all the contingent love that we know comes. This is what the prophetic tradition has alluded to.

> Allah has divided mercy into 100 parts, and He retained with Him 99 parts, and sent down to earth 1 part. Through this one part creatures deal with one another with

compassion, so much so that an animal lifts its hoof over its young lest it should hurt it. (al-Bukhari & Khan, n.d.)[2]

The necessary love is the love of the Divine for Himself. Whoever knows the Divine directly and experientially gets an idea of what true love and mercy is.

My experiences are shared by many other people who found a meaningless void in the life of material hoarding. They turned to the spiritual traditions of Islam to seek guidance and have found wholesome answers to the big questions that had puzzled them. Shaykh Nuh Ha Mim Keller, an American Muslim translator and specialist in Islamic Law, is one of them.[3] In his account of becoming a Muslim he mentions:

> I wondered if I hadn't gone down the road of philosophy as far as one could go. While it had debunked my Christianity and provided some genuine insights, it had not yet answered the big questions. Moreover, I felt that this was somehow connected I didn't know whether as cause or effect to the fact that our intellectual tradition no longer seemed to seriously comprehend itself. What were any of us, whether philosophers, fishermen, garbagemen, or kings, except bit players in a drama we did not understand, diligently playing out our roles until our replacements were sent, and we gave our last performance? But could one legitimately hope for more than this? I read "Kojève's Introduction to the Reading of Hegel," in which he explained that for Hegel, philosophy did not culminate in the system, but rather in the Wise Man, someone able to answer any possible question on the ethical implications of human actions. This made me consider our own plight in the twentieth century, which could no longer answer a single ethical question.

I read other books on Islam and came across some passages translated by W. Montgomery Watt from *That Which Delivers from Error* by the theologian and mystic Ghazali, who, after a mid-life crisis of questioning and doubt, realized that beyond the light of prophetic revelation there is no other light on the face of the earth from which illumination may be received, the very point to which my philosophical inquiries had led. Here was, in Hegel's terms, the Wise Man, in the person of a divinely inspired messenger who alone had the authority to answer questions of good and evil.

I also read A. J. Arberry's translation, *The Qur'an Interpreted*, and I recalled my early wish for a sacred book. Even in translation, the superiority of the Muslim scripture over the Bible was evident in every line, as if the reality of Divine revelation, dimly heard of all my life, had now been placed before my eyes. In its exalted style, its power, its inexorable finality, its uncanny way of anticipating the arguments of the atheistic heart in advance and answering them; it was a clear exposition of God as God and man as man, the revelation of the awe-inspiring Divine unity being the identical revelation of social and economic justice among men.

After his experience of reading the Qur'an, Shaykh Nuh Keller went on to study Arabic, the language in which the Qur'an is revealed. What affected him the most during his study were encounters with simple people when he was in Egypt. He writes:

> In Egypt, I found something I believe brings many to Islam, namely, the mark of pure monotheism upon its followers, which struck me as more profound than anything I had previously encountered. I met many Muslims in Egypt, good and bad, but all influenced by the teachings of their Book to a greater extent than I had ever seen elsewhere.
>
> ....Another was a young boy from secondary school who greeted me near Khan al-Khalili, and because I spoke some Arabic and he spoke some English and wanted to tell me about Islam, he walked with me several miles across town to Giza, explaining as much as he could. When we parted, I think he said a prayer that I might become Muslim.
>
> ...Another was a woman I met while walking beside a bicycle on an unpaved road on the opposite side of the Nile from Luxor. I was dusty, and somewhat shabbily clothed, and she was an old woman dressed in black from head to toe who walked up, and without a word or glance at me, pressed a coin into my hand so suddenly that in my surprise I dropped it. By the time I picked it up, she had hurried away. Because she thought I was poor, even if obviously non-Muslim, she gave me some money without any expectation for it except what was between her and her God. This act made me think a lot about Islam, because nothing seemed to have motivated her but that.
>
> Many other things passed through my mind during the months I stayed in Egypt to learn Arabic. I found myself thinking that a man must have some sort of religion, and I was more impressed by the effect of Islam on the lives of Muslims, a certain nobility of purpose and largess of soul, than I had ever been by any other religions or even atheism's effect on its followers. The Muslims seemed to have more than we did. (Keller, n.d.)

After his mind, body, and soul were convinced that Islam is what he had been looking for, Shaykh Nuh became a Muslim and came under the spiritual tutelage of Shaykh Abdul Rahman Shagouri, a pious saint from Damascus. After years of hard work he connected with the legacy of saints.

I have had the honor of meeting Shaykh Nuh who is now a guide in the way of Sufism and to me is a living example of a verse in the Qur'an in which Allah says:

> ... and Allah will increase the ones who seek Guidance in Guidance ...[4]

In my spiritual quest, what had struck me was how some of the people who had converted to Islam around my campus were more knowledgeable and connected to the Islamic spiritual tradition than I, who had grown up in a Muslim country. One of my first influences was Carl, a student of Islamic studies, who was a convert to Islam. He had acquired fluency in the Arabic language. He was married to a Moroccan lady who was very well educated. Although they both were fluent in English and French, they spoke classical

Qur'anic Arabic in their home. To speak classical Arabic is very difficult, especially making sure that all the case-endings are in their proper places, but Carl and his wife had grown comfortable doing so. I was later to observe that most native Arabs do not speak classical Arabic properly. Carl tutored me privately in the Arabic language, without ever wanting me to pay him money in return. I still cannot forget the magical moment when the beautiful recitation of the Qur'an first started making sense to me. This encouraged me further to study Arabic and read the Qur'an in its original language. A Greek friend of mine, who had converted to Islam, told me that he had memorized a large portion of the Qur'an. I was amazed at the fact that the Qur'an was still preserved through an oral tradition that could be easily traced back to the Prophet Muhammad who knew the book by heart. It was preserved verbatim and passed from generation to generation, with even the pronunciation of every letter unchanged.

A verse of the Qur'an reads, "And We have indeed made the Qur'an easy to understand and remember: then is there any that will receive admonition?"[5] Reciting the Qur'an had become a spiritual experience, which I wanted to be with me all the time. I decided to commit the book to memory and by the Divine grace was successfully able to do so.

During my quest, I went to visit my family in Pakistan. My visit was only for two weeks; however, I had an ardent desire to understand the spiritual culture which I had been veiled from during my upbringing. Some friends of mine offered to take me to visit an old saintly man. I agreed. I remember that it was a relatively cold winter day, with some welcome sunshine. We encountered an old man who was seated on the floor with his legs folded. He was adorned with simple, yet elegant clothes. His eyes had a lot of depth to them. His manner was humble and majestic at the same time. He had a genuine smile on his face, and his entire being radiated happiness. When I looked at him, I found myself speechless. It seemed as if he understood what was going on within me. I remember how my entire being was filled with pristine joy in his presence. His temporal aura made me forget who and where I was. The old man talked very little. From what I remember he said, "You are our masters and we are nothing but your servants." He seemed to be delighted that someone had come to visit him from the big city in the rural suburb where he lived. I remember clearly that his humility was straight out of his heart and that there was nothing about his demeanor that was artificial.

Visiting the old man made me wonder who he was and why I had felt so cleansed in his presence. I later learned about a prophetic tradition that read, "The example of a good companion and a bad companion is like that of the seller of musk, and the one who blows the blacksmith's bellows (respectively). So as for the seller of musk then either he will grant you some, or you buy some from him, or at least you enjoy a pleasant smell from him. As for the one who blows the blacksmith's bellows then either he will burn your clothes or you will get an offensive smell from him" (al-Bukhari & Khan, n.d.). The old man who I met had indeed put some musk of his other worldliness on the slate of my memories. I had heard how my ancestors, once non-Muslims, had embraced Islam just by meeting spiritual saints. I now knew what it was to be in the presence of such a person. The kind of certainty that I got out of this experience was beyond what a logical proof or a concrete description could provide. The experience, in short, had much more depth than what my words can possibly express.

Guidance

The Qur'an is a source of guidance and a way to live my life. What I found in the Qur'an is what people have said about it from the bygone centuries. Busairi,[6] a poet, says in his famous poem of the mantle:

> *Its meaning is like the waves of the ocean in vastness*
> *Its wonders cannot be counted nor comprehended.*
> *Nor would you (be) satiated by its constant repetition.* (Busiri & Tunji, 2002)

There is something timeless about this holy book, which I have not found elsewhere. It talks directly to the reader and gives him advice on the situation he is at the current moment. A beautiful passage of the Qur'an, which gives us an ideal to live by, is found in the chapter of *Furqan* (The Criterion).

> *Blessed be He Who hath placed in the heaven mansions of the stars, and hath placed therein a great lamp and a moon giving light!*
>
> *And He it is Who hath appointed night and day in succession, for him who desireth to remember, or desireth thankfulness.*
>
> *The (faithful) slaves of the Beneficent are they who walk upon the earth modestly, and when the foolish ones address them answer: Peace;*
>
> *And who spend the night before their Lord, prostrate and standing,*
>
> *And who say: Our Lord! Avert from us the doom of hell; lo! the doom thereof is anguish;*
>
> *Lo! it is wretched as abode and station;*

And those who, when they spend, are neither prodigal nor grudging; and there is ever a firm station between the two;

And those who cry not unto any other god along with Allah, nor take the life which Allah hath forbidden save in (course of) justice, nor commit adultery—and whoso doeth this shall pay the penalty;

The doom will be doubled for him on the Day of Resurrection, and he will abide therein disdained for ever;

Save him who repenteth and believeth and doth righteous work; as for such, Allah will change their evil deeds to good deeds. Allah is ever Forgiving, Merciful.

And whosoever repenteth and doeth good, he verily repenteth toward Allah with true repentance—

And those who will not witness vanity, but when they pass near senseless play, pass by with dignity.

And those who, when they are reminded of the revelations of their Lord, fall not deaf and blind thereat.

And who say: Our Lord! Vouchsafe us comfort of our wives and of our offspring, and make us patterns for (all) those who ward off (evil).

They will be awarded the high place forasmuch as they were steadfast, and they will meet therein with welcome and the ward of peace,

Abiding there for ever. Happy is it as abode and station!"

This passage provides hope to sinners who wish to turn away from their past life and mend their old ways. A prerequisite for such a return is humility and not thinking oneself as better than others. Eternal felicity is promised to people who have transcended the superficialities of righteousness, and their entire being has been imbued with the Divine light. The Prophet Muhammad (Peace be upon him) said ,"Allah has greater joy at the repentance of one of His slaves when he turns towards Him than one of you would have over his mount, which, having escaped from him with his food and drink in the middle of the desert so that he has despaired of finding it and gone to a tree to lie down in its shade, suddenly appears standing by him while he is in that state, so that he takes its reins and then says out of the intensity of his joy,

'O Allah, You are my slave and I am Your Lord!' getting confused because of his intense joy."[8]

And Thou Shalt Not Murder

As I write this chapter, I am compelled to write something about President Barack Obama's speech on June 4, 2009, in Cairo. Many of the points he mentioned about Islam are the actual orthodox positions of Islam held by major scholars within the normative tradition of Islamic scholarship. President Obama said:

> ...Indeed, none of us should tolerate these extremists. They have killed in many countries. They have killed people of different faiths—but more than any other, they have killed Muslims. Their actions are irreconcilable with the rights of human beings, the progress of nations, and with Islam. The Holy Koran teaches that whoever kills an innocent is as—it is as if he has killed all mankind. (Applause.) And the Holy Koran also says whoever saves a person, it is as if he has saved all mankind. (Applause.) The enduring faith of over a billion people is so much bigger than the narrow hatred of a few. Islam is not part of the problem in combating violent extremism—it is an important part of promoting peace....

I have personally told my friends, at the faculty of education, the very same thing that President Obama mentioned. Our students in schools and educators as well should know that the traditional scholars of Islam have reached a consensus from the primary texts of Islam that the killing of innocents is forbidden in Islam. Some statements of prominent Muslim scholars regarding this consensus follow.

Hamza Yusuf, American Muslim leader who is founder of the Zaytuna Institute in California and has trained traditionally in the Islamic scholastic tradition says:

> Religious zealots of any creed are defeated people who lash out in desperation, and they often do horrific things. And if these people [who committed murder on September 11] indeed are Arabs, Muslims, they're obviously very sick people and I can't even look at it in religious terms. It's politics, tragic politics. There's no Islamic justification for any of it. ... You can't kill innocent people. There's no Islamic declaration of war against the United States. I think every Muslim country except Afghanistan has an embassy in this country. And in Islam, a country where you have embassies is not considered a belligerent country. In Islam, the only wars that are permitted are between armies and they should engage on battlefields and engage nobly. The Prophet Muhammad said, "Do not kill women or children or noncombatants and do not kill old people or religious people," and he mentioned priests, nuns and rabbis. And he said, "Do not cut down fruit-bearing trees and do not poison the wells of your enemies." The Hadith, the sayings of the Prophet, say that no one can punish with fire except the lord of fire. It's prohibited to burn anyone in Islam as a punishment. No one can grant these attackers any legitimacy. It was evil.[9]

Nuh Ha Mim Keller, an American Muslim author whose story of conversion to Islam was mentioned earlier in this chapter, writes:

> Muslims have nothing to be ashamed of, and nothing to hide, and should simply tell people what their scholars and religious leaders have always said: first, that the Wahhabi sect has nothing to do with orthodox Islam, for its lack of tolerance is a perversion of traditional values; and second, that killing civilians is wrong and immoral.[10]

It might be worth noting that Al-Qaeda and its membership come from the Wahabi sect, which takes a Machiavellian approach to trying to "fix problems." Among the ignoble means that they use are killing of innocents and suicide bombings. According to traditional authorities on Islam, the Wahabi sect does not have anything to do with orthodox Islam.[11]

Al-Azhar in Cairo has traditionally been one of the most recognized authorities of Islam in the Muslim world. Shaykh Muhammed Sayyid al-Tantawi, Imam of al-Azhar mosque in Cairo, Egypt said:

> Attacking innocent people is not courageous, it is stupid and will be punished on the day of judgement.... It's not courageous to attack innocent children, women and civilians. It is courageous to protect freedom, it is courageous to defend oneself and not to attack.[12]

What I quoted is just a small excerpt of the voices within Islam condemning the killing of innocents. The list of contemporary authorities in orthodox Islam that condemn terrorism is quite large.[13]

The misconceptions that surround Jihad in popular media can be partly attributed to some contemporary Muslims losing touch with their tradition. According to Karen Armstrong:

> Fundamentalism is not conservative. Rather, it is highly innovative—even heretical—because it always develops in response to a perceived crisis. In their anxiety, some fundamentalists distort the tradition they are trying to defend. The Pakistani ideologue Abu Ala Maududi (1903–1979) was the first major Muslim thinker to make jihad, signifying "holy war" instead of the traditional meaning of "struggle" or "striving" for self-betterment, a central Islamic duty. Both he and the influential Egyptian thinker Sayyid Qutb (1906–1966) were fully aware that this was extremely controversial but believed it was justified by Western imperialism and the secularizing policies of rulers such as Egyptian President Gamal Abdel Nasser. (Armstrong, 2009)

The traditional understanding of Jihad, as Armstrong has noted, is that of "struggle" or "striving" for self-betterment. The spiritual sages of Islam have clearly explained the meaning of the greater Jihad, which is against one's lower self, caprices of the lower soul, the devil, and worldly lusts. The purpose of the greater Jihad is to achieve a sound heart, free from spiritual diseases. A verse of the Qur'an while describing the day of judgement reads, "On that day nothing of wealth and children will benefit; except for one who brings Allah a sound heart." The traditional understanding of Islam is that the greater Jihad is the obligation of every Muslim and whoever leaves it is not safe from the perils of this world and the next. Jihad also carries the meaning of struggle to better living conditions for the society. A prophetic tradition mentions that the most virtuous action of Jihad is speaking a word of truth in front of an oppressive ruler (Nasai & Shams al-Din, 2005). Jihad is not an end within itself. Thus, the use of ignoble means such as that of suicide bombs or the killing of civilians cannot reconcile with its noble purpose.

Being Part of the Solution

One of the major messages that Islam gives to Muslims is to be part of the solution in the society that they live in. It thus encourages Muslims to earn one's bread with one's own hand and not to be a burden on the society. A hadith states: "No one earns his food better than the one who worked with his hands, and the prophet of Allah, David earned his food by working with his hands" (al-Bukhari & Khan, n.d.). The Prophet Muhammad also taught people not to deny the good they found in their societies. His way was to perfect the good that he found. He said "Verily, Allah loves that when anyone of you does a job he should perfect it." Muslims serious in practicing Islam give immense importance to this message. This is why President Obama in his address in Cairo said, "....Much has been made of the fact that an African American with the name Barack Hussein Obama could be elected president. But my personal story is not so unique. The dream of opportunity for all people has not come true for everyone in America, but its promise exists for all who come to our shores—that includes nearly seven million American Muslims in our country today who enjoy incomes and education that are higher than average...."

I would at this point like to conclude by writing that I have not been able to deal with many of the issues that I would have liked to write about in this chapter. But hope that by this effort of mine, readers will get a general idea of how to look for answers to puzzling questions about Islam from within the religious tradition of Islam. The people who are given authority to speak about this religion are its scholars. Specifically these scholars preserve a chain of narration from the Prophet Muhammad to the present day. One of the very early authorities of Islam, Abdullah bin Mubarak said "The chain of narration is part of religion. If not for this chain, anyone would have said what they wanted."[14]

The Qur'an is preserved verbatim because of this chain; the prophetic traditions are preserved immaculately in canonical works and exegeses on these two primary sources by authorities of the bygone centuries and are also preserved and well known among scholars.

It is also of great importance for people trying to gain a better understanding of Islam to meet with simple people who practice Islam by personal choice. I hope that we will move closer to making a world of dialog and mutual understanding and accepting one another as brothers and sisters in humanity. The prophet of Islam is described in the Holy Qur'an by a verse "We have not sent you except as a mercy to Creation."[15] There is no other verse in the Qur'an that defines the statement of purpose of the Prophet Muhammad better than this. Scholars commenting on this verse have said that everything that the Prophet Muhammad brought was mercy. A way of finding out whether something is a part of Islam is to ask a simple question: Is it merciful? It is my wish that Muslims or non-Muslims wishing to understand Islam better would keep this question in mind as they begin their quest.

Endnotes

1. al-Tirmidhi relates this and says that it is an authentic hadith (or prophetic tradition).
2. This hadith has been related by al-Bukhari.
3. Born in 1954 in the north-western United States, he was educated in philosophy and Arabic at the University of Chicago and UCLA. He embraced Islam in 1977 at al-Azhar in Cairo, and later studied the traditional Islamic sciences of hadith, Shafi'i and Hanafi jurisprudence, legal methodology (*usul al-fiqh*), and tenets of faith (`aqidah`) in Syria and in Jordan, where he has lived since 1980. His English translation of `Umdat al-Salik` by Ibn al-Naqib, A. i. L. and N. H. M. Keller (1994): *Reliance of the Traveller: The Classic Manual of Islamic Sacred Law Umdat al-salik*. Evanston, IL: Sunna Books, is the first Islamic legal work in a European language to receive the certification of al-Azhar, the Muslim world's oldest institution of higher learning. He also possesses ijazas or "certificates of authorization" in Islamic jurisprudence from sheikhs in Syria and Jordan.
4. *Surah Maryam*.
5. *Surah Qamr*.
6. Imam Sharafuddin al-Busiri is one of the most celebrated poets in Islam. He was a pious saint and the spiritual disciple of Abu Abbas al-Mursi. His *Qasida Burda* (Ode of the Mantle) is the most widely sung and memorized poem in the Muslim world.
7. From *Surah Furqan* from verse 61–76. It is very difficult to translate the Arabic to English without losing a lot of the richness found in the original. However this is a good attempt to translate by Marmaduke Picthall.
8. Related by al-Nawawi in *Riadul Saliheen* (The Gardens of the Righteous).
9. *San Jose Mercury News*, September 15, 2001,http://www0.mercurycenter.com/local/center/isl0916.htm
10. From the Amman message website. See http://www.ammanmessage.com/
11. See also *Al.la.madhabiyya* by Said Ramadan al-Buti, one of the foremost scholastic theologians in Islam.
12. Agence France Presse, September 14, 2001
13. Please see http://www.ammanmessage.com/ for more about the contemporary authorities of Islam and their stance on terrorism.

14. Abdullah bin Mubarak is *Emir ul Muminin fi al hadith*, a title given to a scholar who memorizes at least one million prophetic traditions with their chain of narrations and biography of narrators. He was the companion of notable jurist Abu Hanifa, who is the founder of the Hanafi school of jurisprudence. His origins are from Khurasan in Persia.
15. *Surah Anbiya.*

References

Abdullah II bin Al-Hussein. (2004). The Amman message. Retrieved from http://www.ammanmessage.com/

al-Bukhari, M. i. I. l. & Khan, M. M. (n.d.) *Sahih al Bukhari* [the Arabic text of Bukhari's *al-Jami' al-sahih* with Khan's prefatory matter and English translation]. Cairo: Dar al-Fikr.

Armstrong, K. (November/December, 2009). Think again: God. *Foreign Policy Magazine.* Retrieved from http://www.foreignpolicy.com/articles/2009/10/19/god_0

Busiri, S. a.-D. M. i. S. & Tunji, M. (2002). *Diwan al-Busiri.* Bayrut: Dar al-Jil.

Ibn al-Naqib, A. i. L. & Keller, N. H. M. (1994). *Reliance of the traveller: The classic manual of Islamic sacred law Umdat al-salik.* Evanston, IL: Sunna Books.

Keller, N. H. M. (n.d.) Becoming Muslim. Retrieved from http://www.masud.co.uk/ISLAM/nuh/bmuslim.htm.

Nasai, A. i. S. & Shams al-Din, A. (2005). *Sunan al-Nasai.* Bayrut, Lubnan: Dar al-Kutub al-Ilmiyah.

Tirmidhi, M. i. I. & Mahfuz K. A. a.-G. (2003). *Sunan al-Tirmidhi wa-huwa al-Jami al-Sahih.* Bayrut, Lubnan: Manshurat Muhammad Ali Baydun; Dar al-Kutub al-Ilmiyah.

Part Two

Reading Islamophobia

Five

Islamophobia: The Viewed and the Viewers[1]

Shirley R. Steinberg

My student from Brooklyn College called on September 13, 2001, to say she could not attend that evening's class. An observant Muslim, this student wore a modest veil to school. As she attempted to shop on September 12 in her predominantly Muslim part of Flatbush, she was spat upon and called names. She realized that her safety was in danger, and she should not go to school that week. We saw several instances that echoed this student's experience. My husband, Joe, called the CNN news desk and asked to speak to a researcher. He related the student's story and suggested that CNN investigate and cover the anti-Muslim incidents in Brooklyn during this period. The reporter laughed and told him that they had more important events to cover, and that, indeed, maybe these incidents should happen more often—maybe his student got what she deserved.

After September 11, I continually watched each breaking news story, in every venue. I knew I had to write about what I saw, heard, and felt. Moreover, I was curious to see how others responded to the barrage of media stemming from that fall day. What emerged in my media-saturated brain? What was it that kept my attention? Romping through the construction of my consciousness dealing with Muslims and Arabic-speaking people, I realized how very easy it was to hate Arabs, to hate Muslims. As soon as those two planes had hit the Twin Towers, the American public was spewing volatile observations about all Arabs, all Muslims. It really took no time at all for an entire country to explode into rampant Islamophobia.

How long had I been aware of Muslims? Of Arabs? As a Jew, I have always been aware of my sister religion. In early religious classes I learned that a slave woman, Hagar, had borne Ishmael from Abraham and this lineage begat those considered Arabic. The children of Sarah and Abraham became the Jews. Religious mythology followed me throughout my life—stories of how Arabs became dark-skinned, versions of nomadic existence, and exotic tales from *The Arabian Nights*. I remember watching many early films with Arabs as grand fighters, usually brandishing swords, fighting the white man. I recall veils, belly dancing, tents, camels, large-toothed men with rifles and dirty robes.

The Collision of Popular Culture and My Religion

When did popular culture collide with my religious stories? In 1962, I sat through *Lawrence of Arabia* (Spiegel, Lean, Lawrence, & Lean, 1962). It did not take long to get the point, and the remainder of the show was tedious: a minor officer from England was sent to visit Prince Faisal and ended up leading an army of Arabic tribes to fight the Turks—he was a hero. I guess that was my earliest media exposure to Arabs.

Sometime around 1968, *Time Magazine* featured a cover story on the plight of the Arab refugees. I recall giving a speech based on the issue; my 16-year-old brain could not understand why the Arabic countries surrounding Israel would not let their Muslim brothers and sisters into their homelands. I understood why the Israelis did not make room—the country was too small and had been given to Jews. My social studies teacher didn't know anything about it.

In June 1968, just down the freeway from my school, Robert Kennedy was shot by Sirhan Sirhan, defined in the news as "a man of Jordanian descent." Many readers may remember the dark and swarthy photos of the murderer, who quickly disappeared from the limelight. A lot of Americans thought all hopes of social equity and freedom died with Bobby that day, at the hand of the Arab.

Four years later, when I began a new college semester, the news hit that Israeli athletes had been kidnapped at the Munich Olympics by Arab terrorists, a group known as Black September. We were glued to the television as we watched cameras cover the occupied residences; we saw shadowy figures identified as the kidnappers on the phone negotiating with authorities. Then we saw the German police shoot and kill the terrorists and athletes on the tarmac of the Munich airport. I have flown to Munich once, and I assumed the tarmac was still there. No one was able to show me where it was. Almost a quarter of a century later, Steven Spielberg produced *Munich* (Kennedy, Mendel, Spielberg, Wilson, & Spielberg, 2005). Ironically, the film did not deal with the city or with much of the terrorists and athletes. It was typical Spielberg stylized re-historization, a story of the supposed retaliation of the kidnappings by the Israelis. The film followed the murders of many of the Muslim suspects and was problematic on almost every level: the justification of the revenge killings; the fact that the German authorities were never implicated in the shootout at the airport, and the image of the Twin Towers on the horizon at the end of the film. What knowledge did this loosely-historical/fictional film give to the viewers? Many people with whom I spoke had never heard of the Munich massacre, and now Spielberg has given them their history.

I had not visited New York City after the Twin Towers had been built. When the World Trade Center was bombed in 1993 it was shocking, but very removed from my life. I had never seen the buildings. Few were killed, but lots of expensive cars were destroyed. The news reported it was the work of Arabic terrorists. In 1994 we went to New York and scanned the World Trade Center to see where the bomb had hit. We were astounded at how huge the buildings were and how small the bomb damage had been. The buildings were obviously indestructible.

In 1996, I was watching CNN in a hotel in San Francisco—a bomb had destroyed a federal building in Oklahoma City. All of the first reports from the radio, TV, and newspapers indicated that Arabic terrorist groups had planned the mass attack. Hours later, a white man was in custody. No apology was offered to the previously identified, supposed perpetrators. Some Arab Americans complained about the erroneous accusation, but the news quickly moved on to the unfolding Timothy McVeigh story. Upon reflection, I do not recall any attempts by American citizens to spit upon Irish Catholics (McVeigh's background), attack McVeigh's hometown, or pull over white men of 30 who resembled the lanky terrorist.

A network break-in to regular programming in 1997 revealed the headline that Princess Diana had been killed in an auto accident along with her boyfriend, Dodi Fayed. Fayed was a Muslim, an Egyptian, whose wealthy father had been denied British citizenship by the Queen—the elder Fayed owned Harrod's of London. Continued tabloid coverage over the years has claimed that Diana could have been murdered in order to keep her from humiliating the royal family by her relationship with an undesirable man.

By the time the first plane hit in lower Manhattan that Tuesday in September, many Americans' cultural curricula had been imprinted and validated. I believe that was why it was so easy to hate Arabs and Muslims. Naturally, we would be able to hate terrorists, but McVeigh was a terrorist, and our hatred and outrage were limited only to him, not his entire culture, religion, state, or community. Media literacy being my field of study, it was obvious that I would analyze the cultural pedagogy of Hollywood—How had Muslims and Arabs been depicted by Hollywood?

I maintain that if pedagogy involves issues of knowledge production and transmission, the shaping of values, and the construction of subjectivity, then popular culture is the most powerful pedagogical force in contemporary America. The pedagogy of popular culture is ideological, of course, in its production of commonsense assumptions about the world, its influence on our affective lives, and its role in the production of our identities and experiences (Grossberg, 1995). Movies help individuals articulate their feelings and moods that ultimately shape their behavior. Audiences employ particular images to help define their own taste, image, style, and identity—indeed, they are students of media and film pedagogy.

Audiences often allow popular culture vis-à-vis films, to speak for them, to provide narrative structures that help them make sense of their lives. This emotional investment by the audience can often be organized in emotional/ideological/affective alliances with other individuals, texts, and consciousness formations. Thus, this effect mobilized by the popular culture of film provides viewers with a sense of belonging, an identification with like-minded individuals—this feeling becomes progressively more important in our fragmented society (Grossberg, 1995). Keeping in mind the complexity of the effects of film popular culture, the effect produced is different in varying historical and social contexts. With these notions in mind, I went in search of the assumptions that may have been made in the viewing of films having Arab or Muslim characters. I did have a couple of research questions in mind: Why is it so easy for many North Americans to hate Muslims? Why are they so easy to fear and blame? With these questions, I hoped the films I viewed would shed some tentative answers, and, more importantly to my own scholarship, provoke more questions.

I selected movies when my viewing signaled that there was sufficient depiction of Arabs and/or Muslims to discuss. I asked others if they recalled any films that I should be viewing. Consequently, these films were culled out of our combined cultural collective. I did not consult written research in order to gather my films; I wanted to know what stood out in our minds from films that depicted Arabs and Islam. I viewed 17 films and scripted scenes and/or dialog that needed re-examination. After I had gathered these data, I revisited my notes in order to identify themes, archetypes, and authorship in the films.

Film and Islam

Most of the films I viewed dealt with Muslim Arabs. However, *Not Without My Daughter* (Ufland, Ufland, & Gilbert, 1990) and *East Is East* (Udwin, Khan-Din, & O'Donnell, 1998) are films about Muslims, not Arabs (those from the Arabian Peninsula). Sally Field's compelling, yet whining performance in *Not Without My Daughter* (based on a true story of one woman's experience) dealt with an American woman married to an Iranian doctor who deceitfully brought his wife and daughter to his home in Iran. Sally did not want to go: "We can't go to Iran—it's much too violent." Swearing on the Qur'an, "Moody" promises they will be safe. After reaching Iran, greeted by a slain goat (in their honor), Sally is horrified. Cultural analysis is attempted by Sally and her spouse: "It just seems so primitive." "Beliefs seem primitive when they aren't your own." Mother and daughter become prisoners as the husband reverts to Ayotollah-generated fundamentalism. "Islam is the greatest gift I can give," assured Moody. Persian women (in full black *burqahs*) are yammering, scheming, whispering, and occasionally beaten by their husbands or other available men—this was a dark, frightening, and smothering world to the former Sister Bertrille. Field's character is starkly white in comparison to the darkness that cinematographically depicts the Muslims in the film. Women peering out of slits in their *burqahs* are routinely belittled, demeaned, and marginalized by their husbands. There are occasions when Field's character attempts to bond with women and ask for their help. Alas, everyone turns against her, shuns her, or turns her in to her husband. Islam is depicted as unreasonable, and Moody is equally unreasonable, as he immediately becomes a tribalized tyrant to his wife and little girl. When Field reminds Moody of his promise made on the Qur'an and tells a holy man of this breach of faith, she is met with verbal attacks by everyone within earshot. A message is sent to the viewer that Islamic vows on holy books are not kept, and holy men are indeed as evil as everyone else. *Not Without My Daughter* is based on a true story. Obviously, I am in sympathy with anyone whose child is stolen and who is abused by a spouse. However, the film does not center on the marital issues as much as it is an indictment of the entire community in Tehran.

East Is East is BBC-produced and deals with a lower-middle class Pakistani man who marries a British woman. He insists on being a traditional Muslim, and his wife respects that—as long as her husband does not catch the children carrying the statue of Jesus during the Easter Parade. As the children are proudly marching in the parade, someone warns them that their father is approaching. They toss the religious statues to other people, peel off their costumes, and dash home to be there before their father opens the door. The father is depicted as stupid for not catching on, and the family continues the ruse, being Muslim to their father, but really being Christians. Dad is devastated by his older son bailing out of his own arranged wedding. He tries to match-make the other sons: "I'm not marrying a fucking Paki." As a father he is overbearing in his desire to see his children as happy Muslims—he adds insult to injury as he insists on giving his gift of an Arabic watch to each child. He had saved the watches for a special time and ceremoniously presents each of them with the watch. They explode with anger and disgust imagining that they would actually wear a watch with strange symbols.

They are furious when he insists they go to a school to learn the Qur'an. After various defeats, a broken man, he begins to beat his wife and children. Once again, cinematography plays an important role as the camera angles began to change; as the father gets meaner, his character is filmed from below the nostrils of his huge, sweating, bulbous nose—he also had yellowed, crooked teeth. Within an hour of the film, he transforms from a princely, kindly father and husband (in both appearance and context) to an evil fool. Frustrated, he bemoans that neighbors think he is a barbarian. When interviewed about *East Is East*, the actors (most of whom were South Asian) agreed that the film was an important document of immigration and acculturation into British society. None of them even alluded to the racist, Islamophobic depictions of Pakistanis and Muslims.

Tontos, Sancho Panzas, and Ed McMahons: Hollywood Sidekicks

The other films I viewed were about Arabs—those from Arabia (or countries divided from Arabia). With the exception of *Lawrence of Arabia* (Spiegel et al., 1962), all movies were filmed in the West. *Lawrence of Arabia* is a dramatic (and long) saga about a blond, blue-eyed Englishman who, caught up in the myth of Arabia and the desert, convinces marauding rival Bedouin bands of "barbarians" to unite in their fight against the equally barbaric Turks. Peter O'Toole's character is a prototype to Sean Connery and Mel Gibson and is accompanied by Omar Sharif, once an enemy—now a converted sidekick. Angering the British; "Has he gone native?" Lawrence eventually leaves Arabia—naturally, in better condition than he found it: "I did it." "Arabia is for the Arabs now."

Sharif, as a desert sheikh, begins as a proud, brilliant warrior. However, as he is tamed by O'Toole, he becomes his bodyguard, brother-in-arms, and gives his life for O'Toole. He is reduced in the film from a man of stature to a colonized camel rider. Sharif's character is the example for others to follow. It is obvious to all who watch that the Arabs in tribal form could never survive and that the British and Lawrence were sent as divine leaders to organize and unite the different groups. Interestingly, even as Lawrence exoticizes the natives—wears their clothing, rides camels, and imitates their lives—he never forgets that he is an Englishman and that they are barbarians: "Any time spent in a bed would be a waste—they are a nation of sheepskins." "They (the Arabs) are dirty savages." "Arabs are a barbarous people."

As with Sharif in *Lawrence of Arabia*, many of the films introduce a sidekick character for the white male lead. Loyal and faithful to death, the Tonto-ized friend is simpler, devoutly Muslim, full of Islamic platitudes and premonitions, and is frightened easily. In two of the Indiana Jones films, *Indiana Jones and the Raiders of the Lost Ark* (Lucas, Kazanjian, Kasdan, & Spielberg, 1981) and *Indiana Jones and the Last Crusade* (Lucas, Marshall, Boam, & Spielberg, 1989), both of which are set in the Middle East, Indy is accompanied by his Egyptian pal who fears that Indy's ideas are dangerous and will create anger from Allah. He attempts to convince Indiana that he is not stupid: "even in this part of the world we are not entirely uncivilized." Endangered at times, this minstrelized sidekick puts his hands in the air, opens his eyes widely, and shouts for safety. Tonto is a Spanish word for stupid or idiot.

Filling in the Scene with Arabs

Ironically, films that were Arabic in context and content, had little to do with Arabs. *Abbott and Costello Meet the Mummy* (Christie, Grant, & Lamont, 1955), *Casablanca* (Wallis, Philip, Epstein, & Curtiz, 1943), *The Mummy* (Daniel, Jacks, & Sommers, 1999), *The Mummy Returns* (Jacks, Daniel, Sommers & Underwood, 2001), *Ishtar* (May, 1987), and *The Jewel of the Nile* (Douglas, Rosenthal, Konner, & Teague, 1985) contain plots directly concerned with Arabic/Islamic themes. Actors with dialog, though, are western. Depending on the film, extras appeared to be Arabic. Action shots with Arabic peoples are almost exclusively shot in loud marketplaces. No heads are left uncovered; the fez is an accessory of choice for comical extras. The militaristic extras (sword carrying) most often wore a *kaffiyeh* (couture Arafat), and several Arabs sported turbans. What struck me about the extras was the "clumping" in which they would always appear. Let me borrow from Joe Kincheloe as he describes the French Fry Guys of McDonaldland: "The most compelling manifestation of conformity in McDonaldland involves the portrayal of the French Fry Guys. As the only group of citizens depicted in the Hamburger Patch, these faceless commoners are numerous but seldom seen" (Kincheloe, 2004). They intend to look, act, and think pretty much alike. Parent French Fry Guys are indistinguishable from children, and vice versa. They are so much alike that, so far, no individual French Fry Guy has emerged as a personality identifiable from the others. They resemble little mops with legs and eyes and speak in squeaky, high-pitched voices, usually in unison. They always move quickly, scurrying around in fits and starts (McDonald's Customer Relations Center, 1994). Kincheloe goes on: "As inhabitants of a

McDonaldized McWorld, the French Fry Guys are content to remove themselves from the public space, emerging only for brief and frenetic acts of standardized consumption—their only act of personal assertion." In these films, Hollywood's French-frying of Arabs leaves them to stand in clumps, to surround the action, to yell loudly in the background, and to run the market. They are incompetent in keeping their shop area organized as someone is always running through it, knocking the wares down and leaving a fist-flinging *kaffiyeh*-clad merchant screaming from behind.

White Boy Saviors and Dirty, Smelly Arabs

Included in my content/discourse analysis of these films was woven the weft of the white, male leader: sent to save citizens or artifacts from unscrupulous individuals. Lawrence and Indiana serve as perfect Aryan messiahs to these dark, mysterious Muslims. The word barbaric (or barbarous, barbarian) was used in each film. *Aladdin* (Disney Studios, 1992–1996) opens with an overture and opening song that describes the mysterious, dark, barbaric East. Indeed, after the first release of *Aladdin*, American Muslims were irate that the opening song talked about cutting off an ear....The music was changed; however, references to "it's barbaric, but, hey...it's home," were kept.

Physical characteristics of the Arabs generally show bad teeth, large hooked noses, and unclean tunics and caftans, and headgear that are just a tad too exaggerated. Once again, *Aladdin* does not run more than five minutes without describing one of the Arabic characters as "pungent." The films I viewed metaphorically included aroma vision, as one could vividly smell the camel dirt smeared, sweat clinging clothing of Muslim characters. The market scenes imply that Islamic countries center their cities and livelihoods on the marketplace. The Shylockization of these people is obvious in their attempts to barter and cheat consumers. Indeed, once again, in *Aladdin*, the fat, toothless, dirty Arab "businessman" flings out his tablecloth and "for-sale" sign and indicates that anything can be bought for a price. As I take in his hooked nose and sales pitch, the Semite in his character reminds me vividly that both Jews and Arabs share many of the same stereotypes: they lie, cheat, and steal.

Prototypes for Hatred

Islamic characters are not only compared to other Semites through an analysis, but also to other marginalized groups. There were many, many visible comparisons to Hollywood depictions and assumptions about African Americans. Many times I was sure that the negrofication of these characters served to show that any hated group can be exchanged with another. Exemplifying this is the language that served to incant slurs to African Americans:

sand nigger and dune coon were among the nastiest I heard in the films. Negative characteristics of Arabs and Muslims are not compared to those of white people.

While Indiana Jones deals with Nazis in *Raiders*, their characters adhere to the traditional expectations of viewers. The Nazis are anal, obsessive (anal-obsessed?), cruel—but clean and human. The characterization of Arabs always has an underlying implication that puts them on the borderline between human and animal. In each film, whiteness is the standard to which all Arabs and Muslims are measured. In addition to the racism that whiteness nurtures, the categories, the lexicon, the otherization, all become stenciled from one race and ethnicity to the other. When a group of people has been defined and depicted with such singular definition, it seems apparent that viewers can become complicit in fear and racism.

24 Ways to Stereotype on Television

When I first published a version of this article in my and Joe Kincheloe's book, *The Miseducation of the West: How Schools and the Media Distort Our Understanding of the Islamic World* (Kincheloe and Steinberg, 2004), I concentrated on the images of both Arabic peoples and Muslims in films. 9/11 had just happened, and the public was quick to make connections to the stereotypes of Arabs and Muslims seen in the cinema. Television had, for the most part, ignored, avoided, or just didn't bother with much in the way of Islamic or Arabic themes, characters, or even plots. The short-lived *Whoopi* (2004–2004) sit-com did include Whoopi Goldberg's sidekick, Nasim Khatenjami, played by London-born Iranian comedian, Omid Djalili. The interplay of the two characters was indeed refreshing, and Djalili's character asides were insightful and addressed issues that were at play in anti-Arabic sentiments (naturally, the show was cancelled within a year). Other than *Whoopi*, Arabic, and Islamic characters had seldom been part of American TV landscape.

When the 24-hour-a-day broadcasts of 9/11 had become yesterday's news, there was a period in which television seemed to have declared a silence on all things Arab. Occasionally a show would mention September 11, and a few dramas would bring in racist behaviors against Muslims. *Law & Order*, *NYPD Blue*, and other dramas were some of the first TV shows based on racism against Arabs. A common scenario included a store or restaurant owner, and a terrorized and tortured family, victims of those who blamed 9/11 on them. The Islamic families were portrayed as hardworking and honest, and the show was well received. Thematic shows grew around the issue of white/American hatred and fear of Arabs and Muslims. It began to appear on television that different shows were willing to tackle the notion of Islamophobia by association to 9/11. Possibly television would be a medium which would equalize the overt racism associated with cinematic Muslims and Arabs. My hopes were brief, the warm vibes that television had begun to radiate cooled off and Arabic and Muslim-bad-guy-themed shows emerged. Kiefer Sutherland's blockbusting hit, *24*, was supposed to debut in September 2001. After the World Trade Center attacks, Fox network and Sutherland determined it would be prudent and politically sensitive to delay the show until late fall. Based on a fictional American Counter Terrorist Unit, Sutherland's *Jack Bauer* would save the day each season fighting world-threatening terrorist threats. Due to the nature of the show, producers felt it would touch nerves. So close to September 11, it would be in bad taste. The show finally began late in 2001, ranking between 29th and 74th for the first three seasons. Jack Bauer saved the world three years in a row, having fought biological weapons, South American terrorism, and a manipulative and sociopathic First Lady.

In 2004, the Season 4 of *24* featured a Muslim family: mother, father, and teenaged son engaged in a deadly day. An upstanding, middle-class, suburban family, Navi, Dina, and Berooz Araz are thrown into chaos by Turkish Muslim terrorist Habib Marwan's desire to destroy the United States. Navi and Dina had been planted in Los Angeles as part of a small cell whose existence was based on waiting for Marwan's signal to join the jihad. Sixteen-year-old Berooz had not been aware of his parents' other life, and faced his own father's attempt to kill him when Berooz tried to stop the terrorists. Familial love was replaced by Navi's barbaric allegiance to Marwan's evil goals. As I began to view that new season of *24*, I watched the first episodes waiting for the foil—the twist, one that would take us away from the plot that was starting to develop. My media-viewing mind was begging Sutherland to not *go there*. I started to see that Hollywood's détente with Arabs and Muslims was over. They became fair game for directors and producers, and a support system for American governmental policies in the Middle East. The only twist was the tension produced in a new narrative: the evil terrorist Muslims were counterbalanced by the good Muslims. Young Berooz rebelled against his terrorist inheritance, never wavering from his commitment to goodness and the United States. Dina reluctantly worked with Jack Bauer to bring down Habib Marwan, and Navi, the evil father, was killed. The season ended with Jack victorious, and viewers were torn between the terrorist threat of the Turkish Muslim cell and the innate goodness of young Berooz. A polarized view of the Muslims was left with the audience; for every bad Muslim there was a good Muslim.

Other than the depiction of the terrorists as evil, dark-skinned, and determined fundamentalists, Fox could claim plausible deniability as to anti-Muslim sentiments. Themes were established that:

- Muslims are in our midst, hiding among us, they can be upscale; can be our next-door neighbors.
- They would do anything; even kill their own child for the cause.
- Occasionally there are good Muslims who step up to serve the greater good of America.

Season 4 brought *24* into the top 25 shows of the year. I certainly never expected an Islamic-themed *24* again, Fox had pushed it as far as it could go and was lucky to get away with it. Smartly peppering the bad guys with the redeemable Muslims, they had made it through a highly-rated season.

Season 5 returned Jack Bauer to a terrorist plot that dealt with internal political terror. Before the premiere of Season 6, the United States was going through political changes. The Bush Administration suffered an overwhelming loss to the Democrats in the November election and the American public was ostensibly becoming anti-war in regard to the occupation of Iraq. Television news was a hotly contested venue between the far-right via Fox news and conservative talking heads and the newly vocal "liberal" reports. After losing Republican seats and acknowledging that Iraq was not working out as planned, the Bush regime began to repeat their worries of losing to not only the angry Iraqi people, but to the terrorists who wanted to take away our freedom and occupy our own country. There became a need to re-vilify Muslims.

An unprecedented media campaign on major news programs highlighted the January 2007 return of Jack Bauer. As in previous seasons, no one was privy to the plot of the new year, and since Jack had conquered Latin American, Russian, Turkish, and presidential terrorists, Fox would have to come up with something new. The first four episodes of the show were aired back-to-back, indicating that again the show was relying on Muslim-themed terrorists.

The premiere of Season 6 of *24* begins with Jack Bauer's realization of urban unrest. Terrorist attacks are taking place all over the United States; the entire country is in a state of panic and alert. The man who is blamed for the attacks is Assad, and the audience is quickly aware that the plot will again be Muslim terrorists in 2007: "These people are in the Stone Age," a government agent explains. This time Fox had not anticipated the public and media uproar created by the first six episodes. Within the first two nights, Islamic terrorists had exploded the first of the five nuclear bombs in urban Los Angeles. (As the story was told, I was convinced that someone in production had read my work on Hollywood stereotypes and made a point of planting them in every frame possible.)

Jack Bauer joins reformed terrorist Assad, to apprehend Abu Fayed, the author of the domestic chaos and death. Fayed has been running a cell out of Los Angeles. Scene switches to a Los Angeles upscale suburb, and we see two large white men beating the teenaged Muslim Ahmed. He is saved by his best friend's father and brought to the safety of their home. The father and his son are astonished at the unreasonable racism demonstrated toward an innocent family. Ahmed's father was not home, and they insist he stay with them. Very quickly Ahmed's demeanor changes and he is an irrational Islamicist who is indeed part of Fayed's cell. Somehow Fayed has recruited this young American Muslim into his plot, unbeknownst to even his father. Ahmed holds the family hostage and threatens to kill them. We learn again that suburban, upscale "nice" Muslim families can, indeed, be sleeper cells.

Meanwhile, in Washington, the president's sister, who heads the Islamic American Alliance has been arrested along with her colleague, Walid. They have been unlawfully held against their will, she calls her brother who reminds her that these are terrible times and there is no protection from unreasonable search and seizure, and that the terrorist activities demand that war measures be taken. The two are taken to a holding camp full of Muslims. Quickly, the sister is released, leaving Walid in the prison yard. Walid overhears men discussing terrorist activities and quickly realizes they are involved in the attacks all over the country. The viewer is given a second lesson, there is a reason for unlawful arrest, because chances are that bad guys will be included in the sweep. The shell-shocked Jack Bauer had planned to quit CTU, however, after realizing what the Muslim terrorists had done, he remarks that "he is back, he [is not quitting], not after this."

Again, themes are established:

- They can be anywhere, hiding in our best neighborhoods.
- Even the youth are involved in terrorist endeavors; they will kill you, even a best friend who has saved your life.
- Suspension of habeas corpus is justified because in the 21st century world of jihad, it works to identify Muslims and Arabs, thus possibly stopping the terrorists and thwarting their actions.
- Even if some innocents are involved—it is indeed, for the greater good.

24 is Dick Cheney's favorite show.

Terrorists Are Everywhere

Cable TV's *Sleeper Cell* reinforces the fears that *24* has begun but takes them miles further. *Sleeper Cell* first aired in December of 2005 on Showtime; its first two seasons went unchallenged and flew far below any entertainment news or network news radar. Created by writing partners, Ethan Reiff and Cyrus Voris, the show features the first American Muslim protagonist, Darwyn, played by African American Michael Ealy. The show taglines delineate important points:

> Friends. Neighbors. Husbands. Terrorists.
> The enemy is here.
> Know your enemy.
> (2005; www.http//indb.com/title/H0465353/taglines)

Sleeper Cell: American Terrorist uses different opening credits. One of the most significant openings played in Season 1: the music was distinctly soft, a cello playing an Arabic tune, a map appears, it shows the boundaries of Iraq on the top and Arabia as the "country" on the bottom of the map; as the credits flash faster, the music picks up, becomes louder, and has women wailing indistinguishable Arabic sounds. Quick vignettes of white children in swimming pools, white people shopping, flashes of the American flag, dark Arabic-type men, flash back to American flag, white kids playing in a park—music gets louder, long shot of a GPS centering in on a neighborhood, then a large, suburban home, the GPS locks on the home, close-up, show begins.

To eliminate long summaries, I will bullet some of the episodes from the first two seasons:

Season 1: *Sleeper Cell: American Terror*
- Episode 1: American Muslim Darwyn goes undercover for FBI to uncover sleeper cells. He is recruited at a synagogue by a Holy Warrior. Taken to the desert, Darwyn is encouraged to stone a traitor to the group, he shoots him instead.
- Episode 2: Anthrax becomes the threat, probably for a shopping mall. Darwyn makes more connections.
- Episode 3: Mexican money is to come through the border to finance the plot.
- Episode 4: The Mexican money dries up, so it will come through Canada.
- Episode 7: A young Afghani boy approaches the terrorists to become a jihadist.
- Episode 8: White supremacists cooperate with the Holy Warriors in order to get explosives.

- Episode 9: A truck is hijacked; it is disguised as a LA Airport Mobile Emergency Command Vehicle. Two more cells in the United States have been discovered.
- Episode 10: The cell escapes FBI surveillance.

Season 2: *Sleeper Cell: American Terror*
- Episode 1: Darwyn tries to leave FBI and cell, but his FBI contact, a woman, is beheaded in the Sudan by terrorists.
- Episode 2: The leader of the cell, Farik, played by Israeli Oded Fehr seems impossible to break under questioning.
- Episode 3: Farik is deported to Saudi Arabia in hopes that he can be tortured legally there and give up the cell. Cell orders Darwyn to get a weapon.
- Episode 4: Darwyn saves the life of an Islamic televangelist. One of the terrorists watches the evangelist on TV as he runs on a treadmill between two blonde women. Farik escapes Al-Qaeda prison in Saudi Arabia.
- Episode 5: Nukes become the next threat to Los Angeles.

And so it goes. A search of the Showtime website allows the surfer to play a game in which he or she becomes the member of a sleeper cell. An Islamic dictionary is featured:

> Learn the definition and history behind some of the Islamic phrases used during the show. Study now!

At the end of a particularly violent episode, Farik is in a palace in Saudi Arabia, dressed in traditional clothing, he is considering Darwyn becoming the leader of the cell in Los Angeles. The closing credits roll, and a rap song is played loudly. I could not find the artist or all of the lyrics on line or on the episode, so forgive my not crediting the lyrics. Here are some of the phrases from the song:
"Tell me what you think at this"
"You can never understand till we do what we do"
"I can prove what we do given a situation"
"I can come up with a plan"
"Never be ashamed, always be proud"
"So go and do what you do, keep watching the news"
"I got a question for y'all,"
"You think we goin' to let another building fall?"
"Never Again."
"Fuck that....Send me back to Iraq."

Using a type of affective ideology (see Kincheloe & Steinberg, *Changing Multiculturalism: New Times, New Curriculum*, 1997), the audience is given no reason or argument in a scenario or storyline; instead, the music behind the credits goes directly to our primal affect. It bypasses any filters within the brain that may use logic or rationale and leaves us with a visceral impression. One does not expect the listener to politically deconstruct these lyrics, the affective part of the mind draws the connection between a falling building and Iraq and consequently, the invasion and occupation of Iraq are justified by patriots.

Sleeper Cell may be the very best of the worst in the genre. Each episode is produced with cinematic mastery, every hour with the quality of a fine Hollywood film. The writers and actors are not Arabic, neither are the creators. While Jewish names appear in the credit, distinctly Arabic or Middle Eastern names do not appear. Showtime is a network which has always run edgy and topical shows; however, it has usually leaned to the liberal or left in its ideology. The cell is extremely threatening to viewers; sites chosen for detonation or exposure to deadly chemicals are baseball parks, shopping malls, places in which the normal middle American exists. The cell is insidious and impossible to break; even with Darwyn planted as a mole, the threat is never extinguished. Ending a season with Darwyn "saving the day," he is handed back his pocket copy of the Qur'an; he then finds a lost little blond boy, and the mother thanks him with deep appreciation. He is the Muslim Jack Bauer; he saves the day but is always aware that the cells grow and that he must stay with the job. Any bad guys that are caught, under the laws of war, are "non-privileged" combatants; they are not put in jail, will not go to trial, and will be placed in holding by the Defense Department. Darwyn's conflicted self is always close to the surface, and when he finishes saving his day, he often retreats to the mosque to receive spiritual solace.

The themes are repeated and added upon:

- They are everywhere, they have penetrated to every part of our society.
- Even vehicles are suspect; an official vehicle can easily masquerade as an emergency vehicle.
- There may be good Muslims, but there always will be bad Muslims.
- We are in Iraq for a purpose, to avenge the 9/11 attacks, and to keep Middle Eastern terrorists from American soil.

Again, this content analysis demands that we recognize the advent of *Sleeper Cell* and the seasons of *24* that correspond with the loss of faith in Republican leadership and the demand to leave Iraq from the American public.

Media does matter; it speaks to us, and it can be a better tool than any other to reach viewing citizens.

Everyone Is a Bad Guy

An episode of *Law & Order* (Makris, 2006) opened with an American flag covered by a poster: UNITED AMERICANS FOR ONE AMERICA: ARABS GO HOME. We hear an Anglo voice yelling: "Get up, get up, you Arab pig." A masked man in camouflage pushes a man hooded in black in front of the flag. The entire scene is being videotaped. Another man joins the assailant and they both stand with the victim on his knees flanked by the stars and stripes. The first man speaks: "Lolliyops, towelheads, camel jockeys, you are not Americans, you are parasites living off our citizens, you cheer when our GIs die in Iraq. Why do you live in our country if you hate our way of life?" His partner speaks: "You think we're scared of your jihad? After today, be scared of us, this is our jihad." He takes a knife to the throat of the now-unhooded, crying Arabic man, "God bless America!" he slices the throat of the young man. Cut to the law examining the scene. Following the discovery of the videotape, the investigators spend a great deal of time looking for this white supremacist group which is targeting Arabs and Muslims. Going from one dead end to another, the case resolves itself when a cousin of the dead Muslim is found to be guilty. He had created the scenario of supremacists to keep suspicion from falling upon him. Justice is served; the Arabs are the bad guys, and any white supremacists are relieved from suspicion.

In January 2007, an episode of *Law & Order: Criminal Intent* (Shill, 2007) revolves around the brutal murder of a young Pakistani woman, Meena, who films a group of white and Jewish men beating Latino immigrant workers. The men are seen chasing the woman, trying to take her camera; her film leaves evidence of these white assailants. Hearing a news story of a Jewish woman hit by a car filled with Mexican immigrants on her way to synagogue, the detectives surmise: "this has got to be payback." Discussing the case with a Jewish man (wearing a blue yarmulke with stars of David surrounding it) who admitted being at the beating, he queries: "Some illegal alien runs over a mother and her baby and you arrest me?... We didn't hurt the Mexicans, or that Arab girl. We just want these people out of our neighborhood, before they kill any more of our children." Turns out he was telling the truth; his group merely chased her, scared her, and then he went to the synagogue to teach Hebrew. His rabbi backs him up.

The investigators view a film that Meena had made about her family living in New York. Affluent restaurant owners, Meena's parents had lost everything after patrons stopped coming to dine post-9/11. The detectives are emotionally touched as they view this family's experiences as they are punished for being Muslim. After investigation, the men who had been filmed beating the men were exonerated. The plot leads detectives to find the Pakistani woman had been in love with an Italian, and indeed, it seems obvious that he killed her. She was pregnant with his child. The Pakistani parents mourn the death of their daughter and her sexual violation. The father shows his fury by lashing out at the Italian boyfriend. Her brother watches silently as his family disintegrates. A *Romeo and Juliet* story emerges. The families are intent on blaming one another. A marriage had been arranged with a man who has just come to the States from Pakistan. He is gruff and swarthy and much older than the young murdered victim. He is a suspect for a few days but makes it clear he would have never hurt her as he had no emotional ties to her. Her pregnancy ruled her unfit to be his wife, and he intended to return to Pakistan.

After Chris Noth's (Detective Logan's) crackerjack psychological cop intervention, Meena's brother breaks down and admits he murdered his own sister to protect the good name of his family: she had humiliated them all. It had been an honor killing.

Both these *Law & Order* episodes promote themes:

- Even when you think all the Arabs and/or Muslims are not guilty, one of them is guilty.
- Mexican or Arab, immigrants are not welcome in our country.
- Familial honor is more important than love and loyalty; killing one's sister is honorable.
- Arabic and Muslim peoples create white scenarios to deflect attention from their own criminal activities.

Teaching against Islamophobia: Critical Media Literacy

Do we ask why it is easy for many North Americans to hate Muslims? Why are they so easy to fear and blame? We have had concrete reasons to deplore the actions of any terrorists. Islamic terrorism has been tapped as a vehicle to move the causes of many different organizations all over the globe. As a Jew I have always been conflicted as to who has rights over Jerusalem, over the Temple Mount, over Israel. However, my own research has allowed me to reconsider how the construction of my own consciousness has been formed, in large part, by media. Through my own content analysis of a few TV shows and films, I believe I have isolated dangerous themes which are potent enough to infuse the minds of both children and adult viewers. We offer little or no way to read these themes, to learn how to safely and intelligently view media. Many believe that if it is on TV or placed on film by a legitimate source, then the text is accurate and correct. That text directly feeds our emotional and intellectual selves into making political decisions, personal decisions. If we are able to work with students and parents to learn how to "read" film, the news, the papers, perhaps conversation involving injustice could surround the actions of those that do wrong, not their nationality or religion. We must create a curriculum that enables students to read the media, not to eliminate or censor, but to read. I maintain my contention that indeed popular culture is a curriculum—an overt, influential curriculum that feeds our need to consume entertainment. This Hollywood diet is not innocent: It is constructed on obsession, stereotype, fear, and, most importantly, on what sells. As teachers, it is our social responsibility to facilitate our students when reading the menu.

Endnote

1. An earlier version of this chapter appears in *Media Literacy: A Reader*, Macedo, D. & Steinberg, S. (2007, 2009). New York: Peter Lang.

References

Grossberg, L. (1995, Spring). What's in a name? (one more time). *Taboo: The Journal of Culture and Education*, 1–37.
Kincheloe, J. L. (2004). McDonald's, power, and children: Ronald McDonald (aka Ray Kroc) does it all for you. In S. R. Steinberg & J. L. Kincheloe (Eds.). *Kinderculture: The corporate control of childhood*. Boulder, CO: Westview Press.
Kincheloe, J. L. & Steinberg, S. R. (1997). *Changing multiculturalism: New times, new curriculum*. London: Open University Press.
Kincheloe, J. L. & Steinberg, S. R. (2004). *The miseducation of the West: How schools and the media distort our understanding of the Islamic world*. Westport, CT: Praeger Press.
Macedo, D. and Steinberg, S. R. (2007). (eds.) *Media Literacy: A Reader*. New York: Peter Lang.
Steinberg, S. R. (2009). (ed.) *Diversity and Multiculturalism: A Reader*. New York: Peter Lang.

Filmography

Christie, H. (Producer), Grant, J. (Writer), & Lamont, C. (Director). (1955). *Abbott and Costello meet the mummy*. United States: Universal Studios.
Daniel, S., & Jacks, J. (Producers), & Sommers, S. (Writer/Director). (1999). *The mummy*. United States: Universal Studios.
Disney Studios (Producer). (1992–1996). *Aladdin*. United States: Disney Studios.
Douglas, M. (Producer), Rosenthal, M., & Konner, L. (Writers), & Teague, L. (Director). (1985). *The jewel of the Nile*. United States: Twentieth Century Fox.
Jacks, J., & Daniel, S. (Producers), Sommers, S. (Writer), & Underwood, R. (Director). (2001). *The mummy returns*. United States: Universal Studios.
Kennedy, K., Mendel, B., Spielberg, S., & Wilson, C. (Producers), & Spielberg, S. (Director). (2005). *Munich*. United States: Universal Studios.
Lucas, G., & Kazanjian, H. (Producers), Kasdan, L. (Writer), & Spielberg, S. (Director). (1981). *Indiana Jones and the raiders of the lost ark*. United States: Paramount.
Lucas, G., & Marshall, F. (Producers), Boam, J. (Writer), & Spielberg, S. (Director). (1989). *Indiana Jones and the last crusade*. United States: Paramount.

Makris, C. (Director), Nathan, R. & Postiglione, S. (Writers). (2006). *NBC: Law & order*. Season 17, Episode 17006, "Fear America." Airdate: 10/13/06.
May, E. (Director). (1987). *Ishtar*. United States: Columbia Pictures.
Shill, S. (Director), & Reingold, J. (Writer). (2007). NBC: *Law & order: Criminal intent*. Season 6, Episode 06012, "World's Fair." Airdate: 01/02/07.
Spiegel, S., & Lean, D. (Producers), Lawrence, T. E. (Writer), & Lean, D. (Director). (1962). *Lawrence of Arabia*. United States: Republic Pictures.
Udwin, L. (Producer), Khan-Din, A. (Writer), & O'Donnell, D. (Director). (1998). *East is East*. United Kingdom: Miramax.
Ufland, H. & Ufland, M. (Producers), Gilbert, B. (Director). (1990). *Not without my daughter*. United States: Metro-Goldwyn-Mayer.
Wallis, H. (Producer), Philip, J., & Epstein, G. (Writers), & Curtiz, M. (Director). (1943). *Casablanca*. United States: Warner Bros.

Six

Holy Islamophobia, Batman! Demonization of Muslims and Arabs in Mainstream American Comic Books

Jehanzeb Dar

Introduction

During a panel at the 2006 WonderCon, the comic book convention in San Francisco, legendary comics' writer Frank Miller sparked controversy when he announced the title of his new comic book: *Holy Terror, Batman!* As one can probably guess from the title, the plot involves Batman defending Gotham City from the Al-Qaeda terrorist organization (Mount, 2006). Miller, who is best known in the comic book industry for critically acclaimed works such as *The Dark Knight Returns* and *Batman: Year One*, described the book as "a piece of propaganda" where "Batman kicks Al-Qaeda's ass." When asked about the progress of the book in an interview with "Rotten Tomatoes" (2007), Miller said he was still working on the project and that "it's bound to offend just about everybody." Based on extremely stereotypical and insidious representations of Middle Easterners in Miller's other work, the immensely popular *300*, which will be discussed later in the chapter, one can already envision the Al-Qaeda villains setting the stage in his latest title: dark-skinned, black-bearded, garbed in Arab headdress and robes, and wielding an AK-47. This villain, however, is not unique to Frank Miller's work, but rather has been seen throughout the comic book industry. The villain is the comic book Muslim, a poorly developed caricature based on Islamophobic and Orientalist stereotypes. Even if you have never read a comic book, you have most likely seen this portrait before.

Sinister, violent, and stereotypical depictions of Muslims and Arabs have persisted in Hollywood cinema for more than a century and continue to sustain today with films like *United 93* and hit television shows like *24* (Shaheen, 2003; Faber, 2007). In his book, *Reel Bad Arabs* (2001), Jack Shaheen documented and discussed over 900 Hollywood films to expose the industry's unapologetic degradation and dehumanization of Muslims and Arabs. In Shaheen's study, almost all of the films that featured Muslims or Arabs depicted them in an extremely negative light: "brute murderers, sleazy rapists, religious fanatics, oil-rich dimwits, and abusers of women." Similarly, when the mainstream media covers current events in Muslim majority countries, Muslim men are typically seen as angry mobs rioting in the street, shouting in Arabic, and burning an American or Israeli flag, while Muslim women are projected as secluded, fully veiled, and oppressed victims of Muslim men and the religion of Islam. In Hollywood films, these images do not change, but are rather reproduced in order to reinforce Islamophobia and misconceived notions that Muslims are the threatening "Other" and completely antithetical to Western Judeo-Christian values. As the late Edward W. Said noted in 1981:

> The media, the government, the geopolitical strategists, and although they are marginal to the culture at large—the academic experts on Islam—are all in concert: Islam is a threat to Western civilization. Now this is by no means the same as saying that only derogatory or racist caricatures of Islam are to be found in the West.... What I am saying is that negative images of Islam are very much more prevalent than any others, and that such images correspond, not to what Islam "is"...but to what prominent sectors of a particular society take it to be: Those sectors have the power and the will to propagate that particular image of Islam, and this image therefore becomes more prevalent, more present, than all others. (Muzzafer, 1994, p. 3)

The repetition of these images, argues Shaheen, has a profound impact on how viewers shape their attitudes and perceptions of Muslims and Arabs. When one considers how Hollywood films reach a remarkably wide audience, not just in the United States but in over 100 countries as well, the importance of challenging Islamophobia in film is critical. The less an issue is addressed, the easier it becomes for ignorance to perpetuate. For example, being an Arab does not automatically make someone a Muslim (and vice versa)—the former refers to an ethnic group, while the latter is a religious group. An Arab, just like a person of any ethnic background, can practice any or no religion, while a Muslim can be of any race or ethnicity. However, since filmmakers fail to make this distinction in their work, the two groups are often conflated as the same people and the equation reads something like this: Arab = Muslim = Terrorist.

Such misconceptions persist due to Hollywood's repetition of the "Reel Arab/Muslim," and the industry's massive appeal around the world further elevates the importance of breaking stereotypes, but there is another industry that is also popular and worth examining, especially considering how it often inspires blockbuster Hollywood film adaptations: the realm of comic books. It is a medium with compelling narratives, fantastic imagery, heroic characters, and is frequently considered, "the post-industrial equivalent of folk tales" that "touch the innocent part of us that can wonder, aspire, be amazed" (Shaheen, 1991). Superheroes and Superheroines are meant to embody the values of truth, justice, liberty, and equality, and yet the comic book industry suffers from the same injustice that plagues American cinema: negative representations of Muslims and Arabs. As in Hollywood films, realistic portraits of Muslims and Arabs are almost absent and in their place are caricatures of ugly Islamophobic and Orientalist stereotypes. What are the influences for these poor and singular representations and what do we learn about Muslims, their diverse ethnic backgrounds, and their religion? In this chapter, I aspire to answer these questions by (1) examining the prevalent "Muslim terrorist" stereotype and how it correlates with U.S. foreign policy, (2) analyzing the exoticized depictions of Muslims women, and (3) concluding with highlights of some positive representations of Muslims and Arabs in a new comic book series that serves as a potential model for breaking stereotypes and establishing inter-faith/inter-cultural understanding.

The Muslim Terrorist and U.S. Foreign Policy

In Jack Shaheen's study, "The Comic Book Arab" (1991), at least 50 instances of Arab terrorist activities were recorded and, unsurprisingly, all of the Arab characters were associated with Islam. The characters often make references to "Allah," the Arabic word for "God," in a violent and anti-American context. While God is addressed as "Allah" by all Muslims around the world, the word is also used by many Arab Christians as well, but this fact goes without mention (most likely because the writers themselves are unaware of it). What is also important to note is how frequently the Muslim terrorist characters are seen expressing their anger and hate against Americans and Jews, which arguably reflects the way U.S. foreign policy perceives Muslims, i.e., as threats and polar opposites to Western values. In each character I discuss, the Muslim terrorist is always seen as the enemy of the United States and its allied nations, particularly Israel.

In *Batman: A Death in the Family* (DC Comics #426–429, Jim Starlin, 1988), Batman's arch-nemesis, the Joker, concocts a plan to sell a nuclear cruise missile to Muslim terrorists for "much needed funds." Batman discovers the Joker's plot, fights his way through "suspicious-looking Arab men"

(Shaheen, 2001), and stops the terrorist leader, Jamal, from attacking the Israeli capital, Tel Aviv. The Joker, meanwhile, accepts the job offer from none other than Ayatollah Khomeini to become the Iranian Ambassador to the United Nations. Donning an Arab headdress and robes (even though he is in Iran, a non-Arab country!), the Joker stands before the United Nations' Grand Assembly and delivers a speech that only fuels Islamophobia through the guise of "humor":

> I am proud to speak for the great Islamic Republic of Iran. That country's current leaders and I have a lot in common. Insanity and a great love of FISH. But unfortunately we also share a MUTUAL PROBLEM. We get NO RESPECT. Everyone thinks of Iran as the home of the TERRORIST ZEALOT! They say even worse things about ME, would you believe? We've both suffered unkind ABUSE AND BELITTLEMENT! WELL, WE AREN'T GOING TO TAKE IT ANYMORE!! You'll no longer be allowed to kick us around. In fact, you aren't going to be able to kick ANYONE around ever again!

Without further delay, the Joker tears off his Arabian garb and releases deadly laughing gas in the entire room. Fortunately, Superman, disguised as a security guard, inhales the toxic fumes and flies out of the building to get rid of the gas while Batman and Joker do battle. Not only do we see Arabs, Iranians, and Muslims conflated in the same group and depicted as terrorists, but we also see political themes that parallel current events and U.S. foreign policy. Shaheen elaborates:

> Thus, Arabs are equated with terrorists who are equated with Iranians who are equated with Batman's insane arch-nemesis, the Joker. (It is clear that the writers of Batman do not know the difference between a Persian and an Arab. Batman speaks Farsi in Beirut!) The Joker's insanity is their insanity; his destructiveness is their destructiveness. Batman's archenemy finds his home with Arabs/Iranians, America's enemies. This is the most prevalent of the themes involving Arabs in comic books, that is—Arabs [Them] vs. the West [Us].

The writer's and publisher's disregard for cultural, religious, and political accuracy simply points to a crude and racist generalization: Arabs, Iranians, and Muslims are all the "same" and "hate" the West.

Other representations of the Muslim terrorist appear in popular titles such as *Action Comics* (DC Comics, #598, John Byrne & Paul Kupperberg, 1988), where Superman and Checkmate join forces to stop Muslim terrorists who have hijacked an American nuclear aircraft carrier in Metropolis. When Superman tries to negotiate with one of the terrorists, the response is loaded with anti-Muslim stereotypes: "SILENCE, capitalist tool! I am the FIST OF ALLAH—I will do the SPEAKING! The ANGELS OF ALLAH have seized this American warship." At one point, one of Checkmate's companions calls the Arab defense minister a "towel-headed bozo" when he leaves on a private plane. Since the Arab defense minister was "responsible for God knows how many deaths," Checkmate pushes a button and watches the Arab's jet explode. The acceptability of killing an Arab or Muslim, as well as using a racial slur, is quite disturbing, especially when it's in a Superman comic book. A similar theme is found in *The Punisher: Nuclear Terrorists over Times Square* (Marvel Comics, #7, Mike Baron, 1988), where Muslim terrorists steal a kilo of plutonium and plot to "blow a hole in the American dream." The protagonist, Rose, is an agent of the Israeli Secret Service and a young woman "whose parents were killed by fanatical terrorists (presumably Arab) when she was sixteen" (Shaheen, 1991). To combat the Muslim terrorist leader, Yassir, Rose seeks the aid of the American Superhero, the Punisher. Wearing sunglasses and a turban, Yassir is seen shouting in a videotaped message:

> To the garbage eating dogs of the West! We have brought this war to your homes, your cities! Because your values are garbage, we have reduced your greatest triumph, the symbol of your colonial brutality to garbage! Death to the enemies of Islam! Long live the revolutionary Jihad!

As Rose and the Punisher fight the terrorists on the rooftops of Times Square, an obese Muslim man in a turban named Ahmed attacks Rose with a jagged knife. As the Punisher arrives at the scene, Ahmed picks up Rose and hurls her to the streets below, killing her instantly. The Punisher follows up by throwing Ahmed off the building and then mourns Rose's death. The political message in the comic book not only reflects America's long-standing alliance with the state of Israel but also its relentless vilification of the Palestinians. The terrorist leader, Yassir (who notably shares the same name as former Palestinian leader, Yasser Arafat), condemns the "colonial brutality" of the West with such primitivism that actual realities, such as the suffering of Palestinians under Israeli occupation, are seen as illegitimate concerns or distorted perspectives. Given the fact that unyielding U.S. support for Israel has persisted in the modern age, it is not difficult to see how these cruel presentations of Muslims and Arabs, especially Palestinians, stigmatize the credibility of intellectuals—both Muslim and non-Muslim alike—who "dare" to question and criticize Israeli policy. In other words, to criticize U.S. support for Israel would only link one's views with Muslim terrorists like Yassir. Although this issue of *The Punisher* was published in 1988, the same image of Muslims threatening the United States and its allies are only repeated in post-9/11 comic books.

The very first page of *New X-Men: Dust* (Marvel Comics, #133, Grant Morrison, 2002) shows Wolverine standing over a pile of slaughtered Taliban militants in Afghanistan—all dark-skinned, mostly bearded, and wearing turbans. Later in the book, Pakistani terrorists hijack an Air India plane while Professor Xavier and Jean Grey are aboard. Xavier uses his psychic abilities to convince the Pakistani hijacker, whose name happens to be Muhammad, to put down his weapon and surrender to the Indian authorities. Muhammad begins to cry and as he is arrested, he says, "It's true, I don't know what I'm doing with my life!" When one considers the date of the comic's publication, 2002, it is not difficult to make an association between the U.S. invasion of Afghanistan and the glorifying image of Wolverine butchering Taliban militants. Once again, since Muslims are projected as religious fanatics and heartless murderers, the notion of killing them is acceptable and inoffensive in the mind of the reader. Similarly, the Pakistani hijacker represents political tensions between Pakistan and the United States—during a time when U.S. deputy secretary of state, Richard Armitage threatened to "bomb Pakistan back to the stone age" if it did not commit fully to "the war on terror" (Ali, 2008, p. 145)—while the Indian authorities reflect India's cooperation and strong alliance with the United States. The distinction is visualized quite clearly: Pakistanis are "evil," Indians are "good," and the Americans make the rules for such judgment. As with *The Punisher* issue discussed earlier, Muslims are assigned to terrorist roles while members of U.S.-allied nations, such as Israel and India, are rewarded with positive and sympathetic representations.

It is no doubt that Frank Miller's upcoming title, *Holy Terror, Batman!*, will feature similar, if not worse, caricatures of Muslims and Arabs. As mentioned earlier, Miller has expressed his hostility against Muslims and Middle Easterners before, not just in his work but also in interviews. In 2007, many Iranian Americans voiced their concern and outrage when Miller's comic book, *300*, was adapted into a major motion picture (Constable). Perhaps the most noticeable offense in *300* (the comic book and the film) is how the Persians are horrifically demonized as disfigured monsters and savages. It is not hard to notice the punctuated differences in skin color either: the white-skinned Spartans versus the dark-skinned Persians. While *300* takes place in the pre-Islamic and pre-Christian world, the ancient Persians are linked with the same stereotypes that are attributed to Muslims: violent, oppressive, and garbed in typical Oriental fashion, i.e., turban-clad, robed, and bearded. As a result of these familiar stereotypes, the Persians get perceived, in modern terms, as "terrorists"—monstrous beings that are mysteriously driven by an innate desire to conquer, slaughter, and oppress. In an interview with NPR (2007), shortly after the film adaptation of *300* was released, Frank Miller made some incredibly offensive statements about Islam and Muslims:

> ... let's finally talk about the enemy. For some reason, nobody seems to be talking about who we're up against, and the sixth century barbarism that they actually represent (emphasis added). These people saw people's heads off. They enslave women, they genitally mutilate their daughters, they do not behave by any cultural norms that are sensible to us. I'm speaking into a microphone that never could have

been a product of their culture, and I'm living in a city where three thousand of my neighbors were killed by thieves of airplanes they never could have built.

Miller uses the phrase "sixth century barbarism" as a coded reference to Islam (even though Islam began in the 7th century) and then accuses Muslim civilizations of never contributing anything to the world. Perhaps it would benefit Mr. Miller if he learned that the Islamic empires preserved many of the Greek philosophical and scientific works by Aristotle, Plato, Socrates, Euclid, and Pythagoras (Morgan, 2007, p. 52). He should also be informed that algebra was invented by a Persian Muslim named Mohammad Al-Khwarizmi. The English word "algorithm" actually comes from "Al-Khwarizmi" and the significance of algorithms in computers, programming, engineering, and software design is immensely critical. As stated by Michael H. Morgan, author of *Lost History: The Enduring Legacy of Muslim Scientists, Thinkers, and Artists*:

> [Al-Khwarizmi's] new ways of calculating will enable the building of 100-story towers and mile-long buildings; calculating the point at which a space probe will intersect with the orbits of one of Jupiter's moons; the reactions of nuclear physics... the language and intelligence of software; and the confidentiality of a mobile phone conversation. (2007, p. 92)

Ironically, the Western achievements that Frank Miller boasts about could not have been possible without the *collaboration* of civilizations.

So far, we have seen the Muslim terrorist as an incredibly one-dimensional villain. Whether he is trying to nuke Israel, hijack planes and aircraft carriers or is disguised as an ancient pre-Islamic Persian, the Muslim terrorist is no one to sympathize or empathize with. He has no story, no family, and no other purpose but to cause war and destruction against the West. When nothing appreciative is learned about Muslim and Arab characters, the stereotypes blur the distinction between real-life extremists and the overwhelming majority of Muslims and Arabs, who are peaceful and multi-dimensional human beings like everyone else. In the next section, we will see if the stereotypes persist when Muslim women are portrayed in comic books.

Exoticizing Muslim Women

In an industry where readership is traditionally comprised of mostly preteen and young adult males (Lavin, 1998), the images and roles of women in comic books require close examination. Historically, in the late 1930s, women assumed the role of "damsels in distress"—victims that needed to be rescued by the male protagonist; a prize that needed to be won by either the male villain or hero. For example, in the first issue of *Superman*, news reporter and future love interest, Lois Lane, is kidnapped by criminals and eventually rescued by Superman. No relationship is developed and nothing else is learned about who Lois is; Superman simply saves her, hurries her to safety, and then flies away. Over the years, when empowered female characters, or Superheroines, emerged, the industry saw a new wave of female and male readership. However, despite these new portrayals of strong and powerful female characters like Wonder Woman, something else was occurring: women were being depicted as sex objects. Superheroines "like DC's Wonder Woman or Marvel's She-Hulk may easily overcome the most overwhelming threats and obstacles, but they are invariably depicted as alluring objects of desire, wearing the scantiest of costumes" (Lavin, 1998). This is known as the male gaze, where female characters are illustrated and presented in ways their heterosexual male writers, artists, and audiences would like to see them (Mulvey, 1975). Such skimpy and erotic images in comic books became increasingly popular, especially among male readers, and still persist to this very day. With this image of women in mind, it is interesting to examine how *Muslim* women fare in the male-dominated world of comic books. In this section, I will briefly outline the exoticized Muslim woman found in Jack Shaheen's study and then critique a Muslim Superheroine who appears in Marvel Comics' *New X-Men*.

Prior to the character of "Dust," which I will discuss in the next paragraph, Muslim women were "doomed to one of two illustrations, either a scantily-clad and salivated-upon belly dancer, or a faceless housewife, whose thick-set form is bundled up in dark robes" (Shaheen, 1991). As the belly dancer, Muslim women are able to attract the attention of notable Superheroes, who in turn perceive them as oppressed and second-class citizens who need to be saved. Subsequently, as an America hero sets his eyes on an "oppressed" Muslim woman, a villainous Muslim male figure appears and tries to keep her for himself. In *G.I. Combat "Stop at the Corner of Hades"* (National Periodical Publications, #139, Jan 1970) an American G.I. falls in love with a Muslim woman named Princess Azeela after he rescues her from Muslim men. The mufti, a Muslim scholar, is outraged and screams: "Do not be deceived by the American! They care NOTHING for Princess Azeela!" When the G.I. and Princess Azeela get married, the mufti, demonic in appearance, attempts to shoot the American hero. In an effort to save her husband, the princess shields him with her body and is killed instead. Although the belly dancer Muslim woman receives some attention and sympathy, the otherization and vilification of Muslim and Arab men suggest that there is something inherently wrong with her ethnic background or religious faith. As with Muslim men, realistic portrayals of Muslim women are missing. However, in the post-9/11 era, Marvel Comics has made an effort to introduce an empowered Muslim Superheroine. Her name: Sooraya Qadir, or "Dust."

Dust is a relatively popular character in *New X-Men* and, unlike the previous Muslim women mentioned, she has superpowers: the ability to hide in dust, shape into violent sandstorms, and even tear the skin off of her enemies. Created by Grant Morrison, Dust is of Afghan descent and wears an *abaya* and *niqab*, the former is a long outer garment and the latter is veil that covers a woman's entire face except for her eyes. While it is nice to see that Dust *chooses* to observe the *abaya* and *niqab*, as opposed to being forced, stereotypes about Muslims and Islam are still evident in her stories. In several instances, we can make the argument for the Western male gaze: She is an "oppressed" Muslim girl who was rescued from Afghanistan by Wolverine, a Western male mutant. Wolverine is told that the Taliban were trying to remove Dust's clothes, obviously to molest her, and since there weren't any "good Muslim men" around to take a stand against the Taliban's perverted behavior, who better to rescue her than Wolverine, or rather, "Western democracy?" The scenario of Dust fighting the Taliban, as admirable as it is, occurs many times in later issues, which makes one question: Is this is how Western male writers, artists, and readers want to see a Muslim Superheroine, i.e., to rebel against her oppressors, the mutual enemy of the U.S. government? When Wolverine carries Dust back to an X-Men headquarters in India (apparently there aren't any X-Men headquarters in Muslim countries like Afghanistan and Pakistan), Jean Grey tells Dust to reveal herself from concealment. "It's ok, Sooraya," Jean says, "You can turn back into human form now." Finally, Dust appears in her black *niqab* saying "Toorab! Toorab!" Wolverine remarks, "It means 'dust.' It's all she says." Not only does Morrison introduce us to a super-powered Muslim girl, but also to a character who can only say the Arabic word "Toorab!"

Dust made her next appearance in January 2005 in *New X-Men: Academy X* #2, where she is officially a member of the mutant team. This time under the authorship of Nunzio DeFilippis and his wife, Christina Weir, Dust is explored and further developed (and can actually say a lot more than "Toorab!"). However, stereotypes about Muslim women are still present, especially how Muslim women observe their faith. In issue #2, for instance, Dust meets her roommate, Surge, who wears a tight tank top and pink shorts that are seemingly slipping down her waist. Provocative lyrics play from her boom box: "Yeah I drive naked through the park, and run the stop sign in the dark…" Surge is immediately hostile toward Dust because of the way she dresses. "So you don't like my music, huh?" she says. Dust responds shyly and explains she doesn't understand American music. Surge replies, "Yeah whatever, and speaking of things we don't understand, is that outfit you're wearing actually a *burqah*?" Dust tries to explain, but Surge interrupts and says wearing a *burqah* is shameful to women and makes them "subservient to men." Dust replies politely, "No, the *burqah* is about modesty. There are boys and men on campus, and it is not right for me to show off by exposing myself or flesh to them." Surge snaps back, "Are you saying I show too much flesh?" Again, Dust politely tries to explain, "No I do not judge the way you dress, I only ask that you do the same for me." Surge walks to the door and says, "You do judge me... I don't need to be lectured by someone who's setting women back 50 years just by walking around like that." Surge exits the room and slams the door, leaving Dust dejected and discouraged. In a place where mutants are supposed to feel accepted, Dust is misjudged because of the way she chooses to dress.

It is important to note that Dust wears a *niqab* not a *burqah*, which is actually a fuller covering than the *niqab*, but either way, her reasoning to cover herself is somewhat inaccurate and stereotypical. This may be due to the writers' apparent misunderstanding of Muslim women and Islam in general (hence the confusion between *niqab* and *burqah*). Quite frequently, Dust speaks about "protecting herself from men," which not only make men sound lustful and perverted, but it also sexualizes herself and makes her an object of desire. The beautiful teachings of modesty for both genders in Islam tend to be mistaken for the stereotypical notion of "protecting women from men." These beliefs sideline her and keep her in the background, while the rest of the young mutants interact with one another and participate in extra-curricular activities. It is her religion that divides her from others, which not only plays into stereotypes about how "religion divides," but also how Islam in particular places "harsh restrictions" on Muslim women in general. Almost every time the reader sees Dust, she is praying and asking God for forgiveness for whatever sin she may have committed. Unfortunately, Dust fulfills the negative stereotype that Islam is restrictive and that God is someone to constantly ask forgiveness from, especially if you're a woman. It makes the reader perceive her as a "religious nut" as Surge calls her at one point. Other than her religious beliefs, Dust's personality is almost non-existent. What are Dust's hobbies, one may ask? What does she do on her free time? Who sits at her table during lunch breaks? These unanswered questions keep Dust's character underdeveloped and incomplete.

In this section, we have seen several renditions of Muslim women in comic books. While Dust is an immense improvement from the stereotypical representations we've seen of both Muslim women and men in comic books, there are still adjustments that need to be made. Since Dust is the only Muslim character in the *X-Men* universe so far, her character's depiction tries to represent all Muslim women, which is problematic because it marginalizes many Muslim women who don't wear either the *hijab* or the *niqab*. What better way to express the diversity of the Muslim community than create multiple Muslim characters? The concluding section will explore this idea and more.

The Future of Muslims and Arabs in Comic Books

What have we learned so far about Muslims, Arabs, and the religion of Islam based on the images we see in comic books? If readers were to base their knowledge on comic book representations, the conclusion might be: Muslims, Arabs, and Iranians are projected as the same—violent and aggressive, rabidly anti-American and anti-Israel, uncivilized and misogynistic; Muslim women are beautiful, but need rescuing because they are victims of their own people; and the religion of Islam is restricting and encourages violence. We can draw these conclusions because the majority of comic book depictions about Muslims and Arabs are overwhelmingly negative. One may ask: Where are the positive images? Where are the everyday Muslims? Where are the Muslim Superheroes and Superheroines? Frustrated readers searching for accurate representations of Muslims and Arabs may find hope in Naif Al-Mutawa's new comic book series, *The 99*.

First published in May 2006 by his own publishing company (Teshkeel Comics) Al-Mutawa's *The 99* shows us the best depictions of Muslim and Arab characters to have ever appeared in comic books. The title of the series refers to an Islamic teaching that God has 99 Beautiful Names or Attributes. Al-Mutawa draws inspiration from this tradition and produces remarkable Superheroes and Superheroines—most of them teenagers, each embody one of the 99 Names of God via magical gem stones known as "Noor Stones." For example, if a Noor stone possesses the Divine attribute of "Al-Rafi," which means "The Lifter," then the gem-bearer will take on the superpower of "lifting" objects, people, and even one's own self through telepathic means. Unlike the sinister caricatures we've seen in other comic books, *The 99* presents Muslim women and men as three-dimensional characters and heroes. They have stories, families, and character flaws, and their identities are not limited to the context of terrorism and misogyny. The series also consists of characters from multiple racial and religious backgrounds, which promotes Al-Mutawa's aspirations for dialog and coexistence. In an interview with PBS (2007) Al-Mutawa expresses his ambitions with *The 99*:

> ...there is nothing fundamentally different between Islam and any other belief on Earth or any other way of being human.... For me, in the end, the 99 attributes of Allah are attributes that not only all Muslims value, but humanity values. Things like generosity, strength, wisdom, foresight, mercy.... So my point of what I was trying to do was try to bring us together, versus pull us apart.

The 99 is a breath of fresh air in the comic book world, and Al-Mutawa and his creative team should be applauded for their positive representations of Muslims and Arabs. The comics sell 1 million copies per year and "enjoy a high profile in the Middle-East" (Butt, 2009). As DC Comics plans a crossover between *The 99* and *Justice League* (Butt, 2009), one can only hope that this will mark the beginning of countering negative stereotypes and a much-needed change for Muslims and Arabs in mainstream comic books.

References

Ali, T. (2008). *The duel: Pakistan on the flight path of American power.* New York: Scribner.

Butt, R. (2009, July 5). *DC Comics' superheroes join forces with characters inspired by Allah.* Retrieved from http://www.guardian.co.uk/books/2009/jul/05/comic-collaboration-superheroes-dc-teshkeel

Constable, P. (2007, April 9). *Iranian community offended by film's take on ancient battle.* Retrieved from http://www.washingtonpost.com/wp-dyn/content/article/2007/04/08/AR2007040801205.html

Faber, J. (2007, January 17). *"24" under fire from Muslim groups.* Retrieved from http://www.cbsnews.com/stories/2007/01/18/entertainment/main2371842.shtml

Interview: Naif al-Mutawa. (2007, June 26). Retrieved from http://www.pbs.org/frontlineworld/stories/kuwait605/creator.html

Lavin, M. (1998). Women in comic books. *Serials Review*, 24, 93–100.

Morgan, M. H. (2007). *Lost history: The enduring legacy of Muslim thinkers, scientists, and artists.* Washington, DC: National Geographic Society.

Mount, H. (2006, February 15). *Holy propaganda! Batman is tackling Osama bin Laden.* Retrieved from http://www.telegraph.co.uk/news/worldnews/northamerica/usa/1510556/Holy-propaganda-Batman-is-tackling-Osama-bin-Laden.html

Mulvey, L. (1975). Visual pleasure and narrative cinema. *Screen*, 16(3): 6–18.

Muzzafer, C. (1994). *Dominant Western perceptions of Islam and Muslims.* Retrieved from http://www.newdawnmagazine.com/Articles/Dominant%20Perceptions%20of%20Islam%20and%20the%20Muslims.html

Shaheen, J. (1991). The comic book Arab. *The Link*, 24(5), 1–11. A brief essay.

Shaheen, J. (2001). *Reel bad Arabs.* Northampton, MA: Interlink Publishing Group.

Shaheen, J. (2003). Reel bad Arabs: How Hollywood vilifies a people. *The Annals of the American Academy*, (588), 171–193.

Utichi, J. (2007, May 30). *Rt-uk exclusive: Frank Miller on "the spirit"...in 3d? (and delays on "sin city 2"?).* Retrieved from http://www.rottentomatoes.com/m/sin_city_2/news/1648879/rt_uk_exclusive_frank_miller_on_andquotthe_spiritandquotin_3d_and_delays_on_andquotsin_city_2andquot

Seven

"Mad Man Hassan Will Buy Your Carpets!" The Bearded Curricula of Evil Muslims

Özlem Sensoy

Hassan chop!
—Hassan the slave, *Ali Baba Bunny*, 1957

Make your storytelling entertaining to the sultan, oh long-eared one. Or it's the crocodile pit for you!
—Sultan's vizier, *Hare-Abian Nights*, 1959

Mwaaaaaaahhhrrrrrr!!! Give me that lamp!!
—Caliph Hassen Pheffer, *A Lad in His Lamp*, 1948

Introduction

In the spring of 2009, the Vancouver Canucks made the first round of the Stanley Cup playoffs. Like any hockey town, the city quickly transformed into a landscape of car-flags, team jerseys, spontaneous chants of "Go Canucks Go," and traffic no-go zones on game nights. The bars and streets of the city were buzzing with Canucks fever. But remaining buzz-free were the barber shops and bathrooms of Vancouverites, as another well-known playoff tradition began: the playoff beard.

Playoff beards were on display in classrooms, offices, and restaurants all over town. In fact, the male hosts of a local *Breakfast Morning*[1] TV show chatted about this daily: they compared their beards, asked female hosts on the show whether they preferred their boyfriends with or without beards (sexual innuendo implied), and initiated a web-poll wherein the audience could vote on which host's beard was the best.

Yet there was one member of the motley team of six *Breakfast Morning* TV show hosts, the one who read the news updates to the audience every 10 minutes, who was forbidden by producers from growing a playoff beard of his own. Lamenting with the others about this exclusion, the hosts all quickly agreed that the decision was wise because, "as the person reading the news, it wouldn't look professional to have a beard."

This explanation has lingered with me since I heard it. I began to inspect the upper lips and jowls of newsreaders more closely, and wondered: How many news men actually had beards? The only one I have been able to find is CNN's Wolf Blitzer. But did his even count since his closely sheared white beard virtually disappears on his white face? This was quite different from the young white news anchor on *Breakfast Morning* who had dark brown hair, and was in his mid to late-thirties. His facial hair would certainly stand out on his face. And if the Canucks went all the way, that would mean a playoff beard that could be rather long and dark. Not anything close to Wolf's Santa Claus-like whiskers.

Avoiding the lure of a masculinist analysis the playoff beard tradition calls for, it offers an interesting symbolic entré to studying the representation of Muslims in societal curricula. Why is it that a man with a long, dark beard would be deemed not professional and (implied) not reliable in reading the daily news?

While most canonized knowledge about the Middle East and Islam is transmitted formally in school curricula (most often via the Social Education/Social Sciences), in this chapter I consider whether the school curricula are as powerful, as enduring, as organized and canonized an educator about the Middle East and Islam as are the societal, media-based curricula. This suggestion is not new. Scholars in fields such as critical multicultural education (Banks, 1996; Cortés, 2001; Gay, 2000), cultural studies (Hall, 1997; Kellner, 1995), and critical pedagogy (Giroux, 1999; Steinberg & Kincheloe, 1997, 2004; Sensoy & Stonebanks, 2009) have indicated how significant an educator about racial, ethnic, and other diversities popular culture and mass media can be, functioning as both a curriculum (reinforcing normative representations) as well as a "teaching machine" (Giroux, 1997) or a form of "cultural pedagogy" (Steinberg & Kincheloe, 1997) that is not simply a reflection of but also a producer of culture.

This conceptualization of popular culture demands that we move away from the commonsense tendencies among teachers, educators, and parents to dismiss popular culture texts as fun, harmless entertainment, and instead apply criticisms that we might of any educative text. And given the overwhelming power of mainstream corporate media to circulate their messages in a manner, format, and consistency that classroom texts rarely enjoy, media texts may in fact demand closer scrutiny than any other curricula with which students engage. Kellner and Share (2005) argue that, "[t]here is expanding recognition that media representations help construct our images and understanding of the world" (p. 370).

In this chapter, I argue that by the time students study the Middle East and Islam (usually in upper elementary, and at length at the secondary levels), they have already received a lifetime of media-based schooling about it. I will track the representation of the Middle Eastern/Muslim man in Bugs Bunny cartoons in order to examine how a cultural pedagogy about the Middle East and Islam can occur. I will then examine how these cartoon discourses continue to circulate in contemporary representations of and discourses about the Middle East and Islam, specifically, the triangulation of Islam, violence, and men of color. Finally, I will offer some strategies educators can use to address these discourses with their students.

Bugs Bunny Pedagogy

Despite the fact that I was born in the Middle East, Western-produced popular culture, and television in particular, had already organized the way I viewed Islam and the Middle East. One of my key tutors was Bugs Bunny. There were at least five Bugs Bunny shorts that were set in the Middle East or North Africa, featuring Arab and/or Islamic contexts.

The earliest, in 1948, was *A Lad in His Lamp*.[2] The basic plot involves Bugs inadvertently coming upon a "piece of junk" (Aladdin's lamp). He shines it up to use as "an ashtray or something" and as he rubs it, a genie manifests.

Bugs thinks that the genie is a phony. But in the course of events, and in passing, he makes a wish that he could go to Baghdad. Then, whoosh, we are transported to Baghdad, recognizable by its flashy Vegas-style "Baghdad" sign, barren, desert-like streets, and Mad Man Hassan's used rug lot where you can sell your carpets.

Soon, we come upon the royal palace of the caliph (also named Hassen). Caliph Hassen's palace was, we learn, built on a GI Loan (a mortgage guaranteed by the U.S. government to veterans)—and the next scene explains why. The caliph is lazily reclined on pillows, smoking a water pipe when Bugs flies in to the caliph's lap.

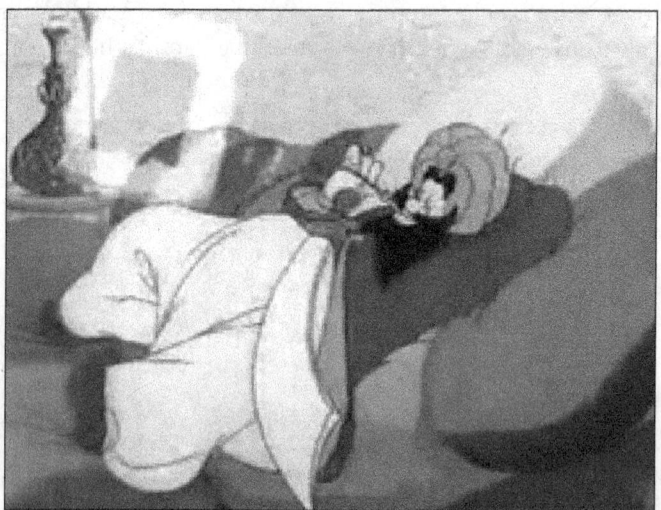

The caliph, startled at Bugs' arrival, greedily pursues our hero when he discovers Bugs has Aladdin's magic lamp.

One of the most startling and swift transformations of the caliph is his shift from laziness to child-like glee at the discovery of the lamp…

to the grotesquely grim facial expressions of the caliph when pursuing Bugs for the lamp.

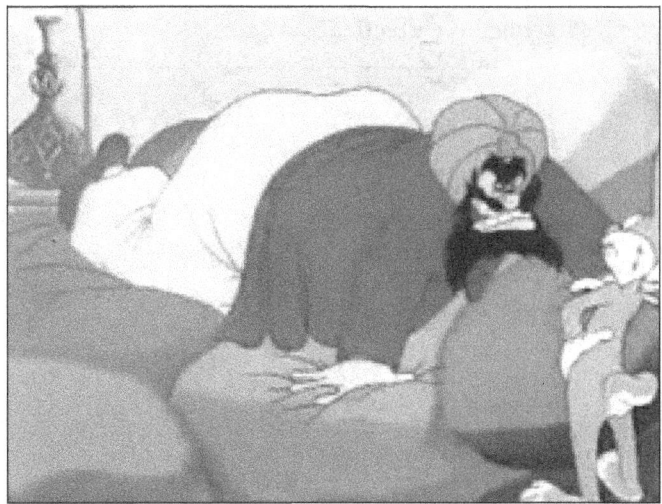

Apparently, for something as trivial to our hero Bugs as a lamp that he would have used as an ashtray, this lazy caliph is willing to growl and fight Bugs in a most ferocious manner. The caliph emits little more than a primitive growl preceding his arrival on the scene, often waving his big sword. In the end, the caliph loses out, and Bugs gets away unscathed.

Sahara Hare[3] (1954) is another example of a Middle Eastern bad man. But this time one that is recognized by Bugs Bunny fans. Yosemite Sam, the classic Bugs Bunny villain, returns as another kind of villain. Bugs calls him Mr. Ay-rabb.

Mr. Ay-rabb wears a towel on his head (literally, since in one scene Bugs wipes his face with it), and a "dress" from which, as Bugs puts it, his slip is showing (thus rendering his garb effeminate).

Our villain rides a direction-less camel through the Sahara Desert—marked by a sign of jibberish script standing in for Arabic.

This time, once again, Bugs is chased around the Sahara by the mad/evil Sam/Arab for another clearly irrational reason: Bugs leaving footprints on the desert sand. As mad/evil Sam/Arab puts it, "a trespasser getting footyprints all over my desert!" Our hero is, of course, able to outsmart Sam/Arab quite easily and escapes unscathed.

In 1957, Merrie Moldies released another Middle Eastern themed Bugs Bunny short film called *Ali Baba Bunny*.[4] In *Ali Baba Bunny*, the bumbling, diaper and turban-wearing oaf Hassan (yes, again the name Hassan) is charged by a nondescript vizier with guarding a cave full of gems.

The oaf slave Hassan is very stupid, which we quickly learn from his inability to remember the magic words, "open sesame" that will open the cave and allow him to enter and protect the jewels.

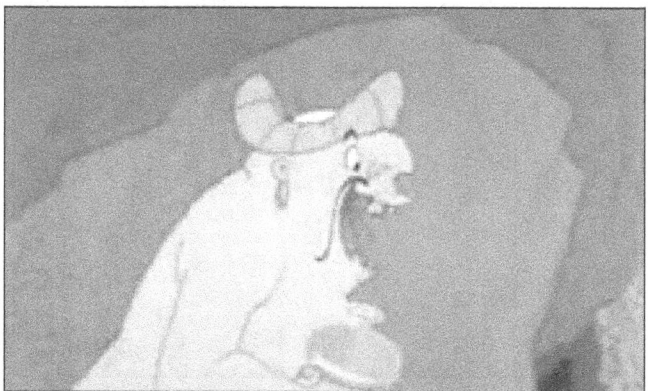

When he does manage to enter the cave, he is easily tricked by a wish-granting genie (Bugs in disguise) who performs a jibberish hocus-pocus genie dance so he and Daffy can escape (Daffy with the stolen gems, of course).

In 1959's *Hare-Abian Nights*[5] we have the return of our "regular" villain, Yosemite Sam, playing a sultan again.

He is sitting in a lavish palace where a series of entertainers are performing for his pleasure. The sultan is indiscriminate with the punishment he doles out for performances that are displeasing to him.

118 | "Mad Man Hassan Will Buy Your Carpets!"

Bugs inadvertently comes to the palace, thinking it's a theatre, and is instructed by the guard to "perform!" for the sultan.

As the sultan's vizier warns him, "Make your storytelling entertaining to the sultan, oh long-eared one. Or it's the crocodile pit for you!" Once again the indiscriminate and violent responses to something as seemingly trivial as singing a bad song or telling a bad story are rationalized by the context and characters. Bugs, of course, regales the sultan with his escapades. Yet the sultan, still wants to kill him but is ultimately tricked by Bugs and falls into the crocodile pit himself.

Lessons from Bugs Bunny on the Middle East and Islam

It is important not to write off these kinds of representations as relics of a particular moment in history, a racist past, or as mere cartoons—just harmless fun. These characters and plots are intimately connected to mainstream narratives about good versus evil, industriousness versus sloth, modernity versus backwardness, intelligence versus stupidity. And the manner in which these particular character-types are cast reflects how these characteristics are thought to be distributed among particular cultural groups.

So what kind of pedagogy about the Middle East, Islam, and Middle Eastern men in particular occurs in Bugs Bunny? What character types, stories, and plots are normalized? What "lessons" are learned?

Lesson 1: Muslim, Middle Eastern Men Are Scary

One of the main discourses normalized in these representations is that Muslim Middle Eastern men are prone to indiscriminate violence. Often this violence is beyond the scope of the "crime." For example, footprints on the desert sand or singing a song off key are both grounds for death. Muslim men are large, carry big menacing weapons, or exert power through authority (such as the viziers or sultans). Their physicality is part of their scariness. Often, their skin is clearly colored brown. All of the Middle Eastern villains in these cartoons have full large bushy eyebrows, and long moustaches and/or beards. They frequently furrow their brows, and physically posture intimidation.

The Bugs Bunny pedagogy perpetuates longstanding stereotypes about Muslim men—that they are violent and intolerant and thus require some degree of monitoring and caution (al-Qazzaz, 1983; Said, 1997; Shaheen, 1997, 2001; Steet, 2000). This popular narrative about Muslim men goes hand in hand with the narrative of oppressed Muslim women (Steet, 2000; Sensoy & DiAngelo, 2006; Sensoy, forthcoming).

Muslim men are sometimes made powerful by Western supports (such as GI loans that built the Caliph Hassen's palace in Baghdad in *A Lad in His Lamp*), or sometimes by coincidences of geography (such as coming upon treasures by accident). Triangulation of evil violence, race, and Islam dominates much of popular and formal curricula about Islam and the Middle East. There is rarely a separation of "Arab" and "Muslim" and "Persian," which are all completely interchangeable in much of popular culture about the Middle East and Islam (Shaheen, 1984). Also, in popular culture jibberish, short-hand scribbles and the meshing together of desert oases and urban centers occur without caution. The "logic" of the narrative over-rides the inaccuracies of the representations.

Lesson 2: Muslim, Middle Eastern Men Are Irrational

As we learn through Bugs Bunny, mad Muslim men are either oaf-ish thugs, sly viziers, or lazy irrational sultans/caliphs. All have extensive facial hair, often depicted as big bushy black beards. They exert indiscriminate violence, and have irrational impulses.

If he's an oaf, he wears diapers or pantaloons, arm-bands and ear rings. Oafs are malleable when the riches of the sultan/caliph are dangled before them (such as access to a genie or riches from the cave as in *Ali Baba Bunny*).

If he's a caliph/sultan, he is lazy and tends to lounge and partake in pleasure more than substance. He is easily angered. And if angered, his wrath is usually disproportionate to the crime, and death is the default punishment. Thus, not only is the violence of Muslim Middle Eastern men indiscriminate, it is also often irrational: out-of-sync with the offense committed. While both authoritarian and slavish groups of mad Muslim men will, if they are angered, act out, their violence emerges somewhat differently. Whereas the powerful ones might drop you into a pit of crocodiles, the oaf slaves will use intimidation and the threat of violence to carry out the orders of the powerful mad Muslim men (who give them their orders from behind the scenes).

In fact, not only is their violence irrational, not much else in their environment makes sense either, as we see in the "keep off the grass" sign placed in the middle of the Sahara Desert.

Even though our hero Bugs must be wary and tread lightly around them, all mad Muslim men can be easily outsmarted. The powerful ones can be tricked by shiny objects, trinkets, and other pleasures (such as a harem girl in *A Lad in His Lamp*). While the big oafs can usually be outsmarted by pretending to be an authority figure whom they will blindly obey (like in *Ali Baba Bunny*).

Lesson 3: Muslim, Middle Eastern Men Are Lazy, Laughable, and Easy to Fool

While mad Muslim men of authority (such as sultans and caliphs) prefer to lie around, be entertained, indulge in hedonistic pleasures like grand gifts and wine, food, and leisure, thuggish mad Muslim men are stupid and often need to be reminded of what's valuable. Either way, all Muslim men are undesirable. They have no wisdom, no smarts, no rationality, no kindness. They have no families. Some have a harem, or camels, but evidently no friends.

While all mad Muslim men carry large menacing weapons (often swords, sometimes rifles, and often their own menacing bodies), they are frequently inept at using them. They can easily be tricked, fooled, or cajoled by our Western hero into doing his will.

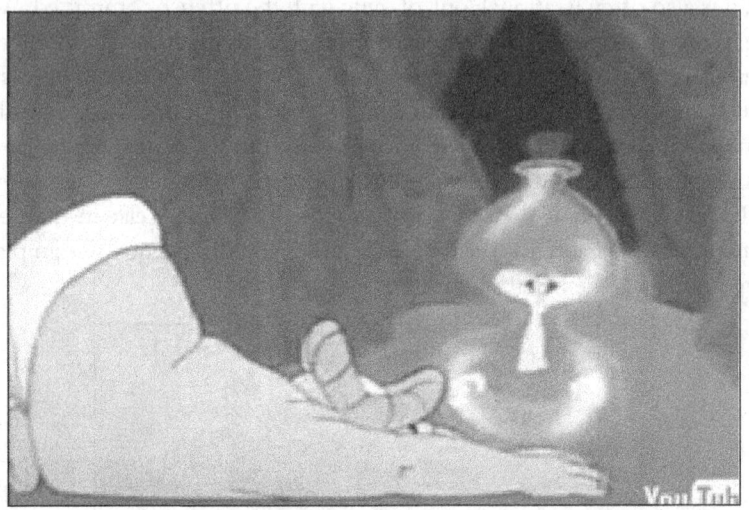

The laziness and stupidity of mad Muslim men is in line with another popular discourse about Arabs and Muslims: laziness and stupidity are often assigned to the Middle East and serve as a de-facto "logic" or explanation for why there is a lack of modernity there. The discourse is: because Muslims are lazy, they don't have the rewards of hard work. In other words, the lack of hard work might be evidence for the dearth of modernity and overall decay of cities in the Middle East as exemplified in popular culture representations as well as in textbooks depicting the Middle East (Jarrar, 1976; Sensoy, 2009; Shaheen, 1997, 2001; Steet, 2000). In mainstream Western culture, meritocracy, exceptionality, and hard work all determine the degree of access to the rewards of that labor (Appleby, 1992). If it's "normal" that Muslims don't work very much, or very well, then it won't be surprising to see few markers of modernity (such as technology, high rise buildings, cars, cell phones, and computers) in their societies.

Connected to the depiction of little hard work among Arabs and Muslims is the barren nature of life in the Muslim "world" in general. Few, if any, tools, technologies, or advancements are represented as being found there (Sensoy, 2009). For example, try this quick thought experiment: When was the last time you saw a media representation of a major urban center in the Middle East (Cairo, Istanbul, Tehran, Damascus) in all of its rush hour madness? Can you picture in your mind's eye Cairo-ens talking on cell phones? Istanbul-ites hailing taxis? Tehran-ians joining friends for dinner out? Or Damascans enjoying an evening stroll in a local park? Our capacity to conceptualize the range of life experiences of various groups is in part determined by the scripts and characters that we have been most socialized, through repetition, to see as normal.

What Educators Can Do to Resist Bugs Bunny Pedagogy

While students may no longer be watching Bugs Bunny, they are watching Disney's *Aladdin* (1992), playing with Bratz's Genie Magic dolls, reading Deborah Ellis' *The Breadwinner* about a young girl in Afghanistan (Sensoy & Marshall, 2010), watching the news coverage of the ongoing "War on Terror," watching the rioting young men of France, the Swiss voting down the building of minarets, and popular movies like *The Mummy* (1999). As Jack Shaheen (2000) put it:

> Writers give cartoon Arabs names like "Sheikh Ha-Mein-ie," "Ali Boo-Boo," "The Phoney Pharaoh," "Ali Baba, and the Mad Dog of the Desert, and his Dirty Sleeves," "Hassan the Assassin," "The Desert Rat," "Desert Rat Hordes," "Ali Oop," "Ali Mode," and "Arab Duck." While monitoring cartoons on November 23, 1996, I saw "Well-worn Daffy" on the Nickelodeon channel. Wearing a white kuffiyeh and armed with a shotgun, Daffy shoots at three winsome Mexican mice. The mice call Daffy, among other things, "Arab Duck!" Adult viewers may be able to separate fact from animal, but for many children the animated world of cartoons consists of good people versus bad people, the latter often Arabs. (p. 34)

Collectively, these lessons (as well as many others that organize the plot of the cartoons) support mainstream Western discourses that Arabs/Muslims and people of the Middle East in general are uncivilized. The familiar stereotypes of nomadic lifestyles, oppression, lack of progress, and violence mutually confirm these elements of the story.

This type of media pedagogy is all around, so what can educators do? To study, understand, and ultimately unsettle the manner in which particular ideas about Islam, men of color, and criminality/evil come together, it's important for educators to understand (and to guide their students in understanding) two interrelated concepts: identity and representation.

Understanding Identity

In many ways, *identity* is the starting point for any study of a culture. Identity refers to the characteristics, beliefs, behaviors, ways of being, and ways of making meaning that define an individual and that are common within a group.

One's identity depends *both* on how a person thinks about her/himself, *and also* on what others believe and think about her/him. *Individual identity* refers to the particular set of life conditions and experiences that we are each born into, and experience throughout our lifetime. Whereas *group identity* refers to the historically based, political, and culturally organized experiences of groups. Group histories may not apply to all members of the group, but there are observable patterns and documented histories. In its simplest form, identity is the details of the response to *who am I?* or *who are we?*, and *who are you?* or *who are they?* We can't answer the first set of questions without knowing the answer to the second set, and vice versa.

Helping students acquire a deeper understanding of the nature and manifestations of identity can benefit students in at least two ways: enhanced *self*-understanding and enhanced understanding of *others*. Enhanced self-understanding will benefit students who may struggle to identify and feel proud of who they are, have trouble finding their "roots" so to speak, and manage what might be conflicting identities. Enhanced understanding of others means helping students to develop accurate, nuanced understanding of others by appreciating that their definitions of others may not match how others see themselves and that people will identify with and attach importance to different beliefs and practices.

Despite good intentions to learn about the identities of others, much is missing from curricular prompts that often remain superficially addressed, such as *who are the Ottomans?* or *who are the ancient Persians?* Studies of *who they are* hold potential for engaging in complex and ongoing issues in the study of societies and cultures.

So what might educators do after we ask students to engage in a familiar curricular activity about culture like *who are the ancient Persians?* that could facilitate a more complex understanding?

Studying identity can be approached by examining the following three principles:

Identity is shaped by individual as well as group conditions and experiences
One's *individual* identity is determined by the unique configuration of experiences that a person has as a member within multiple *social groups* s/he belongs to. These groups are primarily of: race, class, gender, ethnicity, ability, sexuality, first language, religious acculturation, and age. They can also include a myriad of other, more and less-visible social group memberships: being a student, being a badminton player, a sibling, an oldest sibling, and so on.

One could ask, how are one's *personal* preferences to, for example, wear jeans and runners related to one's socialization as a girl (i.e., what it means to "act like a girl")? As a girl in *a particular* cultural context (what it means to be a Muslim girl)? As a student (what it means to be a Muslim girl going to university)? And so on.

Many kinds of shared, *group* memberships come together to frame who "I" uniquely am, as an individual (a Muslim, a girl, who grew up in a working class family, a teenager, a person with a visual impairment, a hockey fan, and so on).

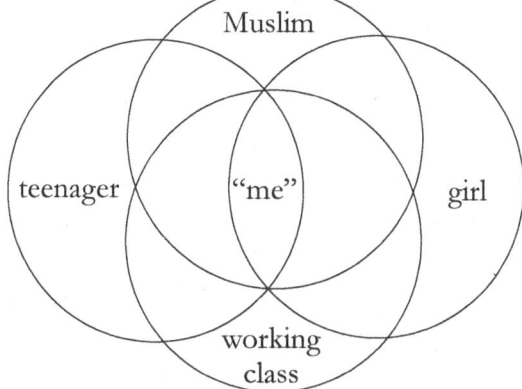

Individuality manifests in all aspects of what makes you uniquely you: your name, the language you (prefer to) speak, your favorite foods, drinks, activities, and books, your choice of friendships, the neighborhood you grew up in, the one you now live in, the clothes you wear, and so on. It is established, but not fixed, because it can change over time. The process begins at birth and develops over one's lifetime.

What we do (practices, customs, activities) and how we communicate (words, mannerisms, dialects) provide clues to our identity.

Some of the most common elements of cultural identity are:

- Dress style (a Muslim woman's scarf, a Sikh man's turban, a Scotsman's kilt, a businessman's suit and tie, a teenager's jeans and t-shirt)
- Music (Irish fiddle, Polish folk dance, Chinese opera, U.S. hip-hop)
- Rituals (Jewish bar/bat-mitzvah, First Nations potlatch, a Western European contemporary bridal shower)
- Family norms (nuclear family living together, large extended family living together, families headed by two moms or two dads)
- Eating styles (breakfast most important meal to eat together, dinner most important meal to eat together)

Students must understand how one's identities are not fixed or rooted in one particular domain—and how individual identity is not *separate from* but *shaped by* one's multiple group memberships. They must understand that one's identity is shifting, fluid, and relational. The particular contexts in which we are at any given time may determine which of our identities are most active.

Thus, students can begin to understand the relationships between individuality and multiple social identities as they manifest in their own lives but also in the lives of the groups they study in their textbooks. In the case of Bugs Bunny's mad Muslim men, there is little to distinguish one Muslim man from another. The construction of an individual identity is virtually interchangeable with the construction of shared group identifications, as is most evident by the almost exclusive use of the name "Hassan."

Integrating this level of identity analysis from the start of the school year, and pulling this thread through everything done in the classroom will enable educators to analyze representations of Muslims and Arabs in a way that is part of an on-going process and an on-going approach to studying cultural others, rather than as an isolated or additive event.

Identities may be both claimed (self identified) and assigned (identified by others)
A person's or a group's perceived identity may not be the same as the identity assigned by others. People are sometimes mistaken about who others are. Many students will have heard of "mistaken identity" where a person is taken to be other than who s/he is. This may arise because someone had deliberately misled others or because of an honest mistake.

This is a good opportunity for students to deeply explore the relationship between group and individual identification. If I (as an individual) am sought by the police, the group identities I share with others are how I will be described. If the police stated that, "we are looking for Özlem," only those who knew *me specifically* would really know who to look for! However, the police may be looking for: an adult female, Turkish, white person, professor, and so on. The picture painted of an *individual* suspect is based on a collage of group (or shared) identifications. Mistaken identifications can occur if assumptions are made about what any of the group identities represent. For instance, if someone assumed that all Turkish people are Muslim, and therefore an adult Muslim female would be wearing a veil, they would be mistaken in my case since I do not wear a veil.

Thus, mistaken (or false) identification brings up an opportunity for students to learn about "essentialism." *Essentialism* is a concept in social science that refers to the attribution of some group characteristics to *all* members who are (or are assumed to be) a member of the group. These characteristics are presumed to be unchangeable. For example, to state "all sultans are lazy" is to essentialize the group "sultan" (and by extension, Muslim men of authority) with a stereotype that some in the group may fit. Similarly, to state "we are looking for a Turkish woman," all Turks are Muslim, so look for a woman with a veil results in problems like: not all Turks are Muslim, not all

Muslim women wear a veil, and Muslim women are not the only women who wear veils and scarves.

Exercises that guide students in understanding the tension and interaction between self-identification and assignment by others can develop their skills in critical thinking, reflexivity, and critical media literacy. Guiding students in identifying when their self-identification was in conflict with how others defined them can engage them and help them understand the impact that the same process has on others. For example, young teens may feel identified by others as rude and as trouble-makers when they walk into a restaurant or store yet self-identify as amiably hanging out with their friends. How would this change if it were a group of all boys versus all girls walking into a store? All brown boys versus white boys? All brown boys wearing turbans or *kuffiyeh* and not speaking English? And so on. Engaging students with these types of thought-experiments and discussion of experiences can facilitate their understanding of how identity assignment and self-identification differ and can impact the object of that identification in various ways.

Identities are shifting and relational
Actions, words, and objects offer clues about identity. It is important for students to learn that their preferences, choices, likes, dislikes, careers, and other aspects of their lives are not *simply* the outcome of choice or preference, but they are also the outcome of the options available to the social groups they belong to at any particular time or context.

Whereas people have multiple identities (I can be Canadian and Muslim simultaneously), there are also many different identities within any group. Thus not all Canadians are Muslims, not all Muslims are Arabs, and so on.

Also, while identities may shift and change (for instance, one grows from the identity group of *child* to *adult*, and sometimes from single person to married person, etc.), it is always in relation to previous identities. In order to understand one's own, and others' identity, we must help students see, talk about, and understand this complex relational aspect of group identities and identifications.

Consider guiding students through this thought experiment, which is intended to guide students into the shifting nature of our identity constructs. Imagine yourself going about your day and engaging in conversations with the following players: your friends, your parents, and your teacher. You might be joking with your friends, talking with more formality to your teacher, and whining irritably with your parents (my experience is that students eagerly and excitedly engage in these types of thought experiments!). Now go beyond the players and add a layer of context: your friends in class versus on the weekend at the mall, your parents when they are pleased with you versus when they are disappointed, and your teacher when you are confidently answering a question in class versus explaining a poor performance on a test. In each of these scenarios you are navigating identity relations, and these relations inform *how* you speak—your tone, the kinds of words you use, and even your facial expressions.

Guiding students in an awareness of themselves as a socialized member of a number of intersecting social groups within a particular culture in a particular time and place (social location) will increase their critical capacity related to identity. They will be able to recognize general patterns of their identity socialization and be aware of themselves in shifting contexts (DiAngelo & Sensoy, forthcoming).

Understanding Representation

As I have argued thus far in this chapter, one of the primary ways in which we develop our understanding of the identities of others is via media representations. Thus, to understand the identities of others, it is useful for students to understand the concept of representation.

Representation refers to self- and other-generated images and knowledges about cultural and social groups. What stories are told? How are they told? Who tells whose stories? Whose interests are served? And how do group and individual resistance (or reclaiming of identity) determine social representation?[6] Because much of this resistance occurs in a space relegated as "outside" the mainstream, understanding representation invites us to examine the separation of "high culture" and "low" or "pop culture," to examine representations characterized as "good" and positive, and compared to those that are "bad" and negative. Also important is the question of what stories are *not* told.

Studying representation in classroom settings can be organized in the following way:

Studying the Accuracy of a Representation

One method of addressing issues of representation is by examining the accuracy of the portrayal of a group in any particular setting (textbook, newspaper, movies, etc.). Thus, the study would include the measure of accuracy or inaccuracy—how right, true, or real—any particular representation is. For example, in studying the representation of Arabs in the Disney film, *Aladdin*, we might ask students to consider the accuracy of those representations as a starting point:

- Is the representation of Arab peoples' dress and practices right for the time and place?

- How true is the representation of the life of royalty in ancient Arabia?

Such measures can be useful because it is important to note distortions and examine the reasons for such distortions by mass media or textbook-based representations. This discussion could be extended to ask comparative questions about similarities and differences among accounts: the movie account, as well as other accounts supplied by textbooks and other sources.

However, limiting the study of representation to this level creates challenges because it can lead to essentializing or stereotyping group characteristics. Thus, the danger of this exploration of accuracy becomes establishing "the" correct interpretation of what was right at a particular time, and applying that to all cases. In order to correct for this possibility, it is important to extend students' study of representation beyond *accuracy* to include knowledge about the context in which the image is circulated.

Studying the Context of a Representation

The study of representation can proceed from the study of the accuracy of an image to the study of the *context* of the image (the time, audience, and setting for/in which it was produced). To examine the context of an image invites us to explore how various groups make meaning of any particular representation and how that representation reflects or challenges dominant ideas in society. A famous and illustrative example is given by sociologist Stuart Hall. It is the example of a ball. We may all agree that a ball is a spherical object, and if we were to simply study the accuracy of a representation (say, a photograph), we might all say "yes that is an accurate picture of a ball," or, "no, that picture looks more like a balloon than a ball." However, Hall suggests that the ball has no *meaning* until it is in the context of a *discourse* about the ball. Thus a football gains its meaning as a football only when the rules of the game are simultaneously in place around it. That is, when it (the object) is given a context (the rules of a particular game).

In a similar way, earlier I offered a discussion about the relationship between the meaning and context of an object like a beard and what it "means" in the social context in which it is represented. In predominantly Muslim societies, it may mean just another manner of presentation (like wearing business suits to work, or jeans and t-shirts to school), something quite unremarkable. However, in parts of Europe, the United States, or Canada, it will carry very different meanings. So the *context* of the representation is part of what gives meaning to the objects. Returning to my opening example of the *Breakfast Morning* playoff beards, in that context, a male sporting a full beard while reading the news means at least that such a look is incompatible and, at worst, unprofessional for someone who tells the viewers what is happening in the world. This has profound implications for someone who may wear a beard for cultural or religious reasons and will function to discriminate against his doing so. Yet in the context of the hockey playoffs, it was normal for the male hosts to grow beards. And as soon as the playoff run ended, the beards were also gone. In this way, the audience learns what kind of appearance is "normal" for men in various social, cultural contexts.

Studying the Motivations/ Interests for a Representation

To study the motivations for a representation means to incorporate knowledge about the production of the image in its analysis.

- Who produces any particular representation? For whose consumption?
- What motivations might any group have for putting forward particular representations?

In the context of the Muslim Middle Eastern men in the images in this chapter, we may ask questions about the motivations for depicting beards, violence, camels, deserts, grand palaces, slothful sultans, and oafish slaves. Setting aside the accuracy (i.e., were sultans of Middle Eastern Islamic courts truly lazy?), there is the question of motivation—both the motivation of the Bugs Bunny producers to tell these stories, as well as mine to re-organize and re-present them here.

The discussion of motivation/interests can be taken to other realms. For example, students can study the (in)famous photographs of the toppling of Saddam Hussein's statue in Baghdad's Fardus Square to further discuss the discourse on motivation. The two photographs of the incident—one close up and one wide-angle shot—offer a very different *picture* of what took place at the Square and invite discussion on why one photograph might have been more widely circulated than the other. For instance, the close-up photo gives the impression of a large crowd being present during the toppling of the statue. The second photo, taken at a wide angle, reveals how small the crowd was in reality. The first photo, which was widely circulated in western countries, served to uphold the idea that the general Iraqi public was mainly in support of the destruction of the statue, and the toppling of the Saddam Hussein regime that it symbolized.

Good and M/Bad, Us and Them/Him

Shaheen (2001) offers a compelling thought about representations of Arabs and Muslims in media: "al tikrar biallem il hmar. By repetition even the donkey learns. This Arab proverb encapsulates how effective repetition can be when it comes to education.... For more than a century, Hollywood has used repetition as a teaching tool" (p. 1).

Alongside this thought is the scholarship in education which informs us that for many young people, media provide the only contact with ethnically diverse people and that media-based representations shape our consciousness about social groups, sometimes in very subtle ways (Steinberg, 2004). To live and actively participate in a pluralistic democratic society means making decisions and dialoguing within the context of shifting identity relations.

I believe that representations today are built upon representations of the past, and that one's ideas about Muslims are intimately connected to the characters and stories told and re-told in various popular culture texts. While Bugs Bunny's mad Muslim men may no longer be around, discourses about Muslim men's violence, indiscriminate and sometimes irrational responses to events, and at times their laughable ineptness responding to challenge are familiar patterns in the ongoing representations in media. Thus, they inform meaning-making about Muslims and the Middle East at large. Through these ideologically consistent messages, the inherent incompatibility of Muslims and the West is reinforced. In a time of multiple and interconnected wars and incursions when this perceived incompatibility literally means life and death, the need to develop critical media literacy in our students at all ages and grade levels is at its most urgent.[7]

Endnotes

1 The name of the TV show has been changed here.
2 Freely available on various websites such as: http://www.jogyjogy.com/watch.php?id=198ec and: http://www.dailymotion.com/video/x1i9z2_bugs-bunny-a-lad-in-his-lamp_fun
3 Freely available online on websites such as YouTube: http://www.youtube.com/watch?v=PbI8HtpLoWo
4 Freely available online on websites such as YouTube http://www.youtube.com/watch?v=sTRD3mFX1-0
5 Freely available online on websites such as Daily Motion: http://www.dailymotion.com/video/xa4fsb_merrie-melodies-hareabian-nights-19_shortfilms
6 This discussion of representation is extended upon in Sensoy (forthcoming). Ickity ackity open sesame: Learning about the Middle East in Images. In B. Subedi (Ed.), *Critical Global Perspectives: Rethinking Knowledge about Global Societies* (pp. 39–55). Charlotte, NC: Information Age Publishing.
7 The author would like to thank colleagues Ann Chinnery, Robin DiAngelo, Elizabeth Marshall, and Gerald Walton whose thoughtful feedback helped improve this chapter.

References

Appleby, J. (1992). Recovering America's historic diversity: Beyond exceptionalism. *The Journal of American History*, 79, 419–431.

Banks, J. A. (1996). The canon debate, knowledge construction, and multicultural education. In J. A. Banks (Ed.), *Multicultural education, transformative knowledge, and action* (pp. 3–29). New York, NY: Teachers College Press.

Cortés, C. E. (2001). Knowledge construction and popular culture: The media as multicultural education. In J. A. Banks & C. A. M. Banks (Eds.), *Handbook of research on multicultural education* (pp. 169–183). San Francisco: Jossey-Bass.

DiAngelo, R. & Sensoy, Ö. (forthcoming). "OK, I get it! Now tell me how to do it!": Why we can't just tell you how to do critical multicultural education. *Multicultural Perspectives*.

Gay, G. (2000). *Culturally responsive teaching: Theory, research, and practice*. New York: Teachers College Press.

Giroux, H. (1997). Are Disney movies good for your kids? In S.R. Steinberg & J.L. Kincheloe (Eds.), *Kinderculture: The corporate construction of childhood* (pp. 164–180). Boulder, CO: Westview Press.

Giroux, H. (1999). *The mouse that roared: Disney and the end of innocence*. Lanham, MD: Rowman & Littlefield.

Hall, S. (Ed.). (1997). *Representation: Cultural representations and signifying practices*. London: Open University.

Jarrar, S.A. (1976). *Images of the Arabs in the United States secondary schools social studies textbooks: A content analysis and unit development*. Unpublished doctoral dissertation, Florida State University.

Kellner, D. (1995). *Media culture: Cultural studies, identity and politics between the modern and the postmodern*. London and New York: Routledge.

Kellner, D., & Share, J. (2005). Toward critical media literacy: Core concepts, debates, organizations, and policy. *Discourse: Studies in the Cultural Politics of Education*, 26(3), 369–386.

Kincheloe, J. L., & Steinberg, S. R. (Eds.). (2004). *The miseducation of the West: How schools and the media distort our understanding of the Islamic world*. Westport, CT: Praeger.

al-Qazzaz, A. (1983). Image formation and textbooks. In E. Ghareeb (Ed.), *Split vision: The portrayal of Arabs in the American media* (pp. 369–380). Washington, DC: American-Arab Affairs Council.

Said, E.W. (1997). *Covering Islam: How the media and experts determine how we see the rest of the world*. New York: Vintage.

Sensoy, Ö. (2009). Where the heck is the "Muslim world" anyways? In Ö. Sensoy & C.D. Stonebanks (Eds.), *Muslim voices in school: Narratives of identity and pluralism* (pp. 71–85). Boston: Sense Publishers.

Sensoy, Ö. (forthcoming). Ickity ackity open sesame: Learning about the Middle East in images. In B. Subedi (Ed.), *Critical global perspectives: Rethinking knowledge about global societies* (pp. 39–55). Charlotte, NC: Information Age Publishing.

Sensoy, Ö., & DiAngelo, R.J. (2006). "I wouldn't want to be a woman in the Middle East": White female student teachers and the narrative of the oppressed Muslim woman. *Radical Pedagogy*, 8(1), 1–14.

Sensoy, Ö., & Marshall, E. (in press). Missionary girl power: Saving the "Third World" one girl at a time. *Gender and Education*, 22(1).

Sensoy, Ö., & Stonebanks, C.D. (Eds.). (2009). *Muslim voices in school: Narratives of identity and pluralism*. Boston: Sense Publishing.

Shaheen, J.G. (1984). *The TV Arab*. Bowling Green, OH: Bowling Green State University Popular Press.

Shaheen, J.G. (1997). *Arab and Muslim stereotyping in American popular culture*. Washington, DC: Center for Muslim-Christian Understanding.

Shaheen, J.G. (Spring, 2000). Hollywood's Muslim Arabs. *The Muslim World*, 90, 22–42.

Shaheen, J.G. (2001). *Reel bad Arabs: How Hollywood vilifies a people*. New York: Olive Branch Press.

Steet, L. (2000). *Veils and daggers: A century of National Geographic's representations of the Arab world*. Philadelphia: Temple University Press.

Steinberg, S. R. (2004). Desert minstrels: Hollywood's curriculum of Arabs and Muslims. In J. L. Kincheloe & S. R. Steinberg (Eds.), *The miseducation of the West: How schools and the media distort our understanding of the Islamic world* (pp. 171–179). Westport, CT: Praeger.

Steinberg, S. R., & Kincheloe, J. L. (Eds.). (1997). *Kinderculture: The corporate construction of childhood.* Boulder, CO: Westview Press.

Bugs Bunny Short Film References

Burton, J. (Producer), & Harris, K. (Director). (1959). *Hare-abian nights.* [Merrie Melodies (Bugs Bunny) short]. US: Warner Bros.

Selzer, E. (Producer), & Freleng, F. (Director). (1954). *Sahara hare.* [Merrie Melodies (Bugs Bunny) short]. US: Warner Bros.

Selzer, E. (Producer), & Jones, C. (Director). (1957). *Ali baba bunny* [Merrie Melodies (Bugs Bunny) short]. US: Warner Bros.

Selzer, E. (Producer), & McKimson, R. (Director). (1948). *A lad in his lamp.* [Merrie Melodies (Bugs Bunny) short]. US: Warner Bros.

Eight

Barack Obama, Islamophobia, and the 2008 U.S. Presidential Election Media Spectacle

Michael D. Giardina

[Barack Obama] is not a Muslim, he's a Christian. He's always been a Christian. But the really right answer is, What if he is? Is there something wrong with being a Muslim in this country? The answer's no, that's not America.
— Colin Powell, on *Meet the Press*, 10/19/08

Our data shows that only 34 percent of Americans say that they have no prejudice against Muslims. That figure compares to 74 percent who say they have no prejudice against Jews. So while anti-Semitism is certainly not a relic of the past, anti-Muslim sentiment is at an alarmingly high rate right now in America, and because of that it's used as a political tool against politicians.
— Dalia Mogahed, Gallup, 2008

Proem

October 2001: A few weeks after the events of September 11, 2001. A time when the nation was not only on edge, but a number of its citizens were also showing an increased predilection within some quarters to openly slur 'the Other' with invective essentializing of those who appeared to be Middle Eastern and/or adherents to the Islamic faith. Right-wing media personalities, in particular, fanned the flames of intolerance, such as when Ann Coulter (2001) wrote in a *National Review* article, just days after the tragedies, that the United States "should invade their countries, kill their leaders and convert them to Christianity."[1] Or when Franklin Graham, who delivered the benediction at George W. Bush's inauguration, declared Islam "wicked, violent, and not the same as God." Or when Dr. Jerry Vines, pastor of the First Baptist Church of Jacksonville, Florida, stated that Islam's founder and most sacred figure, the prophet Mohammed, was a "demon-possessed pedophile." Or when the hebetudinous Rev. Jerry Falwell stated bluntly that Mohammed "was a terrorist."

****

Closer to home in Illinois, a proud Mexican American doctoral student with a deep commitment to social justice issues solemnly recounted to me an incident in which two white, college-aged men in a black pickup truck yelled at him to "Go back to Iraq" and called him a "dirty sand nigger" as they drove by while he pumped gas into his fuel-efficient car at a service station near campus.

* * *

September 2008: Seven years after 9/11/01. Barack Obama, the junior Senator from Illinois, had just a few weeks prior accepted the Democratic Party's nomination for president. Teaching a course on classic advertising campaigns and their location to the broader socio-historical formations in which they were located, deployed, and made meaningful, I covered the then-unfolding media spectacle of Obama's quest for the presidency, looking especially at the narrative structure of his television advertisements and online digital presence: I was shocked when one of my students, a senior from the Chicago suburbs who was carrying an "A" in the course, noted aloud and with self-assurance that many of Obama's television ads seemed to play up narratives of him being "an ordinary American" because "he's a Muslim, and some people are uncomfortable with the idea of a Muslim president."

But I know that I should not have been shocked.

Not in the least.

Consider the environment from whence this student's comments were always already contextually bound:

> Obama had for the last three years found himself cast within an echo chamber of right-wing discourse as un-American, a terrorist sympathizer, a socialist, a Marxist, an Afro-Leninist, a Muslim, and more. One popular e-mail making its way across the universe, for example, asked "Who is Barack Obama?" and recited a litany of lies about him and his family background before ending with an ominous, scare-mongering declaration that, "The Muslims have said they plan on destroying the U.S. from the inside out, what better way to start than at the highest level—through the President of the United States, one of their own!!!!"[2]

On the Rupert Murdoch-owned Fox News Channel—which many, including the White House under the Obama administration, have called an outright media wing of the Republican party rather than a legitimate news gathering organization—on-air hosts repeatedly deployed racial and ethnically tinged misinformation, such as when Steve Doocy, co-host of the *Fox & Friends* morning show, claimed live on air that Obama had spent "the first decade of his life raised by his Muslim father as a Muslim and was educated in a madrassa," which Doocy went on to define as a radical school "financed by Saudis, [that] teach the religion that pretty much hates us. The big question: Was that on the curriculum back then?"[3] Of course, this was demonstrably false (and was easily debunked by actual journalists at CNN who traveled to the school Obama had attended, conducted interviews, and reported the facts)—not that it mattered to Fox News.

Print media fared no better. *Investor's Business Daily*, a national newspaper in the United States focusing on international business, finance, and global economics, published a scorching editorial during the primary season that asked, among other questions posed as valid, whether Obama would "put African tribal or family interests ahead of U.S. interests?" and whether or not he was spending "an inordinate amount of his campaign time on the crisis unfolding in Kenya."[4] And, even after he had been elected president, columnists for the Rev. Moon-owned *Washington Times*, such as Frank Gaffney (2009), continued to argue that Obama would be "embracing the agenda of Muslim Brotherhood—an organization dedicated to promoting the theo-political-legal program authoritative Islam calls Shariah and that has the self-described mission of 'destroying Western civilization from within'" (n.p).

Sadly, mainstream news outlets were not immune to such lapses in journalistic integrity, either. To give but two glaring examples, *Newsweek* entered the fray of the absurd, publishing an article by senior editor Lisa Miller (2008) titled "Is Obama the Antichrist?," which gave column inches to Christian fundamentalist rapture adherents who believed Obama's election might fulfill end times prophecies, and *Time*'s Mark Halperin (2008), a noted political analyst, offered a list of 16 things Sen. John McCain (R-AZ) could do to increase his chances of defeating Obama during the general election, including such pithy observations as "Emphasize Barack Hussein Obama's unusual name and exotic background through a Manchurian Candidate prism" and "Allow some supporters to risk being accused of using the race card when criticizing Obama."[5]

However, talk radio—ever a teeming bastion of hate-speech in contemporary America—was and has remained the most pronounced location of fear-mongering with respect to the intersection of Obama and "Muslim" identity. Consider:

- Tom Marr, guest hosting on the equally detestable radio show of CNN's resident xenophobe, Lou Dobbs, forwarded the notion that he believed Obama had "an inner Muslim" that "has some sympathy

> [with] Islamic terrorism" (see *MediaMatters for America*, 25 August 2009).
> - Lee Rodgers, host of the syndicated *Lee Rodgers Show*, brazenly pronounced that Obama, "clearly is more sympathetic with the long-term goals of world communism, and, let's be blunt about it, Muslim terrorists, than with any legitimate American goals" (see *MediaMatters for America*, 11 March 2009).
> - Dan Caplis of Clear Channel Radio rhetorically asked, in the aftermath of a photo appearing of Obama dressed in traditional attire of a tribal elder during his 2006 trip to Kenya, whether Obama would wear "the same type of clothing and turban that Osama bin Laden wears," while another Clear Channel host, Bob Newman, likened the outfit to "Somali warlord garb" (see *Colorado MediaMatters*, 2008).
> - During his syndicated radio show, host Neal Boortz posited the need to "[A]sk Obama how many prayer rugs he has" (see *MediaMatters for America*, 25 August 2009).
> - And, not to be undone, Rush Limbaugh argued on his hugely popular April 27, 2009, radio show that his friends believe "Obama is terrorist attack number two" and that "Obama is the follow-up to 9/11" (see *MediaMatters for America*, 27 April 2009).

So perhaps my young student can be forgiven for assuming that then-Senator Obama—who often referred to himself during the campaign as "the skinny kid with a funny name," and who had openly spoken with pride of growing up a citizen of the world through roots laid in Hawaii, Kenya, Kansas, and Indonesia—might actually *have* been a Muslim. After all, a *Research 2000* poll taken during July 2009—that is, six months *after* Obama was sworn in as the 44th president of the United States—found that 58 percent of self-identified Republicans were "not sure" or "doubted" whether Obama was born in the United States (Thrush, 2009). Such was the power of the mediated pedagogies circulating in the popular-political sphere, which affected our received knowledge concerning Obama.

In this chapter, I examine three case studies concerning Barack Obama's (not) "Muslim" identity; two from his time as a presidential candidate, and one from his time as president. First, I will examine the so-called "madrassa story," which originated in January 2007 just prior to Obama's official announcement that he was running for president, and which situated him as having attended a radical madrassa while living in Indonesia. Second, and building on the first, I discuss the growing tide of anti-American charges that was to envelop Obama's candidacy, especially as read through the brazen campaign rhetoric of Republican vice-presidential nominee, Sarah Palin. And third, I briefly comment on the intersection of the so-called "birther" and "deather" movements as it related to Obama's push for health care reform in the summer and fall of 2009. My overarching goal is thus to pull back the veil of fear, misinformation, and racialization of politics as it relates to a three-year arc in which the mediated body of Obama operated as the site for the playing out of debates concerning the future of the nation.

In Which Obama Becomes "a Muslim"

> Senator Obama has never been a Muslim, was not raised as a Muslim, and is a committed Christian.
> — Robert Gibbs, Obama Press Secretary, 2008

It is both one of the great ironies and great tragedies of the 2008 presidential election that Barack Obama was to be so callously painted by his detractors as, for lack of a better umbrella term, "un-American," when his life story is by its very nature an *inherently* American one. In one of the first national newspaper articles to focus on Obama the politician,[6] Harold Meyerson (2004) wrote in a *Washington Post* article titled "A bright hope in Illinois" that, were Obama to win his then-forthcoming Senate race, he "would not only become the sole African American in the Senate: he would also be the most distinctly American of its members" (p. A23). By that, Meyerson was directly referring to Obama's transracial, transnational, transcultural biography, which he outlined thus:

> His father was Kenyan, his mother a white girl from Kansas. The two met and married at the University of Hawaii in 1960 (when miscegenation was still a felony in more than half the states). His father disappeared from his life when Obama went to college at Columbia, then moved to Chicago for five years of community organizing in a fusion of civil rights crusading and Saul Alinsky house-to-house plodding. He then went to Harvard Law School, where he became the first black president of the *Law Review*, returned to Chicago to run a program that registered 100,000 voters in the '92 elections, entered a civil rights law firm and became a senior lecturer in constitutional law at the University of Chicago. (p. A23)[7]

Although Obama himself has often said of his 2004 Senate race that, "I think it's fair to say that the conventional wisdom was we could not win. We didn't have enough money. We didn't have enough organization. There was no way that a skinny guy from the South Side with a funny name like Barack Obama could ever win a statewide race" (quoted in Davey, 2004, p. A1), he was mainly speaking about the fact that he had been up against self-funded multi-millionaires such as Blair Hull and well-established political figures such as Illinois State Comptroller Dan Hynes in the Democratic primary rather than a tidal wave of negative ads and press for his so-called "exotic" background or even his "funny" name.[8] Prior to his dramatic keynote address at the 2004

Democratic National Convention (DNC)—which many mark as Obama's debut on the national stage—feature-length news stories began to appear (such as William Finnegan's *New Yorker* article in May 2004, or Bob Herbert's *New York Times* article in June 2004) casting Obama in glowing terms and characterizing him as a breath of fresh air; a statewide poll of voters in June 2004 registered Obama with a sparkling 91–9 favorable–unfavorable rating in Illinois (see Pierce, 2004, p. A05), and the free trade and globalization favoring newsmagazine, *The Economist*, referred to him in an editorial as a "dream candidate" ("Obama heads for the convention," 2004).

Likewise, and following his soaring oratorical keynote—which emphasized that his story "was part of the larger American story…that in no other country on Earth is my story even possible" and deployed inclusive rhetoric that spoke of participating in a "politics of hope" rather than a "politics of cynicism"—he was lavished with praise from all corners of the globe, with many observers openly speculating on the potential for a future presidential run by the otherwise "obscure state legislator" who was nonetheless a "rock star" in the making (Smith, 2004, p. 6A). For many in both the political establishment and the nascent grassroots blogosphere, Obama held Tiger Woodsian (see Cole & Andrews, 2001) crossover appeal to voters moving forward in a rapidly changing America facing an onrushing future of global uncertainty.

One might wonder, then, how the "uniquely American" Obama characterized above could morph so quickly into the *un*-American discursive caricature that played on still-simmering fears of "the Other," especially Muslims, by a fair portion of the population.[9] Or, to put it differently, and following the work of David Altheide (2008) on the evidentiary narrative process—How is it that large swaths of the American public so readily began to believe as undeniably true such counterfactual knowledge about Obama?

By all accounts, it was an article in the far-right publication, *Insight Magazine*, which is owned by the same company that owns the *Washington Times*, in late January 2007 that served as the opening salvo in a loosely coordinated effort to frame Obama as the "scary" "Other," to introduce a (false) counternarrative to his glowing (true) personal biography. The article began: "Are the American people ready for an elected president who was educated in a madrassa as a young boy and has not been forthcoming about his Muslim heritage?" Howard Kurtz (2007), an inside-the-beltway media reporter for the *Washington Post*, detailed the story's near-immediate "vortextual" promotion—the "short-term compression of the media agenda in which other topics either disappear or have to be connected to the event" (see Whannel, 2001, p. 206)—within the right-wing media:

> Fox News picked up the *Insight* charge on two of its programs, playing up an angle involving Hillary Clinton. The magazine, citing only unnamed sources, said that researchers "connected" to the New York senator were allegedly spreading the information about her rival for the Democratic presidential nomination. The *New York Post*, which, like Fox, is owned by Rupert Murdoch, also picked up the article, with the headline: "'OSAMA' MUD FLIES AT OBAMA." Thus, in the first media controversy of the 2008 campaign, two of the leading candidates find themselves forced to respond to allegations *lacking a single named source*. (p. C1, emphasis added)

Such is the nature of corporate media in America. In response to the baseless allegation, the Obama campaign released a statement denying the charge, and Obama himself noted at a press event: "When I was 6, I attended an Indonesian public school where a bunch of the kids were Muslim because the country is 90% Muslim. The notion that somehow at the age of six or seven, I was being trained for something other than math, science and reading, is ludicrous."

Despite the denials, the right-wing noise machine—led by Fox News—kept spewing forth the charge, which like in a game of Pass It Around, grew evermore outrageous. One such interlocutor falsely stated with indignation *after* Obama's public statement on the matter: "Why didn't anybody ever mention that man right there was raised—spent the first decade of his life, raised by his Muslim father—as a Muslim and was educated in a madrassa?"

As the madrassa story ebbed and flowed around the fringes of right-wing media throughout the spring months of 2007, it was becoming increasingly clear that the not-so-subtle attempt to link "Obama" with "Muslim" was having its desired effect of seeping doubt about Obama's background into the minds of some voters, especially those already leery of Muslims—or, it is fair to say, of minorities, of "Others," in general. As if to confirm these sentiments, a Pew Research Center for the People and the Press poll (cited in Bacon, 2007), conducted in August 2007, found that 45% of respondents would be less likely to vote for a candidate for any office who was a Muslim (compared with 25% for a Mormon [i.e., Mitt Romney], and 16% for an evangelical Christian [i.e., Mike Huckabee]).

In December 2007, the Obama = Muslim storyline, which had been fabricated and reiterated in various mediated forms for nearly the entire year, had become a standard campaign dynamic. At a campaign event held in an Iowa coffee shop, a public exchange between Obama and an attendee underscored the extent to which nearly a year of dismissing this one particular rumor had still not succeeded in convincing everyone of the truth, as well as revealing how "Muslims" continued to be viewed in the main of America's public sphere. Michael Saul (2007) of the *Daily News* (NY) reported the exchange in this manner:

Obama was asked to explain his "Muslim background" by a 58-year-old white Iowan, who stated that her reason for asking the question was because "It's not so important that he is a Christian, although I'm very thankful he is. But it's very important that he's not a Muslim. I'm glad I got an answer because the Middle East is being run by the Muslims. And their kind of freedom is not the freedom that America has fought for all our lives, and I want to know that the next President of the United States, if it's Barack Obama, will be fighting for the freedom that America has fought for."

These types of exchanges and anecdotes picked up in steam when the calendar turned to January 2008, just as the primary season was starting to reach a fever pitch. Covering the candidate in South Carolina, Lisa Wangsness (2008) of the *Boston Globe* encountered potential voters who exhibited confusion over Obama's background: One person she interviewed believed that Obama had been sworn into his Senate seat on a Koran instead of the Bible (which was false), while another indicated that "The only thing I can stand here and tell you tonight is I have heard he's a Muslim, and I heard him say on TV the other night he was a Christian. How do I know?" (p. A8).

By mid-April 2008, roughly 10% of the electorate had come to believe Obama was in fact "a Muslim," and by September, noted Nicholas Kristof (2008) of the *New York Times*, almost one-third of likely voters "knew" "that Barack Obama [was] a Muslim or believe[d] that he could be. Even among *Democrats*, 23%of those holding negative views of Obama believed he was a Muslim, with the same poll finding that only 61 percent of the electorate viewed him as patriotic (versus 76 percent for Hillary and 90 percent for McCain)" (Reid, 2008, p. 9). Kristof's article further contained a quote from Gallup's Dalia Mogahed, who noted that:

> Our data shows that only 34 percent of Americans say that they have no prejudice against Muslims. That figure compares to 74 percent who say they have no prejudice against Jews. So while anti-Semitism is certainly not a relic of the past, anti-Muslim sentiment is at an alarmingly high rate right now in America, and because of that it's used as a political tool against politicians.

Additionally, the fringes of the American Right no longer remained as the solitary drivers of this non-story; elected officials, such as Rep. Steven King (R-IA) (2008), were now openly propagating a discursive creation that aligned Obama not with the United States but with "Muslims" and "terrorists." Offered King, "And I will tell you that if he is elected president then the radical Islamists, the Al-Qaeda and the radical Islamists and their supporters, will be dancing in the streets in greater numbers than they did on Sept. 11th" (ibid).[10]

And there we have the first piece of the puzzle: what began as a false statement in the right-wing fringe press moved effortlessly into the right-wing corporate press a la Fox News and syndicated radio shows (e.g., Limbaugh, Dobbs, etc.), grew steadily across the entirety of 2007, seeped into the consciousness of numerous voters, and was finally embraced wholeheartedly by various elected Republican members of Congress—all predicated on a cultural context in which the abstract "Muslim" was viewed with heightened suspicion by many whose only understanding of or interaction with "Muslims" came from the mediated public sphere itself, whether in the form of Hollywood movies (see Kincheloe & Steinberg, 2004) or cable news coverage of "9/11." And all of which made it that much easier to, as the next section discusses, cast under suspicion the very fact of Obama's "American" identity and his intention to protect the nation.

In Which Barack Obama 'Pals Around with Terrorists'

> There is no indication that [William] Ayers and [Barack] Obama are now "palling around," or that they have had an ongoing relationship in the past three years. Also, there is nothing to suggest that Ayers is now involved in terrorist activity or that other Obama associates are.
> — CNN Political Ticket, 10/5/08

For the first month or so following the respective party nominating conventions in late August and early September 2008, the official direction of McCain's campaign toward Obama was essentially one that painted his rival as politically inexperienced and overly liberal on social and economic concerns—typical red meat political rhetoric aimed at drawing a clear policy distinction between the two men whilst highlighting the former's military background and long political experience in the U.S. Senate at the expense of the latter. However, an avalanche of vituperative rhetoric shown toward Obama—especially as related to the public persona and actions of McCain's running mate, Alaska Governor Sarah Palin—was soon to escalate among the various cultural intermediaries associated with Conservative interests in general and the Republican party specifically. Palin herself led the charge, declaring at one campaign rally that:

> Our opponent is someone who sees America, it seems, as being so imperfect, imperfect enough that he is palling around with terrorists who would target their own country.... This is not a man who sees America as you see America and as I see America. (10/5/08)[11]

This statement was meant as a direct reference to Obama's passing association with former 1960s activist Bill Ayers (now a Distinguished Professor of Education at the University of Illinois-Chicago), yet it worked to stoke further fears about Obama and his imagined association to those "Other" terrorists. Two weeks later, Palin increased the racialized tenor of her rhetoric, this time at a Greensboro, North Carolina, fundraiser. Said Palin:

> [John McCain and I] believe that the best of America is not all in Washington, D.C. We believe that the best of America is in these small towns that we get to visit, and in these wonderful little pockets of what I call the real America, being here with all of you hard working very patriotic, um, very, um, pro-America areas of this great nation. (10/17/09)

What this statement implies, of course, is that not only are there "pro-America" parts of the country, but that there are likewise by definition "anti-America" parts of the country. It is important to note that the composition of the audience Palin spoke to was in line with most of her previous public appearance. To wit, Palin had held 44 public events (rallies, town halls, etc) between the time she was introduced as McCain's running mate and the time she made the earlier statement. As deconstructed by Nate Silver (2008) at FiveThirtyEight.com, home to the leading number crunchers in terms of polling data during the 2008 election, there was a distinct racial element in play: 34 of these 44 cites held voting-age (18+) populations whiter than the U.S. average, and on average were 83.3% non-Hispanic white, 7.5% black, 5.2% Hispanic, and 4.0% "Other" (by comparison, the US composite average of the same voting-age population was 72.0% white, 11.2% black, 11.0% Hispanic, and 5.9% other).[12]

The introduction of anti-American tropes into the presidential race, like the previous instance involving the baseless story of Obama's childhood education, quickly dispersed into the public sphere, with both members of Congress and the right-wing media using Palin's comments as a jumping-off point to slander Obama (and Democrats more generally). Most visible among political figures was Michelle Bachmann, a first-term Congresswoman from exurban Minnesota who has since gone on to be the Poster Girl for conspiracy theorists and anti-government adherents.[13] Asked by host Chris Matthews while a guest on the MSNBC political program *Hardball with Chris Matthews* if Obama worried her, Bachmann replied:

> Absolutely. I'm very concerned that he may have anti-American views.... What I would say, what I would say is that the news media should do a penetrating expose and take a look. I wish they would. I wish the American media would take a great look at the views of the people in Congress and find out, are they pro-America or anti-America? I think people would love to see an exposé like that.[14]

As if on cue, the *Washington Times*, in its on-going propaganda campaign, followed suit by accusing Obama of aiding in funding "extremist Afrocentrists who shared [Jeremiah] Wright's anti-Americanism," as well as having "ties" to the "militant advocacy group" ACORN (which isn't militant), and which in his article titled "Funding Extremists," Greg Pierce (2008) negatively defined as "various affiliated groups [that] agitate for 'a living wage,' for 'affordable housing,' for 'tax justice' and union and environmental goals, as well as against school choice and welfare reform" (as if those goals were somehow *bad*). And, moreover, W.F. Walker Johanson, a regular contributor to the far-right WorldNetDaily online publication, was given space in the newspaper to stoke Red Scare-like fears about Obama, arguing in his column:

> Barack Obama is a true wolf in sheep's clothing. On the outside, he's nice, pleasant, handsome, well-spoken, has cute little kids, dresses well, looks like someone we would all like to know. But underneath, he resembles an anti-American Marxist who believes the following [insert lengthy screed on immigrants, abortion, gay marriage, bigger government, etc].[15]

As these campaign rallies and press clippings collided in the public sphere of public opinion, questions began raining down on the McCain campaign, with calls inciting violence toward Obama becoming more and more regular. Khaled Hosseini (2008), the famed author of *The Kite Runner* and *A Thousand Splendid Suns*, openly wondered in a *Washington Post* editorial if the McCain-Palin ticket was:

> willfully inciting the angry and venomous response that we have been witnessing at their rallies? If not, then what reaction are they hoping to evoke by their relentless public suggestions that Obama is basically an anti-American liar who won't put 'country first' and has an affection for terrorists? Do they not understand the kind of fire they are playing with?

Although McCain pushed back half-heartedly for his supporters to remain "respectful" of Obama, it was his running mate Palin that was driving ahead full force, and it was likewise clear that the newfound aggressive rhetoric was taking hold among some of ticket's most ardent supporters. As reported by Colbert I. King (2008) for the *Washington Post*, supporters of the McCain-Palin ticket attending a Palin rally in St. Clairesville, Ohio (a "white, working class community"), recounted the following observations to videographer Casey Kaufman, who was covering the event for *Al-Jazeera*); I quote directly:

- From an older white woman: "I'm afraid if he wins, the black [sic] will take over. He's not a Christian. This is a Christian nation! What is our country gonna end up like?"
- An older white man: "When you got a Negro running for president, you need a first-stringer. He's definitely a second-stringer."
- A young white man holding a child: "He seems like a sheep—or a wolf in sheep's clothing to be honest with you. And I believe Palin—she's filled with the Holy Spirit, and I believe she's gonna bring honesty and integrity to the White House."
- An older white man: "He's related to a known terrorist, for one."

- An older white man: "He is friends with a terrorist of this country!"
- An older white man: "He must support terrorists! You know, uh, if it walks like a duck and quacks like a duck, it must be a duck. And that to me is Obama."
- A young white woman: "Just the whole, Muslim thing, and everything, and everybody's still kinda—a lot of people have forgotten about 9/11, but . . . I dunno, it's just kinda . . . a little unnerving."
- A white woman: "Obama and his wife, I'm concerned that they could be anti-white. That he might hide that."
- An older white woman: "I don't like the fact that he thinks us white people are trash...because we're not!"[16]

While Palin herself could be written off as a cartoon candidate in over her head on the national stage—and Tina Fey's priceless turn as Palin on the long-running NBC sketch comedy show *Saturday Night Live* went a fair way in doing just that—it was ever more clear that her words were having real effects on real people. Ta-Nehisi Coates (2008) teased this out, arguing that by the end of the campaign, McCain's crowds weren't even necessarily there to support him (as they were for his running mate); rather, "they were there because they believed Obama was a Muslim," that "they just hated a specter of the dude [who McCain] was running against" (p. 1). This was played out time and again, whether it was an older woman telling McCain at a Lakeville, Minnesota, town hall that Obama "is an Arab" during the question and answer period (which forced McCain to correct her) or a woman at a similar event in Las Cruces, New Mexico, decrying the "illegal aliens" ruining the country.

Yet it is not solely a question of Obama's falsely perceived "Muslim" identity, nor his transracial background, nor the vague connotations of his name, nor necessarily his center-left politics. Rather, it's the reiterative discursivity of the whole package, wrapped up and cast as "anti-American" to a group of potential voters for whom "the Other" has been continually deployed by politicians on the Right (and more generally in the right-wing media) as the source of their constituents' personal ills. Arlie Hochschild (2003) chronicled one such version of this story, arguing that George W. Bush parlayed a strong sense of manufactured fear and white male resentment into a *campaign of fear*, one that, during the 2004 presidential election, offered the (power of the) vote as recourse to those who felt frightened, passive, and concerned for their safety, future, and well-being, especially to those still shaken by 9/11:

> Unhinging the personal from the political, playing on identity politics, Republican strategists have offered the blue-collar voter a Faustian bargain: we'll lift your self-respect by putting down women, minorities, immigrants, even those spotted owls.

> We'll honor the manly fortitude you've shown in taking bad news. But (and this is implicit) don't ask us to do anything to change that bad news.... Paired with this is an aggressive right-wing attempt to mobilize blue-collar fear, resentment, and a sense of being lost—and attach it to the fear of American vulnerability, American loss. By doing so, Bush aims to win the blue-collar man's identification with big business, empire, and himself. The resentment anyone might feel at the personnel officer who didn't have the courtesy to call him back and tell him he didn't have the job, Bush now redirects toward the target of Osama bin Laden, and when we can't find him, Saddam Hussein. [...] He speaks to a working-man's lost pride and his fear of the future by offering an image of fearlessness. He poses here in his union jacket, there in his pilot's jumpsuit, taunting the Iraqis to "bring 'em on"—all of it meant to feed something in the heart of a frightened man. (n.p.)

Issues of race, class, gender, and sexuality (both seen or unseen) and their location to contextually significant backlash politics are burned into every word of Hochschild's cogent analysis; in the 2004 election, fear and loathing of "the Other" became embedded within a modern-day "Southern" electoral strategy.[17]

But this is not to deny that this constituency does not have *real* anger and resentment. Speaking at The Commonwealth Club of California, Noam Chomsky (2009) made the following point about the reach and effect of right-wing media personalities such as Beck, Limbaugh, and so on who drive the narrative:

> I'm thinking about the part [of the right-wing media] that has substantive content—crazy content—but it *is* substantive. It does give answers, to the people who for the last thirty years have seen their wages, income, stagnate or decline, benefits decline, services decline, there's nothing for their children, world's out of control. These are the people who on polls, maybe 80 percent of them, say the country's going in the wrong direction, the government's run by the few and the special interests, not the people, and so on—you know, *they're not wrong*. This *is* all happening to them. And the answers that they're getting, from say, you know, Rush Limbaugh, Michael Savage, the rest of them, are, well, we have an answer: the rich liberals own everything, they own the corporations, they run the government, they run the media, and they don't care about people like you, they don't care about the fly over people between the East Coast and the West Coast. They only care about giving everything you worked for away, to illegal immigrants, or gays, or something. So we gotta protect ourselves from them. And furthermore they run the government, when they put up a health program, it's not to give you health, it's to kill your granny. And that's an answer to something. It's a terrible answer. But it *is* an answer. And if you do suspend disbelief, if you forget about what's happening in the world, really, it's a coherent answer. Now they're not hearing anything else. [emphasis original].

In the final section, I want to tease out Hochschild's and Chomsky's general point more closely, using the post-election health care reform debate—especially the town hall fiascos of summer 2009—as my example. In particular, this debate coalesces around the so-called "Birthers" (individuals who doubt whether Obama was a natural-born citizen and therefore ineligible to serve as president) and "Deathers" (anti-reform supporters who, taking a lead from Palin, Bachmann, and the right-wing media, believed that Obama's health care plan would, in effect, mean "kill their granny").

In Which Barack Obama Faces Down "Birthers" and "Deathers"

> The white Southern base of the GOP strongly doubts the legality of the 2008 election and the legitimacy of the man elected. They see him as alien, foreign and suspect.
> — David Frum, former Bush speechwriter, 2009

> Too many political and media leaders are deliberately fanning the flames of ignorance and fear, and they should be ashamed.
> — Errol Louis, 23 July 2009

Following Obama's landslide electoral victory and subsequent inauguration, the misrepresentation, obfuscation, and outright slander aimed at him did not simply fade away. If anything, it increased to hyperactive levels in the mediated spheres represented by the usual suspects such as Fox News and talk radio of the Limbaugh/Beck/Dobbs ilk. However, there was also a noticeable uptick in backlash narratives among everyday folks, some bordering on pure anger and hatred toward the newly elected president. Some of this backlash had to do with specific policy orientations—such as the way the Obama administration was directing U.S. foreign policy (e.g., putting an end to Bush's torture policy), or whom he had nominated to the U.S. Supreme Court (Sonya Sotomayor, the first Latina to serve on the Court). However, much of it was manifest in the complex cultural politics of the contemporary moment, the two most visible points of intersection for both coming in the very public debate of health care reform, which was informed by angry, mob-like protest not only in relation to the policy, but to the figure of Obama himself.

But let's step back for a minute. In mid-2009, a bevy of stories began to appear amid the far-right questioning the Constitutional legality of Obama's presidency, driven by the notion that he was not a native-born citizen. Never mind that similar stories about his place of birth were debunked nearly a year previously (as tied up with the "Muslim" background stories); the so-called "Birther" phenomenon would for a time vortextually dominate the chattering class of cable news pundits, as well-known mainstream figures including Larry King, Chris Matthews, and Lou Dobbs all waded into the discussion as if it was a legitimate question in the first place. But this was not solely a media fixation, reporting on some obscure right-wing smear to gin up ratings—it was being mirrored in the general public. To give but one example,

Rep. Michael Castle (R-DE) was confronted by a woman at his own town hall meeting who vociferously argued that Obama "is not an American citizen, he is a citizen of Kenya," which brought with it raucous applause, and Castle himself was heckled by his own constituents when he clarified for the woman that in fact Obama was an American citizen (Stelter, 2009, p. 2). Lending added weight to the ridiculous charge, Sen. Richard Shelby (R-AL), who had served in the Senate with Obama, refused to dismiss the premise, stating later: "Well his father was Kenyan and they said he was born in Hawaii, but I haven't seen any birth certificate. You have to be born in America to be president" (quoted in Winant, 2009, p. 2).

It is worth noting the absurdity of the story, but also the intent behind it. To begin, the only way for the story to be empirically true was if, as Michael Tomasky (2009) outlined:

> Obama would have had to persuade the state of Hawaii to collude in forging a birth certificate that has been verified by its Republican governor and director of health as well as the nonpartisan factcheck.org. Moreover, his mother would have had to have the foresight to place birth announcements claiming he was born in the US in both the *Honolulu Advertiser* and the *Hawaii Star Bulletin*, 48 years ago, in anticipation of a future presidential run.

That a group of individuals bought into what was and is effectively a conspiracy theory is not unique in American politics (see Bratich, 2008). Historian Kathryn Olmstead, for example, has argued that, "The best historical parallel for the Birthers is the far-right John Birch Society, or 'Birchers'…[who] saw the US government as filled with agents of the enemy, the Communists. They viewed President Dwight Eisenhower as a secret Commie, which is analogous to the Birthers who see Obama as a secret Muslim" (quoted in Potter, 2009, p. A14). What is so problematic about this particular group of true-believers, notes (Sullivan (2009a), is the common tie that binds their paranoia together:

> The demographics tell the basic story: a Black man is President and a large majority of white Southerners cannot accept that, even in 2009. They grasp conspiracy theories to wish Obama—and the America he represents—away. Since white Southerners comprise an increasing proportion of the 22% of Americans who still describe themselves as Republican, the GOP can neither dismiss the crankery nor move past it. The fringe defines what's left of the Republican center…. The chilling implication is that a large number of Americans believe the President has no right to be in office and has fraudulently maneuvered himself there. (p. 4)

By the time the debates over health care reform were dragging into the summer months, protestors attending town halls organized by their elected representatives were turning loud, angry, and occasionally violent, many marked by individuals holding signs "featuring swastikas and Obama with a 'Hitler' mustache" (Harris, 2009, p. 31). Others held signs stating "Say No to Socialized Medicine," "Save Granny," and "No to ObamaCare," while still others brought firearms and "touted signs complaining they paid too much tax, that Obama planned to increase government control, turn America into France, take away their guns and was illegally serving as President" (Davies, 2009, n.p.). Talk radio was certainly contributing to this discourse, led in many respects by the perpetually unstable Fox News host, Glenn Beck, who, in addition to promoting the idea that *Obama* was "a racist," openly discussed on his television show that Obama was "setting up a network of secret internment camps and joke[d] about poisoning Democratic congresswoman Nancy Pelosi" (Harris, 2009, p. 31).

All of which would be laughable if it wasn't so serious. Unlike the so-called Brooks Brothers "riots" in Florida 2000 (see Krugman, 2009), what we were seeing at these town halls was, by and large, legitimate anger on the part of those attending, but an anger exploited by those on the Right for their own political ends. Correlatively, that this anger—at government, at politicians, at corporations, and their own financial situations, etc.—outwardly manifested itself in racialized terms was not entirely surprising, stoked as it was by those media personalities who were "making the explicit case that white Americans [were] losing something precious with the election of a black president" (Serwer, 2009, n.p.). Leon Hadar (2009), a research fellow at the non-partisan Cato Institute (a pro-market, libertarian think tank) summed up the general tenor of that argument in this manner:

> These people believe that 'their America' is being robbed from them by an African-American president who has just nominated a Hispanic woman to the Supreme Court and who, together with a cabal of secular multiculturalists and radical socialists, is going to 'de-Christianize' America; force white Americans out of their jobs; provide reparations to American-Africans to compensate them for slavery; nationalize the entire economy under the control of bureaucrats in Washington; and open the country's gates to millions of Latin immigrants who are bound to demand that California and Texas be returned to Mexico.... While this End-of-Old-America scenario has nothing to do with reality, its popularity among the 'birthers', 'deathers' and the Republican Party's electoral base exposes genuine fears among those who find it difficult to adjust to the new political realities that are driven in part by dramatic demographic changes, including a growing non-White and non-Christian population and a more tolerant and secular generation of young Americans. (n.p.)

Looking back a year hence, to one particular McCain campaign rally, loops the historical legacy of this paradigm back into sharp relief: a middle-aged, white audience member who, when given the microphone to ask a question of McCain, exclaimed:

> I'm mad! I'm really mad! And what's going to surprise you is it's not the economy—it's the socialists taking over our country.... When you have Obama, Pelosi, and the

rest of the hooligans up there going to run the country, we have to have our head examined.... It's time that you two represent the rest of us. So go get 'em.

As if on cue, the sea of white, middle-aged folks cheered, bursting into loud chants of "U-S-A! U-S-A!" Hooligans: a multicultural man and a white woman, each holding relative positions of power, reduced to "socialists" who don't represent said sea of white faces, and who would be "running" the country.

But as Hadar suggests in the earlier quote, "their America" never really existed in the first place, other than perhaps from the mid-1950s to early-1960s television fictions of *Father Knows Best*, *The Donna Reed Show*, *The Andy Griffith Show*, *Ozzie and Harriett*, and most notably *Leave It to Beaver*, which exemplified the idealized post-WWII suburban nuclear family in America. In other words, while some of the louder voices on the Right, such as Patrick J. Buchanan (2009) continue to argue that "traditional Americans are losing their nation"—and by this he means an America once defined by its *whiteness*—it is an historically inaccurate view which survives only in narrative form. Sullivan (2009b) makes this point in very concise terms, noting that:

> [T]his axiom, while useful as myth, has a problem. It is untrue. And this "country" that white Americans are allegedly losing is not, in fact, a country. It is merely a self-serving and solipsistic illusion of a country that some white Americans *feel* they are losing. From its very beginning, after all, America was a profoundly black country as well. (emphasis original).

Obama's transnational American blackness (Parameswaran, 2009)—his very existence as a global citizen of empire elected to the most powerful position on Earth—may not usher in the kind of wholesale, systemic change his ardent supporters are hoping for, but the very *fact* of his presidency, to rework Inderpal Grewal (2006), does have the potential to produce and empower "identities within many connectivities in a transnational world, whether as the source of imperial power or as a symbol of freedom and liberty" (p. 196), especially those who are, or who are from, historically marginalized communities and locales. And that, it would seem, most surely ruffles the feathers of those individuals still holding on to a fiction of an America that never was.

Coda

> [Obama] has already done more to heal the open wound between the West and Islam than anyone else on the planet.
> — Andrew Sullivan, 2009

> I am proud to carry with me the goodwill of the American people, and a greeting of peace from Muslim communities in my country. As-Salamu Alaykum.
> — Barack Obama, Cairo, Egypt, June 4, 2009

Despite the critics who attempted to marginalize or discredit Obama during his candidacy for the presidency, as well as those who still seek to derail his policy initiatives by regurgitating baseless personal accusations, the first year of the Obama presidency has for many signaled a sea-change in the direction of the country, as well as resulting in an avalanche of goodwill cascading down upon the United States from its partners abroad.[18] It has also signaled, if in words but not yet forcefully in deeds, an intention to engage in dialogue with the Islamic world(s), witnessed most notably by his June 2009 speech in Cairo, Egypt, which *Der Spiegel*'s Gabor Steingart (2009)—an early critic of the president—characterized as a "courageous speech" that acknowledged:

> that Islam is a power for peace, that the Koran is a call for peacefulness, and that the U.S. president finds nothing wrong with women who wear the *hijab*. He added that the U.S. must, once and for all, stop trying to export its particular vision of democracy. No Western leader before him had been as empathetic and obliging in an address to the world's 48 countries with majority Islamic populations. Obama offered the Muslims nothing less than reconciliation and partnership.

It is interventions such as these into the arc of history on the part of Obama, which, while their ultimate political utility may never fully materialize in foreign policy, carry with them the possibility of changing the hearts and educating the minds of many Americans as to their particular—if not entrenched—understandings of Islam. For all of the fear-mongering, race-baiting, dirty politics unleashed against Obama for the last three years, there *is* reason to be hopeful: lest we forget, Obama *won* the election, even in the face of it all, and continues to remain popular, both at home[19] and abroad.[20] So while the Limbaughs, Becks, and Palins of the world continue to pontificate irrationally into any live microphone they can find about how Obama is ruining "their" country, they've been outed as the fringe that they are, because their center does not hold. There are most assuredly problems in this country that need to be dealt with, from health care reform to the reform of Wall Street. But, to quote from Frank Rich (2008), and this is important, "We will only begin to confront the magnitude of our choice when and if we stop being distracted by small, let alone utterly fictitious, things."

Endnotes

1   Coulter, who was fired for the article, wrote three years later that "I am often asked if I still think we should invade their [Muslim] countries, kill their leaders, and convert them to Christianity. The answer is: Now more than ever!"

2   A version of this e-mail can be found at http://www.snopes.com/politics/obama/muslim.asp

3   Airdate January 19, 2006.

4   In a similar vein, right-wing pundit Debbie Schlussel posted an anti-Obama diatribe on her website that stated in part: "[I]s a man who Muslims think is a Muslim, who feels some sort of psychological need to prove himself to his absent Muslim father, and who

is now moving in the direction of his father's heritage, a man we want as President when we are fighting the war of our lives against Islam? Where will his loyalties be?"

5   To be fair, Halperin does qualify his remarks in a footnote by stating, "This is analysis of what is likely to happen, not advice or endorsement."

6   Robert Draper (2009) notes that the first national coverage Obama received was a little-remembered February 6, 1990 article by Fox Butterfield that appeared in the *New York Times* covering Obama's selection as the first African American editor of the Harvard *Law Review*. In an article that appeared in the *Boston Globe* the following week, Obama said of his election to the *Law Review* presidency, "[M]y election was not about me, but it was about us, about what we could do and what we could accomplish" (Matchan, 1990, p. 29). In a foreshadowing of things to come, Matachan's article quotes John Owens, a former co-worker of the then-28-year-old Obama in Chicago, as stating: "This guy sounds like he's president of the country already" (*ibid*).

7   In nearly every major newspaper or magazine article on Obama, in 2004, some variation of this paragraph was used to describe his background.

8   Truth be told, his acknowledgment that he had smoked marijuana and experimented with cocaine while in college—which he had previously written about in his heartfelt memoir, *Dreams From My Father*—and the perception that he was overly professorial (read: wonky, aloof, etc.) in his demeanor, were seen as a far greater disadvantages for him in the Senate race, both garnering significant media attention in Illinois. Additionally, the notion that he was not "black enough" for some was also portrayed as a potential negative. In response to this latter problematic, Obama was quoted as saying: "If I was arrested for armed robbery and my mug shot was on the television screen, people wouldn't be debating if I was African-American or not. I'd be a black man going to jail. Now if that's true when bad things are happening, there's no reason why I shouldn't be proud of being a black man when good things are happening, too" (quoted in Davey, 2004, p. 1).

9   In researching this chapter, I was unable to find one mainstream print article during the 2004 Senate campaign from a legitimate news organization that even suggested Obama was Muslim, had been at any point a practicing Muslim, or was in any way sympathetic to "radical Islam." Even those articles emanating out of such quasi-news outlets as the *Washington Times* remained focused primarily on pointing out his liberal positions on issues ranging from abortion to NAFTA to foreign policy.

10 This rhetoric was not only limited to fringe politicians. Mitt Romney, the former governor of Massachusetts and a leading Republican candidate for president who was ultimately defeated in the primary by McCain, characterized Islam during one of the debates as: "Violent, radical jihadists want to replace all the governments of the moderate Islamic states, replace them with a caliphate. And to do that, they also want to bring down the West, in particular us. And they've come together as Shi'a and Sunni and Hezbollah and Hamas and the Muslim Brotherhood and Al-Qaeda with that intent" (http://www.nytimes.com/2007/05/15/us/politics/16repubs-text.html). Romney also made it clear that he would not have had any Muslims serving in his Cabinet or as national security advisors.

11 Lost among the traditional media was that Palin was the one figure in the race who actually had real connections to someone who had preached armed insurrection against the U.S. government—John Vogler of the Alaska Independence Party. Palin's husband, Todd, had for seven years been a member of the AIP, and earlier, in 2008, Palin herself recorded a message of support for the AIP.

12 Silver extended his analysis to the public events Obama held during the same interval, which covered 48 distinct cities, and found that the racial composition of these cities were: 69.8% white, 17.4% black, 8.9% Hispanic, and 4.0% other (here the percentage of whites very nearly matches the U.S. average of 72.0%, with 22 of Obama's cities whiter than average, and the other 26 were less white than average). For detailed analysis, see http://www.fivethirtyeight. com/2008/10/real-america-looks-different-to-palin.html

13 Michael Tomasky, a veteran journalist currently serving as editor of *The Guardian*'s American offering, characterized Bachmann thusly: "She's a first-term backbencher from exurban Minneapolis who says the Lord told her to run for Congress. She declared herself 'a fool for Christ' in 2006 when she announced her candidacy. By all accounts she's down with the whole right-wing Christian package: immigrants bring disease and pestilence, homosexuals want to indoctrinate straight children, and so on."
14 Even the otherwise sensible Sen. George Voinovich (R-OH) joined in with harsh—and nonsensical—rhetoric, commenting in regards to Obama, "With all due respect, the man is a socialist."
15 Although first printed in the *Washington Times*, ABC News's political newsletter, the *Note*, included it on its list of daily Must Reads (10/22/08). Thus was its readership enhanced significantly, as well as given legitimacy.
16 Alexandra Pelosi's (2009) HBO documentary *Right America: Feeling Wronged—Some Voices from the Campaign Trail* revealed similar comments from McCain-Palin rallies, such as those calling him the "Anti-Christ" or stating "He reminds me of Hitler." It should also be noted, as is later taken up in this chapter, that, as Pelosi offered in an interview, "There are lots of normal people in this movie…they just don't agree with us on, like, moral and cultural and political issues. They don't agree with us on anything, really" (quoted in Schone, 2009). http://www.salon.com/ent/tv/int /2009/02/16/alexandra_pelosi/
17 For more, see Giardina and Newman, 2008.
18 According to the annual Anholt-GfK Roper Nation Brands Index report (2009), the United States "is now ranked #1 by global citizens," up from the seventh place in 2008. Anholt, an internationally renowned branding expert who advises more than a dozen governments, notes the implications of this move: "What's really remarkable is that in all my years studying national reputation, I have never seen any country experience such a dramatic change in its standing as we see for the United States in 2009.... Despite recent economic turmoil, the U.S. actually gained significant ground. The results suggest that the new U.S. administration has been well received abroad and the American electorate's decision to vote in President Obama has given the United States the status of the world's most admired country." (http://www.gfk.com/group/press_information/press_releases/004734/ index.en.html)
19 As of October 2009, Obama pulls a general 55–37–8 favorable–unfavorable–no opinion rating, with regional differences as high as 82–7 in the Northeast and as low as 27–68 in the South, and as high as 79–14 among voters aged 18–29 and as low as 41–53 among those over the age 60. Source: DailyKos/Research2000 (10/12-10/15 polling sample; http://dailykos.com/weeklypoll/2009/ 10/15
20 In May 2009, Obama's approval rating was exceedingly high throughout Europe than the United States, with continental Europe giving him a 78% approval rating, with those numbers much higher in Italy, Spain, and France.

References

Altheide, D. (2008). The evidentiary narrative: Notes toward a symbolic interactionist perspective about evidence. In N. K. Denzin & M. D. Giardina (Eds.), *Qualitative inquiry and the politics of evidence* (pp. 137–162). Walnut Creek, CA: Left Coast Press.

Bacon, P. (2007, November 29). Foes use Obama's Muslim ties to fuel rumors about him. *The Washington Post*, p. A01.

Bratich, J. Z. (2008). *Conspiracy panics: Political rationality and popular culture*. Albany, NY: SUNY Press.

Buchanan, P. J. (20 October, 2009). Traditional Americans are losing their nation. WorldNetDaily. Retrieved 4 February 2009 from http://www.wnd.com/index.php?pageId=113463

Chomsky, N. (2009). Speech delivered to the Commonwealth Club of California.

Coates, T. (2008, November 20). This really won't end well… *The Atlantic Monthly.* Retrieved October 15, 2009 from http://ta-nehisicoates.theatlantic.com/archives /2008/11/this_ really_ wont_end_well.php

Cole, C. L., & Andrews, D. L. (2001). America's new son: Tiger Woods and America's multiculturalism. *Cultural Studies: A Research Annual,* 5, 107–122.

Colorado MediaMatters. (2008, February 26). Clear Channel hosts likened African outfit worn by Obama to "the kind of garb you often see Osama bin Laden in" and to "Somali warlord garb". Retrieved October 15, 2009 from http://colorado.mediamatters.org/items /200802270001

Coulter, A. (2001, 13 September). This is war: We should invade their countries. *National Review.* Retrieved 4 February 2009 from http://web.archive.org/web/20010914225811/ http://www.nationalreview.com/coulter/coulter091301.shtml

Davey, M. (2004, July 26). A surprise Senate contender reaches his biggest stage yet. *The New York Times,* p. A1.

Davies, A. (2009, September 19). US politics has shifted swiftly from health care to race relations. *The Age* (Australia), p. 16.

Draper, R. (2009, November). Barack Obama's work in progress. *GQ.* Retrieved October 20, 2009 from http://www.gq.com/news-politics/politics/200911/barack-obama-writing-books-writer-robert-draper

Finnegan, W. (2004, May 31). The candidate: How the son of a Kenyan economist became an Illinois everyman. *The New Yorker,* p. A05.

Gaffney, F. (2009, March 16). Shariah's brotherhood. *Center for Security Policy.* Retrieved October 15, 2009 from http://204.96.138.161/p17940.xml

Garofoli, J. (2008, October 9). Veiled racism seen in new attacks on Obama. *San Francisco Chronicle.* Retrieved October 15, 2009 from http://www.sfgate.com/cgi-bin/article. cgi?f=/c/a/2008/10/08/MNB313DUTE.DTL

Giardina, M. D. (in press, a). From Howard Dean to Barack Obama: The evolution of politics in the network society. In G. Kien & M. Levina (Eds.), *Everyday life in the (post) global network.* New York: Peter Lang.

Giardina, M. D. (in press, b). Toward a politics of hope: Performing political reality in the age of Obama. *Cultural Studies/Critical Methodologies,* 9(6).

Grewal, I. (2006). *Transnational America: Feminisms, diasporas, neoliberalisms.* Durham, NC: Duke University Press.

Hadar, L. (2009, August 18). Birthers, deathers, and the fear of change. *The Business Times* (Singapore), p. 14.

Halperin, M. (2008). *ABC's the note.* Retrieved October 19, 2009 from http://thepage.time. com/ halperin'-take-ways-mccain-can-beat-obama -that-clinton-cannot

Harris, P. (2009, August 16). Obama becomes target amid fear that hate will turn into violence. *The Observer* (London), p. 31.

Herbert, B. (2004, June 4). A leap of faith. *The New York Times,* p. A27.

Hochschild, A. (2003, October 2). Let them eat war. *CommonDreams.org.* Retrieved March 12, 2007 from http://www.commondreams.org/views03/1003-12.htm

Hosseini, K. (2008, October 12). McCain and Palin are playing with fire. *The Washington Post,* p. B05.

Johanson, W. (2008, October 22). Obama, a wolf in sheep's garb. *The Washington Times.* Retrieved October 15, 2009 from http://www.washingtontimes.com/news/2008/oct/22/ voting-america-away/

Kincheloe, J. L. & Steinberg, S. R. (2004). *The miseducation of the West: How schools and the media distort our understandings of the Islamic world.* Westport, CT: Praeger Press.

King, C. I. (2008, October 18). A rage no one should be stoking. *The Washington Post,* p. A15.

Kristof, N. D. (2008, September 21). The push to "Otherize" Obama. *The New York Times,* p. 1.

Krugman, P. (2009, August 6). The town hall mob. *The New York Times.* Retrieved August 8, 2009 from http://www.nytimes.com/2009/08/07/opinion/07krugman.html

Kurtz, H. (2007, January 22). Campaign allegation a source of vexation. *The Washington Post*, p. C01.
MediaMatters for America. (2008, January 16). *Investor's Business Daily*: "Would Obama put African tribal or family interests ahead of U.S. interests?" Retrieved October 15, 2009 from http://mediamatters.org/research/200801160003
MediaMatters for America. (2008, August 25). Boortz: "Let's ask Obama how many prayer rugs he has". Retrieved October 15, 2009 from http://mediamatters.org/research/200808250016
MediaMatters for America. (2009, April 27). Limbaugh says his friend believes "Obama is terrorist attack number 2; Obama is the follow-up to 9-11". Retrieved October 15, 2009 from http://mediamatters.org/mmtv/200904270023
MediaMatters for America. (2009, August 25). Dobbs fill-in Marr "believes" Obama has "an inner Muslim" that "has some sense of sympathy" with "Islamic terrorism." Retrieved October 15, from http://mediamatters.org/mmtv/200908250051
MediaMatters for America. (2009, March 11). Rodgers claims Obama "clearly is more sympathetic with the long-term goals of world communism, and let's be blunt about it, Muslim terrorists, than with any legitimate American goals." Retrieved October 15, from http://mediamatters.org/mmtv/200903110032
Meyerson, H. (2004, March 12). A bright hope in Illinois. *The Washington Post*, p. A23.
Miller, L. (2008, November 24). Is Obama the antichrist? The winning lottery number in Illinois was 666, which, as everyone knows, is the sign of the Beast. *Newsweek*.
Newman, J. I., & Giardina, M. D. (2008). NASCAR and the "Southernization" of America: spectatorship, subjectivity, and the confederation of identity. *Cultural Studies/Critical Methodologies*, 8(4), 479–506.
"Obama heads for the convention." (2004, July 17). *The Economist*.
Parameswaran, R. (2009). Facing Barack Obama: Race, globalization, and transnational America. *Journal of Communication Inquiry*, 33(3), 195–205.
Pierce, G. (2004, June 1). Inside politics. *The Washington Times*, p. A05.
Pierce, G. (2008, October 15). Inside politics: Funding extremists. *The Washington Times*, p. A06.
Potter, M. (2009, August 1). Birthers' fiction takes on a life: Claims that Obama wasn't born in the USA live on in media, despite facts. *The Toronto Star*, p. A14.
Reid, T. (2008, June 11). Obama to counter Muslim rumors. *The Australian*, p. 9.
Rich, F. (30 August, 2008). Obama outwits the bloviators. *The New York Times*. P. WK10.
Rooney, K. (2008, October 16). Palin's unreal remark. *Time*. Retrieved October 15, 2009 from http://www.time.com/time/specials/2007/article/0,28804,1643290_1643292_1855139,00.html
Saul, M. (2007, December 23). I'm no Muslim, says 'Bam: Christian Barack lays rumors on his ties to rest. *Daily News* (New York), p. 23.
Serwer, A. (20 October, 2009). Pat Buchanan: White Americans are 'losing' their country. The American Prospect. Retrieved 4 February 2009 from http://www.prospect.org/csnc/blogs/tapped_archive?month=10&year=2009&base_name=pat_buchanan_white_americans_1
Silver, N. (2008, October 18). "Real" America looks different to Palin, Obama. *FiveThirtyEight.com*. Retrieved October 15, 2009 from http://www.fivethirtyeight.com/2008/10/real-america-looks-different-to-palin.html
Smith, A. C. (2004, July 27). Party's new 'rock star' to give keynote. *St. Petersburg Times* (Florida), p. 6A.
Stein, S. (2008, October 17). Michele Bachmann channels McCarthy: Obama "very anti-American," Congressional witch hunt needed. *Huffington Post*. Retrieved October 15, 2009 from http://www.huffingtonpost.com/2008/10/17/gop-rep-channels-mccarthy_n_135735.html
Steingart, G. (4 June, 2009). Obama's unfinished speech in Cairo. Spiegel. Retrieved 4 February 2009 from http://www.spiegel.de/international/world/0,1518,628547,00.html

Stelter, B. (2009, July 25). A dispute over Obama's birth lives on in the media. *The New York Times*, p. 2.

Sullivan, A. (2009a). Obama still isn't president in the South: Denying the leader's American birth is just another form of racism. *The Times* (London), p. 4. (9 August).

Sullivan, A. (2009b). Whose country. *The Daily Dish*. Retrieved October 22, 2009 from http://andrewsullivan.theatlantic.com/the_daily_dish/2009/10/whose-country.html

Thrush, G. (2009, July 31). 58 percent of GOP not sure/doubt Obama born in US. *Politico*. Retrieved October 15, 2009 from http://www.politico.com/blogs/glennthrush/ 0709/58_of_GOP_not_suredont_beleive_Obama_born_in_US.html

Tomasky, M. (2009). The unencumbered man. *The New York Review of Books*. July 2.

Wangsness, L. (2008, January 26). Obama fighting false e-mail rumors in South Carolina: Some voters say they are not sure of candidate's faith. *The Boston Globe*, p. A8.

Whannel, G. (2001). *Media sports stars: Masculinities and moralities*. London: Routledge.

Winant, G. (28 July, 2009). The Birthers in Congress: Seventeen men and women who are either enabling the fringe movement or having trouble admitting Obama is president. *Salon*. Retrieved 4 February 2009 from http://www.salon.com/news/feature/2009/07/28/birther_enablers/

Younge, G. (2 Auguest, 2009). To engage the Birther fantasists is futile; to dismiss them, reckless. *The Guardian* (London). Retrieved 4 February 2009 from http://www.guardian.co.uk/commentisfree/2009/aug/02/obama-birthers-us-presidency

Part Three

Categories on the Board: "Muslims You Never Knew"

Nine

The Undercover Muslim:
An African American Perspective on Transitions of Muslim Identity

Preacher Moss

Preamble

To give clarity to the level of this conversation I'm about to offer you, the reader, let's start with the fact that this isn't actually a conversation, but a "covertsation." Should you be identified and caught with this information you can tell the authorities that you got it from Preacher Moss, and they'll let you go because they only have a reference to me potentially being a funny black man. I suggest you stick to that line as well. I do. The truth is that comedy is my cover, and education and social change have been my mission from a very young age and disposition. The enemy doesn't like liberation talk, thus our conversations is covert.

I would like to mute the argument that people will say that I'm not a scholar, cleric, mufti, mulana, imam, or minister on the issue of Muslim identity, but I am indeed much more. I'm brutally, and humorously, honest, void of having to observe ceremonial good will, or pleasantries. People don't always know I'm Muslim, so sometimes I let them blame the liberation talk on the "black guy" most of the time. No disrespect, but the battle for the meaningful transitioning of the Muslim image will be won in the streets, and schools, and educational formats where people are able to understand the value of maintaining the humanization. To further understand what I'm saying it, this battle won't be won by the Muslims, but quite possibly in spite of the Muslim community. Let's stop here a moment, because I can see where you may possibly need a framing of our "covertsation." You may have momentarily forgotten that you are talking to an "Undercover Muslim" (UM).

What Does Being an Undercover Muslim Actually Mean?

Being an Undercover Muslim means several things depending what side of the Muslim image you find yourself on. First, the main characteristic of the UM is that despite historical attempts to silence, and diminish value, the UM has developed an affinity to create a similar or superior understanding to reverse the processes that would attempt to oppress, or worse, silence. Indeed, the greatest aspect of the UM is that he/she is highly efficient at understanding and engaging multiple domains. This would be especially true for the ultimate UM, the African American here in the United States, or anywhere in the world.

Second, the UM is a specialist at engagement protocols as they would apply to liberating the overall human condition. Islam propagates that our work is for the benefit of all of humanity, the same as Prophet Muhammad (Sallalahu Alayhi Wa Salaam (SAW)) was sent as a mercy for all of mankind.

Third, and possibly the most important, is that the UM has undergone the actual program of dehumanization, and at some level remains to struggle, thrive, and ultimately succeed despite the program. Like every superhero you may have grown up watching, or idolizing, all of them had some kind of superpowers. The superpower of the UM is using history as a means of taking marginalization and allowing it to be the means by which we acquire information needed for organizational, political, and infrastructural changes. The UM has by nature become a specialist at acquiring skills for gathering intelligence in a multi-domain knowledge capacity.

The best of the UMs are encyclopedic in their historical knowledge of how dominant minorities have captured and manipulated the hearts, minds, and spirits of those they would not serve, but rather have serve them. To be real, the Muslim issue is clouded by the fact that (1) many Muslims on one hand only have book or Google knowledge of their oppression, specifically here in North America, and (2) those that would begrudge religious freedom here in the 21st century, do so now because current events have allowed them to expedite a process that would have taken them untold years to develop. On both cases, in some varying degrees they are pretenders to the throne as they seek opportunities to cheat history and outright re-write it. Let me give you a bit of a history lesson.

Something a Pimp Told Me...

A long time ago on one of my travels through life, a pimp named Divine befriended me. I know he took his name from the mercurial figure named Father Divine. Father Divine was precursor to the idea of the mega preachers that we presently witness on television today. Divine used to try to pass himself off as being a part of the 5% Nation of Islam, later called the Nation Gods and Earth. Anyway, a prostitute came over to Divine to complain that a "customer" wanted to pay X, when she wanted Y. Divine told her to do it for X and he would make up the difference with a nice dinner. She went for it. Immediately after this exchange he told me something that I had forgotten until a Muslim brother named Dawud Al-Haqq would repeat to me as an UM. Divine told me, "Shorty, believe this sho' nuff. As long as you got people needing something, they'll act funny for the money, and strange for the change."

Flash Forward...September 10, 2001

I was analyzing the fact that U.S. policy toward kicking the snot out of Iraq was getting out of hand, and the domestic issues confronting us at the time needed attention, as the budget surplus was getting a lot smaller, but I felt no one was noticing. I could tell the difference because it seemed everyone had begun hating on the poor since the presidential election of 2000 was concluded, and George W. Bush was inaugurated. Now keep in mind this was before I was a full-fledged UM. I was doing my internship as an African American and a Muslim. Ironically, the only Muslims America was possibly afraid of, at the time, were Minister Louis Farrahkan, and the lingering transformative memories of Malcolm X. While the world was asleep on the eve of the biggest terrorist attack in U.S. history, I was contemplating taking my mission to bring together African American Muslims, Immigrant Muslims, and eventually non-Muslims through humor. This mission would two years later be launched, "CODE: Allah Made Me Funny-The Official Muslim Comedy Tour." It was ambitious for me to accept the mission of bring people together, but not as important as it was to lay the ground work of being able to effectively address several facts.

1. African American Muslims are marginalized as African Americans in America, and ignored as African American Muslims. It would seem that the average citizen reads "African American" and stops. Symbolically, it's as Joe Citizen says, "I stop at what I know."
2. African American Muslims are overlooked Muslims by many Muslim countries and cultures because of the tendency to only want to understand and engage in what is comfortable, and value added to

their understanding, not what's different, and potentially valuable. Sadly, we continue to have the differentiation of mosques not upon the relevancy of scholarship, and community value, but maintenance of the "cultural imperative."

Thus the UM constantly deals with the potential for marginalization, with the threat of being invisible, while using these things as a means of growing intelligence. This is the heavy lifting of growing value on both sides of the Muslim image conundrum. The only way to achieve success in transitioning the Muslim image is to hold it up as a "mirror of human history" and not an aberration disconnected from it.

History Lesson on Muslim Transition Efforts

The concept of UM didn't start with 9/11 or me. Let me clarify that the original UMs were Muslims brought here as slaves. In keeping this real, they weren't undercover...*they were under siege*. I categorize them differently, and respectfully, as they were forced to do more than the requisites for the modern UM, and they were not affected by a definitive event. Quite simply, they were the defining event. The "Original Undercover Muslims," and the "Run for Cover Native Americans" were dealt a raw hand, left to be history rather than understand it. Their excellence is that in their many expressions they were able to achieve incredible results despite their obvious handicaps.

The idea of Muslim transition has always been integrated with the emerging thought of making meaningful contributions. The second generation of UMs was actually from the Ahmaddiya Movement in Islam, which espoused the idea of a multi-racial society based on equality and justice. Islam was the context for achieving this goal. They were true UMs as they were a collaborative of African American, Subcontinent Asians that had migrated to the United States and were propagating Islam in the early 1900s. This was also the period of introduction for Eastern/Oriental religions staking a claim in the open landscapes of religious expression available after the Civil War. What is important is that it was established as a reformist religion that, indeed, worked with mainstream organizations, and ideology. Whether the movement of the time was the Woman Suffrage Movement, Unionization, protection of children, or equal access to resources the Ahmaddiya Movement of Islam had obvious synergies. Being that the understanding of Muslims, and Muslim countries, at this time grew out of the understanding from a Muslim world that was largely colonized at this time; its effectiveness was not fully realized. If you're reading about this transitional movement of Muslims here in the United States for the first time, don't worry or feel embarrassed. It just means that the dominant minority in your town has managed to do their job, with expert skill and execution. To really understand UM, (1) be clear that the UM has never been the possession of one group, and (2) you, with certainty, need to know some history about the "haters." There are "haters" on both sides of the Muslim image. The "haters" are Muslim and non-Muslim. The dominant minorities of your city, town, state, or country are as uncreative, as they are unrelenting. The formula is pretty basic. Here in the United States the cookie-cutter approach to valuing minority groups is a simple two-step dance of "Annihilate-Vilify, Annihilate-Vilify, Annihilate-Vilify." Be it Hip-Hop, R&B, Blues, Tejano, Ska, or Tango, this dance can be executed to any form of music of the racially, economically, religiously, and culturally oppressed. My personal favorite is Samba.

If you carefully examine the "Annihilate-Destroy" tandem, you see that it has no room for reason, understanding, logic, or fairness, unless you are part of the team doing the annihilating, and vilifying. Some would say this strategy keeps us a stone's throw away from blasting ourselves back to the Stone Age. Can you say yabaa dabba doo? If so, can you translate it into Arabic for me?

If you need a better understanding of this dance then ask yourself questions like:

- Why don't you ever see black people hawking/promoting tanning lotions?
- Why don't you ever see Native Americans in commercials selling real estate?
- Why don't you see Asians in promotions for Uncle Ben's Rice?
- When was the last time you saw gay men highlighted in condom ads?

The reason is that your local dominant minority has excelled at controlling the image or deleting images that may induce historical recall of any oppression, denial of life, liberty, access, and opportunity. In other words, the dominant minority doesn't want to do stupid things like…tell the truth, especially on themselves. I developed a not-so-funny, but true skit to assist in understanding the difficulties of transitioning for the Muslim Image, but also for minority images in general. I called it, "The Dominant Minority Report."

Fade In
Two gentlemen stand across the street watching another gentleman load items into his house. They stare intently as they appeared to be confused. Both gentlemen wear shirts displaying the words: "Preserve the dominant minority or else." They shake their heads simultaneously.

Gentleman 1

Will you just look at that! Who does that guy think he is?!

Gentleman 2

Exactly, who does he think is? (beat) Umm who is he?

Gentleman 1

I've never seen him before. I don't even know where he's from, but I know he's not from here.

Gentleman 2

Well, let me take the bull by horns and find out what his intent is.

Gentleman 2 departs across the street toward the unknown gentleman. After a brief conversation Gentleman 2 pulls out a gun and shoots the unknown gentleman. He crosses back over the street rejoining Gentleman 1.

Gentleman 1

Looks like that went well.

Gentleman 2

It actually did. I had to shoot him though. You can't take chances.

Gentleman 1

Well, was he going to present any problems to our mode of operation?

Gentleman 2

I don't know, but this way we have plenty of time to make up problems he would have caused us.

Gentleman 1

Yeah. You've gotta be forward thinking these days.

Fade Out

The toughest mission for the UM is to take all of the unnatural challenges of society and humanize them just enough whereby people focus back on their core values just enough to have them realize that we all have value. In a nutshell the transition of the Muslim image/identity is an all-consuming battle to keep the image human in the eyes of the mainstream, as opposed to mired in the lies in the mainstream (controlled by the Dominant Minority). Maybe the issue of the Muslim image has more to do with the motivations, intent, and negative agenda driving the fear rather than the fear itself. Why would I say that? Let us continue our very, very profound "covertsation," if you will.

"They Act Funny for the Money, and Strange for the Change": Understanding the Anti-Muslim Industrial Complex

No before I get started, I know that the astute among you will claim that I got this saying from my pimp friend, Divine. That's true. Next some among you will say that I am calling those beneficiaries, propagandists, and proponents of the Anti-Muslim Complex whores. That's true, but not just yet. My point here is that the Muslim image has long been a value added proposition for those that would fully commit to it. The proliferation of experts on the issue of Islam, terrorists, Islamist, Islamo-Fascism is in abundance. Let's face facts: *It's big business to hate Muslims, and advance whatever theories are out there to keep business robust.* On the extreme, at the other end of the spectrum this complex allows some of the non-lettered people within the religion their 15 minutes of fame or whenever the detonator goes off. My point is that when peace, as the most viable option to human suffering, is no longer value added, we are no longer a stone's throw from the stone age, we are the stone age. Hence, you may have to decide for yourself, in light of this lunacy, whether it is better to be "Underground (type your own definition here)" or just plain ole' buried under the ground. The potential lies in all of us.

And Now for My Dismount...

There are many pieces of information, and philosophies about understanding transitional aspects of the Muslim identity. I chose to provide a historical and conceptual understanding as to not how we got here but how we may get out. Admittedly, it would be awesome to give some great inspirational message to you the reader. Ideally, I would like to blow you away with some profound statement on the meaning of life and love. However, it would blow my cover, as I'm still on a mission as an "Undercover Muslim." Nonetheless, I'll leave you two pieces of advice from my many travels and experiences.

1. In the critical moments, when you have to lay it all on the line, don't look at your condition to change, but look inside yourself to change the condition. Keep as pure a heart as you can.
2. Beware, and guard yourself from being someone who, "Acts Funny for the Money, and Strange for the Change."

Well, I'm done. It's time for me to get back to walking the earth. You may see me disguised as a Muslim, a black man, a Native American, illiteracy, poverty, or the guy that cleans your windows at the end of the expressway. I am all of these things and at the same time none. Tell the Dominant Minority I'll see them later, because they won't be able to see me. As Salaamu Alaikum.

Ten

Faith or Fight:
Islam in the African American Community

Samaa Abdurraqib

When considering the idea "Muslims in America," what inevitably comes to mind are the Muslim immigrants who have, over the course of several decades, come to the United States and become a part—whether welcomed or not—of U.S. society. What, in most cases, does not come to mind are the Muslims who have been here since the early beginnings of the New World; the Muslims we would not consider immigrants; the Muslims who are "home-grown" Americans. These Muslims, the ones whose images we are often unable to conjure, are the African American Muslims who have been rooted in the United States for centuries. More recent estimates place the number of Muslims in America at approximately six million. According to Sherman Jackson (2005), approximately 42% of these Muslims in America were "blackamericans" (Jackson, 2005, p. 23). Considering the large number, not recognizing the history black people have with Islam is a gross oversight.

As a person who falls into this category and who grew up recognizing that African American Muslims were an integral part of the Muslim American landscape, I think overlooking this segment of the Muslim population in the United States is a bit nonsensical. The first Muslims I was cognitively aware of were African American Muslims; many of the Muslims my parents told me stories about were African American; the first images of Muslims I was exposed to were African American. To be fair, when my family moved to the Midwest, the Muslim communities represented in the Masajid were overwhelmingly non-black, mostly immigrant Muslims. However, being in the minority in these spaces didn't make me question the legitimacy of the nexus between my heritage and my faith. And although there weren't overwhelming large numbers of African American Sunni Muslims in the city I lived in, my Islam still made sense in the black communities I moved within. Islam was considered as part of a legacy of black expressions of faith that diverged from normative Christianity. Islam was not a foreign presence in the black communities I grew up in.

Although I was young, and relatively unaware of the discourses of religion and faith that were at work in my communities, I am certain that my faith was seen as just that—an expression of spirituality and religiosity. And while the political history of Islam in the black community was not ignored, this history was understood as a sort of seamless lineage. Of course, this is not to say that everyone in the black communities I was a member of completely understood the tenets of Islam or that they understood Islam as theologically acceptable—I mean, black Christians still believed their path was the right path, just as black Muslims believed their path was the right path. This is just to say that Islam was a recognizable expression of faith and religion in the black community. It was not only seen as an expression of a political consciousness. People around me, as far as I can recall, acknowledged and claimed historical figures who were black and some derivation of Muslim—people like Malcolm X and Elijah Muhammad, for example —as both political and religious leaders from our shared African American past.

At this point, I think it is important for me to highlight that I am *not* espousing a position on the Nation of Islam (NOI) or any other early incarnations of black Islam. While I am an African American Sunni Muslim, I don't see my task in this chapter to be one in which I pass judgment on people's faith and/or their expression of that faith. I see my goal in this piece as twofold. I first want to point to the ways in which the legacy of Islam in the black community has been overlooked. And I want to offer up what I see as two primary reasons for this oversight.

When Spike Lee's 1992 film *Malcolm X* was released, it seemed that mainstream society expressed a new (or renewed) interest in Islam as a political force in African American communities. The film received excellent reviews and was one of the most popular films of the season. Malcolm X, as both a political and a religious figure, has been well known among black people, but to bring his life, his politics, and his religious practices into mainstream light seemed like, well, a fruitful but perhaps risky undertaking. Many of us, both black and white, recall the era of Malcolm's popularity as an era of opposing viewpoints on the Black Civil Rights movement—one side advocating peace, the other side advocating violence. Malcolm stood on one side of the spectrum, while Martin Luther King, Jr. stood on the other. One photograph that, for me, aptly illustrates the division between these two camps is the "Malcolm and Martin" photo which depicts the two Civil Rights leaders shaking hands upon meeting on March 26th, 1964.[1] Prior to the meeting, Malcolm X had broken ties with the NOI and had expressed interest in working with Civil Rights leaders he (and other members of the NOI) had previously disparaged. However, despite the realities of Malcolm's political and religious shifts, the photograph of the two leaders smiling and shaking hands seems to represent the two different factions (as iconicized by the two leaders) coming together and shaking hands as if to say "we don't like each other, but we can be cordial." And this is how Malcolm is cemented in many of our minds: a political leader, a black nationalist, and a black separatist who belonged to the NOI. In all of my early experiences learning about Malcolm outside of my house—inside was a different matter—Malcolm's faith and spirituality were rarely addressed. I eagerly awaited the release of Spike Lee's film, hoping that it would portray what I knew to be the *full* life of Malcolm X.

I was about 15 when the film was released. To me, *Malcolm X* (the film) represented a groundbreaking moment. I cannot articulate the excitement in our household: *finally* we were going to see ourselves—our complete selves—rendered on the screen. We'd seen our share of mainstream films about African American history and life. We'd seen a few mainstream films about Muslims (many of them maligning). But never had we seen a cinematic representation of African American Muslims. For me and my family, our connection with Malcolm circled around a shared religious affiliation as well as a racial affiliation. My brothers and I had been taught about Malcolm's life from a very young age. Both my older brother and I had read his autobiography at a fairly young age. His life with the NOI and his subsequent conversion to Sunni Islam left quite an impression on us. I can still remember the day we went to see it—November 19th, two weeks after my birthday. Going to the theater to see the movie was quite a big deal. We didn't go to the theater often, definitely not as a family. As we walked into the theater and sat down, I felt excitement and I was proud to see someone who was so important to my history immortalized on film.[2]

While Lee's movie did receive good reviews, one criticism that I personally have is that the film focused on Malcolm's politics in his early life and merely skimmed over his religious life: his religious investment in the NOI; his pilgrimage to Mecca; his later life as a Sunni Muslim. This isn't to say that one aspect of his life is more important than the other. Quite the contrary. What I find problematic is the way in which these two aspects of his life are presented as fragmentary—as if his politics didn't inform his faith and vice versa. As if, being Muslim, he could only deploy a political ideology and not a religious one. And, on the other hand, when his spirituality is represented in the film, it is presented as being devoid of any political inspiration. For me, by rendering these two parts of his life as incommensurable, the historical importance and the potency of Malcolm's political and spiritual influences were slightly diminished.

I believe that Lee's treatment of Malcolm was indicative of widespread mainstream perspectives of the history of Islam in African American history. Generally speaking, when Islam is discussed or taught, experiences of black Muslims in the United States are missing. On the other side of the coin, when black history is discussed or taught, black incarnations of Islam as a spiritual and religious force are neglected. And thus we're left with a strange gap in our knowledge—our understanding of the history of Muslims in the United States and, even more crucial in these post-9/11 times, our understanding of what "American Islam" can look like.

More often that not, when taught, Islam in the black community falls into the category of African American political movements and ideologies. At least this is how I was exposed to people like Malcolm X while I was in my elementary, secondary, and college classrooms. That is to say, it is *when* we learned about Islam in the black community. To be honest, figures like Malcolm X were considered a bit too militant for my elementary and secondary classrooms. If we learned about Malcolm at all he was, as mentioned earlier, cast as the antithesis to Martin Luther King, Jr., the other side of the peaceful protest coin. When dealing with African American communities, Islam, it appeared to me, could either be a faith or a political way of life. Yet, the fact is that black Muslims are generally never mentioned in discussions of Islam or Islam in the United States; what we're left with is a gap that fails to address the full religious lives of African Americans in the United States while simultaneously failing to address the presence and evolution of Islam in the United States.

Islam has been practiced within the United States since some of the first Africans were brought over on slave ships. Some slaves from West African countries had already, as a result of trade, travel, and invasion, been practicing Islam. Historians and scholars debate the numbers and percentages of Muslim slaves brought to the "New World"—Dennis Walker, for example, places the number somewhere between 15 and 20%. Regardless of the exact number, the mere presence of these Muslims demonstrates that Islam was a religion that was a part of the black experience in the Americas. Many of these slaves knew Arabic; many of them brought over pieces of the Qur'an with them. Others who were Hafiz (a title of respect for a person who memorized the entire Qur'an) carried their knowledge of the Qur'an with them.[3]

While there have been many recent books written on the Muslim presence in the United States during slavery,[4] the mention of Islam in the black community has historically been omitted in the classroom, in discussions of religion, slavery, and race in the United States. This erasure—disconnecting African Americans from an Islamic past—began early during slavery. There were clearly Muslim slaves brought over, scholars reference and cite slave traders who recognize differences and religious related hierarchies among their slaves.[5] Yet, records are scarce. In an early article, Michael Gomez (1994) attributes this scarcity to historical practices. First, he writes, slave owners and whites during the antebellum period "were ignorant of the Islamic faith, did not accurately record the variegated cultural expressions of African slaves" (Gomez, 1994, p. 672). Gomez continues by arguing that the "cumulative evidence suggests that such observers could distinguish the Muslims from other slaves but had neither the skills nor the interest to record detailed information about them" (Gomez, 1994, p. 672). Another reason he cites is a lack of dialog between African and North American historical scholars. Whatever the case may be, the paucity of the records gives the impression that Islam is new to America, that the only Islam that has come to America has been brought by recent immigrants.

In all actuality, Islam has been and continues to be a strong force in the African American community. The number of Sunni Muslims has grown as well as the numbers of people who practice different incarnations of Islam. But a lack of circulated information about the history of Islam and black people in the United States leads to substantive gaps in our understanding of both Islam in America and the religious lives of black people in America. These omissions leave us with only the mainstream stories about black people's Islamic practices. And, unfortunately, this has meant that Islam, as a force within the black community, has generally been spotlighted in terms of its political agendas and trajectories rather than its spiritual and religious importance.

In my estimation, the marriage of Islam and politics in the black community, at least as far as the "external world" is concerned, comes from two different places: racism and xenophobia. Gomez's arguments help solidify the racist implications in these omissions by tracing them historically. In the past, African Americans who chose alternate expressions of blackness—expressions that didn't adhere to the dominant Christian society of the United States—were seen as being subversive. Their subversion was threatening. Early incarnations of Islam in the black community, such as the NOI, for example, were seen as threats to the political fiber of the United States. The response to these movements illustrated the extent to which black determination, through religion and politics, was problematic for those who had the power to legitimize religion.

In looking at the more recent side of the U.S. history (especially post-9/11 history) I would say that the nature of this exclusion has changed. This is, of course, in part not only due to the rising number of Muslim immigrants resettling here in the United States, but it is also, and more largely I would say, due to the persuasive and persisting post-9/11 rhetoric that insists on asserting that Islam is a foreign and transplanted religion. This kind of rhetoric is a necessity in the "War on Terror" because it first allows us to construct an image of what "the enemy" looks like—one whose specific nationality may be ambiguous, but they are definitely brown and definitely not American-born. This rhetoric then allows Islamophobic people in the United States to deploy their own hate speech and hate rhetoric, demanding that Muslim immigrants "go back home" and letting them know that they "don't belong here." In order for this rhetoric to have any staying power, Islam in the black community must be forgotten.

Viewing Islam as a vehicle for nationalist politics in the black community began, generally speaking, at the turn of the 20th century when early incarnations of "black Islam" began to crop up. Organizations like Noble Drew Ali's Moorish Science Temple of America played an influential role in the political landscape during this time. They appeared on the scene as a sort of precursor to larger Afrocentric movements, such as Marcus Garvey's Back-to-Africa movement of the 1920s. Although these different incarnations of Islam started early in the 20th century, most of these emergences, in our cultural imaginary, are eclipsed by the massively and politically charged Nation of Islam.

The Nation of Islam, being the most well-known black Muslim organization, probably doesn't need an explanation. But I'd like to present a brief and partial presentation of their beliefs and politics. In 1930, a man named Wallace Dean Fard appeared in a predominantly African American community in Detroit. He was a business man—a salesman. He claimed to have come from Mecca but was ambiguous about his nationality, ethnicity, and life in general. He began proselytizing to the lower-class African Americans in this community, telling them that he was their "brother" and that he could tell them about their homeland. His proselytizing contained messages about diet (abstain from pork, for example), behavior (no alcohol, adultery, smoking, and dancing), on dress and on ethics (hard work, family, respect for authority, etc.). Early on, he identified himself as a prophet who "had a startling message of African American identity and destiny" (Turner, 1997, p. 149). As his preaching "mission" gained momentum, Fard named his organization the Allah Temple of Islam (ATI). Fard's message grew out of his idea that whites and blacks in America would one day face off in what would be a final battle, which he called the "War of Armageddon." He told his audience that the only way to win this war was to become Muslim, to "convert to their 'natural religion [Islam] and to reclaim their original identity as Muslims'" (Turner, 1997, p. 150). In August of 1931, W.D. Fard gave a speech in which he renamed the "black men of North America," rather than Negroes, the black men of North America were members of the "lost tribe of Shabazz" who were taken from Mecca some 379 years prior. This speech introduced Elijah Muhammad—born Elijah Poole—to W.D. Fard and the Islam preached by this self-proclaimed prophet. After having several run-ins with law enforcement agencies, Fard left Detroit and turned the organization over to Elijah Muhammad.

Elijah Muhammad led the organization from 1934 to 1975, the year he died. Under his leadership the ATI became the NOI. During Muhammad's reign, the NOI cemented its hold in the African American community as a religious alternative to the hegemony of Christianity. Muhammad and other NOI members saw Christianity as a tool of oppression—further distancing African Americans from their heritage and roots, keeping them tied to the chains of slavery. In order to break these chains, members of the NOI were required to reject all traces of the dominant white culture from their lives. Members rejected European American forms of dress, education, and politics. The NOI even asked members to reject their slave names—Christian names given to slaves by their masters—to symbolize emancipation from white slavery and ideologies. In both their religious practices and in their political practices, the NOI was a separatist organization. For those who practiced with the NOI, they saw themselves as combining their politics with their faith. As Sulayman Nyang (1991) writes, NOI members saw their faith as "a political weapon, a strategy for physical and spiritual survival" (Nyang, 1991, p. 239). So while their religious tenets were strongly political and strongly separatist, they were still able to combine spiritual aspects of Islam as well as ethical aspects of Islam (dress, diet, and modesty, for example). This rejection of dominant European American religion and thought was, as can be imagined, threatening. The threat—of black militancy, of racial upheaval, and so on—made it easier to ignore the religious and faith-oriented aspects of the organization.

Throughout most of its time in the public spotlight, the NOI has been seen as a "cult" that was a by-product of and was fueled by white racism in the United States. This "cult" in turn fueled hatred in black communities. Rather than considering NOI as an expression of faith and religiousness in the black community, critics saw the group as a political force which was "neither legitimately religious nor authentically Islam" (Curtis, 2006, p. 5).

Critiques leveled at the Nation weren't solely from outside the black community. Both Roy Wilkins of the NAACP and C. Eric Lincoln, an African American religious scholar, argued that the NOI came from a place of hatred and was a response to white racism and hegemony.

Acknowledging the NOI's political goals as primary casts this particular incarnation of Islam in the black community as empty in terms of religious motivations and inspirations. In fact, the Islam practiced by the NOI was seen as a means to an end—the end being black political power, black nationhood, and black self-determinism. It was seen as being, first and foremost, a subversive response to the dominant white Judeo-Christian ideology. In fact, in Lincoln's seminal text, *The Black Muslims in America* (1961), he writes that "It would be difficult, probably impossible, to separate the Black Muslim teachings on Christianity from those on race. A fundamental tenet of the sect is that all Black Men are Muslims by nature and that Christianity is a white man's religion. Thus there is not even a *possibility* of awakened Black Men accepting Christianity" (Lincoln, 1961, p. 76, italics in original). In his estimation, black nationalist politics was inseparable from the black Islam of the time.[6]

Critiquing this inseparability seems quite ironic to me, especially considering the political climate witnessed in the United States today. We're currently experiencing a moment in our political history where politicians, if they want to be elected and/or stay in office, are obligated to cater to the needs and desires of powerful religious groups; groups whose loyalty to a candidate hinges on the candidate's ability to formulate a political platform based not only upon policies but also upon politically charged morality issues. Edward Curtis IV argues that in Lincoln's case, politics and religion were "diametrically opposed…politics were this-worldly and religion[s] were otherworldly." For Lincoln, Curtis continues, "'true' religion dealt mainly with issues of theology, salvation, and meaning" (Curtis, 2002, p. 2).[7] Yet theology, salvation, and meaning are not only reserved for Judeo-Christian faiths or even Sunni Islam. Members of the Nation of Islam, as I mentioned earlier, felt their practices offered salvation from enslaved mindsets and gave new meaning to their lives as black people living in America. But Lincoln's segregation of faith and politics demonstrates the ways that black people's passion for religion, when mixed with a passion for racial politics, immediately becomes uncomfortable and dangerously subversive. And the repercussions of this segregation were and continue to be apparent. Aligning black Muslims with vehement political ideologies results in a double erasure. On the one hand, Muslims (foreign Muslims, Sunni Muslims, etc.) have tried to distance themselves from the Nation, calling it, as other critiques did, not a "true" religion. For example, Curtis cites a letter written by an Algerian Muslim that implores readers not to "confuse the sect of Muhammad with that of true Islam. Islam does not preach hate...it does not preach racism, it only calls for love, peace, and understanding" (Curtis, 2006, p. 5). This letter was published in a historically black newspaper in the late 1960s, but even today, immigrant Muslims and Sunni Muslims fervently distance themselves from the NOI and Louis Farrakhan by calling the NOI a political group. Another interesting, more recent and non-Islamic example of this is the controversy that cropped up surrounded President Barack Obama's former reverend, Jeremiah Wright. During Obama's bid for the presidency, Wright's sermons were highly scrutinized and several quotes were taken out of context and deemed "un-American." Wright immediately became a "poster child" for black present-day militancy, and the Right Wing accused him of using his church as a breeding ground for black militants.

I'd like to return to the figure of Malcolm X in order to illustrate my point. While in primary and secondary school, if I learned about Malcolm X at all, I learned about him within the context of Black History month, namely in units about the Black Civil Rights Movement of the 1960s.[8] In these units, we learned about Malcolm X in just the ways I mentioned earlier: the militant antithesis to Martin Luther King, Jr.'s peaceful and pacifist Civil Rights Movement.[9] We're not really taught about the NOI, Malcolm's religion, his pilgrimage, or anything remotely related to his religion. It's as if there is no real correlation between his religiosity and his politics. Meanwhile, we learn that Martin Luther King was revered and, although not in detail, we learn that the Civil Rights Movement—at least as it is conceptualized in the mainstream—was built upon the foundation of black churches.

This treatment of Malcolm X is not limited to primary and secondary schools. I've taken college courses on African American history that segregate Malcolm's politics from his religion in similar ways. These courses differ from our black history units in grade school in that they do provide more in-depth information on the Civil Rights Movement in general and Malcolm's politics specifically. However, we still only delve into his politics. His religion is not described as faith; it is only described as the catalyst for his "black supremacist" politics. Malcolm X fares no better in religion classes. Now, to be honest, I have never taken a class on religion that even mentions the U.S. incarnations of Islam. Both classes on "world religions" and classes on "eastern religions" present Islam as a foreign religion that—if at all mentioned in the U.S. context—was brought to the United States by recent immigrants. However, I was recently told by a friend that in her university course on "eastern religions," the professor both talked about Islam in the U.S. context and spent a brief amount of time discussing Malcolm X and the NOI.[10]

While C. Eric Lincoln disparages the NOI for its political, rather than religious leanings, he is at least able and willing to trace Islam in the United States back beyond the emergence of the NOI, something mainstream histories of Islam in the United States fall short of doing. Both he and a few other historians[11] begin their discussion of black Islam with the Moorish Science Temple movement, whose leader, Noble Drew Ali, proselytized that a new religion would liberate the "everyday-Negroes" living in the United States. The Moorish Science Temple was founded in 1913 and attempted to bring salvation to African Americans by connecting them to their national origin. In essence, Ali configured a new identity for black people living in the United States—they were now Asiatic black people, or more specifically, Moorish Americans. Ali felt that constructing a new identity, a new lineage for African Americans would help liberate their consciousnesses from the racist environment of the United States. To this end, Ali created "Nationality and Identification Cards," which were adorned with Islamic symbols (star and crescent). Lincoln writes that the cards "announced that the bearer honored 'all the Divine Prophets, Jesus, Muhammed, Buddha, and Confucius' and pronounced upon [the followers] 'the blessings of the God of our Father, Allah'" (1961, pp. 51–52). The card identified Ali's followers as "'Moslem[s] under the Divine Laws of the Holy Koran of Mecca, Love, Truth, Peace, Freedom, and Justice'" (p. 52). The card also proclaimed that the holders had, in a sense, dual citizenship—not only did they belong to the "Moorish" or "Asiatic" nation, but it also declared that the holder was "A CITIZEN OF THE UNITED STATES" (p. 52).

Although the religion Ali created was in many ways considered apocryphal—the Qur'an he spoke of, for example, was a religious text of his own creation—practitioners saw themselves as a part of a larger, global Islam. Ali saw this new "Moorish" faith as a complete way of life, a mobilization of "eclectic *religious, cultural, and political* motifs to construct a new black American cultural and political identity" (Turner 72, italics added). So while a black nationalist ideology was crucial for the formation of this new identity, black nationalist politics were not isolated from religion and faith. Ali recognized that Islam, as it was practiced globally, was considered a *deen*, or a way of life. Therefore, his inspiration for his movement came from the notion of Islam "as a global religious, political, and cultural phenomenon" (Turner 72).

C. Eric Lincoln also briefly recognizes a lesser known and often overlooked group who claimed religious ties to the both the Moorish Temple and the NOI: The Five Percenters. To be honest, the belief system professed by the Five Percenters is still somewhat of an enigma to me. However, it seems to be summarizable: black men and women as supreme beings, or gods, and the 5% who recognize this "truth" have the key to the most essential piece of knowledge. Hence the name, Five Percenters. According to their ideology, the world is divided into three groups. 85% of the world does not understand who the "true gods" are; 10% of the world knows the truth but preaches lies; and 5% are the "poor righteous teachers" who understand and preach that the black man is the "true god." This doctrine is, of course, seen as apocryphal to Sunni Muslims, and perhaps even to the NOI. The Five Percenters were considered an off-shoot of the Nation. The group saw its start around 1965 when Clarence X, a disenfranchised member of the NOI, began to preach his own interpretations of NOI and Islamic doctrines.

Growing up, I spent the formative part of my life (late 1980s–early 1990s) amidst a resurgence of Afrocentricity. I was raised in a rather large, fairly diverse Midwestern city and this resurgence manifested itself as a celebration of all things African and African American. This was presented in a variety of areas of life: dress (kente cloth, "black" medallions), music (Afrocentric rap), academic thought (Frances Cress Welsing, Mualana Karenga, Haki Madhabuti, to name a few intellectual forces from this time), and religion. Afrocentric religious expressions meant, at least as far as I could tell, an emergence (or rather, reemergence) of the NOI as well as other black variances of Islam—the Ansaaru Allah[12] and the Five Percenters. I saw these religious expressions as a nexus of black religion, culture, philosophy, and politics. And although the young me wasn't exactly aware of the complexity of their beliefs (beliefs that I feebly tried to articulate and summarize previously), I knew that those who aligned themselves religiously with these groups saw their religious practices as contained under the "umbrella" of Islam. While our faiths weren't exactly synonymous—me as a Sunni Muslim, and them as a Fiver Percenter, for example—those I met and knew saw our spiritual paths as being similar; we belonged to the same religious legacy and tradition.

This common legacy seemed to be founded in a shared black identity and in, what was considered to be, a rejection of hegemonic forms of religiosity. This era of Afrocentricity had its resonances with earlier Afrocentric movements—to truly be a black person, or an African, it was necessary to reject the cultural, religious, and intellectual manifestations of whiteness and to, instead, embrace African cultural productions and symbols. Falling in line with this call, the new Afrocentric look became all the rage. During my last two years in junior high, I can remember a marked change in fashion—gone were all of the large, gold accoutrements. Black medallions bearing symbols of Africa and kente cloth took their place. Women began to wrap their heads and traded tighter clothes for looser ones adorned with "ethnic" prints. These expressions of Afrocentricity were welcomed by my parents (and other older

African Americans in my circles) with open arms because they saw it as being connected to the Black Power Movement many of them participated in.

This historical moment made quite an impact on me because it played a large role in the framing of my sense of identity and cultural awareness. Shortly after I was born, my parents left the ethnic and cultural diversity of New York City for the relatively homogenous cultural landscape of Ohio. While I was almost always surrounded by other African Americans, I only knew of two other African American Muslim families—one of which traveled from New York with us. The fact that my burgeoning awareness coincided with this shift in black cultural life meant that I saw both my blackness and my Muslimness as fitting into the large landscape of what it meant to be a black person in the United States. My Islam wasn't antithetical to my blackness, and vice versa. So, while the vast majority of my friends and classmates were black and Christian, my Islam made sense to them in some way; my Islam was a manifestation of embracing my "African" roots. On a regular basis, I could walk around the city and be greeted with "As Salamu Alaikum" by black people who may or may not have identified as Muslim. My *hijab* and looser clothing afforded me a kind of respect in African American neighborhoods—rather than having to fend off misogynist slurs or xenophobic epithets, I was called "sister" and was treated, generally speaking, respectfully.

Black and Islamic heritage/history was also affirmed and confirmed by the different ways black Islam manifested itself in my communities. I could ride through certain key intersections in certain neighborhoods and, while stopped at a light, I would inevitably be met by a brother from the NOI selling newspapers and other wares. I could walk downtown and be guaranteed to share words and brief conversations with a member of the Ansaaru Allah who set up shop on the corners to sell their incenses, medallions, perfumes, and oils. I could recognize that we all possessed divergently different belief and faith systems, but I could also recognize that our histories converged. I could recognize that our presences in that particular city and at that particular time were all connected back to an Islamic idea of a supreme ruler.

By the time the Five Percenter movement encountered the late 1980s (and I encountered it), the ideology had become synonymous with other expressions of black pride. To me, the complex belief system and science were lost—all that remained was an ambiguous message about black pride and a rejection of white ideas. black hip hop brought me face to face with the rhetoric of the Five Percenters. Rappers like Rakim (of Eric B and Rakim) and groups like the Brand Nubians explained Five Percenter symbolism in his lyrics. Other groups, like the Poor Righteous Teachers, wove Five Percenter doctrine into the majority of their lyrics. Songs like "Holy Intellect" and "Gods Earths and 85ers" attempt to explain the ideology behind their faith. In retrospect I can recognize that the ideology of the Five Percenter movement was diluted by the time the music hit my ears, but in that era of Afrocentricity, it felt like recognition for me. My parents had always taught me about my African heritage alongside my Muslim heritage and even though I didn't understand their precise beliefs as they expressed them, I could recognize that they too were expressing a synergy between their faith and their politics.

Now in the early part of the 21st Century, African American Muslims are still marginalized, yet that marginalization seems to come from a different direction. Now, rather than Islam (insofar as it is practiced in the black community) being primarily associated with nationalist political ideologies, Islam has become synonymous with foreignness. This shift can arguably be attributed to the recent influxes of immigrant Muslims to the United States and, of course, the post-9/11 images of Muslims that are disseminated and circulated widely here in the United States. This shift doesn't merely apply to a trend that is seen from outside of the group (i.e., non-Muslims looking at and categorizing/classifying Muslims as they see fit), but also from within the group (immigrant Muslims defining what Islam is and what Islam in America should look like). Jackson (2005) characterizes this shift from within thusly:

> following the settling of critical masses of Muslims from the Muslim world, the basis of religious authority in Blackamerican Islam shifts to the sources, authorities, and interpretive methodologies of historical Islam. On this development, given their presumed mastery over this intellectual legacy, immigrant Muslims came into a virtual monopoly over the definition of a properly constituted "Islamic" life in America. Meanwhile, Blackamerican Muslims found themselves increasingly unable to address their cultural, political, and social reality in ways that were either effective in an American context or likely to be recognized as "Islamic" in a Muslim one. Like the Blackamerican Christians of an earlier era, struggling to find their voice in the context of a Christianity dominated by white Americans, Blackamerican Muslims found themselves struggling to reconcile a dignified black, American existence with the super-tradition of historical Islam, on the one hand, against the presumed normativeness of a historically informed and culturally specific Immigrant Islam, on the other. (p. 4)

This marginalization that Jackson writes of has, I would argue, simply worsened since 9/11. Out of necessity, the available image of a Muslim living in the United States must be foreign-born, recently arrived, or, at most, the product of immigrant parents. Muslims as U.S. citizens are highly problematic and somewhat illogical within anti-Muslim/Islamophobic rhetoric. How are we supposed to "go back to where [we] came from" if this is the place we've come from? The notion of a "pure blood" American Muslim is almost inconceivable. White converts to Islam are considered race/cultural traitors—a sort of anathema. Black converts to Islam, let alone African Americans who have generational ties to Islam, well, aren't exactly considered. Black converts are, according to Jackson (2005), the only American-born Muslims whose conversions "connote neither cultural nor ethnic apostasy" (p. 130). This, he argues, is why the connection between Islam and the black community must remain intact and black Muslims must not be marginalized. African American ties to Islam work to legitimate Islam as a "bona fide American religion," he writes. Were it not for African American Muslims, "Islam would be orphaned in the United States, with no indigenous roots to complicate attempts to relegate it to the status of an alien, hostile intrusion" (p. 130).

Of course we can see evidence of this alienation circulating everywhere, throughout everyday interactions with different media outlets, entertainment outlets, and even within the classroom. The fact that, in religion classrooms, Islam is segregated and relegated to discussions about Eastern religions is one clear example of this alienation. An understanding of Islam as a religion that has evolved over time in the United States would do wonders in terms of combating the Islamophobic and xenophobic vitriol that we encounter on a day to day basis.

On a lesser note (or at least less dramatic note), divorcing Islam from African American life presents complications in my personal life. When I spent the majority of my time around black people and in black communities, I found that being Muslim translated into an articulation of my blackness. However, moving out of these communities meant that my expression of my faith was translated differently.[13] I have experienced people's confusion. Recent comical examples include *two separate* instances when I was asked if I was a "foreign exchange student." One situation occurred mid-semester in a college language classroom where, prior to the question, I'd been speaking both English and Spanish without (as far as I could tell) any detectable foreign accent. The other situation occurred on a city bus when a (I suppose) well-meaning white woman assumed that I was unfamiliar with riding a bus—because I was a foreign exchange student—and tried to let me know that I was exiting at the wrong stop.[14] I've also experienced people's hatred. Less comical examples include one day, while I was still an undergrad, I was told on *two separate* occasions that I didn't belong in the United States. One person yelled that I should "go back to where I came from;" another person told me that I should "get back on my camel."[15] There are numerous other more threatening and more violent hate-related incidents that Muslims experience in the United States on an everyday basis,[16] the only thing I want to point to is the way in which a lack of recognition of Islam's history in the black community leads to assumptions about who I am.

To move beyond the assumptions about my identity and move toward the larger picture: How would a different understanding of the history of Islam in the United States help combat Islamophobia? It's been ages since I've been a student in a grade school classroom, and it's been several years since I've been a student in a university classroom. So I feel like I can't exactly speak to the ways in Islam or African American history is taught now. But I have very clear recollections of the ways I was educated on these matters outside of my home, in these kinds of classrooms. I can't imagine a drastic change. I say this because the idea of Islam being a "newly imported religion" is still part of common parlance and discourse. There still is no concept of Islam as an American religion—at least in the eyes of mainstream America. And there's still a lack of understanding that Islam has a history in the United States, and a large part of that history lies within the black community. This still seems difficult to comprehend.[17] I think that incorporating this history, the legacy of Islam in the African American community, into classroom discussions of Islam and black history will begin to change our perceptions of what Islam in the United States can look like and will provide a fuller presentation of the ways in which black religious and political life work together.

Endnotes

1 The two men met in Washington D.C. They were there to attend the debate on the senate's Civil Rights bill. Their meeting was a short one and it was the only time the two met.
2 I should probably be honest here, I wasn't at all "proud" to be going to the movies with my family. I was actually rather embarrassed. Especially when my mother pulled out the sandwiches she'd made for us to eat while watching the movie. I was utterly embarrassed. Mostly because I was 15 and definitely thought I was too cool to be seen with my family.
3 For obvious reasons, slavers liked to find Africans who were young and bring them into slavery. According to Walker, many of these young Africans were literate, had already memorized the Q'uran, and were able to write parts of the Q'uran on paper and disseminate it.
4 Sylviane Diouf's *Servants of Allah: African Muslims Enslaved in the Americas* (1998), Allan Austin's *African Muslims in Antebellum America* (1997), and Michael Gomez's essay "Muslims in Early America" (1994) just to list a few. There are several other texts, some of which are included in the References section of this chapter.
5 Both Michael Gomez and Henry Brent Turner discuss this in their work along with others such as Dennis Walker in his text *Islam and the Search for African-American Nationhood* (2005).
6 I think it's important to note here that although Lincoln discounted the religious aspects of the NOI and earlier inceptions of Islam in the black community, his 1961 text is still considered one of the more thorough treatments of Islam in the black community.
7 Curtis points to Lincoln's own Protestant Christian identity as a possible reason for his inability to consider the religious aspects of the NOI's teachings.
8 The emphasis here is on the word *if*. We didn't always cover Malcolm X in these units. Mostly because (I think) he was considered a bit too "militant" for a unit that is supposed to be mild and uplifting.
9 Not only does learning about the Civil Rights Movement de-contextualize and polarize Malcolm X, it also presents an uncomplicated story of Martin Luther King, Jr. and the Civil Rights Movement in general.

10 It's probably important to mention that she called this particular professor "exceptional," further cementing my impression that the content of his course was not, by any means, standard.
11 Robert Dannin's *Black Pilgrimage to Islam* (2002) and Richard Brent Turner's *Islam and the African-American Experience* (1997) are two texts that provide a more complete historical treatment of Islam in the African American community.
12 Kathleen Malone O'Connor writes an interesting study of the connections between the Ansaars and Jewish tradition. Her article entitled "The Nubian Islamic Hebrews, Ansaaru Allah Community" is featured in *Black Zion: African American Religious Encounters with Judaism* (2000). The book in general offers fascinating discussions of a frequently overlooked aspect of African American religious history.
13 Two things I should mention: (1) I wear *hijab*, so outside of the black community, which often gets read as "foreign." (2) The city I was raised in experienced a large influx of Somalian refugees in the early 2000s. This meant that people's immediate reaction to me was not necessarily "Oh, she's a black woman." For example, while I was in college (I attended college in the same city), I was often asked if I was Somalian.
14 I, of course, knew where I was going—I'd been riding the same bus for at least three years. Her assumption that I was a foreign exchange student was ridiculous, but her assumption that a foreign exchange student wouldn't understand how to ride the bus or wouldn't understand how to ask the bus driver for directions was insulting. She appeared to be embarrassed; she appeared even more so when I told her that she should be.
15 Both of these situations were driving related.
16 I receive emails from The Council on American-Islamic Relations that, on something like a weekly basis, contain some sort of horrific and terrifying story of a Muslim man or woman (increasingly more women) who was a victim of a hate crime or some other public harassment.
17 The incomprehensible nature of this fact was exemplified for me while listening to a presentation by Dr. Sherman Jackson. After Jackson had given an hour-long talk about the various ways Islam had manifested itself in the black community throughout history, one Muslim man in the audience (we were predominantly Muslim) asked, essentially, how "we" could bring all of these Black people into the "true" Islam. Dr. Jackson reiterated some of the points of his lecture, specifically his points about immigrant Muslims presenting Islam as a "full bottle," thus making it difficult to incorporate African American culture into their Islamic practices. However, a few questions later, another Muslim man asked virtually the same question!

References

Curtis, E. E. (2002). *Islam in Black America: Identity, liberation, and difference in African American Islamic thought.* New York: State University of New York Press.

Curtis, E. E. (2006). *Black Muslim religion in the nation of Islam, 1960-1975.* Chapel Hill, NC: University of North Carolina Press.

Dannin, R. (2002). *Black pilgrimage to Islam.* New York: Oxford University Press.

Diouf, S. (1998). *Servants of Allah: African Muslims Enslaved in the Americas.* New York: NYU Press.

Gomez, M.A. (1994). Muslims in early America. *The Journal of Southern History*, 60(4), 671–710.

Jackson, S. (2005). *Islam and the Black American: Looking toward the third resurrection.* New York: Oxford University Press.

Lincoln, C. E. (1961). *The Black Muslims in America.* Boston: Beacon Press.

Nyang, S. (1991). Convergences and divergence in an emergent community: A study of challenges facing U.S. Muslims. In Y. Haddad (Ed.), *The Muslims of America* (pp. 236–250). New York: Oxford University Press.

Turner, R. B. (1997). *Islam in the African-American experience*. Bloomington, IN: Indiana University Press.
Walker, D. (2005). *Islam and the search for African-American nationhood: Elijah Muhammad, Louis Farrakhan, and the Nation of Islam*. Atlanta, GA: Clarity Press.

Eleven

The Dialectics of Islamophobia and Homophobia in the Lives of Gay Muslims in the United States

Younes Mourchid

Introduction and Background

In light of recent events related to acts of terrorism around the world affecting the Muslim communities and the political and public reactions resulting from these events, there is an increasing anxiety and uncertainty of how today's societies are developing and what direction they are taking with respect to identity and partiality. The key questions are whether there are any missing elements of understanding about the construction of society and whether there are approaches to safeguard each person's opportunity to live a life of choice, without diminishing the freedom of others.

These events have triggered an increased attention on all Muslims, particularly in countries of the European Union and the United States (Abbas, 2005). Although the effects of recent events on Muslims are moderately discussed and differentiated in academic research, political debate, and media, the unseen implications for the youngest and the minority members of society, such as gay Muslims, may often be overlooked or neglected. However, considering the fact that in the EU and the United States, approximately one-third of all Muslims are under the age of 15 and one-fifth are aged 16–24 (Muir and Smith, 2004), there is an urgent need to investigate possible implications of the unwilling focus upon Islam and Muslims for the growing generations and matters of equity. International surveys, such as the collection of country reports of anti-Islamic reactions in the EU issued by the European Monitoring Centre on Racism and Xenophobia (EUMC/RAXEN, 2001), provide for various accounts of immediate reactions of politicians and the public toward Muslims in the aftermath of the said events. However, these surveys, while acknowledging the explicit xenophobic behavior increasing toward the Muslim communities in the West, fail to depict and predict a picture of what inherent and long-term consequences Islamophobia could have for young and gay Muslims.

This chapter critically explores and lays out the numerous factors which could be contributing to Islamophobia, attitudes entailing non-differentiated views of Muslims in relation to what today is referred to as "homophobia." With respect to community, the main objective of this enquiry is to point out the high level of significance this type of dialectic between Islamophobia and homophobia can have for gay Muslim, non-gay Muslim, and the non-Muslim members of the society. By being the target of homophobic and Islamophobic attitudes, the gay Muslims are unwillingly placed in a conflict between their Muslim and sexual identities, which is currently the cause of much debate among gay Muslims about community belongingness. This chapter highlights the themes of this debate through multiple voices of gay Muslims living in the United States. As a recommendation for educators, this chapter further argues that it is possible for traditional Muslims to adopt a religious framework that is critical of homosexual behavior without being accused of homophobia, just as it can be possible for gay Muslims to criticize Islamic teaching about sexual behavior without contributing to the existing discourse of Islamophobia.

I outline the different facets of Islamophobia as manifested in countries of the EU and the United States. This inquiry will review the different facets of homophobia as identified in Islamic canonical texts and as displayed in community members' reactions and behaviors in Muslim communities throughout the Muslim world and in the West to the topic of homosexuality and community members identifying as gay Muslim. After discussion of the research methodology employed in this study, this chapter will evolve into the presentation and analysis of interview data. The presentation will focus on three major question themes which emerged from the interview data:

1. How militant intolerance toward homosexuals as imbedded in core Islamic values correlate with stigmatization and fear experienced by gay Muslim within their Muslim communities and thus with their internal Islamophobia?
2. Do Muslims who show intolerance toward homosexuality deserve a respectful hearing in the liberal market place of ideas?

3. Should Muslims be taught and teach about homosexuality in schools?

The Different Facets of Islamophobia

Before surveying the different facets of discrimination and how these relate to homophobia, it is useful for the mission of this chapter to define the term Islamophobia as a contemporary phenomenon. Generally speaking "phobia" means an "unfounded or irrational fear." On the basis of this generality, Haque (2004) conjures that *Islamophobia* can be understood as an "unfounded fear of Islam and its followers." In this sense, the fear of Islam and its followers could be seen as the result of limited knowledge about the religious Islamic culture, values, beliefs, and their practical application to reality on a day-to-day basis. However, with respect to Islamophobia in today's context, lack of knowledge may be assisted by distorted perceptions and interpretations. The Runnymede Trust identifies seven aspects within Islamophobia: "Muslim cultures are seen as monolithic, Islamic cultures are substantially different from other cultures, Islam is perceived as implacably threatening, Islam's adherents use their faith to gain political or military advantage, Western criticism of Muslim cultures and societies is rejected out of hand, the fear of Islam is mixed with racist hostility to immigration, and Islamophobia is assumed to be natural and unproblematic" (Abbas, 2005, p. 29).

Islamophobia is not a new phenomenon. This is evidenced by the fact that few days prior to 9/11, in the World Conference against Racism in 2001, the UN formally recognized Islamophobia as a "discriminatory and exclusionary" phenomenon, similar to Anti-Semitism or Anti-Roma (World Conference against Racism, Racial Discrimination, Xenophobia and Related Intolerance, August 31–September 8, 2001, Durban, South Africa; in Allen, 2005, p. 2). As a case in point, covering the span of 1999–2004, the Commission on British Muslims and Islamophobia, set up by the Runnymede Trust, released a report about the issues, challenges, and actions of Islamophobia, after having held numerous meetings, counseling, and interviews with many national organizations—governmental and private. Particularly significant in the report is the claim that despite many joint efforts being undertaken toward tackling religious discrimination against British Muslims, the situation seems to have only superficially or "cosmetically" improved and that the legal framework remains insufficient in formulating explicit protection and progress (Muir and Smith, 2004, p. 3). A positive step toward creating such a framework has been established through the introduction of the Religious Hatred Bill, recently issued as an amendment of the Public Order Act of 1998, which aims at protecting persons from acts of religious hatred (Racial and Religious Hatred Bill 11, 2005).

The Different Facets of Homophobia in Islam and Muslim Communities

There is a general consensus amongst notable scholars of Islam, past and present, that homosexuality is a deviation of man's true (heterosexual) nature. Thus the act of homosexuality is sinful and perverted and is viewed with contempt in most Muslim societies and Islamic countries. There are approximately seven verses in the Qur'an (the holy text of Muslim faith) that supposedly refer to homosexuality and same-sex acts. The majority of these verses refer to the nation of Lut (the biblical nation of Sodom and Gomorrah). The following are examples of a few verses:

> We also sent Lut (Lot):" he said to his people: "Do ye commit lewdness such as no people in creation ever committed before you? For ye practice your lusts on men in preference to women: ye are indeed a people transgressing beyond bounds. Surah VII (Araf), Verses 80–81

> Of all creatures in the world, will ye approach males. And leave those whom Allah (God) has created for you to be your mates? Nay, ye are people transgressing all limits? Surah XXVI (Shu'araa), Verses 165–166

> If two men among you are guilty of lewdness, punish them both. If they repent and amend, leave them alone: for Allah (God) is Oft-Returning, Most merciful. Surah IV (Nisaa), Verse 16

There are approximately four Hadiths (sayings attributed to Prophet Muhammad) in reference to homosexuality, same-sex acts, and cross-dressing. A few include the following:

> When a man mounts another man, the throne of God shakes.—Prophet Muhammad (pbuh)

> Kill the one that is doing it and also kill the one that it is being done to. (in reference to intercourse) —Prophet Muhammad (pbuh)

> Cursed are those men who wear women's clothing and those women who wear men's clothing.—Prophet Muhammad (pbuh)

During the time of Prophet Muhammad (d. 632 CE), there was not one single case of a reported punishment or execution for homosexuality or same-sex acts. The first execution ever to have been carried out was during the time of the third Caliph, Umar (586–590 CE), who ordered a homosexual man to be burned alive. Scholars at the time differed in opinion on this form of punishment, arguing that no human should be burned (according to the traditions of Prophet Muhammad), thus it was decided that homosexuals should be thrown off the highest building and then stoned to death.

Islamic schools of thought and jurisprudence differ on the issue of homosexuality. Sex between males was treated differently by the various legal schools, on the basis of differing interpretation of the traditional literature. All the legal schools regard sex between males as unlawful, but they differ over the severity of the punishment. The Hanafite School, in South Asia and Eastern Asia today, maintains that same-gender sex does not merit any physical punishment. The Hanabalites, of the Arab world, believe that sex between males must be punished severely. The Sha'fi school of thought, in the Arab world, argues that punishment for sodomy can only be carried out if there are four adult male witnesses who actually see the penetration.

According to the Ahmadi Muslim Jama'at (a small sect within Islam), homosexual behavior is a symptom of the decadence of society. Members of this sect go on to argue that homosexuality is contrary to natural laws and immoral. Imam Siraj Wahaj, an African American convert to Islam and a prominent cleric and scholar of Islam in the United States, was quoted saying the following, in 1992, in reference to the supposed opening of a gay mosque in Toronto: "I would burn down the masjid (mosque) myself, if I could." (Solomonia, 2004).

Answering a question posed on homosexuality, Dr. Muzammil Siddiqi of the Islamic Society of North America responded, "Homosexuality is a moral disorder. It is a moral disease, a sin and corruption.... No person is born homosexual, just like no one is born a thief, a liar or murderer. People acquire these evil habits due to a lack of proper guidance and education." In an attempt to elaborate why homosexuality is a sin, he maintained, "There are many reasons why it is forbidden in Islam. Homosexuality is dangerous for the health of the individuals and for the society. It is a main cause of one of the most harmful and fatal diseases. It is disgraceful for both men and women. It degrades a person. Islam teaches that men should be men and women should be women. Homosexuality deprives a man of his manhood and a woman of her womanhood. It is the most un-natural way of life. Homosexuality leads to the destruction of family life" (Siddiqi, 2000).

More liberal progressive imams, such as Sheikh Zaki Badawi of the Ealing Muslim College, refuse to pigeonhole homosexuality in this way. Speaking to *Gay Times*, he said that "the film *My Beautiful Launderette* [which centers on the love of a gay Muslim man for a white former racist] should serve as a useful reminder to the Muslim community that they cannot simply sweep gays and lesbians under the carpet. Homosexuality has always existed and continues to exist in all Islamic countries. Indeed, many high-ranking leaders in the Islamic world are gay." Sheikh Badawi categorically rejects homophobic violence. "In Britain," he says, "we Muslims are in a minority, and it should not be our task to encourage intolerance towards other minorities." (Badawai, 2007) He is one of the few Muslim figures who advocates the teaching of homosexuality in the context of sex education lessons in schools, as long as it does not challenge the "normality" of the traditional heterosexual family by "promoting" homosexuality. However, toleration does not equal acceptance, and even he considers homosexuality to be a "problem" similar to alcoholism, which is against Islamic teaching, even though being an alcoholic or gay does not disqualify one from being Muslim.

Compared with homosexuals from other faith denominations, the situation for gay Muslims of faith has been noticeably bad. For many years now, gay and gay-friendly Christian organizations and individuals, such as the Reverend Richard Holloway, the Bishop of Edinburgh, have publicly denounced homophobia while affirming the possibility of being gay and remaining true to one's faith. Recently, the homophobia of Islamic orthodoxy has begun to be challenged by gay Muslims themselves with the formation of a progressive organization for gay Muslims, Al-Fatiha, in the United States in 1997.

The name Al-Fatiha is inspired from the title of the first chapter of the Qur'an signifying "the beginning" or "opening." It consists of an invocation for guidance from Allah, who is referred to as "the Compassionate, the Merciful One." The founders of Al-Fatiha believe that these qualities and not the views of the extremist groups represent the true essence of Islam. The "Opening" for Al-Fatiha members represents the hope of a dialog through which the mainstream Muslim community will come to acknowledge the millions of gay Muslims in its midst and open its arms to them. Despite the severe hostility gay Muslims had experienced from their communities, some Al-Fatiha members were wary of provoking an Islamophobic backlash by highlighting exclusively Islamic homophobia maintaining that "there is considerable Islamophobia in Britain, and the last thing we as gay Muslims want is to be marginalized twice over, once for being gay and again for being Muslim."

Yet this dilemma is little understood by the wider gay community. An Al-Fatiha spokesperson argued that "we have to be very careful to make a distinction between the two so as not to alienate potential straight Muslim supporters and to offer homosexual Muslims the possibility of being true to their faith. We have to emphasize the fact that interpreting the religious texts is a dynamic process and that application of religious laws must take into account the changing social context. While we recognize that we have many powerful allies in the non-Muslim community, we must also recognize that, ultimately, the situation for gay Muslims of faith can only be improved by changing attitudes from within the Muslim community itself. This is the revolutionary task Al-Fatiha is attempting to carry out."

Settings and Methodology

This inquiry is follow-up part two to an initial inquiry I pursued to investigate how certain members of the gay community who were raised in Muslim households have come to embrace or reject the identity of gay Muslim (Vis. Mourchid, 2009). The second part of the inquiry goes beyond identity issues and explores how individuals who identify as gay Muslims navigate the terrain of Islamophobia and homophobia. Initially, this inquiry was inspired by multitude of conversations, which took place during the Arab Youth Symposium on September 20, 2003, at the campus of the University of California at Berkeley. The symposium participants voiced different identities, which in some instances are converging and in others are diverging. Accounts and stories told by gay Muslims were particularly striking. This group's representatives, in addition to the challenges of Islamophobia and Arabophobia, also have to navigate the terrains blazed by homophobia not only in the general society but within their immediate Muslim community, which generally condemns any romantic form of same-sex relationships. In the light of this background, the identity "gay Muslim" invokes a great deal of curiosity. Energized by a kinship I share with participants in such struggle and the questions entailing from aforementioned invoked curiosity, I set out to understand how the Muslims who identify as gay in United States conciliate the challenges they face from Islamophobia and homophobia and how they integrate any learned lessons in shaping their identity as gays Muslims. I employed three descriptive field-work methods throughout my project: focus group interviews, individual in-depth interviews, and participant observation.

Initially, I made contact with the research participants using a referral snowball sample technique through key non-profit organization such as Al-Fatiha Foundation, which promotes the progressive Islamic notions of peace, equality, and justice for Muslim who explore their sexual orientation or gender identity, and their allies, families, and friends and the South West Asian and North African Bay Area Queers (SWANABAQ)—a group and discussion forum for lesbian, gay, bisexual, trans-gendered, and inter-sexed (LGBTI) people who are Afghan, Arab, Armenian, Assyrian, Azerbaijani, Berber (Amazigh), Chaldean, Copt, Cypriot, Greek, Iranian (Persian), Kazakh, Kurd, Kyrgyz, Maltese, Tajik, Turkmen, Turk, or Uzbek living in Northern California.

I employed one-on-one, semi-structured interviews as the principal form of data collection. I conducted 20 individual interviews, each lasting between 45 to 90 minutes, and two focus group interview discussions. Many of the participants were interviewed two or three times during the two-year period of this inquiry. Nine of the participants were women and eleven were men. The participants ranged in age from 20 to 65 years. Most of the participants were second-generation immigrants, who were primarily raised in the United States and planned to stay in this country. The interviewees reported a wide range of ethnic backgrounds. Forty percent of participants were of South or Southeast Asian descent; 45% of students identified as Arab or Arab American and 5% as other. Interviews were conducted in three languages: Arabic, English, and French. Interviews conducted in a language other than English were translated into Standard English and checked by the interviewee for accuracy. The names used to report the testimonies are fictitious to preserve the identity of the participants.

Data Presentation and Analysis

Members of the gay Muslim community experience a wide range of reactions, stigmatization, and different forms of prosecution and discrimination that can be as mild as disowning by the family and the community and as grave as death. Participants of this study report that they have made important life-long decisions about their residence and work, mostly based on the fear of prosecution and stigmatization that can result from living openly as a gay person in their Muslim communities. Youssef, an immigrant from Algeria, expounds further:

> I did not know for sure that I was gay when I was living in Algiers as there were no gay role models around, but I was captivated by other men. I knew I was different and did not fit in at home, among the neighborhood kids, and at school. I was a good docile kid, but my father always found a pretext to get mad at me and beat me up. It was as if I had scripture on my forehead saying, "beat me up please." I was terrorized everywhere and was called pejorative names such as "faggot." I did not know what I was doing and what my destination was. I just knew I had to get out and go somewhere else where I could feel safe. When I came to America as a student, I then learned why I was different and why I incited aggression towards me; I was queer and everyone could sense the queer energy but me. At that point, I deployed my utmost efforts to stay in the States and acquire legal status as an immigrant. I had some catching up to do, some thinking to do about my faith as a Muslim, and some serious rage and intense need for approval from the outside world to come to terms with.

In his testimony, Youssef highlights an important element in his experience as a different kid growing up in Algiers. Although he did not know he was queer by the mere fact that he was different, he inspired negative reactions from those in his immediate environment. He thus experienced severe levels of homophobia, which caused him to feel afraid and unsafe. His relentless effort to make his home in the United States is indicative of his indelible fear of returning home and facing prosecution. Youssef ends his testimony on a poignant point—that of the long-term consequences of being directly or indirectly subjected to homophobic prosecution: questioning of Islam and the Muslim identity, associated rage, and a range of psychological handicaps. It is at the heart of these handicaps that the seat of internal Islamophobia resides.

Nora, a second-generation immigrant from Syria, sheds further light on the struggle of being estranged from her immediate community as a direct result of being gay and on the ensuing psychological and mental complications:

> For years I could not tell and I did not know how to say to my family I was gay. I just left home to go far away to school in California. After college, I got a decent job in the East Bay of San Francisco and started developing my own community. But then my father got ill and I moved back to Chicago to help my mother take care of him. During that period I succumbed to my mother's and extended family pressures and agreed to marry a nice guy whose family is close to mine. This decision did not sit well with my conscience and few weeks before the wedding I told my folks I changed my mind about the marriage and told them the truth about my sexuality. My mother had a nervous break-down out of embarrassment in the community. In our culture, such a turn of events brings a great deal of shame to the families. I did not know what to do, so I came back the Bay Area. Few weeks later, my father passed away from a combination of grief and illness. I was blamed for his death by many and I was not allowed back home to attend the funeral. I was heartbroken and attempted suicide.

The events and traumas Nora experienced as a result of living her truth and making difficult decisions solicit a great deal of empathy and reflection from those of us in the observation deck. It is clear from Nora's testimony that in her community, community well-being, voice, and cohesion supersede the voice and the well-being of the individual, which is typical of Muslim communities around the world. This community characteristic is an emblem of Islam as a religion established during the time of Prophet Mohammed in the 7th century. Nora's report also underscores the severe consequences that a gay Muslim can suffer as a result of honoring her individual conscience and needs in defiance of community honor and well-being. Her report highlights the untenable positions gay Muslims find themselves in and the non-sustainability of making one choice over the other. Either choice comes with a hefty price. As Nora tells her story, she alludes to the heart of the issue: her fear of Islam and Muslims and thus her acknowledgment of an Islamophobic psychological make-up. I further probed Nora on this make-up and she elaborated:

> When I looked deeply at the source of my tragedy relative to family, I can simply point out that the core cause is the common inflexible belief system stemming from Islamic thoughts and traditions. My folks were good people in their hearts, but they were drunk on an ideology that served none of us. I see us all as victims of an anachronistic belief system where room for flexibility and adaptation to reality is a no more than a strait-jacket. My early reactions to such system were extreme and anarchist to say the least. I disowned my Islamic heritage and identity; I removed

the Qur'an from my home; I shunned any social settings where discussion of Islam and Muslims was taking place, I reprimanded those who assumed I was Muslim just because I had a Muslim name, and as a matter of fact, I was close to changing my name legally.

Nora's reaction to the source of her troubles as a gay woman within her Muslim community is typical of the experience of other participants in this study. Nora's perception of lack of flexibility in interpretation of Muslim canonical thoughts and ability to adapt to current realities as "strait-jacket" is poetic. This perception is indicative of the intensity of homophobic attitudes and pressures a gay Muslim has to endure to belong to a Muslim community. As a counter-response to such costly attitudes, Nora developed a reverse hatred toward anything and anyone Muslim. Her reactions are understandable given the intensity of pain and loss she sustained as a result of narrow-minded attitudes and actions toward homosexuality. The pertinent question that emerges in this debate is: Do Nora's reactions qualify her as an Islamophobe? Nora's strong feelings toward Islam and Muslims were related to the hurt, pain, and anger she experienced at the hand of Muslims who disapprove of homosexuality and a gay lifestyle. Her reactions and feelings did not originate from an anti-Islamic ideology and did not go further to cause hurt to Islam and Muslims.

The psycho-dynamic of turning self-hatred into outward Islamophobia is more apparent in the account of Mohamed, a gay Muslim male originally from Saudi Arabia, who came to the States and acquired a refugee status based on sexual orientation. Mohamed discusses the dynamics of internal homophobia and internal Islamophobia and how these have brought him close to self-destruction enmeshed in a cycle of drug and sexual addiction and acting out:

> I was walking around with this seismic rage, which cost me jobs and friendships. I spent most of my time online looking for sexual hook-ups or sometimes a full weekend in bath-houses getting high and having unsafe sex with multiple partners. As my sexual acting out and use of drugs begun to get out of control and the consequences worsened, I sought professional help and joined a twelve step program for sexual and drug addiction. I suffered from an acute case of internal homophobia. At a deep level I blamed my homosexual identity for the loss of family love, country citizenship, and the ability just to be normal like everyone else. At the same time, I had a deep resentment towards Islam and its backward values. I blamed these values for the absence of a framework where my sexual identity can be embraced. I renounced Islam as soon as I moved to America and unlike other gay-Muslims I met here, I have not come to the defense of Islam and Muslim.

Mohamed's testimony highlights the sufferings a gay Muslim endures to begin to entertain the possibility of personal internal freedom. This journey to such freedom is laced with deep psychological handicaps manifesting in the form of self-hatred for being gay and as a symptom of internal homophobia. This self-hatred reverts into a behavior of self-destruction and self-medicating to take a distance from reality and the suffering of coming out and standing up for oneself. Mohamed was lucky to find support in psychotherapy and within recovery rooms and the 12 steps of NA and SAA.

For Mohamed, his struggle with homophobia could not be separated from his internal Islamophobia. As a matter of fact, he seems to blame Islam and its dogmas for his own homophobia. In this vein, he went beyond the rejection of Islam as a religion and culture in the spirit of disapproval into complete denunciation and condemnation of anything with the semblance of Islam. It is important to note that when the interview was conducted, Mohamed was still early in his recovery and healing process from the insanity of his drug and sexual addiction. His stance toward Islam and his identity as a gay Muslim are expected to soften and improve, and he continues to trudge the road toward full recovery.

There is no existing past and present civil constructive dialog between gay members of the Muslim community and their traditional heterosexual counterparts who condemn homosexuality as deviant and unnatural. In the absence of such conversation, the status quo is bound to be perpetuated. As a potential starting point for such dialog to take roots, this inquiry posed the following argument to the participants for reflection and debate in a focus group setting: Is it possible for traditional Muslims to adopt a religious framework that is critical of homosexual behavior without being accused of homophobia, just as it can be possible for gay Muslims to criticize Islamic teaching about sexual behavior without contributing to the existing discourse of Islamophobia? In a spirited discussion about this argument, Selma, a female second generation American Iranian and graduate student, retorted:

> I would very much like to have a constructive and honest dialogue with any conservative Muslim who has a problem with me being gay. Traditional Muslims denounce and condemn homosexuality outright and refuse to hear or entertain any alternative interpretation to the events surrounding the people of Lut upon which the rejection of homosexual identity and behavior is based. Allah condemned the people of Lut not because they engaged in same-sex relationships, but because they forced others to have sex which is considered by today's standards rape and because they had sex with children and committed incest. Many of my gay Muslim brothers and sisters and I condemn sexual acts of incest, pedophilia, and rape. However, in the absence of "Ijtihad" among Muslim clerics, such interpretation has not seen the light in mainstream Islam and those who have the courage to bring it up are silenced.

Mahera, a second generation female Palestinian, interjects:

> I agree that "Ijtihad" is a necessary pre-condition for us to have a conversation about the status of homosexuality in Islam. There is a pressing issue for me though,

which I consider the most important pre-condition. The killing and violence against gay Muslims must stop and be addressed by authority figures and issuers of Fatwa. The principles of human rights and compassion that both the Quran and the Prophet Mohamed advocated must be extended to gay Muslims. Yes, we can agree to disagree, as other religious groups do, about the rights and wrongs of homosexuality, but basic human right must be upheld. In the West, we begun to see some progressive clerics who speak against violence and homophobia, but the message has to travel and take effect in other Muslim countries and in other Muslim communities in the West where thousands are living in the closet hiding from the terror of being killed or hurt for being gay.

The pre-condition of "Ijtihad" is a common theme featuring in the testimonies and interjections in regard to whether those who condemn homosexuality deserve a respectful hearing in the liberal market place of ideas. It is a valid argument that the scales by which homosexuality and same-sex relationships are weighed and judged derive from a narrow interpretation of the events surrounding the dealings of the people of Lut. The context is unaddressed and so is the distinction between destructive sexual behaviors and same-sex love and consensual erotic relationships. In the absence of Ijtihad and the interpretations of the acts of people of Lut taking into account the context and current science and realities surrounding the discourse of homosexuality, a constructive dialog between gay Muslims, civil society, and conservative Muslims is pointless and is doomed to widen further the rift.

As an organic precondition for Ijtihad to take place in the currently closed and narrow discourse of homosexuality, a discourse and initiative of sex education must take place in the evolution of Islam as it seeks to adapt to the current world realities. As a necessary precondition for a possible dialog to take place and attitudes to improve and change, Muslim clerics and men of authority are behooved to condemn any form of violence and prosecution against gay Muslims. They can use the mechanism of fatwa, a religious decree, to break the cycle of violence which has taken the lives of hundreds of gay men and women in the Muslim world and has kept millions in unauthenticated hiding. As will be understood from the participants' perspective, it is this violent treatment of homosexuals which leads many gay Muslims to question, relinquish, and hate their Muslim faith and identity and thus bear the burden of Islamophobia.

Sima, a female Iraqi, a college professor of gender studies and activist for gay rights in the Muslim world, comments further on the issue:

> Homophobia as we know it today is a product of the era during 18th and 19th century Europe. In the context of sexuality, Europeans enacted sodomy laws, which they outsourced to the Middle East and North Africa in the 19th and 20th centuries through the mechanism of imperialism and protectorates. As Muslim countries became nation states post World War I and II and still under control of the colonial powers, they adopted these same sodomy laws. Later in the 20th century and these

days, as Occidental countries created a discourse of human rights and a movement of tolerance and emancipation of the gay communities and as this discourse was again outsourced and imposed on Muslim countries, a backlash from the Muslim countries led to the perception today among Muslims that homosexuality is a Western phenomenon and that Muslims should protect their communities and future generations from Western decadent values. It is this perception today that is at the core of homophobia in Muslim countries and incentive for our work as gay-Muslim activists. We are not looking to change Islam and its core values, but we are working on changing perceptions and on highlighting the tolerant and gentle path of Islam which advocates the rights and the freedom of the individual.

It is clear from the experiences and perspectives of many gay Muslims who engaged in soul searching and in critical thinking using historical discourse analysis tools of deconstruction that most gay Muslims do not engage in Islamophobic practices, but in the questioning and rejection of homophobic Islamic attitudes. Engaging in such critical exercise, some gay Muslims are distinguishing between core Muslim values, people's interpretation of these values throughout history, and European outsourcing of their discourse of homophobia to Muslim communities through the mechanism of imperialism. In a sense, European discourses of homophobia have contributed to the institutionalization of homophobic laws such as the sodomy laws, which are still in effect in 95% of Muslim countries today and which serve as a basis for the prosecution of gay Muslims. It is interesting that as Europeans and North Americans began to change their attitudes and laws toward more tolerance of homosexuality in the context of human rights, the permissible practices of homosexuality in the West have been perceived by Muslims as a sign of societal and value decadence and they proceeded to enforce the sodomy laws and interpret the Qur'an and the Hadith in a manner that lends support to the condemnation of any same-sex relationships. The pressing question in this vein pertains to whether Muslims of all stripes are willing to create the educational opportunities for learning and for such distinctions to take roots in the knowledge repertoire of young Muslims around the world.

Open-mindedness and fair-mindedness are essential components of a civil dialog to take place and for a middle way in viewpoints to be attained. At the heart of these concept of the middle way is the principle of "fairness." The distinction between open and closed minds corresponds to the distinction which Muslim anthropologists draw between inclusivism and exclusivism referring to two different ways Muslims understand and practice their religion and relate to others. In the view of several participants of this study, creating a space between the closed and the open views and between the inclusive and the exclusive approach is where a possible dialog between two different parties can take place, each listening to one another, and eventually moving toward a middle way. Imad, a male gay Muslim of Egyptian origin and an inner city teacher, elaborates:

> School can serve as the middle way for opposing viewpoints to find a common ground. In my school, there are many Muslim kids. Sex Education classes in my district are optional. However, 65% of parents opt for their children to attend sex-education classes. Many parents consulted with me regarding the content of these classes. I had a chance to tell them what I tell every parent: In a diverse and complex world where we live today, it is important for your children to learn about their bodily functions, proper sexual conduct, sexually transmitted diseases, pregnancy, birth control, rape, sexual orientation, and all the legal aspects of sexual conduct in society. For the parents who opt out, I say to them: Please take a look at the curriculum we teach in school regarding sex education. You the parents have the opportunity to supplement this curriculum with your own take, deriving from Muslim teaching. Many parents change their mind and some are afraid to take the risk.

Imad's account provides an example of how the educational system can bridge the divide between two different views creating thus an opportunity for a middle way to emerge—a middle way where the discussion is not about who is right or wrong or about who holds the ultimate truth about human affairs, but about the presentation of objective facts, diversity of perspectives, and, above all, about tolerance and respect of the differing points of view.

The movement toward the middle way invoking principles of tolerance and respect for the "other" on the part of Muslims, non-Muslims, and homosexuals for the sake of co-existence constitutes the driving force of the discourse of "Peace Education." The principles and processes of peace education can enhance the existing discourses of multiculturalism and antiracism education and provide a fresh paradigm to deal with challenges of the 21st century emanating from diversity and clash of cultures and ideologies. The peace education paradigm provides the prospect of "hope" and an element of "empowerment" whereby community members do not need to wait for policies and laws to be enacted to feel safe and connected in their communities, towns, and countries. It is a prospect that opens the door for the basic elements of human relationships to take root: dialog, empathy, and compassion.

Conclusion and Discussion

This inquiry sought to recognize and discuss the disagreement between gay Muslims and their conservative heterosexual counterparts over sexuality education and the difficulties a multicultural society faces in attempting to deal justly with minority groups that hold diametrically opposed views. In the process we came to identify, on one side, a "homosexual perspective," which sees homosexuality as morally acceptable and as part of the legitimate diversity of liberal societies, and on the other, a "Muslim perspective," which maintains that homosexuality contravenes divine law and is a denial of God's creative purposes. The present discussion suggested that one consequence of the increasing acceptance of homosexual lifestyles in the liberal West has been the marginalization or rejection of the "Muslim perspective" based on the belief that the "Muslim perspective" is a homophobic one, with no place in a liberal society.

The accounts of this inquiry seem to affirm that if groups with differing views are to co-exist in harmony in a liberal society, they must develop mutual respect through open dialog based on empathy and compassion. However, dialog is not easy for people who speak different languages and expound different worldviews. There is a need for cultural interpretation so that the beliefs of conservative Muslims can be expressed in language comprehensible to homosexuals and vice versa. The process and agents of Ijtihad can perform the role of the cultural interpreter in order to communicate in a language that is accessible to all parties of the debate with their respective Islamic and liberal teachings and values, fully and fairly, and as far as possible without distortion.

The second major question of this inquiry focused on the militant intolerance toward homosexuals as embedded in core Islamic values. In this vein, the participants of this study provided poignant accounts. In order to further interpret the validity of these accounts, it is important to revisit what is meant by "homophobia." In the view of this inquiry, not everything judged or perceived as "homophobic" these days actually warrants the judgment, especially when drawing a parallel between Islamophobia and homophobia. "Islamophobia" signifies bullying, discrimination, abuse, and social avoidance directed at Muslims because of unjustified fear or hatred of them. In the same manner, "homophobia" signifies bullying, discrimination, abuse, and social avoidance directed at homosexuals because of unjustified fear or hatred of them. Under the guidance of these respective yet related definitions, we can clearly see a distinction between expressing disapproval of homosexual behavior and being homophobic. In the same way Catholics, for example, can maintain that according to Catholic teaching abortion is wrong, Muslims can say that according to Muslim teachings homosexual practices are wrong without being accused of homophobia. Disapproval is not necessarily incompatible with tolerance especially if we define tolerance as "a deliberate choice not to interfere with conduct of which one disapproves." (Horton, 1993, p. 3)

With regard to the "stigmatization and fear" experienced by homosexual Muslims within the Muslim community, such fear is valid and warranted. The multiple voices of this study call on the conservative Muslims to employ the tools of Ijtihad and issue a fatwa to put an end to committing violence against gays in their Muslim communities. However, those who base their Islamophobic attitudes on such "stigmatization" are invited to consider the broader context of Islamic beliefs and practices. Islam does not hold individual freedom to be such a central value as liberalism does. It is a tradition in Islam that when a Muslim sees another going astray, he has a moral obligation to encourage him to get back on the right path. From this perspective, it is easier for Muslims to accept practices that conflict with Islamic teaching if these are the practices of other groups within a multicultural society than it is to tolerate them within the Muslim community itself. An emerging pattern among Muslim communities in multicultural settings is that there is a general tolerance of diverse practices and lifestyles, including homosexual ones, outside the Muslim community, and a general policy of noninterference so long as the practices or lifestyles conflicting with Islamic teaching are engaged in private by those within the Muslim community.

This inquiry concludes with the suggestion that for dialog to take place between homosexuals and conservative Muslims, a discourse of Ijtihad and sex education should include lesson packets about homosexuality and peace education. Indeed, there is evidence that Muslim schools, especially in the West, are increasingly seeing it as their role to prepare children for full citizenship. The relationship must be reciprocal and must involve openness and a willingness to listen on both sides. If Muslim children are to learn about Western concepts of sexual identity as well as respect for those who identify as homosexuals, then also other children need to learn about Muslim perspectives and to respect them. Empathy is central to this process as well as critical reflection.

References

Abbas, T. (2005). After 9/11: British South Asian Muslims, Islamophobia, multiculturalism, and the state. *The American Journal of Islamic Social Sciences*, 21(3), 26–36.

Allen, C. (2005). Justifying Islamophobia: A post-9/11 consideration of the European Union and the British contexts. *The American Journal of Islamic Social Sciences*, 21(3), 1–23.

Badawi, S. (2007). http://www.mail-archive.com/lgbtdiscuss@googlegroups.com/msg00002.html. Date of last retrieval March 16, 2010

European Monitoring Centre on Racism and Xenophobia (EUMC/RAXEN) and Commission for Racial Equality (CRE) (United Kingdom). (2001). *Anti-Islamic reactions in the EU after the terrorist acts against the USA*. Vienna: EUMC.

Haque, A. (2004). Islamophobia in North America: Confronting the menace. In B. Van Driel. (Ed.), *Confronting Islamophobia in educational practice* (pp. 1–18). Stoke-on Trent, UK/Sterling, VA: Trentham Books Limited.

Horton, J. (Ed.). (1993). *Liberalism, multiculturalism and education*. London: Macmillan.

Mourchid, Y. (2009). Left to my own devices: Hybrid identity development of religion and sexual orientation among Muslim students in the United States. In Ö. Sensoy & C. D. Stonebanks (Eds.). *Muslim voices in school: Narratives of identity and pluralism*. Rotterdam, The Netherlands: Sense Publishers.

Muir, H. & Smith, L. (2004). In R. Richardson (Ed.). Commission on British Muslims and Islamophobia (England) (2004) *Islamophobia: Issues, challenges and action*. Stoke-on-Trent, UK/Sterling, VA: Trentham Books Limited.

Racial and Religious Hatred Bill (2005), House of Commons. *Bill 11*. Authority of the House of Commons. London: The Stationery Office Limited.

Siddiqi, M. (2000). http://74.125.47.132/search?q=cache:asvKXnE8P7wJ:www.encyclopedia.com/doc/1P3-509413391.html+Muzammil+Siddiqi+Homosexuality&cd=1&hl=en&ct=clnk&gl=ca&client=firefox-a. Date of last retrieval March 16, 2010.

Solomonia (2004). http://74.125.47.132/search?q=cache:E9XvTxoL1sMJ:www.solomonia.com/blog/archives/005004.shtml+Imam+Siraj+Wahaj+gay+mosque&cd=1&hl=en&ct=clnk&gl=ca&client=firefox-a. Date of last retrieval March 16, 2010.

Twelve

"Yes, My Name Is Ibrahim and I Am an Atheist!"
Confessing *Asrar*: Atheism, Arts, Answerability, Imagination and the Muslim You Have Never Known

Awad Ibrahim

> "I am a theist," means "I know that God exists." "I am an atheist" means, "I do not know that God exists." Appending the Greek prefix "a" could in no way be constructed as meaning, "I know that God does not exist."
> —Chester Dolan in "Blind Faith"

Confessions, those processes by which the subject is incited to formulate and state certain truths about herself or himself, are always juicy. They are juicy for two reasons: First, they have the capability to have an effect on the subject herself or himself; and second, like an unexpected scene in a horror movie, they cause the listener's eyes to widen and heartbeats to speed up. To confess is to say the unexpected, to utter *asrar*—the plural of the Arabic word *sir*, with the vowel pronounced like the "i" in "sit." The word "*asrar*" literally means "sit on the fence between telling secrets and confessing." In my understanding, telling secrets involves talking about those furtive affairs that are known to no one but the self, whereas confessing has almost legal ramifications. Yes, my name is Ibrahim, I am an atheist, and this short essay is my *asrar*. The chapter is thus autobiographical: recording my journey with Islam beginning at my birth and my thought processes on "secularism" (as a "reproblematization" of the religion) within the Muslim world and within Islam itself. My *asrar* should be read in relation to accountability, hospitality, and imagination, keeping in mind that my name has already been deciphered within an Islamophobic discourse, especially after 9/11.

Before I proceed, I must "confess" that, on the one hand, some of what is stated here is meant to be provocative; it is thus better read as a description of reality that corresponds not only to my life but also to the lives of a lot of people known to me. In fact, as I make my confessions, I consider the so-called "left" as both a political category and an ideological category. I think, or at least hope, that most members of the political left in the Muslim world will be nodding their heads in agreement with most of the arguments I am advancing here. However, I have two audiences in mind for this chapter: insiders and outsiders. Insiders, who are familiar with Islam and the Muslim world, may find my arguments provocative, but not totally new. This short chapter is, in fact, is directly aimed at you the outsiders.

Face to Faith: A Genealogy

Indeed, the story of an Ibrahim who is an atheist is long, complex, and not easy to tell. It gives rise to fear of retaliation from the very people it tries to talk about. It is written, quite unfortunately, with fear because in Islam, to be or to become Muslim is irreversible. That is, one may convert to Islam but not out of it. Within Islam, one is allowed to convert from one sect to another (from Sunni to Shiite, for example), but Muslims hardly do it. To declare oneself an "atheist," in the crude etymological sense of the term, is an apostasy, which, in Islam, is punishable by death. But the story dares one to tell it.

My name is Awad Ibrahim, born and raised in a very poor Muslim family in a relatively small city called Sinnar in the Sudan, where I did my schooling till high school. As it happens to a number of us, the shift in my intellectual, and thus religious, life happened when I went to the University of Khartoum. There I was introduced to critical and radical thinking, including Marxism and poststructuralism, liberal arts, especially theater, and, above all, to independent thinking. During my freshman year at the university, I joined the Party of Democratic Front, or PDF, an alliance of anarchist, leftist, and Marxist groups. A friend of mine then invited me to join a radical and avid reading group, where nothing was off the table. There I was introduced to Socrates' notion that the most banal is the most difficult, so we asked few fundamental, societal, cultural, and, most significantly, religious questions. The questions were (among many others): Who are we? Why are we here on earth? What is our purpose in life? What is the role of politics in religion, and what is the role of religion in politics? Should there be any connection between religion and the state? What/who is God? What does it mean to be human? A classic Marxist question was: What role does social class play in both politics and social transformation? The realization that I could ask these questions was unsettling yet exceptionally thrilling. I became an intellectual rebel. Ideas gripped my life, and my life at some point was a testimony to the power of ideas. Before then I was a "good boy," as people around me, including my mother, used to say: I went to the Mosque five times, performed my prayers on time (including the painful *Subuh* or dawn prayer),[1] studied and memorized the Qur'an in a *madrasa* (or *khalwa*, as it is called in Sudan), helped my single mother around the house, took on summer jobs when every young person I knew was playing and amusing himself or herself, and did quite well in school.

Then came the big breakthrough. Not only could I ask those questions, but as part of our reading group discussion, I discovered that the question matters (even more) than the answer; that the question we ask influences, if not determines, the answer we come up with, since *no one* has *the* answer; that one of my aims in life can be to research both the question and the answer; and that I was on uncharted territories and ways of thinking and being. In fact, when I raised these questions as part of a panel presentation I organized in my third year of university, I was called names, including *kafir* or "unbeliever." It is worth noting that the prophet Mohammed (peace be upon him) has made it clear that if someone calls you a *kafir*, either you or this person is a *kafir*, since being a *kafir* is punishable by death. That is to say, before you call someone a *kafir*, you should make sure that the person is really a *kafir*, as otherwise you are declaring yourself a *kafir*. Hence, the appellation should not be taken lightly.[2]

Those who called me a *kafir*, a group of Muslim Brotherhood,[3] were aware of the power of the question, especially when it is raised about the fundamentals of Islam. When I raised such a question, I was physically attacked and psychologically tortured for weeks. I was spat at and verbally abused and had to flee the university for three days. This group's policy was (and still is) that if the message cannot be disputed intellectually, then the messenger must be killed. This policy, unfortunately, works in the Muslim world, and we have seen it happen, for example, in the case of Salman Rushdie's *Satanic Verses*, the cartoons of the prophet Mohammed in a Danish newspaper, and currently in Iran.[4] I believe that this malaise, the total hatred toward any intellectual questioning, is the reason for the intellectual decay in the Muslim world.

My quest for a genuine intellectual dialogue has led to difficult paths where there are no certainties. As argued by Chester Dolan in the opening quote of this chapter, the word "a-theism" can in no way be construed as: "I know that God does not exist. My atheism can only be a declaration, a confession of my uncertainty of God's existence.[5]

Face to Faith: Imagining an Ibrahim

[I]s there anything worse, said Nietzsche, than to find oneself facing a German when one was expecting a Greek?
—Deleuze & Guattari (2004, p. 109)

The idea of an Ibrahim being an atheist seems to surprise and trouble the minds of a number of people, both Muslims and Christians, the two groups that are relevant here.[6] I present two incidents to reinforce my point here. The first is a letter I received while teaching at Bishop's University (Lennoxville, Québec) from the Islamic Council of University Professors (ICUP) inviting me to attend a dinner hosted by them in October 2001 in Ottawa, Ontario. The letter of invitation was followed by three phone calls. I did not know how they obtained my address and phone number. I wondered why I was invited to the ICUP since I knew no one in the Council nor had I heard of it until then. My surprise was really no surprise, as it all simply had to do with my name.

The second incident happened three days after the horror of September 11. I received a call at home from a pastor who I worked with in a refugee organization. She explained that she was organizing a religious panel to offer condolences to show solidarity with the victims of 9/11. Each, she added, would recite from the scriptures of his or her religion. She would represent Christians, there was a "Jewish professor" to represent the Jews, and I would represent Muslims, she explained. At this point, I was not sure about what Muslims would think of my representing them, since "representing," in my understanding, meant speaking in their name and occupying their place. I declined the invitation, as I could not bear the responsibility of speaking in the name of Muslims, while my own Islamic faith is shaky at best.

These two incidents illustrate something larger than a simple letter and phone calls. They are telling me in a powerful way how my name is *already* "read," "marked," "positioned," and "imagined." It is imagined and read in ways that can only be performative acts of history. Here, Ibrahim *is*, and *is* already known. That is, purely on the basis of my name, the pastor and the ICUP presumed their knowledge of me (almost with certainty). It is a reading that has little to do with my current being, with *me*. The here and now reveal something radically different. At the risk of my repeating a stereotype, they point to a Black man who speaks Arabic, born into a Muslim family but is a true living example of the contradiction of the postmodern age. And when it comes to my *sir* of being an atheist, I know that it is not meant to highlight something radically new or to indicate an exception. In fact, this is a common description of the Left—mostly Marxists—particularly in the Arab world (as mentioned earlier). And it is a secret or a *sir* only because it is unknown outside the Muslim and Arab world.

Face to Faith: Arts and the Mess of Uncertainty

As an atheist—being uncertain, that is—the arts became my savior, my space of meditation in the world. It has remained the place where I contemplate the mess of existence or being alive. The more I created art, or the more art created me, especially theater, the more I discovered that artists should be afforded the time and space to work through the arduous process of art creation; however, in the Muslim world, there was an exceptionally strong link connecting atheism (that is, having intellectual and religious doubts), secularism, arts, and the Left. In this world, *art is the Left, and the Left is where art is created.*

Most, if not all, art creation in the Muslim, especially Arab, world is either done within or by the Left or is directly influenced by it. The Left in the Muslim world is a confluence of democrats, liberals, nationalists, and Marxists-Leninists, who are central *dispositifs* or components. The all-encompassing ideological desire that drives their world is *secularism*: the separation of the state and religion. A visit to www.secularism.org/skeptics/secularism.htm will show the historical as well as contemporary background of this debate. Here a number of thinkers, such as Nasr H. Abu Zeid and Hussein Mroueh, and books, such as Abdurrahman Badawi's *From the History of Atheism in Islam*, Ismail Adham's *Why am I an Atheist?*, and, of course, the controversial Ibn Warraq's *Why I am not a Muslim*, among so many others, are discussed. But the Left in the Arab, particularly the Islamic, world is still unable to openly endorse secularism in public, since the concept bears the connotation of atheism, and atheism is considered a conversion: a strictly forbidden act in Islam (as already discussed). Confessing to one's affiliation to secularism/atheism would be a danger to one's life, since their *fatwa* could be capital punishment. Yet, throwing off the yoke, a number of authors and those of the general public have declared their secularism and atheism openly. The poet Amal Dangal, for instance, in a verse that is recited by almost every secularist, as well as every atheist, went as far as to say: "Glory to the Satan, beloved of the winds, who said nay in the face of the one who said yea, and lived in eternal pain ever after." Art is the symbolic site through which the confession to secularism or atheism is made, where most affirm their ideological beliefs. They do so in and through astute and indistinct art forms and representations: poetry, painting, sculpting, and so on.

> And I come to your site—my hope
> Throned by angst, and heart divided by grief
> I come to you, to be mesmerized
> Having my guitar, I come to tell you
> His story when he gave his life to your path
> And drew your picture on his voice
> And said: either you or I would die!

In my very crude and literal translation of a small section of "The City of Your Eyes" by Abd el Gadir el Ketayabi, the City is the Sudan, the whole country, and her "eyes" represent the place where the vision of hope is built. El Ketayabi is specifically talking about a secular state, envisioning holding her hand without fear and walking along the Nile on a full-moon night. In the Sudan, the name Mohamed Ahmed, when used in poetry, for example, came to symbolize not only the working class but also all other marginalized individuals. Similarly, the name Fatima has come to signify the powerfully courageous females and feminists.

My point is that art in the Muslim world is tremendously engaging and uses highly metaphoric language. It is hardly talked about either within the Muslim countries or elsewhere. The use of symbolism is conspicuously linked to the contextual nature of political practice in the Arab world, where turmoil and *coups d'état* are commonplace. Here, for one reason or another, the first to be captured and detained whenever and wherever there is a *coup d'état* are members of the art community, most of whom are affiliated to the Left.

Face to Faith: Arts, Imagination, and Answerability

In this concluding section, I am offering the Bakhtinian notion of "answerability" as a way for reimagining "Ibrahim" and for taking secularism, especially atheism, in the Muslim world seriously. As I mentioned earlier, this short chapter is written with fear, as it may again expose me to the same horrific experiences during my undergraduate university years: violence, accusation of apostasy, and maybe even threat of capital punishment. In psychoanalytic terms, this fear can create traumata, and trauma silences a person (Lacan, 1998). But to speak and still continue to live, I need "answerability," as otherwise I am left with silence as my other alternative. Bakhtin (1990) articulated the notion of answerability within the field of art, but it is not necessary to justify its use here.

A piece of art, Bakhtin explains, is one that is yet to be consummated, to be finished, and coauthored. No piece is full in and of itself. It needs a reader/viewer, who will coauthor the piece in the process of reading/viewing. Bakhtin calls this "dialogism," which he sees as the *effort of understanding*, as "the active reception of the speech of the other." Seeing art itself as a form of speech, the adjective "active" is all-important for Bakhtin here: "active reception" means that an art piece has to be worked on, dialogued with, translated, negotiated, and coauthored. If this is so, as most literary and art critics would emphatically argue, how do we explain the "reader" who refuses to coauthor or even look at the piece of art at all? Here, I would contend, a régime of nonanswerability is created. But to understand nonanswerability, one needs to understand answerability first.

According to Bakhtin, answerability is a construct focused on ethical response, a fundamental foundation of dialogic relations, such as reader–text or viewer–art. In other words, we act in response to others and our own experience. This means that "I" need an "other" to respond to, but my response is uniquely and temporally mine. This, by definition, intensifies the ethicality of the response. As Bakhtin put it, and he is worth quoting at length,

> I have to answer with my life for what I have experienced and understood in art, so that everything I have experienced and understood would not remain ineffectual in my life. But answerability entails guilt, or liability to blame. It is not mutual answerability that art and life must assume, but also mutual liability to blame.... The individual must become answerable through and through: all of his constituent moments must not only fit next to each other in the temporal sequence of his life, but must also interpenetrate each other in the unity of guilt and answerability (p. 110).

Here, "the poet must remember that it is his poetry which bears the guilt for the vulgar prose of life, whereas the man of everyday life ought to know that the fruitlessness of art is due to his willingness to be unexacting and to the unseriousness of the concerns in his life." (98) This is because art cannot afford to be too high-flown, too self-confident. If that were the case, then art would in no way be bound to answer for life. And it is this that I referred to earlier as the régime of nonanswerability. As Bakhtin aptly contended, "it is certainly easier to create without answering for life, and easier to live without any consideration of art. [For him,] Art and life are not one, but they must become united in myself—in the unity of my answerability." (102)

If these arguments were to be juxtaposed against the backdrop of the (intense) intellectual closure in the Muslim world, then obviously we as "readers" of Islam were forbidden to read and answer to the religion itself. Instead, it is decided that, at least for most of us, we are incapable of answerability, of reading, and of coauthoring. However, in the West, especially in the discourse of Islamophobia, "Ibrahim" needs a new, and maybe different, kind of answerability. "Ibrahim" is not what most readers of this chapter think. He is contradictory, postmodern, temporal, extremely secular, atheist, feminist, and knows only too well what it means to be a Black person living in the West. Therefore, I think "Ibrahim" needs to be set free and reimagined, and this can only happen when there is an "answer" to his art creation (in its broadest sense), not to what his name invokes in imperial imaginations. Ibrahim just *is*; he *is not* already known.

Following Nietzsche, Roland Barthes (2002) proposed that the author, indeed, dies in the process of reading. That is, the moment I read a text, that text is temporarily mine, although the author still has his or her signature on it. The author can be compared to the artist and text to art. If this is so, then the Barthesian "death of the author" certainly requires "answerability." Ibrahim does not need to be thrown off the window and left to *die* in the cold, he needs to be answered, coauthored, and dialogued with. Dare we all, finally, let the "author" —whatever his or her name—work through the mess of life: our answerability then is not to the author's name but to his or her "text."

And So We Declare: The St. Petersburg Manifesto

We are secular Muslims, and secular persons of Muslim societies. We are believers, doubters, and unbelievers, brought together by a great struggle, not between the West and Islam, but between the free and the unfree.

We affirm the inviolable freedom of the individual conscience. We believe in the equality of all human persons.

We insist upon the separation of religion from state and the observance of universal human rights.

We find traditions of liberty, rationality, and tolerance in the rich histories of pre-Islamic and Islamic societies. These values do not belong to the West or the East; they are the common moral heritage of humankind.

We see no colonialism, racism, or so-called "Islamophobia" in submitting Islamic practices to criticism or condemnation when they violate human reason or rights.

We call on the governments of the world to:

reject *Sharia* law, *fatwa* courts, clerical rule, and state-sanctioned religion in all their forms;

oppose all penalties for blasphemy and apostasy, in accordance with Article 18 of the Universal Declaration of Human rights;

eliminate practices, such as female circumcision, honor killing, forced veiling, and forced marriage, that further the oppression of women;

protect sexual and gender minorities from persecution and violence;

reform sectarian education that teaches intolerance and bigotry towards non-Muslims;

and foster an open public sphere in which all matters may be discussed without coercion or intimidation.

We demand the release of Islam from its captivity to the totalitarian ambitions of power-hungry men and the rigid strictures of orthodoxy.

We enjoin academics and thinkers everywhere to embark on a fearless examination of the origins and sources of Islam, and to promulgate the ideals of free scientific and spiritual inquiry through cross-cultural translation, publishing, and the mass media.

We say:

to Muslim believers: there is a noble future for Islam as a personal faith, not a political doctrine;

to Christians, Jews, Buddhists, Hindus, Baha'is, and all members of non-Muslim faith communities: we stand with you as free and equal citizens;

and to nonbelievers: we defend your unqualified liberty to question and dissent.

Before any of us is a member of the *Umma*, the Body of Christ, or the Chosen People, we are all members of the community of conscience, the people who must choose for themselves.[7]
 Amen!

Endnotes

1. This prayer is conducted around four or five o'clock in the morning. So, imagine a thirteen- or sixteen-year-old boy who is trying to sleep but is being woken up at 4 a.m. to perform his prayer. Not only did I do that, I stayed awake helping my mother get ready for her work at an elementary school. She used to sell lunch and other goods there. After I transported her goods to the school, I came home and got ready to go to my own school.
2. By the way, Christians and Jews are called "The People of the Book," not *koufar* (plural of *kafir*), since they have received the word of God through the Bible and the Torah.
3. See Amyn Sajoo (2009) to read about the radical history and politics of the Muslim Brotherhood.
4. For events around the publication of the book *Satanic Verses* by Salman Rushdie, see Ruthven (1990); for Danish cartoons, see Hussain (2007), and for Iran, see Boroumand (2009).
5. After lengthy conversations with a number of people on the issue of uncertainty of God's existence, including practicing Muslims, one can reach a provocative conclusion that we are all atheists. If "Appending the Greek prefix "a" could in no way be constructed as meaning, "I know that God does not exist," as Chester Dolan explains, and since

no one knows with absolute certainty that God exists, then we are all doubtful (whether we practice religion or not). Therefore, because of and thanks to this doubtful nature: we are all a-theists.
6. Here, I am referring specifically to conservative Muslims, the Muslim Brotherhood or the mullahs, for example, those who stick to the absolute letter of the Qur'an. The only reason I am calling on Christians as my second audience is because the example I am offering in the chapter is related to Christians.
7. The St. Petersburg Declaration (2007). Available at http://www.centerforinquiry.net/isis.

References

Bakhtin, M. (1990). *Art and answerability: Early philosophical essays.* Austin, TX: University of Texas Press.

Barthes, R. (2002). The death of the author. In Stygall, G., Editor, *Academic discourse: Readings for argument and analysis* (pp. 101–106). Mason, OH: Thomson.

Boroumand, L. (2009). Civil society's choice. *Journal of Democracy, 20*(4), 16–20.

Deleuze, G. & Guattari, F. (2004). *A thousand plateaus: Capitalism and schizophrenia.* New York: Continuum.

Hussain, A. (2007). The media's role in a clash of misconceptions: The case of the Danish Muhammad cartoons. *The Harvard International Journal of Press/Politics, 12*(4), 112–130.

Lacan, J. (1998). *The four fundamental concepts of psycho-analysis.* New York: Norton.

Ruthven, M. (1990). *A satanic affair: Salman Rushdie and the rage of Islam.* New York: Vintage.

Sajoo, A. (Ed.) (2009). *A companion to the Muslim world.* New York: Palgrave Macmillan.

Thirteen

Know the Ledge but Don't Hit the Edge: Building with the God Jahmega Allah

Habib Siam

Determining a writer's audience is a delicate process. I intended to produce a manuscript that would connect with both the uninitiated and the well informed. Achieving such a balance was a challenge. My goal was not to present a pamphlet guide to the 5 Percent Nation; however, through stretches, this text is guilty of relying on a succinct approach. This chapter is about individuals and their stories, narrated through a voice other than my own. The result is a collage of conversation and side commentary peppered with reflection. It unfolds in neither a linear nor chronological manner.

> *By the course of Allah, the true and living,*
> *Cream of the planet, Earth God of the universe,*
> *The first soul, black like coal,*
> *That's how old, there's no set birth record*
> *—Lord Jamar*

How Do You Write a Chapter about the Gods and Earths?

Michael Muhammad Knight dedicated an entire opus to the New York based organization commonly referred to as the 5 Percent. The God Wakeel Allah's account of the Nation's founder Clarence 13X, the Father, Allah, spans two comprehensive volumes. While I do not mean to deny conciseness, the value it brings to argumentation and to writing in particular, I do believe that certain subject matter cannot be glossed over. To do so would be a grave disservice.

The dialectics, tensions, and contradictions encountered when reading, talking, or conducting research on the Nation of Gods and Earths (NGE) make this movement all the more intriguing and complex. How will history remember Clarence 13X, a man portrayed by the Federal Bureau of Investigation's surveillance records as "a fascist and a racist (...) gang leader" despite receiving public support from then-mayor John Lindsay for developing a community-based education system? Are claims that the black man is God or that the white race is grafted inherently racist and misguided or historically informed and consciously enlightened? Why have the movement's social contributions and its impact on American consciousness and popular culture gone largely unrecognized and under-examined?

These are but some of the issues with which I grappled in order to write this chapter. Another question I faced is one that begs to be asked of almost any narrative: Where do I begin?

Some accounts chose the Father's split from the Nation of Islam's Temple 7 as their starting point. Others argue it more appropriate to turn the clock back to Noble Drew Ali's founding of the Moorish Science Temple of America after a sojourn in Egypt and the Arabian Peninsula. To assess beginnings as fixed points in time, however, is essentialist and reductionist. The assessment would ignore the influence of events that precede said points and depicts history as pictorially static, rather than diachronically fluid. This is why I've elected to begin somewhere in the middle.

The story picks up at The Fox and The Feather, a British pub in downtown Ottawa, of all places. The conversation that follows is a candid, informal exchange with Jahmega Allah, a former member of the NGE. I say "former" reluctantly because, although the God's worldview has grown to incorporate tenets from a broader range of philosophies, the influence of the 5 Percent is still palpable.

This is story of one God. It is also the story of many others.

Something That Just Sounded Beautiful[1]

So tell me, how old were you when you started?

When I started reading? When I started hearing?

Yeah...

I mean you have to go way back. I guess the first thing was hearing the talk. The talk always got you. "Peace God." You know, you'd hear that. "What's the math God?" And you're kind of like, okay, what's this about? And then, how it worked... I mean, you'd be there, chilling with your little crew, getting ready to play some ball or just sitting on the bench, talking or whatever... and yeah, the guy who approached me, Justice, he was like the God of the neighborhood. There was Justice, there was Prince, there was Knowledge. When you seen them walking around, head high, and everybody giving them respect, right, you were immediately drawn to that, to the power. It's like in traditional, orthodox Islam, you might hear about people being drawn to the light. See, you were kind of drawn to that. You know what I mean? As a 10-year-old, 11, 12, that's a wrap for you.

Almost literally

Exactly, I mean, things rhyme, they flow, sound nice. It was designed to be like that. Attractive. That was the vision. You know, they'd be standing around in the cipher and you're listening, and you're like, that sounds pretty smart right there. Back then, it was great, it was a little different then now and I hate to sound like an old timer, but the Gods, they were the smartest AND the hardest brothers. They were whopping people out but at the same time they were teaching the math. So you respected that, whether you were drawn to one thing or the other. I mean me, I was always impressed by a smart dude. But hey, if you had a knuckle game with that, that was bonus. So that's how it was. You get drawn in. Next thing you know, you're getting your lessons. You're doing your little fast. Maybe you could eat a couple of pieces of fruit over a 48 hour period, if you were weak, you know, or just fast it out. I wasn't really swinging that way, but if you were heavy into that swine, you might have to detox your body and that's pretty much it. You know, not a big ritual. They give you a name, your born name and boom!

What's in a name?

You know, it matches your personality, so you gotta be that dude. Like Justice, a lot of dudes that were on the rougher side, that might be it. You had Knowledge, which was always kind of like a basic name, like John, so maybe a humble cat might have something like that. Then sometimes you might have something like a "Supreme Magnetic" or "Unique Understanding" or something that just sounded beautiful. You know, lots of "Uniques."

And "Jahmega." Do you want to break that down for me?

Jahmega Allah, you know, that's the "Big God" right there (Laughs). I mean, I was always that dude with that personality, always present, always into something. I swear to God man, wherever I'm at now, wherever I was at then, I always had that deep voice, that boom, that bass.... There was a snap to it that E.F. Hutton shit. Ears are marked, listen up. So that was that. It's a beautiful thing.

True indeed... but there's much contradiction in what you've just shared.

Definitely a little bit of hypocrisy there.

I mean a good knuckle game, at least I'm assuming, must have gone hand in hand with a good stick up game.

(Laughs) Yeah, I mean, let's keep it real. The older Gods that blew up in my neighborhood, here's how they met their fate. There was one, like I said, Justice, who took us on, he had a couple of kids with my homeboy's sister, Kiki. Anyway, he had a few seeds with her and I don't know what the fall out was, but it got to the point where God would walk right past the kids and wouldn't even acknowledge them. And he would see them every day. You know what I'm saying? So, then you're like, alright. Then of course, the crack era came in. You know you're going to have a few Gods hitting that pipe, that's automatic. So, now you have that fall out, or pitfall. They had heroic moments, right, and they'd be Supermen again, but then you see them fall victim to this and that. Justice, like I said.... Everybody went down to North Carolina with a package, 'cause that was the thing to do. Couple of cats possied up, as we used to say, they got together, got a couple of packs and took it down South. So what happened was, these dudes got locked up and Justice got his ass beat to death in jail in North Carolina. He died in prison. Then there was Big Un, big fucking brother. He was kind of chilling out, you know, he started doing a little charity work, taking kids to ball games. He started dealing with this chick and I guess he got physical with the woman. The mother had a 14 year old who shot him to death. Then there was Knowledge, who was a younger brother. He was about my age. One day, he got his arm nearly chopped off in Brooklyn. He got hit with an axe. Anyway, he got on the pipe and fell off. I hadn't heard from him in a minute, then somebody, this is years later, was like "Yo, you hear what happened to Darryl man, Knowledge? His daughter died in a swimming pool, his two-year-old." I was like "Damn man, that's fucked up." My man is like "Well, ain't you gonna ask me?" I was like "Ask you what?" He goes "How the fuck Darryl B----- got a swimming pool?" And I was like "Yeah, the thought did kind of cross my mind." Apparently, he had gotten arrested on some drug charge, some crack-head shit, and the judge sent him to the navy, right? So he stayed in the navy for like six years. Got out and he was a ferryboat captain. He was with the ferry, the Staten Island ferry. Seventy-five grand a year, bought a crib, got married, did it lovely. And that's the Gods for you. Crazy, how life turns out.

So what does that say about "Knowledge, wisdom and understanding?"

1, 2, 3... Can't have one without the other. You know what I mean. Man, woman, child, right? I mean look at my situation. It seems like a very simple mathematical equation until you put it into action. Man, woman, child. Sun, moon and stars... but it's not simple at all. Not in my life at least.

That's why there's only 5 percent.

(Laughs) I feel you on that.

Freeze Frame 1: Today's Mathematics

In 1963, [Clarence 13X] left temple number 7. (...) He knew from his lessons while in the temple that the Original Man (blackman) was the Supreme Being, God. Supreme means the most high, being means to exist. God, therefore is the name given to the highest form of existence: the Blackman. This supreme form of life is the vehicle through which Allah's will is made manifest. There is no substance in the Universe or world that the Original Blackman's body does not consist of. Even the forces we see around us, above us and below us have their beginning within us. He also knew from his lessons that 85% of the people were mentally blind, deaf and dumb, while 10% of the people were devils who kept the 85% ignorant and that 5% were the righteous teachers who would lead the people from certain destruction. What he now realized was that this was applied to him individually. That he, as an individual, was God and therefore could not sit by idle and depend on a "mystery God" to do what he himself was blessed with the innate abilities to do. He changed his name from Clarence 13X to Allah and went to the streets of Harlem to do God's job. God's job as he saw it would be to reach his blind, deaf and dumb people and from them raise the 5% Nation.

This excerpt from *The Greatest Story Never Told*, a brief biographical account of the Father, should help those of you who are disoriented find your bearings. It begins to explain notions that are central to the organization's philosophy: the belief that the black man is God and that the black woman is the Earth who receives the God-body's seed (the child). The rejection of a "mystery God in the sky" draws focus to black people's condition in the physical world, the wilderness of America. This Marxist materialist approach encourages members to assume responsibility for affecting change on a personal level through knowledge of self and socially through mentorship and community involvement.

Education has always been a focal point of the Gods' efforts. Though the School of Allah has stood at the same address, 2122 7th Avenue, in Harlem, for over 40 years, the 5 Percenter approach is hardly classroom-based. "I attended U.C.L.A., now how that grab you?" raps Lorenzo Dechalus. "University of the Corner of Lincoln Avenue." There is no confusion here between schooling and education. In fact, the Gods' pedagogical techniques borrow heavily from the Socratic method of instruction. Rather than adopting a didactic format, the lessons are designed as questions and answers, call and response, thus ensuring that the student remains an active participant in his or her learning.

In "What we will achieve," the NGE describes its principal goals:

1. National consciousness: Defined, in part, as the awareness of black people's role in history and of their contributions to World civilization.
2. Community control: Sovereignty over educational, economic, political, media and health institutions.

3. Peace: The absence of confusion or chaos, which is order, the foundation upon which the science of life rests.

The 5 Percenters' understanding and interpretation of the world relies heavily on the science of Supreme Mathematics, an intricate epistemic system that assigns a semantic designation to each of the numbers from 0 through 9. Similarly, the Supreme Alphabet attributes a meaning to each of the letters in the alphabet. The following is an abridged rendering of the 5 Percent Nation's "Supreme Mathematics" pamphlet.

1- Knowledge (Known-ledge)
The foundation of all things in existence. It means to look, listen, observe, learn, and respect any and everything.

2- Wisdom (Wise-dome)
Wise words ways and action, the application of your knowledge.

3- Understanding
The clear picture drawn up from your knowledge and wisdom. When you can see clearly through your "third eye."

4- Culture/Freedom (Free-dome)
Culture is the way of life for the black man, woman and child which is I.S.L.A.M. (I-Self-Lord-And-Master)

5- Power/Refinement
Power is the truth. It is the light that brings one out of triple darkness and into their [sic] true way of life.

6- Equality
The state of equilibrium. Knowledge (1), wisdom (2) and understanding (3) is all being born into equality (1+2+3 = 6).

7- God
The Asiatic black man, the original man who has knowledge of himself and all things around him.

8- Build/Destroy
To add on anything that is positive (build) or to do away with anything that is negative in one's cipher (destroy).

9- Born
To bring into existence physically through the womb of the black woman and mentally through Allah's mathematics.

0- Cipher
A complete circle consisting of 120 degrees of knowledge, 120 degrees of wisdom and 120 degrees of understanding.

In addition to studying Supreme Mathematic, the Supreme Alphabet and the science of life, the Nation's lessons touched on philosophical themes like the nature of time, the relationship between the material and the spiritual or the existence of free will.

More Like Church but You Walk Out Feeling Great

If we rewind just a little, you said you had people of all ages at the rallies...

I mean, the main thing is, you'll go to some of the rallies and you'll see old wisemen, like dukes that were 5 Percenters since the sixties. That's pretty impressive man. To keep your attributes for forty something joints, that's props. But for a lot of us, it was just a phase. A lot of brothers signed up so they wouldn't get whooped up in jail, you know. Then there's a few that stick with it. A lot of us though, we might have lost the attributes but there's still things that stay with you.

Like the lessons.

Yeah, and you think about those lessons when you see things fall into play. Like if I have a bad day on like the 21st of the month, I'm like, ah, the day of confusion right here. You know, the 2 before the 1. You know what I mean? I wonder.

So, the lessons. You have the Lost Found lessons, the 120 lessons.

Yeah, the 120. You got the 1–36, the 1–40, the degrees.

The 1–10.

Yeah, the 1–10 is your foundation. That's the Supreme Mathematics and you know what those are. From that foundation alone, everything spawns off. Then you get into the different elevations, right. I mean there are guys...

That are way out there?

Yeah, and when you think about it, all this stuff has to be committed to memory. Like certain times, people took that more seriously than other times.

I find it interesting that there's so much emphasis placed on memory and word of mouth. I mean, for something that's been around for forty some odd years, there's very little record of what the Gods did or what they were about.[2]

No, it's one of those things.

There's no definitive manual. Manual's not the right word, but...

Yeah, there's no book but maybe that's because it's not a religion.

No, but it's an organization, at the very least.

Yeah, it's a way of life. That's why. I mean, you're not going to find scriptures for it. I mean it's a common misconception, but like I said, there're no scriptures, there's no prayer. And why would you think so? Because there's constant mention of the word Gods, right?

Not just that but the fact that it is a doctrine with ground rules so to speak... and its ends would strike me as similar to those of a religion or spirituality in the sense that the members strive for a raising of consciousness, so there are some parallels.

Yeah, but it started because Clarence was a member of the NOI.

Right.

He was under Master Fard and you know, it was supposed to be this black thing but he was offended because the founder of the NOI, W. D. Fard Muhammad, was Arab or white or whatever he was. A lot of people used to say he was half. He was offended by that and he left and he formed his own Nation.

But there's a lot of overlap with NOI.

There's a lot of common ground but there's also a lot of dissimilarities, and even more so with traditional Islam. I mean you read from both scriptures. You read from both the Bible and the Qur'an. The garb is different. See Elijah [Muhammad—W. D. Fard's successor] was smart enough to understand that what black Americans were at the time, in the 30s. I mean, what are you going do? All of a sudden black guys are going to start wearing full garb and growing long beards and wearing kufis? That would be way too much. That's why if you go to a rally, you'll find that it's very much like a church experience? A lot of call and response, whereas in traditional Islam, there's none of that. I mean, it's a very different experience than praying in a mosque, very different. Like I said, it's more like church, but you walk out feeling great.

Freeze Frame 2: Yakub—It's Arabic for Jacob

The Nation of Islam (NOI) and the Nation of Gods and Earths are secular. The statement seems a little oxymoronic but it is accurate. In this context, the terms Allah and Islam are used as the Arabic words for God and peace respectively and not as Muslim concepts. The NGE emphasizes that its practice of Islam is scientific, rather than religious. Science is concerned with determining exact certitudes about the world through observation. Religion, the Gods argue, is that which cannot be detected by the senses. Once again, this underscores the value placed on the material over the mystic or the unseen. Furthermore, 5 Percent doctrine is not contingent on the 5 pillars of Islam: *Shahada* (possession of faith), *Sala* (prayer), *Zakah* (giving of alms), *Sawm* (fast), and *Hajj* (pilgrimage to the Holy City of Mecca).

Despite the bountiful similarities between the organizations, there remain some important points of contention, most notably the circumstances around the Father's departure. While the God Jahmega states that Clarence took issue with Master Fard's mixed racial background, that explanation is not entirely factual. Both NOI and the NGE classify the world's population into two categories: original man (all non-white races) and people of color (in this case, whites). Clarence's discontent with the NOI lay primarily in the fact that he rejected the notion that W. D. Fard was the physical embodiment of Allah. Instead, he contended that all Original men were Gods—emphasizing the divinity of all non-white people, be they black, Asian, Arab or East Indian.

One of many historical and philosophical convictions that both Nations do share, however, is the belief that the white race was created some 6,000 years ago by a crazed scientist called Yakub. Genetic selection and cross breeding over a 600-year period of time were responsible for increasingly lighter skin complexions. According to the NOI's doctrine, Yakub's progeny, the white devil, is destined for a 6,000-year reign before the Original man can regain his rightful place as Supreme Being.

At a surface level, the plot seems to be a variant of H.G. Wells' *Island of Dr. Moreau*, only the plot unfolds on Patmos, in the Agean sea. I am, however, unsure of how literal the parable is... and this is where we pick up again.

Walking up to Ronald Reagan with a Rifle

To me, there are a few things that seem a little far-fetched... You know, we've talked about the whole Yakub thing. I mean, to me...
Stop. Okay... "The devil is grafted."
Yeah.
Okay, maybe a little farfetched if you see test-tubes, or you know, a petri dish, or whatever. You have that science fiction notion, that might be something in your head that's farfetched. Yeah, but then you take a look at this Earth, right? And then you say, wait a minute. Let's look at what we have here... Latinos. That's a grafted race. That's not, that's nothing pure there. That's white people raping and fucking natives. So you get Latinos. Let's put that in perspective. Look at black Americans, both North and South. That's a whole other nation as compared to the people over in Africa with whom we have no connection whatsoever. So, to say that that's not true, or that it's farfetched, I don't think that at all. I read an article in the newspaper, a couple of years ago. This Danish scientist had determined that all blue-eyed people had one common ancestor. So who's that common ancestor? I mean, I read this article and I got a tingle down my spine.
You kept the clipping.
You know what, I do have that clipping.
I know, that's what I meant. I remember you showing it to me.
Okay. Alright. See that? Now you know I'm not bullshitting. So who was that? Is it that scientist that you might have read about?

Now given the similarities between the two movements, do you find people that pledge allegiance to both organizations? Kind of straddle the fence...

Yeah, I mean... it's weird, it's almost like the Nation [of Islam] never really strived for that membership. I mean the last time you really saw that was before the million man march. The Gods, they kind of made way to gangs, real gangs, Crips, Bloods, you know? The kids these days, they'd rather join that rather than build.

When did you start phasing out?

When?

Yeah.

I guess that came with... that's a good question... Are you looking for a date or for a mind-frame.

A mind frame.

Okay, good... I guess that came when I got into other people in history. I started reading more about the NOI. There's a point in your life when, and I wish everybody did, but not everybody does, but there's a point in your life when you start picking up some revolutionary reading. You might read H. Rap Brown's *Die Nigger, Die*. You might read some Stokley Carmichael, or Assata. So you might get into some of these books. And I guess the difference between the NOI or the 5 Percent and say a Black Panther Party, the Nation taught to separate and start your own, whereas the Panthers, they wanted in. They wanted in, by any means necessary, you know? So I started reading some of this stuff, compared to some of that. And then the 5 Percent, peace God, this, that and a third kind of becomes secondary to that because these guys were doing it on a national scale.

You're saying the Gods never expanded?

No, no. I mean, I've met Gods from San Jose and stuff like that but it was never really a movement in that sense. It's like to join the Black Panther Party you had to read some books.

And get some weapons training

Yeah, and to join the NOI, you had to know a few things. To join the 5 Percent, it was a lot easier to get in, you know, to maybe know your 1 to 10 and you're accepted in. And it's designed for cats that might not be... I mean, the Nation and the Panthers had a discipline to them, and when you think discipline, you think army. It's something you take a bit more serious. I mean, if you're serious about your people, then it's almost like a natural progression. And if you're not, then you stay in, or you fall off your lessons and just become an 85er, walking around with no knowledge. So, it's like, what do you want to be. I just took my knowledge to the next level. I mean, NOI, Panthers, they were changing laws and getting things done. Adding on is great, don't get me wrong. You know, I love that. The math is nice but a few breakfast programs are a little more impressive in my book.

Marching on congress...

Yeah, things like that. Walking up on Ronald Reagan with a rifle. That'll make your heart pump.

So what did the Gods contribute? What would you say their legacy is?

There were some rallies. There was police brutality in Harlem and the mayor [Republican John Lindsay] had actually called the Father to come out and actually stop, you know, to put out a cease and desist order to the Gods in Harlem or that would have got torn apart. That shows the power back then and that was when the Nation was probably at capacity. That's a powerful thing, to have the mayor call a guy to stop a riot. Almost like what you saw Malcolm X pull off a few years later.

But see, when I think of American consciousness as far as black movements are concerned, a lot of people don't know much about the 5 Percent. It's almost like they fell through the cracks or got overshadowed.

I hear you... but it's hard to quantify, right, because how many black boys got that self esteem in them, where they can sit in a science class and say, you know, 93 million miles? *[Referring to a set of lessons called The Actual Facts that teach, among other things that the Earth is 93,000,000 miles from the Sun.]* You know what I mean, be able to break down a few circumferences and be able to sit and stand tall and walk proud... and where did that go for that kid? That's an effect right there. This guy became a good father. So, it's easy say there's not no new stop signs but like I said there are a lot of intangibles there. A lot. Just look at the music. Let's go there, you know what I mean? Wise Intelligent, Brand Nubian. These guys were teaching millions. Millions. Big Daddy Kane's "Young, Gifted and Black." I remember brothers blasting that shit. Everybody was on some chest out shit with the Gods. Everybody. The Wu. Cats like Rakim, Kool Moe Dee, Busta Rhymes. Where did they get their wizardry from? The Nation, so there you go, right there. How many cats did these guys employ? You can take that in a lot of directions, a lot of directions.

So fast-forward a decade or two, where are you at with all this today?

Me? Every brother I come in contact with, I'll drop a jewel. You ask any of these brothers that I play ball with, any of these cats you see me interact with, and if they had to describe me, eventually, somewhere down the line they'd be like "Yo, that brother knows some shit." You know what I'm saying? There's a respect factor that comes with me, because I do do that. I might not be trying to tell a cat today's mathematics, but there's some teaching involved. Whether it's how to build, whether it's just common advice on your day to day, or maybe you'll learn some history on who you are, something that you might not have known yesterday but that you'll take with you for the rest of your life and maybe pass on to your seed. And that's not with no arrogance. So, do I do my duty on the regular? I think so, I can honestly say I think so.

Epilogue: Dog Is God Spelled Backward

While editing this interview, I was amazed by the breadth of topics covered, from the NOI, to religion, racism, and gang affiliation. A good deal of the exchange was left out in hopes that you, the reader, would feel compelled to seek additional information on your own. Adbul Noor's *The Supreme Understanding: The Teaching of Islam in North America* is a solid place to start. Books like *The 5 Percenters: Islam, Hip Hop and the Gods of New York* and *In the Name of Allah: A History of Clarence 13X and the Five Percenters* paint a more in-depth and critical picture of the Gods and Earths.

One stretch of conversation I hated to see go was our talk about the 5 Percent's influence on hip hop and how underappreciated it has been, particularly in the area of linguistics. How many times have you heard, or maybe even spoken, the expression "What up G?" Can I be at liberty to assume that you thought the "G" stood for gangster? Now try dropping the o and the d from God.

And to think you've known about the 5 Percent this entire time.

Endnotes

1. Throughout the interview, my questions and comments are in italics. The God Jahmega's responses are in roman font.
2. McGill's library holds only one book on the Nation of Gods and Earths. This is more indicative of the dearth in 5 Percent literature than it is a poor reflection on the university's catalogue.

Fourteen

Pieces of Iman: The Pilgrimage Home

Yassin Alsalman

I would like to first prologue this chapter by saying the following: I am a human being. I am a man. I am a Muslim. I am an Iraqi. I am a Canadian. All attributes are pieces of my identity. I can only speak for myself and not my entire religious community, cultural heritage, or for all those that look like me. Therefore, if you disagree, then you're probably not me. Peace be unto you... SALAM

> Unfashionable Prejudice, like the mustache I inherited
> What stash *huh*? The evidence so evident,
> No precedent sold, messages so soulless,
> In fact them weapons you own...
> Same brand and barcode
> Slave land in our homes, war of mosque domes on TV
> I watch it GROW, like American waistbands from burgers in their hands
> BUT
> When I mention America, don't assume I'm sent from a cleric or associate pretentious heretical henchmen you're married ta'
> Jury bench stench of an enema pretending to be...
>
> Peace to Allah and Justice
> And Justice and Justice Justice
> Peace To Allah and Justice....
> (*Brand New Being*, The Narcicyst)

Who Would Have Thought That the Ghost of Extremism Past Would Come Back to Haunt Us?

With the advent of September 11th, a new wave of artists started flying high and scorching stages and microphones to clear Islam's name once and for all. Whether enticed or not, Muslim, Arab, or Eastern fetishism infected us all around the new millennium. *Kuffiyah*s became the new accessory; sexy Arabs became the new hot terrorist (coming to a runway near you), and Iraq became the new black. With war, comes product. In this chapter, I will be examining how the growing Muslim artist repertoire began and their weapons of mass dissection—of your stereotype, that is. Without even delving outside my own experience, it will be a personal dissection of the moments in my life and the people I have encountered that led me to be who I am and *why* I am as an "Arab Muslim." The reason I chose this approach is because, there is no one book, no quote or saying, map or land that can describe the emotion of our experience. It is in flux. It is something that is relatively new. How do you footnote your own reality?[1]

Before we delve into the so-called "new" Muslim, I would like to ask the question: What is a Muslim? The word "Muslim" stems from the same word in Arabic that birthed "Islam." The root word is *Salam*, which directly means "peace" and indirectly relates to "giving in" or "offering one's will." Therefore, the word Muslim means "he/she who submits to God"; submission plays a major part in Islam alongside will or, as they say in Arabic, *al-niya*. Let's just say "Where there is a will, there's a way" is the only motto that applies to Islam 100%. Without willing your faith into action, there is no submission, so to speak. In Islam, everyone is a Muslim as long as they will their submission through the religion. This is not to negate any beliefs more than it is to show humanity that we, as in the human species, are created under One source, One Energy, One God. Whether you choose to acknowledge it or not comes down to your own free will. This goes against the Islamic conquest after Muhammad (pbuh) passed, which naturally I did not exist in and cannot necessarily agree with.

Another important point I want to clarify is this: not all Arabs are Muslims and not all Muslims are Arabs. As primitive as this thought may seem to some, it is essential and imperative to be stated. It is a common misconception in the West that all Muslims are in the Middle East. It is now, and has been for decades, a fact that Islam is the fastest growing religion worldwide and is no longer a cluster of people belonging to a certain region; although the religion was born in the land currently known as Saudi Arabia. It should also be noted that a religion does not necessarily dictate the acts of the mass; neither does it reflect the gaze of the media/the watcher. My understanding of Islam, for example, could be interpreted as heathen-esque by the Islamic powers-that-be and vice versa. Therefore, the proverbial box that is our preconceptions and belief system based on "what we've seen," needs to be thrown out of the window for this chapter. Let that picture glass fall and break on the ground. The common representation of a Muslim has to be shattered and reconfigured as a mosaic of its old self—a multi-colored image that constitutes the new whole. The new us.

The echelon of righteous Islam has been in its dark ages for the last two decades. Christianity and Judaism, the two other monotheistic religions in the family, have hit their theological pubescence and grown out of their childhood (some would say not completely either). Islam, being the youngest of the religions, rarely grasped at its chances to grow. My key observation is that most Muslim countries failed to modernize, opting instead to Westernize. I see this as a crutch that may not allow the Muslim world to fully grasp its identity as unique and away from its colonized mentality. Sure, Burj Dubai is a sight for sore eyes but how does it truly represent our capacity to self-govern and attain sovereignty from the colonial ancestry deeply rooted in our Earth? I do not know a solution to this either and can't assume which direction or how to modernize uniquely. A fruit doesn't fall far from its tree, but it can plant its own roots, can't it? From Mecca to Mecca Mall, we've come a long way on our pilgrimage toward Capitalism's "Freedom."

This dichotomy is also present in many artists from the Muslim World. The foot firmly planted on the West tugs at the foot teetering in the East for those who were raised outside of their native lands. Many convictions, thoughts, decisions, and interactions are both cemented in and torn apart by the dual-identity. Not to say this experience is insatiable, it is in fact this duality that allows most "modern-day Muslims" to develop a larger understanding of difference. The interaction of cultures leads one to feel *inter*national. The hyphenated experience of a Muslim comes both through birth or conversion; there is no difference in the distinct drive to separate the X from Y, the Muslim from the Canadian, the West from the East. Furthermore, this relationship is strengthened and re-invigorated with hatred and fear through our social mediation sources; be it FOX News or Hollywood. The relationships between the colony and the colonial powers have lost their romance and are now in the final phases before a bitter divorce. What about its children? Where will they be when the fight is finally over?

Home Bitter Sweet Home

It's hard living in the West, when I know the East got the Best of me.
Could be Looking in my eyes, but you'll never really see the rest of me.
(*Destiny*, Omar Offendum)

I was born to Iraqi parents in Dubai in the early eighties. My mother was my source of warmth and logic, while my father helped me cultivate my expression and artistically passionate side. They were both from Basra, the southern part of Iraq, also dubbed the "city of poets." I grew up around my father's parents for the early years in my life in Dubai, my grandfather would pick me up from kindergarten and let me sit in his lap while he drove the car but made me believe I could. I know this sounds dangerous but think of it metaphorically: my ancestry was taking me home and letting me shape the rest of my journey. I see this now as one of the most pivotal moments in my life. (Anyway, the school was a two-minute drive from my home he could have picked me up by foot if he wanted to for God's sake!) He would pop in Michael Jacksons' *Bad*, which was my favorite album at the time. When Michael Jackson died, I had a flood of memories re-emerge from that era. The way my house looked, the color of the carpeting, my sister's height difference; all these subconscious memories resurfaced with the passing of an icon. But I digress; MJ will do that "to ya." Pop culture meets your subconscious.

My grandparents had relocated to the Emirates after years of exile in Kuwait. My grandfather being part of the political structure in Basra, he and many others were told to leave around the time Saddam ousted the previous leader and the Ba'th regime took a new turn toward violence. He packed up and left Basra, with my father staying in Iraq with his grandmother. He spent a majority of his youth indoors, molding and crafting model airplanes and imagining himself in them. Until this day he tells me he wished he had become a pilot. I think those model planes and flying were the symbols of his life; he would spend the rest of his life traveling trying to establish a home.

My father had left Dubai one winter to visit a place I didn't know. He came back with a leather jacket for me and a promise for the family. My parents thought it was smart, being Iraqi and all, to give their children a second chance at an identity (i.e., passport). My father left Iraq with a traumatic experience. Being an artistic person, the army was not his dream profession nor did it satiate his goal to dream. He studied to be an architect, went to England for his masters and married my mother at the age of 24. He took her back to England, where she also did her masters, and they relocated to the Emirates for work. In the mid-70s, my mother was a microbiologist and my father was a successful architect. Her heart remained in Iraq while my father's longed for a home. Experience is everything.

At the age of five, we went to visit my mother's family in Basra for the third and last time in my life. Slowly becoming accustomed to being in Iraq, I remember looking forward to the sleepless nights in the hot houses and moving up to the rooftops to sleep. I remember my uncle Ghassan's dog being bigger than me. I remember my sister getting electrocuted by the fridge. That summer in Iraq was our transitional period. My father had stayed back in Dubai to bring everything to a close and we were brought to Iraq, in my mind, to say goodbye to a land that will never be the same. The Iran–Iraq war had just come to an end but the face of conflict was still grimacing in the streets. Iraq was under military dictatorship. The slight moan toward a Saddam speech was viewed with suspicion; people feared even thinking opposition to the television appearance of Iraq's Sith Lord. I vividly recall Saddam feeling like a boogie monster more than a president my whole life, even though I didn't understand why until now.

On my last day in Iraq, my mother took me out to buy toys before leaving for Canada. She bought me a water gun and a wooden Lego set of Baghdad city. I never opened that box and showed my family the riot of the century in my last night "home." I pleaded and cried and huffed and puffed until I fell asleep. I just wanted to touch home. Next thing I knew, I was on the plane, on my way to my new step-motherland. Arriving in London, we met my father who was now ready for the next step in his life but obviously anxious from the alienation of immigration. As I pulled out my water gun in the airport, my father reached in for the plastic pistol and threw it in the garbage. He told me that he would never buy me guns again. I rained on that airport floor with bullets of tears ricocheting around my father's lessons. My father was the type to let you learn the lesson. He always said "words are only true if you act them out." Word is bond. I never owned a toy gun after that day. I was later told my father had an experience in Iraq where a major in the military put a gun to his head. This led him to a nervous breakdown and eventually his departure from Iraq. If I could get my hands around the neck of the man that pulled that instrument of hate on my father, I would crush my fate like Marty McFly and his sports almanac. But it was written.

The years in Canada flew by. My father coasted and looked for work while my sister and I attended what I like to call "immigrant school." Classe D'acceuil, French for "Help Class," was where interim students went before they attended real schools. Chinese twins, a Peruvian boy, three Indian siblings, Arabs...everyone was not where they were from. I went to first and second grades until I learned how to think and compute in French. God, I write about it like it was a motherboard! Programmed-to-be-destination-unknown-home. It was interesting to say the least; I was reborn in ways I didn't understand until later in my scholastic life, when I developed my self-understanding and dynamics of people...in grade school. There was the white-as-snow Bully, the one that called me names like "immigrant" or "brown." He was pudgy in his countenance and bouncing on his continent. There was the Korean dude that I always got along with (even later in high school, one of my best friends was a Korean dude). The Harold to my Kumar. There was the sweet innocent girl in class that did everything perfectly and, as a young boy, you would get this weird feeling in your stomach like you want to hang out with her but you don't understand it so it translates as awkwardness. I felt like an Arab Nerd. I was always the extroverted one, the one that wore yellow gym clothes and they would call me Banana man. My asthmatic ass couldn't run a meter in snow without slowing down considerably, so I was also the one that didn't end up in the game. But being the outcast really helped me and I loved it! There were kids that either loved me or hated me. Nowhere in the middle, where me, myself, and I were growing up.

One day, as the bus dropped me home, the snow banks were really high on the front entrance of our house so I started shuffling toward the back, trying to avoid any extra second spent in the minus-god-knows-what weather. As I passed by our garage door, the words emblazoned on the back wood said:

RETOURNER CHEZ VOUS ANIMAUX

Go back home, you animal. I was going back home but now home felt like someone took a shit on our lawn. Home felt alien. Home felt in flux all over again. That incident opened the floodgates to the next couple of years of our family life. We got our citizenship and became "naturalized." My father moved his parents to Canada and sponsored them, while my mother's parents refused to leave Iraq. On the day of our "swearing" into citizenship, we were asked to raise our right hands and pledge allegiance to the Queen. I told my grandmother I didn't want to do it, because I am Iraqi. Isn't that cute? I kept my hand down for the recital until I caught a glimpse of my father's fire-burning eyes. I raised my hand like the question was 1 + 1 for a million dollars.

Fear Makes the World Go Round

Socially we're near the root
Old Folks scared of youth, and we fear the truth
Tell me what's dear to you and who?
(*Nothings' Fair in Love and War*, The Narcicyst)

The garage incident prompted my father to use his rights as a Canadian citizen and express himself directly to the media. This was the early nineties and Bush Part 1 had set action toward his theatres of war. The floor seats were sold out and balconies filled up for the Mother of All Battles. As my mother wailed watching Iraq plummet under clouds of depleted uranium smoke, war sirens became the soundtrack to my family's life back home. I spit on the television as GHWB announced the war. I was proud of that. Then my sister and I went upstairs, my father tucked us in and she hugged me all night while I cried. I was afraid of living. I was afraid of dying. I was afraid of my mother being sad. I was afraid, because I didn't know why I was afraid. This period in my life was the beginning of the identity crisis.

The newscasters from CFCF12 visited us often. My father made sure the local media knew that the prejudice against Arabs was unjust and immoral. He left Iraq to live "free" and he sees his children get bullied; spray paint bombarded his property, judgment at work, people becoming more and more doubtful of Muslims and Arabs. The atmosphere was tense for years. I remember this being the beginning of the end of my honeymoon with the melting pot known as Canada. I started to see the old brick behind the façade of beautiful buildings, the sneer being the smile. To assume that life would have been easier in Iraq would be silly, and I could finally feel the falsehoods of freedom getting uncovered by the aftershocks of bombings in the East.

Fear is the cousin of anxiety. I started developing a sense of paranoia at a young age. Incidents where bullies would chase me home were paramount in my psychological development. I recall running so hard from a bicycle while two French Canadian kids, who used to be my "friends," laughed and scoffed at how weak I had become. With my asthma kicking in, I would slow down and they would smack me from the bicycle. It got out of hand one day and they hit me with the bike, knocking the wind out of me for the first time in my life. Between the impact and my sheer panic, I thought I was dying. They obviously felt horrible. My revenge was a renegade with a cause, a rebel without laws. My exclusion slowly drove me to find a new me, a person that didn't give a damn about the constant finger pointing and difference. With the war passing and people slowly re-shifting their focus on other things, my life resumed and the running stopped. My father had faced some hardship during those years, losing his job and being forced to shift gears to maximum immigrant drive. My parents attempted to open a restaurant, while my father found a job in Ottawa. My mother would wake us up at 6 am, take us to school and head out to the restaurant. Pops would come back every weekend for a couple of days and head back to Ottawa. The strain on their relationship and our family unit proved too much. My father quit his job and headed back to the Emirates. We closed the restaurant and moved to a smaller apartment. My cocoon of comfort was being de-feathered.

At the age of 13, I felt as though I had caught the swing of things. Finally out of grade school, I was about to join my rebellious sister at a high school called FACE in Montreal. This place was like *Fame*; it really did make me want to live forever. My friends cut class, couples were making out all over the place, there was music playing in the hallways, kids learning instruments, dreads, punks, GIRLS. There were things I really didn't pay attention to in grade school. As I was learning to fit in, my parents were searching for a way out. Over the Christmas break, my father came back and told us "we are leaving Canada." My world was in absolute meltdown. What about my friends? What about my French? What about my school? I'm sure my parents understood the fear of leaving what I had been taught all over again was scary. We were moving to Abu Dhabi. My sister was in denial. As I slowly understood who I was to become, I quickly realized this dream wouldn't last. My sister threw a going away party at our house (Don't tell my parents, they haven't found out about it yet.). As the party wound down and friends started trickling out, I saw my future spinning in front of me. There was a tape in the cassette player that was calling my name. Wu-tang Clan's "Enter the 36th Chamber" became my salvation. This album played so much in my Walkman, it ripped into shreds upon landing in Abu Dhabi. I listened to it for the entire 20-hour trip back East, as though trying to memorize the culture that I had become accustomed to, lest I forget it to some corny Arabic pop music. Once again, I was a stranger in my home.

Over the years, I moved back to Canada after years in the Middle East. It was strange because, growing up in the Gulf, I was treated by certain people as "the immigrant" or the "*ajnabee*," the foreigner. I came back to Canada in 2000 to study Political Science and Communication Studies. I became a rapper, a part-time teacher and a master's graduate. I saw three wars on television that meant nothing and destroyed everything. I marched the streets chanting slogans for Justice in Iraq and Palestine. I found out I was an Arab Muslim after all. I found home, but not on a physical plane. My home was with those that were like me, those who were searching for an origin that has been wiped off the map, as we knew it. I found it in the hyphenated Muslim. I found it in the immigrant. I found it in my soul, in my spirituality, in my religion. I married a woman who, in her own light, showed me the path toward enlightenment. I found my best friends and lost some of them to fate. I found God and lost It. I am constantly gaining and losing faith, I am not your average Muslim. The rest, as they like to say, is His story.

Like Immigration, We Keep It Movin'

I write right to left, you write left to right, metaphor of a foreigner's plight.
—(*Destiny*, Omar Offendum)

My story is not unlike other Arabs, Muslims, and any other peoples who needed to leave one place for the chance of a "better life." I look at this as a new form of identity bonding, a social mediation of the nomad, a cross-continental conundrum that has become the catalyst for this century's children. We are a product that cannot be put in a box. These experiences I share with you are the simplest examples of the prejudice that can create an identity crunch that is only rivaled by the pain of losing one's motherland. When I was asked to write this chapter, I thought of many different ways to represent what a Muslim is. Then I thought to myself, who am I to tell you what to believe, how to believe, who believes, and who we are. I am still trying to figure that out myself. I travel a lot these days, crossing airports from New Jersey to the Netherlands, Boston to Beirut. And I am yet to touch Baghdad the way it feels to touch Montreal. I think this is something I am going to have to live with and become it.

Islam is beautiful. Being raised with this religion has taught me vigilance, perseverance, driven me to my goals, it has brought me will power that I never imagined I could muster. I also think it has demons, just as any other ideology does when it is practiced by the most vindictive of mammals, the human. I like to see myself as a member of the so-called "new Muslim." I define that as a Muslim that is practicing, believes in God, but also is not alien to expressing oneself through non-traditional means. A Muslim that wills his/her faith in God, through ways even our brothers and sisters did not think possible. I found my faith on a stage somewhere with a microphone. It was one of those moments I can't describe. I was on stage and someone screamed out "Yo, it's the Osama of this rap shit." I couldn't take it anymore. So I started reading the Qu'ran, searching for God, searching for myself and the answers to the questions I was afraid to ask for two decades of my life. I never knew. In order for them to know, I had to know. Each One, Teach One.

As I mentioned in the introduction to this chapter, Muslims worldwide started reaching for microphones, paintbrushes, cameras and beat machines to be heard over the cacophony of news wires and propagandist television stations feeding us a demonic representation of Islam. The hegemonic order of thought and deceit became the archnemesis to truth seeking; a lot of artists around me ask themselves "Am I even a Muslim? Who am I?" I, of course, stay quiet and have no answer for it. The open-ended nature of our identity and what we are becoming is forever in transition. Daily news reports will affect us more than your average Caucasian resident here, North America. September 11th may have scared the white out of you, but it put us in jails; it placed bags over our eyes and flags over our demise. Since that day in New York City, the death toll has magnified itself to grave proportions. Iraq has become a chessboard for any operative to play his game; from Blackwater to Al-Qaeda. Afghanistan hasn't really changed. Osama Bin Laden aka "The boogieman part 2" is still alive and represents Islam to mainstream America. When I say mainstream, I mean those who don't question what they are told. As I visit places like Lebanon, I see the cultures we all grew up with as separate, binding as one. And I'm not talking Disneyland culture here. Communication, emotion, separation, identity, religion, style—all these personal expressions are becoming inseparable and in common between nations and religions. Idioms no longer shape who we are, we are shaping ethos with our own steeples. Oh, the times they are a-changing.

I am currently sitting on a plane, on my way to Seattle, Washington to rock a show as my professional alter ego The Narcicyst (yes, I quoted myself earlier, how ironic, huh?) I am not too sure how to end this chapter because there is no conclusion to our inclusion. Everything in life plays its part, every moment chains onto the next like a strand of DNA shaping a hybrid culture, skin tone, religion, people. There are no clusters, I like to believe, there is only one whole. The reason I wrote this chapter in this format is for you to know that, we are not a people that can be boxed in. There is no *one*-way to go about finding God, in my opinion. I do not believe in borders (but my passport leads me to believe I have to) just as I don't believe you have to write a chapter or essay in a certain format to get a passing grade. If you want to know who we are, talk to us, live with us, experience with us. Don't believe that a book can tell you who we are, let alone this book. The best way to really learn about Islam is to do what we immigrants do best, travel. All around you there are Muslims that have had different paths to the same goal, life. The same life you share with us. As I approached the security clearance in the States, the man at the counter stared at my ring which says *"Tawakalt 3ala Allah."* He asked me where I got it, I told him my mother got it for me to protect me and it says "may all your actions be blessed by Allah." He answered me with one of the most comforting and elementary sayings of gratitude in Islamic culture *"Hamdulilah,"* praises due to Allah, Thank you. I felt like we were in the Matrix and he was welcoming me as one of the chosen ones. We may be different but we are the same. We may be seen but we are rarely heard. It's time for a new chapter so I leave you here. Don't believe the hype, unless it's playing on a stage, iPod, or theatre near you. Then join in the madness and flourish in the commonality of our differences. We will not be silenced. We are everywhere. We are Muslims. We are the future. We are you.

> First hand experience
> Second class citizen
> Third person verse
> Four fam member immigrant
> 5 sided pentagon, triple 6 presidents
> All led me to never forget where the seven lives...
> The Prince of Poets,
> Delivery or relevance
> The BADdest kid, madness with soliloquy and militance
> In the room between your skeletons and elephants
> Similar to Arabic calligraphy and lettering. (My word is bond)
> Like speaking to a friend you see the deepest of serenity,
> Sleeping with the enemy,
> This beat is just end of me, on the roads like a fender

> But they don't get the picture still rendering
> I stay on like my wedding ring, in reverence of many things
> Never will it ever bring the heaven that I'm leveling
> Around, chasing the sound patient, though I don't talk slow,
> I know, we're groundbreaking like a pothole
> (*Second Class Citizen*, The Narcicyst)

Endnote

1. Like this, September 12th, 2009 7:36 pm. Montreal, Canada. At the dinner table because the desk wasn't ready.

Part Four

Teaching Against Islamophobia

Fifteen

Common Sense, Uncommon Knowledge and Fighting Words[1]

Carolyne Ali-Khan

Introduction

Common Knowledge for a New Generation

NYC, Student: "No disrespect Miss, but don't you be scared to go Pakistan? Aren't your people all terrorists?" "Yo, Miss! Your family is from Pakistan! Do they be blowing themselves up over there?" "Don't Muslims hate us? That's what I heard..."

Pakistan, Taxi driver: "Your President Obama, is better? I hear American peoples they happy, they don't like Mr. Bush.... We don't like our government, and the Taliban, they are very bad peoples, cause too much problems for us here. Pakistan is a very beautiful country but these peoples make too much problem for everyone..."

I have daydreams in which I take my high school students with me to Pakistan. Once there they meet the people "on the street," who (like the taxi driver quoted) are quick to remind us that the people who make the news are not the face of a country. They meet Pakistani teens with their cell phones and Facebook friends. They watch local television and see a hugely popular late night talk show that is hosted by a glamorous, intelligent, political "dame" (who is every bit a diva). Going through bookshelves in Pakistani homes, they read popular local short stories written in English. They notice that the tales are poignant, or romantic, or sardonic and irreverent. Immersed in the rhythm of life "over there," they see for themselves that the notion of the hateful Muslim enemy is an absurd myth, propaganda at its finest (and that "being Muslim doesn't mean that people blow themselves up").

I am not surprised that my students connect Islam to terrorism. It has been eight years now since 9/11. A 15-year-old (young adult) in classrooms today would have been just seven years old when the events of September 11, 2001, began to unfold. An entire generation has grown up in the repercussions from that moment. Anne Bakalian and Mehdi Bozorgmehr (2009) examined in detail the "backlash" from 9/11 on Muslims in America. They conceptualize it as: (1) hate crimes and bias incidents, (2) stereotypes and scapegoating, and (3) governmental initiatives (against people of Muslim/Arab/Middle Eastern origin). Each of these mechanizations of prejudice is mutually reinforcing, with governmental policies "legitimiz(ing) the backlash in the eyes of the American public" (p. 2). Meanwhile the climate of fear and hate has been further legitimized by the media propaganda machines that (historically true to form and largely unchallenged)[2] are churning out endless stories, video games, novels, and movies that reinforce the notion of "Muslims" as bad and dangerous.[3] Unsurprisingly, the majority of Americans report having learned either nothing or only negative things about Islam and Muslims (CAIR, 2006); my experiences in classrooms confirm this (Ali-Khan, 2009). Given this landscape, it is most likely that bias against Muslims is all that my students have ever heard.

The propaganda machines have been noisy but the war machines have been quiet. At the start of this school year only a few of my students knew that the United States is at war with Afghanistan. "Not just Iraq? Are you sure?" they ask me, "We don't see nothing about that on the news." Meanwhile the U.S administration is considering sending up to 40,000 more troops to Afghanistan (Schmitt & Shanker, 2009). As the military keeps reaching into American schools,[4] looking for children[5] to enlist, I worry about students like mine who do not have enough information to be cognizant of all that may be at stake when they formulate their ideas about "terrorist Muslims who blow themselves up." The number of dead and injured is a sobering reminder of one of the repercussions of this ideology of hate: at the time of this writing (October 2009) there are an estimated 1,340,000 Iraqi deaths due to the U.S. invasion (justforgeinpolicy.org), and over 4,000 Afghani deaths[6] with an additional 1,000[7] killed by unmanned U.S. drones[8] in Pakistan. In addition to the dead, there are countless other thousands (probably hundreds of thousands) who have been injured and displaced by the U.S. Department of Defense's "Overseas Contingency Operation" (which is the new, better-sounding title for what was formerly called the "War on Terrorism").

Regardless of how they are named, these conflicts remain bloody as ever[9] and have been largely framed as being against "Muslims"—a tactic that deliberately and erroneously defines them as religious[10] rather than political disputes. Meanwhile, the U.S. President Barack Obama received the 2009 Nobel Peace Prize (presumably for making us all feel good about the future), despite the fact that the United States is (in effect) intransigently at war with three countries (Afghanistan, Iraq, and Pakistan).[11] Obama's nomination came under considerable critique in the international and left-based press,[12] but it is unlikely that this opposition will reach the ears of the majority of teachers and students in the United States. The implicit message of this particular "prize" for peace suggests that symbolic goodwill is more important than actual life and limb. Or perhaps the message is that in the discourse about war/peace, Muslims/"people from over there" simply don't count.

Although I try to remain wide-awake to these social and political moments, it is hard for me to fully digest the extent of Islamophobia present in the United States today, and to really process the way in which this pedagogy, just outside the classroom, can infiltrate more formal teaching spaces. Christopher Stonebanks notes that teachers are likely to hold the ideal of social justice and fighting the good fight in high regard, but reality is a little more difficult (2004, p. 100). I concur. Although conscious of the neoliberal tendency to quickly fault public schooling (Tobin, 2009), I still wonder if perhaps as a teacher I have not done enough; that I have said less than I wanted to, or meant to, or thought I had to; and that I have underestimated the impact of the common knowledge gleaned from growing up in an Islamophobic age. In this chapter I present a few of my experiences, offering a sample of some the kinds of Islamophobic curricula moments that I have encountered. What follows are examples of what we (as educators) can "teach against," how we can "teach from," and where we can "teach about" as I explore a few strategies to fight back against destructive "common knowledge" about Muslims/Islam (and Pakistan).

Teaching against...

"It ain't necessarily so": When Tolerance Isn't

Tuesday morning, 8:20 am, on the street in front of a landmark skyscraper in midtown Manhattan, I am waiting to meet half a dozen eager but still sleepy high school students. We have received a special invitation at my school: We are to be guests at the Simon Wiesenthal Center's museum of tolerance "The New York Tolerance Center." The museum is generally closed to the public, so I have not had a chance to preview the exhibits; this is the description from their website:

> The *New York Tolerance Center*, in the heart of Manhattan, is a professional development multi-media training facility targeting educators, law enforcement officials,

and state/local government practitioners[13]...Through interactive workshops, exhibits, and videos, individuals explore issues of prejudice, diversity, tolerance, and cooperation in the workplace and in the community.

We sign in at the registration desk and descend a long open spiral staircase. Architecturally the entrance spaces are impressive, I expect the exhibits to be equally glossy and engaging; I am glad we came. At the bottom of the staircase we find ourselves...in front of a huge wall, it references the September 11, 2001, attacks on New York. It proclaims, "Global hate has inspired international terrorists to target the U.S as a symbol of freedom and democracy." My heart sinks. There is no wandering allowed in this museum, no deviation from the tour we are given (en-masse with perhaps 100 other students and teachers, lockstep). Our next stop is a giant collage of reproduction racist posters and photographs; many of them are about slavery. Although there are dozens of slogans and images about "race" (with "race" being presented as black/white) I see only one poster about sexism. This poster is the cover of a *Hustler* magazine showing the lower half of a naked woman in a meat grinder, her naked glossy behind is plump, airbrushed and alluring (this is a sex magazine after all), and centrally positioned. Our guide directs our attention to it. A hundred teenagers dutifully try to direct their gaze. Some look at their feet. I wish I could say that things get better as this tour continued, but they don't. We spend the day trapped in a lair of authoritarianism, righteousness, inappropriate material and misleading information. There are a number of unpleasant incidents that occur. I am depressed at having brought my students to this place. More disturbing is the idea that in addition to all the children I am there with, multiple police departments (including New York, the largest police force in the country) and DA offices are "trained" with this "education." "They hate us" is the phrase jumbling around in my head. So much for tolerance.

"We are a symbol of freedom and democracy so they hate us" is a phrase rife with the type of thinking that is antithetical to tolerance, education or understanding. The question "Why do they hate us?" was the "question" echoed over and again in the press about 9/11; it ends with a question mark that lies. It is not a question, nor is it rhetorical. It is however a teachable moment and it bursts with answers that don't begin with "because." As educators we can problematize this sadly all too common "question" as we ask: Who are they? Who are us? What is left out of these constructions? What do they imply about Muslims? What do they assume? How do these words suggest both you and "we" should feel? How would you feel if you were a Muslim or Middle Eastern student (or anyone who could be construed as "they") reading these words? How do these sentiments compare with other inflammatory statements that you have heard about Muslims or other non-dominant populations? How do they fit with your knowledge of stereotypes? Take out the words "why do" and look at what is left, "they hate us." The way in which the "question" is constructed, is there any room to refute this idea? Think about the times that you have heard the question before. What answers have you heard? (Spoken by whom, for whom, and in what context?) Who benefitted from these answers? Who was harmed? How does/doesn't this question fit with work toward peace, and the concept of "tolerance"?

Something Rotten: Islamic Bombs and Soccer Balls

Recovered from the trip and planning for my lessons, I am watching a link from a teacher resource site. The curriculum package is about Pakistan. The lesson is entitled "Forget the War on Terror. Think of World War III" (performanceeducation.com). So I am watching WWIII: Pakistan started it (and, of course, it was televised). This is the story: First missiles flaunting Pakistani flags were paraded through the streets on army trucks (you can see the logo from Pakistani TV, as this is real footage from Pakistan's national Independence Day). Then the rockets were fired. We are given an aerial view. Next, flames engulfed the screen, buildings exploded, forests melted. The obligatory mushroom clouds plumed. (The musical accompaniment to this is credited as the film score for the horror movie *Saw II*.) Figures 1 and 2 show two stills from the film.

Figure 1: Missile with Pakistani flag

Figure 2: The end of the world as we know it

Reality check: 1. The United States is the only country in the world to have *ever* used the atomic bomb (and we used it twice).[14] 2. This footage documents something that *has not happened;* therefore it is not history; it is not a documentary, nor is it reasonable conjecture. I received this lesson in a link e-mailed to me from a teacher resource site, and I remain stunned by it. In a personal correspondence with the publishers about this material they informed me that they estimate their readership of this at "10K."

The site that this educational material comes from is called Performance Education; it carries free lessons for teachers, with a marketing approach that uses mailing lists. This site gets between 20,000 and 39,000 hits per month during the school year (quantcast.com). Their package on Pakistan comprises 20 lessons in 31 pages. It is worth looking at a little more. Lesson 1 (Figure 3) is a graphic organizer named: "How are you connected to Pakistan?" The answers hold both good and bad connections, which I sum up in the following way—Question: What kinds of connections are possible? Answer: (a) Bad connections: Iran (against whom we are considering war, because of their nuclear weapons), Iraq (against whom we are at war because "we thought they had nuclear weapons"), Afghanistan (against whom we are at war "to wipe out the terrorists"), and the "Islamic bomb" (which, although not theirs[15] is a term that simply defies all rational explanation). (b) Good connections: Angelina Jolie (in a film about an American journalist murdered in Pakistan), soccer balls, and Pakistani food.

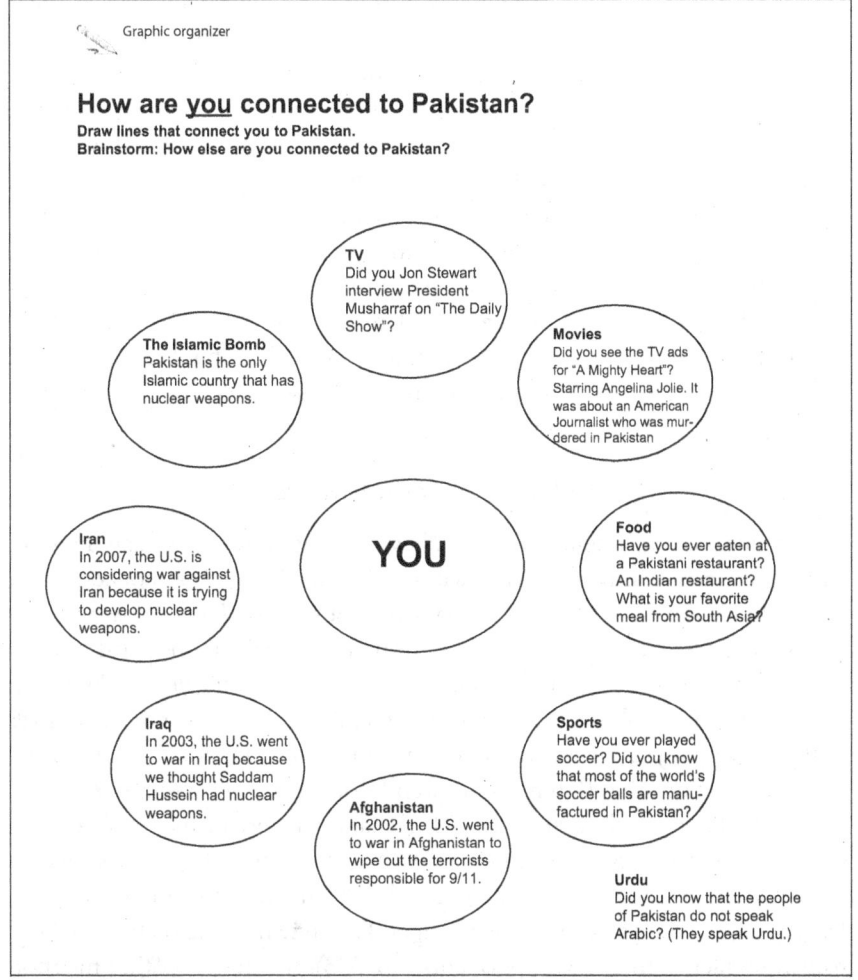

Figure 3: Teacher resources "Connecting you to Pakistan"

The idea that teachers might use this worksheet, to tell students that they are connected to Pakistan because they/we (in United States) might go to war Pakistan (as we should/have with their neighbors) but, "Hey, we all like eating and soccer," strikes me as a comedy skit gone horribly wrong. The sheer inhumanity of this definition of "connecting" is stunning. In addition, this lesson presents a form of multiculturalism that even when "positive" reduces people/s to the objects that they produce/consume. In this, it offers parallels to other troubling renditions of multiculturalism, such as, for example, many of the U.S. representations of Native American populations in which their "pretty costumes" are appreciated but the people in them are rendered invisible.

Besides their overt racism,[16] wide readership, aggressive mailing, and the production sophistication of the materials, I am additionally concerned by the level of care and detail that these materials evidence.[17] The "history maps," "political analysis" activities, graphic organizers, classroom debate activities, YouTube links, and media news links, are all clear and well presented. *They look legitimate.* As teachers and administrators are pushed toward scripted notions of education, teaching[18] and learning it is easy to see how lesson packages that *look* sophisticated and appear to come from a reputable source are tempting to use. But as Shakespeare famously proclaimed in *Hamlet*, something is "rotten in the State of Denmark" (1996, p. 43). As educators we must be attuned to the fact that in a racist and Islamophobic world much that tries to find its way into classrooms (like these materials) may in fact be deeply and thoroughly rotten.

And the Correct Answer Is...

I am preparing my students for the New York State Regents examinations. Among other tasks, the students will need to analyze global concerns and political cartoons. Globe Fearon's classroom textbook, *Using Primary Sources (2004)*, prepares students by using the "primary source" of a political cartoon of Saddam Hussein grinningly rolling a carpet over a giant death (skull-and-cross-bones) symbol as he welcomes the UN inspectors. The correct answer to the accompanying question is that Hussein was in fact hiding "weapons of mass destruction."A different exam prep book, *A Key to Understanding Global Studies* (Killoran et al., 2007), lists "International Terrorism" as a "Global Concern," but makes no mention of war and invasion as global concerns (War matters less than terrorism?). The book informs students that, "Iran, Iraq, Syria, and Libya have not only helped Palestinian terrorists but used terrorism to silence their own opponents" (p. 333), it offers no other mention of Syria and Libya (in over 400 pages) while Iran and Iraq are referenced only in passing. As with the resources from Performance Education, these materials reinforce the message that all that is worth knowing about the Middle East/Arabs/Muslims is that they are dangerous/terrorist.[19]

I would like to say that we need not be overly concerned, as we can rely on textbook watchdogs to guide us. The American Textbook Council bill themselves as an "independent national research organization to review social studies textbooks and advance the quality of instructional materials in history" (2008, p. 2), which sounds promising. They have issued a recent report entitled, "Islam in the Classroom, what the textbooks tell us" (historytextbooks.org, n.d.). In a 55-page report, they argue that American social studies textbooks are *not Islamophobic enough*. On the topic of terrorism they state, "The idea that 'poverty and ignorance lie at the root of the problem' sounds plausible but is not true" (p. 33) and "it is impossible today for American teachers and students not to be exposed to *a belligerent dimension of Islam*" (p. 53, italics mine). They then argue that a failure to connect this "belligerent Islam" to classroom teaching on Muslims represents a "civic failure," a "deficiency" (p. 54), and a misuse of taxpayer dollars. The alternatives they propose include the right wing Fordham Foundation's publication *Terrorists, Despots and Democracy: What Our Children Need to Know*. A closer look confirms that in each of the alternative materials they list as resources for educators, Islam is presented as the cause of violence, all Muslims are characterized as the same, and "we" (the good guys) are obligated as professionals and citizens to stand in collective patriotic educated opposition to "them."

Lunatic?

All of these texts and examples use a conceptual binary that separates the world into two reductionist and opposing categories.[20] The Pakistani American scholar Fawzia Afzal-Khan, who critiques the notion of bad Muslim/good West, eloquently notes that this positioning is both dangerous and so preposterous as to be "cartoonish."

> Battle positions are now hardening on both sides: the avenging (yet seen in their own eyes as "liberating") Judeo-Christian armies of the West on one hand, and the so-called terrorist Muslim barbarian hordes massing on the gates of "civilization" on the other. Such a dangerous but surely cartoonish division of the world into these simplistic binaries was popular only amongst the lunatic fringe, I used to think. However that "fringe" has expanded since 9/11 to include most of the U.S. citizenry today. (2005, p. 21)

Teachers and students can work together to unravel "the lunatic fringe" that Afzal-Khan speaks of. The materials I have referenced are the tip of the iceberg, they exemplify that "the fringe" is organized, systematic, and diligent in producing racist materials against Muslims. As we become more aware of the extent of this cartoonish oppositional positioning and ubiquity of Islamophobic materials, we can use this knowledge to fight back. For example, using vocabulary terms such as "propaganda," "bias," "stereotype," and "inference," educators can work with students to pose questions that unpack the assumptions, silences, and messages evidenced in Islamophobic curricula. After a lesson on propaganda (what it is, how it works, when it is used, examples, and common forms of it) it did not take my high school students long to be able to critique a book entitled *Mesopotamia*[21] (Mayfield & Quinn, 2007) that my school district distributed. Figures 4 and 5 are the pictures from the book.

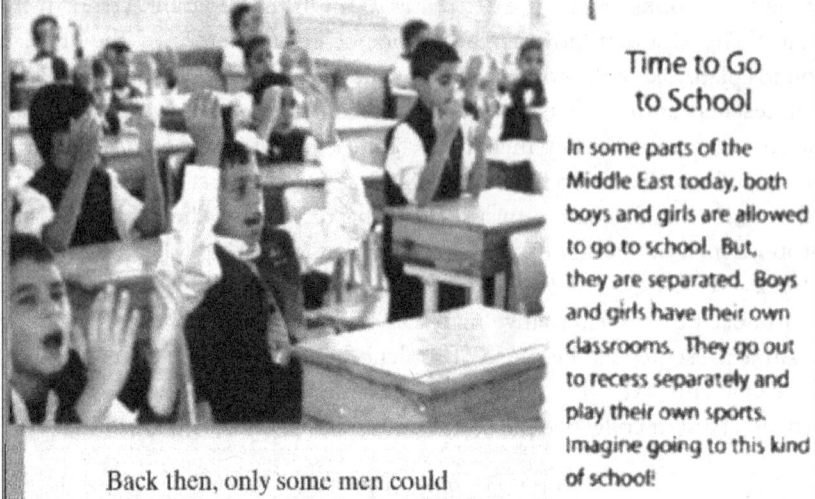

Figure 4: "Imagine!" a page from the textbook *Mesopotamia*

Figure 5: Another photographic image from *Mesopotamia*

"Obsession": Notes on a Bad Film and a Good Tool

I have received an unsolicited free movie. I am not alone. Twenty-eight million DVD copies of *Obsession*, a movie, were sent (free) to homes as an insert in local newspapers and magazines (including, I have been told, the *Chronicle of Higher Education*). Producer Raphael Shore, proclaims, "*Obsession*...a documentary was seen by one out of six Americans" (Obsessionthemovie.com). While it seems unlikely that this is true, it received extensive media coverage.[22] The full title of the film is *Obsession: Radical Islam's War on the West* which was followed (2009) by a film called *The Third Jihad: Radical Islam's Vision for America*. According to the linked website these films uncover the truth that innocent looking Muslims are in fact violent, irrational, and a "lurking danger" to the American way of life "in the land of the free and the home of the brave" (Radicalislam.org). (Upon reading the words "lurking danger," I cannot help but to envision crouching-shrouded-dagger-clutching "Muslims" hiding under kitchen tables across America.) The premise of both pseudo-documentaries is that "fanatical Islam" is about to consume us all. Although this may, too, seem lunatic to many, it has been taken seriously and plays upon old fears. Teachers can use knowledge of media literacy and film criticism to examine how the visual tactics and imagery from WWII has been co-opted and recycled over and again to create "the enemy." More specifically teachers can use Jack Shaheen's *Reel Bad Arabs* (2001), Shirley Steinberg's "Desert Minstrels: Hollywood's Curriculum of Arabs and Muslims" (2004) and Johnson and Blanchard's *Reel Diversity* (2008) as excellent resources on this topic.

My response, joining the outcry against this film, was to use a free downloadable application called "comiclife" (plasq.com/comiclife). Comiclife allows users to insert still pictures (from films or photos) to go along with captioning graphics that together create a comic book. My idea was to illustrate places to pause the film with a brief guide of questions to ask. It was also to encourage teachers and students to use an art-based technological application to create counter-hegemonic narratives. In my thinking, the strategies for a fight against the kind of propaganda evidenced in *Obsession* must both (a) encourage students to a critique of the kinds of tactics used to sway arguments and (b) encourage them to research information that contradicts (and, in effect, "unsilences") the narratives left out of films such as these. Together teachers and students can ask questions about what is represented, left out, or implied, and what other story might be told. They can use media literacy or media literacy classes to play the game of finding the fallacies and inconsistencies in a film.[23] Figures 6 through 9 are samples of a few pages from the comics that I created to support a critical reading of the film. They were accompanied by a list of resources about Muslims. This type of art and media-literacy-based work can be one strategy to teach against Islamophobia to create counter narratives to propaganda.

Figure 6: *Obsession the movie*—Connecting Islam to fear

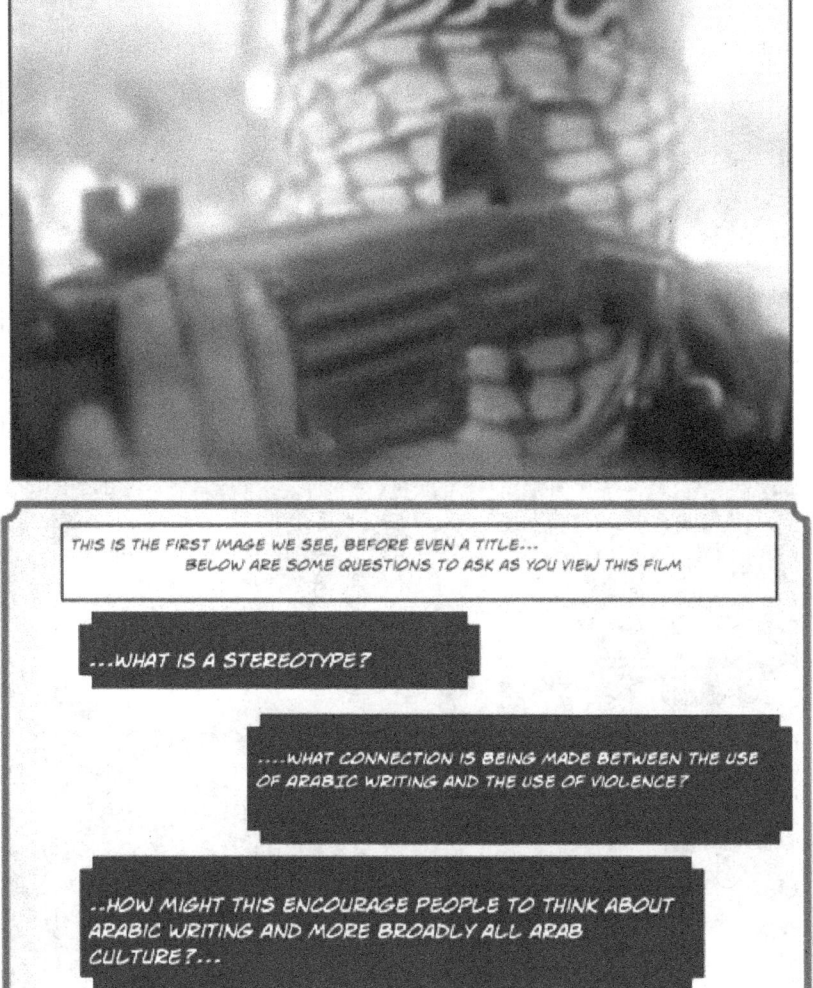

Figure 7: Arabic script = Terror?

Figure 8: Two very different women

Figure 9: The pedagogy of bias

Teaching from...
Beyond Common Sense

"I would say we have to go beyond the common sense of the people, with the people"
—Paulo Freire (Horton & Freire, 1990, p. 100).

Another way to counter Islamophobia is to counter common sense about Muslims and Islam in America. Common sense claims that the United States and her allies are at war with "Muslims" because there is something to be gained and that this moment is not like other moments when we were wrong. Common sense posits that we are always fair people who do not target the innocent; we are just trying to protect "ourselves." Common sense lives in the now, removed from contexts that might taint it. According to the history books found in my classroom no one was ever disadvantaged by U.S. actions. These books, in effect, present us with a "historiographical Disneyland where all of our intentions are good" (Kincheloe, 2004, p. 4). Classroom studies of geography and history can help students go beyond the normative dangerous myths of common sense.

Non-necrophilic Concerns

The truth of American history is that the type of racism presently deployed against Muslims (both on personal and policy levels) is not new. Villaverde, Heylar, and Kincheloe (2006) encourage us toward a history that "gives up necrophilic concern" and instead focuses on looking at the way reality has been constructed and at the forces that have shaped institutions and consciousness (p. 319). They ask us to view history and ask "Who is advantaged and who is disadvantaged?" The United States has a history that (although admirable on many levels) also includes a legacy of oppressive policies against Native Americans and African Americans. In addition, there is a history of targeting immigrant groups who have been held accountable for the actions of the few in their home country and have paid a price for this perception (individually and collectively). Linda Alcoff explains the logic at work, "strongly felt social identities are considered by many to harbor inherent political identities" (2006, p. 22). The assumption behind targeting immigrant groups is that some hyphenated Americans (in this case Muslim Americans) are *not really us*—they are "the others" who are a threat that must be dealt with (of course, other hyphenated Americans such as "Italian Americans" are just *us*).

Cognizant of darker moments in U.S. history, Japanese Americans recently used their own experiences and struggles to understand those of Muslims. In WWII Japanese men, women, and children were placed in internment camps that separated them from the rest of the American population. Several teaching resources exist that speak about their plight.[24] In post-9/11 moment they have publicly come out in support of South Asians in the wave of recent anti-Muslim profiling, "We weren't responsible for Pearl Harbor and we shouldn't have had to prove our loyalty any more than anyone else. They shouldn't either" (Bakalian & Bozorgmehr, p. 58). The treatment of the Japanese was not unique: After 1917 German Americans were subjected to cultural suppression and involuntary assimilation. Considered as part of the "Bolshevik menace," Communist party members (including naturalized citizens and immigrants) were forcibly expelled to the Soviet Union. During McCarthyism and the Cold War, communist party members and sympathizers were detained, blacklisted, and stripped of their livelihoods. During the Iranian hostage crisis, Iranian students and foreign nationals were deported. Currently Middle Eastern and South Asian Immigrants are detained, interrogated, deported, and deprived of normal legal recourse (Bakalian & Bozorgmehr, pp. 32–54). Teaching about these events is moving beyond teaching children to play nice together as Muslims and non-Muslims in the classroom (much as this is also important) but it is a move toward teaching about structural levels of discrimination. The idea here is not to bash the United States but rather to be honest about what has been done, and to use history to help us analyze (and change) the present.

Social studies teachers can examine the history of imperialism and the twinned history of anthropology, to understand how struggles that are often framed as ideological, religious, or racial are often (beneath the surface) struggles over resources. Mark Zuss notes the interplay between struggles for resources and struggles over representation (1999). As teachers we can look at history with our students to pose the question, "What else might be going on?" We can engage students in questions about competing ideologies. For example, in the American logic of common sense Jews and Muslims are often framed as "natural enemies" (like cats and dogs?). Knowledgeable global studies teachers can use history to refute this. Afzal-Khan (2005) argues that much of what has been framed as anti-Semitism against Israel is "the ire of the colonized and neo-colonized people against the colonial Master" (p. 21) and the "legitimate frustration of the worlds have-nots against the haves" (p. 20). Statements such as these raise issues that go beyond the common sense positioning of competing religions and identities to ask deeper questions about power and inequity.

A Sense of Direction

The notion of a monolithic Muslim identity can be dismantled on multiple fronts. Teachers can read Ozlem Sensoy's essay, *"Where the heck is the 'Muslim World' anyways?"* (2009), for a good-sense explanation of the unsound ways that Muslims are often represented in textbooks. One strategy to help school age students unpack the redeployment of Orientalist stereotyping can be to design lessons that give them a sense of the differences between nationalities. A teacher might ask: "Where are you from if you are[25] Egyptian, Iraqi, Jordanian, Lebanese, Moroccan, Palestinian, Yemeni, Syrian, Saudi, Iranian, Israeli, Turkish, Afghani, Bangladeshi, or Pakistani? Who are your neighbors? What is your capital city? What is your average income, life expectancy, climate (etc.)? Students can map the distance between the capital cities of these countries. They can use maps to find populations of Muslims around the world (including, for example, Indonesia). They can look for landforms that lie between or are shared by these countries. They can research and compare the countries using different atlas, Internet and textbook sources to understand the physical, geographic, and cultural range of diversity. As they do this type of research, the notion of the uniform Muslim/Arab/Other quickly falls apart. Using a different approach they can respond to similar stereotypes that refer to peoples they are familiar with and who are different and proud of their identity. The statement, "Oh, Puerto Ricans, Dominicans, Mexicans, Cubans (insert ethnicities here), you're all the same, aren't you?" (said with an exaggerated wink) has worked well to elicit outrage from my students. The absurdity and injustice of lumping people together in a single label/identity quickly becomes apparent when it is applied to groups familiar or close to us.

Teaching about...

Uncommon Knowledge

In this final section, I offer examples of some uncommon knowledge of specific Muslims in the arts. If we are to believe the Western media, Pakistan (like other Muslim nations) is populated entirely by barbaric woman-hating hordes. It is a nation of stern men in flowing garments (whom friends of mine in Pakistan like to refer to as "fundos" or "beardies") who are the most conservative of Muslims. Reality is different; those portrayed in Western press are (unsurprisingly) not the truth of the country. They are often referred to even in the Pakistani press as "the lunatic fringe." In this final section, I offer a few glimpses of a Muslim country and people that make up the Pakistan I know. They are not the lunatic fringe.[26] They are intelligent, complex, and rational; they sing, dance, and read, and (perhaps most shockingly) they laugh, merrily poking fun at themselves and at the world.

Queens and Dangerous Mangos

In essentialist logic "the enemy other" is not only unlike us but also indecipherable. "The other" only laughs sardonically or menacingly or in sadistic glee. A look at the images in the press confirms that Muslims only show their teeth when they are being evil. We all understand that they do not chuckle, giggle, or fall over laughing. Muslims are un-fun. Humor either in its folk or its most profound form is absolutely beyond them. Mikhail Bakhtin notes how laughter has been philosophically and ideologically important and held "a deep philosophical meaning, it is one of the essential forms of the truth concerning the world as a whole, concerning history and man" (1984, p. 66). Part of taking oneself seriously is not taking oneself seriously. Americans know this; *The Daily Show* is serious stuff.

Pakistani TV star Begum Nawazish Ali is also serious stuff; she is popular and adored; a gorgeous, politically savvy, hard-hitting late night talk show host (see Figures 10 and 11). Often clad in elegant saris, she has a sharp tongue and an elegant singing voice; she also can make you laugh. Politicians (even conservative religious politicians like the mayor of Karachi) vie to be on her show. Clips from BBC documentaries (available on YouTube) show her shopping in local markets and being greeted by enormous smiles of admiration and mirth by a range of men and women from all echelons of society. She is not dressed in the elegant attire of her show; she is dressed in the jeans one would expect her to be in. The *begum* (Urdu for "society lady") as everyone knows is a man.

Figure 10: Late night talk show

Figure 11: Gorgeous, smart, sophisticated (and in drag)

Looking at the press in the United States, one would be right to think that Pakistanis don't poke fun at their leaders, past or present. "'This speech is dead. No emotions.' General Zia said, 'People will not only think that I am a prisoner in my own Army House, but that I am also suffering from some kind of dementia.' The Information Minister nodded enthusiastically as if that had been his plan all along" (Hanif, 2008, p. 67). "I mean when they say that thing about your mother, they have absolutely no intention—and I am certain no desire either to do what they say they want to do with your mother.... They have not even *seen* your poor mother" (p. 18). Mohammed Hanif's, *A Case of Exploding Mangos* (2008) from which these quotes are taken, is in places graphic (both with violence and with sexually explicit content).[27] It is not a book to give students unless you have cleared it with parents and school administration, but it has held firm to the top of the bestseller list in Pakistan (available on Amazon) and offers a witty deeply irreverent look at Pakistani politics, culture, religious practices, and military life. It is insightful, poignant, and sardonic. Not only is it widely read, but when I was recently in Pakistan it was the book on everyone's lips. I include it here to point out that Muslims are capable of poking fun at themselves and push readers to ask: If this is not what you expected, what did you expect? Excerpting from this book and books like it, it is a question we can ask our students.

Singers and Rappers

Adil Omar is an 18-year-old rapper/singer/songwriter from Islamabad, Pakistan. He has worked with musicians such as B-Real of Cypress Hill and magician/comedian/actor Penn Jillette.[28] I asked him how he has been received in the United States, "People have assumed that I'm either a religious fundamentalist or fanatic, or that I'm not well educated. I usually break the stereotype when they get to know about my Secular Humanistic views and listen to my music or have a proper conversation with me. People either have crazy assumptions or are very interested and open and welcoming to someone from a different culture and background." On the role of music for Pakistani youth he continued, "Music has an important role for Pakistani youth but I don't feel it's important enough. I believe it should make more of a social impact instead of just being entertainment for young people" (personal correspondence, 2009). His song "Islamabad" reflects the ambiguity of Pakistani youth:

> Pure apathy, establishment's thrusting its hips back and forth as it's robbin' from the public for kicks Under close watch— You, Your's, Your Mother and Sis It's the land of the trapped and the corrupt politicians But it's official that we like it so much.

Adil and his fans in Pakistan are well aware that systemic problems plague their country but they (like many Western youth) are turning to music (including hip-hop, rap, and rock) to argue back against the establishment. Robert Mackey of the *New York Times* recently published an article noting and linking to other Pakistani rock music bands that address political issues (*NYT*, September 11, 2009). DJ Shazia is a woman who has used her dance music mixing radio DJ skills on Pakistan's FM 96 to successfully fight the influence of the Taliban in the war-torn area of Swat (CNN.com, October 30, 2009). Bakhtawar Bhutto (assassinated former Prime Minister Benazir Bhutto's daughter) has a rap-tribute to her mother that is popular on YouTube (n.d), which has played repeatedly on Pakistani television. She raps to footage of her mother (the former leader of Pakistan), "Dear Mom if you can hear me, Crazy intelligence, I've got a few things I never got the chance to say, but if I could have. Yo. I would take the pain away...." Sadly these are themes with which many of my students can identify. For students interested in music, Coke Studio in Pakistan (cokestudio.com/pk) recently filmed MTV style live shows with performances from popular musicians who encompassed a range of westernized and traditional Urdu folk music as well as a hybridized fusion of the two. Each of the episodes was themed (individuality, harmony, equality, spirit, unity); all of the videos can be downloaded.

Conclusion

Against, From, About, and Out

A cautionary note: although I have emphasized similarities here, I do not intend by the examples of work from Pakistan to promote the idea that, "Pakistanis are not barbaric because they are in fact like us in The West." I introduce these examples to offer suggestions for teachers to find organic places where we are most accessible to each other and work outwards from there. There is much to be discovered, a YouTube search will yield a hoard of music and a cache of BBC documentaries about a Pakistan that is not the place of terrorists and the lunatic fringe. A search at Amazon.com will yield a shoal of books that do not play into the stereotypes of oppressed and rabid Muslims, but instead portray individuals who navigate a complex world.

I cannot take my students to Pakistan, and we will probably continue to be bombarded by messages of fear and hate about Muslims in and outside of schools. But I am hopeful that we can work to counter the bloody common knowledge of this racism and all racisms. Remembering my own time in high school I recall a song by the band Pink Floyd, about a lunatic who starts out "on the grass" and ends up "in my head." Cautioned by these lyrics and encouraged by the work of scholars who fight against Islamophobia, I hope that we can go beyond common sense—the lunatic can be contained and one day soon this work will be unnecessary.

Afterword

Words to Chew on

Paulo Freire asks that we problematize the world, in which we are immersed, avoiding easy answers as we reach toward a critical consciousness (1970/1993; 1973/2000).

Hate/Message crimes
"All hate crime is political in the sense that it involves a statement that goes far beyond a particular act of violence or intimidation. It involves the identification of a target, the objectification of the targeted individuals, and the depersonalization of the victim. Often hate crimes have a deliberately public aspect that is meant to convey a warning to a wider community" (MacGinty, 2001, p. 650)

Terrorism
"The concept of terrorism itself is defined in such a way as to serve the interests of those in power. It is the actions of the individuals against the people or property of those in power. However this description disregards a much more significant form of terrorism, namely state can be defined as "terrorizing a whole population through systematic actions carried out by forces of the state" (Gordon, 2004, p. 106)

Facts
All thought is fundamentally mediated by power relations that are socially and historically constituted: Facts can't be isolated room values /ideological inscription" (Kincheloe & McLaren, 2003, p. 452)

Tolerance

"School programs that claim tolerance actually sustain the notion that the dominant culture must tolerate those who are *other*" (Steinberg, 2009, p. xi)

Neutrality and a depoliticization

"As soon as I started looking at that word *neutral* and what it meant it became very obvious to me that there can be no such thing as neutrality. It's a code word for the existing system. Nothing to do with anything but agreeing to what the system is and will always be—that's what neutrality is. *Neutrality is just following the crowd.* Neutrality is just being what the system asks us to be. Neutrality in other words, was an immoral act." (Horton & Freire, 1990, p. 102).

"We live in an era of depoliticization where public discourse around political questions slowly fade away in a world of ideologically charged entertainment. In such a cosmos a literacy of power becomes more and more important, as we struggle to counter the miseducation that continues to shape American views of the world." (Kincheloe, 2004, p. 23).

Oppression

"Oppression differs from discrimination bias, prejudice, or bigotry because these refer to individual acts that anyone can manifest (all humans have learned prejudices). In contrast, oppression occurs when prejudice is backed by social and institutional power. Oppression involves institutional control, ideological domination, and the imposition of the dominant group's culture on the target group" (Sensoy & Diangelo, 2009, p. 345)

Endnotes

1. Small portions in the section "Teaching against…" have been published in a previous form in *Muslim Voices in School* (2009).
2. However, a lengthy recent article (August 15, 2009) in one of Britain's leading newspapers, *The Guardian*, critiques Western hysteria over Muslims. http://www.guardian.co.uk/books/2009/aug/15/eurabia-islamophobia-europe-colonised-muslims.
3. Kincheloe and McLaren use the term cultural pedagogy to refer to the way cultural agents promote hegemony (2003, p. 442).
4. The military places recruiting advertisements in the American Federation of Teachers union-based magazine "helping" educators to encourage youth to enlist. The recruiting practices of the U.S military are addressed by NYCORE, who offer an anti-recruitment package (NYCORE.org).
5. The military enlists youth at 17, while the legal age of adulthood (to drink alcohol, for example) is 21 in most states.
6. The number of Afghani deaths here has been calculated by using the UN estimates for the first half of 2009 and combining them with previous numbers (http://www.cnn.com/2009/WORLD/asiapcf/09/26/afghanistan.deaths/); Szabo comments on the lack of information about this (July 20, 2007) *Civilian Casualties in Afghanistan, Fatal Neglect.* http://www.counterpunch.org/szabo07202007.html.

7. Although Pakistani newspapers issue daily reports on this, the numbers do not seem to be compiled. The numbers I use here are estimates complied from *Kabul Press* (http://kabulpress.org/my/spip.php?article2887) and the longwarjournal (http://www.longwarjournal.org/archives/2009/10/analysis_us_airstrik.php#ixzz0TeOEynDg). They are intended to illustrate a situation rather than to exactly document the number of fatalities.
8. Tellingly, the number of fatalities and casualties in Afghanistan (and Pakistan) are so underreported as to be almost impossible to access.
9. U.S. President Obama is escalating the war and his request for $128 billion for Iraq and Afghanistan is likely to be granted.
10. G.W. Bush called these wars "Crusades," a sentiment that is carried on in right wing media. Emran Qureshi and Michael A. Sells in *The New Crusades* examine the popularity of this idea (2003), New York: Columbia University Press.
11. The Department of Defense request for funding FY 2010 (*http://www.defenselink.mil*) offers a disturbingly detailed insight on the nuts and bolts of military expenditure and involvement around the world. In this document Iraq, Afghanistan, and Pakistan are given detailed sections (everyone else is summed up as "and the rest of the world").
12. Michael Moore and Howard Zinn are two public intellectuals who joined critics in the international press who have spoken out against this nomination. Binyon, in the *British Times*, exemplifies reactions in the foreign press (October 9, 2009) *Comment: Absurd decision on Obama makes a mockery of the Nobel peace prize*. http://www.timesonline.co.uk/tol/news/world/us_and_americas/article6867711.ece.
13. According to their website "past and ongoing participants include the New York and New Jersey State Police Departments, NYPD, New York City Parks Department, District Attorney's offices of the Bronx, Brooklyn, Queens and Staten Island, Grand Central Partnership and various other corporate and Jewish groups."
14. The use of the atomic bombs at Hiroshima and Nagasaki by the United States killed more than a quarter of a million people.
15. The phrase "Islamic bomb" was first used in 1979 by *Time* magazine (http://www.time.com/time/magazine/article/0,9171,920461,00.html), who used it again in 2002 (http://www.time.com/time/magazine/article/0,9171,1003581,00.html). But the authors of these lessons were probably familiar with it from Armstrong and Trento's recent book entitled, *America and the Islamic Bomb: The Deadly Compromise* (Islamicbomb.org).
16. Lesson 2 includes a worksheet entitled: *"What's wrong with Pakistan?"* (This, I think requires no comment.) Lesson 2, p. 5 says this, *"One bright spot?*—In July 2007, an elite force of the military—commandos—stormed the Red Mosque in Islamabad. It was the center of Islamic radicalism in the capital city. But the military shut it down, killing 100 fundamentalists. Since then, suicide bombers have killed 800 people." (I confess to being stumped as to how we could explain to students this designation of "bright spot").
17. Lesson 10 includes a worksheet with the title, *"What do adults know about Pakistan?"* Here are the instructions for students: "Interview 5 adults: teachers, principal, the librarian, parents, relatives." Show the map to each adult. State: "Pakistan is the only Muslim country that has nuclear weapons." Ask: "Which country is Pakistan?" Encouraging students to have active engagement with the adults around them and current events (as proposed in Lesson 10) could be sound pedagogy, yet it takes on a sinister hue when the point of the exercise is to reinforce specious "facts" about a nuclear-armed dangerous Islamic "other."
18. My experience of this scripting includes being guided to lesson plans that look something like this, "have-students-think-critically-for-7-minutes-use-2-graphic-organizers-have-students-work-in-differentiated-groups-for-8-minutes-use-3-Internet-links-on-your-Smartboard-incorporate-4-new-vocabulary-words-explicate-3-literary-strategies-and-2-state-standards, and remain engaging."
19. Implied, of course, is the corollary that "our" hands are squeaky clean.
20. Paulo Freire (1970) and Kincheloe and Steinberg (2004) are critical theorists who offer insightful critiques of binary thinking in educational contexts.

21. This book on "Mesopotamia" is intended for readers who are most comfortable with small books and lots of language support. It is very compact, at under 30 pages, yet includes a large color picture of Jesus and two full pages on the Hebrews with a map of Israel.
22. Jonathan Tobin of the *Jerusalem Post* claimed *Obsession* "does no more than state the obvious about the rise of Islamism, its tactics and its purpose." (http://www.jpost.com/servlet/Satellite?apage=1&cid=1222017586476&pagename=JPost/JPArticle/ShowFull). the *Washington Times* stated, "Viewing this documentary should hereafter be considered a prerequisite for participating in the debate about the national security challenges we face, and what must be done to address them." (March 20, 2006, http://www.washingtontimes.com/news/2006/mar/20/20060320-093053-5818r/). Meanwhile the *New York Times* in a deeply disturbing article reported that, "When a Middle East discussion group organized a showing at NYU recently, it found that the distributors of *Obsession* were requiring those in attendance to register at IsraelActivism.com," (Arenson, 2007). IsraelActivism is an organization of Hasbara Fellowships that is deeply pro-Zionist. This is disturbing as it re/connects anti-Islamic sentiments to being a good Jew. Inherently the argument here is that *of course* if you are Jewish, patriotic or simply someone who does not support violence, you must take a stance against Muslims.
23. This list of logic fallacies can be used as a guide, http://onegoodmove.org/fallacy/toc.htm.
24. Gail Sakurai's *Japanese American Internment Camps* (Children's Press, 2002) is a story told from a child's point of view. This book tells of the fear and injustice of being taken to Japanese American Internment Camps.
25. This list is not comprehensive.
26. I am expecting a charge that the Westernized English-speaking "elite" in Pakistan are not the "real" face of the country. I would argue against this essentialism. Leaving aside the impact of a worldwide globalization, Pakistan's colonial history of British Imperialism and connections to England have rendered it a hybridized culture with strong longstanding Anglo influences. Muneeza Shamsie points out that Pakistan has always had a tradition of English-language writers (2005). There is an abundance of English-language bookstores, several widely read and circulated newspapers and magazines in English, several television channels in English, as well as number of magazines, theatres, etc. To ignore these as inauthentic is to artificially mute an integral part of Pakistani culture.
27. Although shocking to some, Eve Ensler's *The Vagina Monologues* were performed in Islamabad in 2003. Nighat Imran Rizvi, who staged the performance, commented on it "My mother-in-law came to see it wearing a *hijab*. While my mother wept after the readings. And my husband, along with the other men, considered it to be pathbreaking," http://www.mid-day.com/entertainment/news/2004/march/78203.htm.
28. A recent interview with Adil Omar can be found at the online site of the Pakistani magazine *Chup!—changing up Pakistan* at http://changinguppakistan.wordpress.com/2009/01/07/a-rap-artists-perspective-an-interview-with-adil-omar/.

References

Afzal-Khan, F. (2005). *Shattering the stereotypes: Muslim women speak out*. Northampton, MA: Olive Branch Press.

Alcoff, L. M. (2006). *Visible identities: Race, gender and the self*. New York: Oxford University Press.

Ali-Khan, C. (2009). On being us and them: A voice from the edge. In Ö. Sensoy & C. D. Stonebanks (Eds.), *Muslim voices in school: Narratives of identity and pluralism*. Rotterdam, The Netherlands: Sense Publishers.

American Textbook Council. (2008). *Islam in the classroom, what the textbooks tell us*. Retrieved September 10, 2009, from http://www.historytextbooks.org/islam.htm

Arenson, K. (2007, February 26) Film's View of Islam Stirs Anger on Campuses. *The New York Times*. Retrieved October 1, 2009, from http://www.nytimes.com/2007/02/26/movies/26docu.html

Bakhtin, M. (1984). *Rabelais and his world*. Bloomington, IN: Indiana University Press.

Bakalian, A., & Bozorgmehr, M. (2009). *Backlash 9/11: Middle Eastern and Muslim Americans respond*. Berkeley, CA: University of California Press.

Bhutto, B. (n.d.). *I would take the pain away*. Retrieved July 10, 2009, from You-Tube http://www.youtube.com/watch?v=5RxgiLARd5I

Council on American-Islamic relations (CAIR) (n.d.). *American public opinion about Islam and Muslims, 2006*. Retrieved June 6, 2008, from http://www.cair.com/Portals/0/pdf/american_public_opinion_on_muslims_islam_2006.pdf

Coke Studio. (n.d.). Retrieved September 21, 2009, from http://www.cokestudio.com.pk/about.html

CNN. (2009, October 30). *Taliban radio wars*. Retrieved November 1, 2009, from http://www.cnn.com/video/#/video/world/2009/10/30/ctw.sayah.swat.radio.wars.cnn

Freire, P. (1970, 1993). *Pedagogy of the oppressed* (rv/20th ed.). New York: Continuum Intl Pub Group (Sd).

Freire, P. (1973, 2000). *Education for critical consciousness*. New York: Continuum.

Globe Fearon National: Using Primary Sources (2003). Lebanon, IN: Globe Fearon.

Gordon, M. (2004). The United States and Israel: Double standards, favoritism, and unconditional support. In J. L. Kincheloe & S. R. Steinberg (Eds.), *The miseducation of the West: How schools and the media distort our understanding of the Islamic world* (pp. 103–116). Westport, CT: Praeger Publishers.

Hanif, M. (2008). *A case of exploding mangoes*. London, UK: Random House Ltd.

Horton, M.,. & Freire, P. (1990). *We make the road by walking: Conversations on education and social change*. Philadelphia: Temple University Press.

Johnson, B. C., & Blanchard, S. C. (2008). *Reel diversity*. New York: Peter Lang.

Killoran, J., Zimmer, S., & Jarrett, M. (2007). *A key to understanding global studies*. New York: Jarrett.

Kincheloe, J. L. (2001). *Getting beyond the facts: Teaching social studies/social sciences in the twenty-first century* (2nd ed.). New York: Peter Lang.

Kincheloe, J. L. (2004). Introduction. In J. L. Kincheloe & S. R. Steinberg (Eds.), *The miseducation of the West: How schools and the media distort our understanding of the Islamic world* (pp. 1–24). Westport, CT: Praeger Publishers.

Kincheloe, J. L., & McLaren, P. (2003). Rethinking critical theory and qualitative research. In N. K. Denzin & Y. S. Lincoln (Eds.), *The Sage Handbook of Qualitative Research* (3rd ed.), (pp. 433–488). Thousand Oaks, CA: Sage.

MacGinty, R. (2001, December). Ethno-National conflict and hate crime. *American Behavioral Scientist*, 45(4), 639. Retrieved September 20, 2009, from Academic Search Complete database.

Mackey, R. (2009, September 11). An American accent to Pakistani rock. *The New York Times Blog*. Retrieved September 11, 2009, from http://thelede.blogs.nytimes.com/2009/09/11/an-american-accent-to-pakistani-rock/?scp=2&sq=pakistan%20music&st=cse

Mayfield, C. & Quinn, K. M. (2007). *Mesopotamia*. Huntington Beach, CA: Teacher Created Materials Publishing.

New York Tolerance Center, homepage. (n.d.). Retrieved September 1, 2009, from http://www.wiesenthal.com/site/pp.asp?c=lsKWLbPJLnF&b=4441265

Obsession in the Media. (n.d). Retrieved September 3, 2009, from http://www.obsessionthemovie.com/media_TV.php

Performance Education. (n.d.). *Pakistan on the brink*. Retrieved April 1, 2008, from https://www.performance-education.com/lessons.php?prod_set=BZ-4137

Qureshi, E., & Sells, M. (2003) Constructing the Muslim enemy. In Qureshi, E & Sells, M *The New Crusades* (pp. 1-50). New York: Columbia University Press

A New Film Exposes Radical Islam in America. (2009, May 11). Retrieved from http://www.radicalislam.org/news/new-film-exposes-radical-islam-us
Sakurai, G. (2002) *Japanese American Internment Camps.* San Francisco: Children's Press
Schmitt. E., & Shanker, T. (2009, September 20). General calls for more U.S. troops to avoid Afghan failure. *The New York Times.* Retrieved October 1, 2009, from http://www.nytimes.com/2009/09/21/world/asia/21afghan.html
Sensoy, Ö. (2009). Where the heck is the 'Muslim world' anyways? In Ö. Sensoy & C. D. Stonebanks (Eds.), *Muslim voices in schools: Narratives of identity and pluralism.* Rotterdam/Boston: Sense Publishers.
Sensoy, Ö., & Diangelo, R. (2009, January). Developing social justice literacy: An open letter to our faculty colleagues. *Phi Delta Kappan International,* 90(5), 345–352. Retrieved March 20, 2009, from Academic Search Complete database.
Shaheen, J. G. (2001). *Reel bad Arabs: How Hollywood vilifies a people.* New York: Olive Branch Press.
Shakespeare, W. (1996). *Hamlet.* R. Andrews & R. Gibson (Eds.), Cambridge: Cambridge University Press.
Shamsie, M. (2005). Introduction. In Shamsie, M. *And the world changed: Contemporary stories by Pakistani women.* (pp. xi-xx). Oxford: Oxford University Press.
Steinberg, S. R. (2004). Desert minstrels: Hollywood's curriculum of Arabs and Muslims. In J. L. Kincheloe & S. R. Steinberg (Eds.), *The miseducation of the West: How schools and the media distort our understanding of the Islamic world* (pp. 1–24). Westport, CT: Prager Publishers.
Steinberg, S. R. (2009). Preface. In S. R. Steinberg (Ed.), *Diversity and multiculturalism: A reader.* New York: Peter Lang.
Stonebanks, C. D. (2004). Consequences of perceived ethnic identities. In J. L. Kincheloe & S. R. Steinberg (Eds.), *The miseducation of the West: How schools and the media distort our understanding of the Islamic world* (pp. 87–102). Westport, CT: Praeger Publishers.
Tobin, K. (2009). *Global reproduction and transformation of science education.* Retrieved October 1, 2009, from www.cdesign.com.au/.../keynote_tobin_global_reproduction.pdf
Villaverde, L. A., Heylar, F., & Kincheloe, J. L. (2006). Historical research in education. In K. Tobin & J. L. Kincheloe (Eds.), *Doing educational research—A Handbook* (pp. 311–345). Rotterdam: Sense Publishers
Zuss, M. (1999). *Subject present: Life-writings and strategies of representation.* New York: Peter Lang.

Sixteen

Footnotes on Reflective Practice

Anastasia Kamanos Gamelin

> To be carried by shoes, winged by them. To wear dreams on one's feet is to begin to give reality to one's dreams.
> —Roger Vivier

Introduction

Within the post-9/11 landscape, the rhetoric regarding the "truths" of Islam and the single narrative of Muslim females as its victims is compelling and serves to uphold the common misconception in the Western world that Islam is an inherently oppressive religion with regard to women. Furthermore, public discourse on Muslim cultures is increasingly framed around the presumed incompatibility of Islam and Western values and promotes a reinforced sense of "us" versus "them."

In response to the misconception of the Muslim world as a homogenous whole, Kandiyoti (1988) writes:

> So-called Islamic societies embody widely differing histories of state and class formation. The relationships between state and religion have correspondingly varied as they have evolved.... But all have had to grapple with the problems of establishing 'modern' nation-states. This meant forging of citizenship, and finding new legitimizing ideologies and power bases...most Muslim states have failed to generate ideologies capable of coping realistically with social change. This and their histories of dependence on the West have led them to rely on Islam not only as the sole

coherent ideology at their disposal but also as a symbol of their cultural identity and integrity. (p. 275)

This, however, does not negate the chilling reality of honor killings, the torturous practice of female circumcision and the cruelty of female lapidation, which exemplify the multiple forms of violence perpetrated against women in regions that Caldwell (1978) has identified as the "patriarchal belt" of the Middle East. That such acts are carried out in the name of Islam is an example of the appropriation of extremist religious forces for political gain and continued dominance. As Islamic feminists themselves argue, it is the interpretations and cultural influences of the societies in which the religion spread that allowed for the current status of women in Islamic cultures today.

However, Farida Shaheed (2006, p. 245) reminds us that "essential components of patriarchal structure in Muslim societies do not differ from those enumerated by non-Muslim feminists, and, like elsewhere, women's subordination occurs at multiple levels (kinship structures, state-building projects, anti-imperialist and populist ideologies, and national and international policies)."

This said, my intention here is neither to debate nor to provide a historical, theoretical template of patriarchy. Rather, I use the concept of patriarchy to ground the discussion of "reflective practice" as it relates to the diversity of women's "lived worlds" (Smith, 1987, p. 6) and its effectiveness as a practice attuned to emancipatory pedagogy. Such a discussion, I suggest, is an exploration of the conditions which unite women in both our differences and our similarities and offers a perspective of transformative education that is change enacting. In this chapter, the diversity and complexity of women's worlds are explored in the weaving of narratives that describe my experience of living in Saudi Arabia and teaching in the kingdom's first private university for women. My aim here is to participate in a cross-cultural reflection on "women's ways of shaping their realities" (Sizoo, 1997, p. 3) that defies the traditional dichotomous analysis, which pits the "Western" liberated woman against the "subservient" Muslim woman. An example of research-on-action, my objective here is to try to understand rather than explain.

Reflection as Practice

Dewey defined reflection as "active, persistent, and careful consideration of any belief or supposed form of knowledge in the light of the grounds that support it and the further conclusions to which it tends" (Dewey, 1933). For Boud, Keogh, and Walker (1985) reflection is an activity in which people "recapture their experience, think about it, mull it over, and evaluate it."

These authors extend the definition of reflection to include attention to one's feelings along with one's beliefs. In Schön's (1983) interpretation, "reflection" begins when there is a "surprise" a "jolt," and where an unexpected outcome leads us to begin to look at something in a new way. According to Schön, we can respond by reflection in two ways: "reflecting-on-action" by thinking back on what we've done in order to search for the causes of the surprising outcome. Or we can "reflect-in-action," changing a situation while in the midst of it; in other words, by "thinking on our feet." Reflection, then, serves the critical function of questioning the assumptional structure of our knowledge.

Narratives

Stories, writes Edith Sizoo (1997), "tell different things to different people." Certainly, the narratives included in this chapter can be read as indictments of an oppressive political regime, or as examples of ultra-conservative religious practices that serve in the continued oppression of women. And though these may be true, they tell much more as well. They illustrate the means that women use to respond to places, worlds, and situations not of their own making and the strategies they use to cope. Kandiyoti (1988) has used the term "patriarchal bargain" to discuss how women "strategize" within the constraints of different forms of patriarchy and explains:

> different forms of patriarchy present women with distinct "rules of the game" and call for different strategies to maximize security and optimize life options with varying potential for active or passive resistance in the face of oppression. (p. 274)

I suggest that reflective practice, as enacted here, is a strategy of resistance against pressures that seek to oppress and control.

My Repertoire

I'm not a traditional academician by any postmodern re/con/figuration of the term. In some circles this can be considered as either a strength or a shortcoming. However, I have come to realize that in the context of 21st century learning it is more aligned to the former rather than the latter. My journey from the barn-red brick apartment complex of a housing project to the mouse-coloured Victorian walkways of academia was an exodus marked by confusion, fear, and struggle. Poverty, like discrimination, is a language littered with signifiers that when articulated leaves a visible trace on its listeners and speakers. Luckily, as an immigrant, I was literate in the language of oppression, able to identify the halts, jerks, push, and pull of daily life as a mediation between forces that sought to contain, control, and confine. Resistance, I knew, was embodied, articulated in different ways by women who left their sleeping children alone at night to mop sloppy miles of office hall tiles, fill countless stalls with toilet paper, and wipe clean any evidence of the day's work on desks and filing cabinets.

Navigating the hinterland of academia with this baggage was helpful in allowing me to develop a visceral, compassionate understanding of what it means to be nullified, to be present and absent simultaneously. To be directed to perform one's ethnicity, race, gender, or class in light of the shadow cast by the observer's gaze. I am like many women writing culture, caught in a crisis of language. This crisis is of epic proportions. I use epic here in its etymological sense as in "focus" or "center" to identify the root and route of a way of interpreting a world that has traditionally stymied self-knowledge and diverted authenticity and creativity into a sole version of "truth" and "knowing." What author Chimamanda Adcichie (2009) has called the "single story" means that singular versions of human experience become fossilized as exemplary of all human experience and, hence, become almost impossible to disembed from the bedrock of cultural, social, or popular "truths."

The power of stories, then, is not to explain experience but to bring memory into the present in ways that it has not been before. Reflective practice as storytelling creates the possibility to tell and to know the past, and to re-imagine a future.

Walk a Mile in My Shoes

Geertz (1973) reminds us that "culture is public because meaning is" and explains that "what prevents most of us from grasping what people are up to is not ignorance as to how cognition works as a lack of familiarity with the imaginative universe within which their acts are signs" (p. 12). In quoting Wittgenstein, he writes:

> We say of some people that they are transparent to us. It is, however, important as regards this observation that one human being can be a complete enigma to another. We learn this when we come into a strange country with entirely strange traditions: and, what is more, even given a mastery of the country's language, we do not *understand* the people. (And not because of not knowing what they are saying to themselves). We cannot *find our feet* with them. (p. 13)

Contradictions and Paradoxes

A black limousine stops along the sidewalk leading to the gilded doors of the shopping mall. The driver, wearing a crisp white *thobe* and tan sandals quickly gets out and circles around the car to open the rear passenger door. The gleam of white lights bounces off the chest of the car's sleek black body and hits against the crystal-like door panes. I stand to the side, feeling the residue of the day's heat sink into the creases of my black *abaya*. Instinctively, I unwrap a layer of my sequin-encrusted *tarha* and readjust it to allow the tassle to hang fashionably from the side of its folds. Underneath, my hair is damp and beads of sweat trickle down my neck. I watch and wish I could capture this moment on film. The scene is not unusual. It will be repeated hundreds of times during the hot Saudi night. But to capture it would be to catch a moment of the contradiction and paradoxes inherent in my students' young lives.

I watch intently, purposefully. I try to snap the still shot in my mind, remembering each detail of the scene for its re-enactment on the page. In the darkroom of my mind, this image will emerge as black markings on the page. I fear my words and descriptions will be pale in comparison to the scene before me. As the door opens, the bright red polish of painted toenails peek out from black patent sandals. The ivory skin of a pointed foot emerges from the sheaths of flowing black cloth. With measured movements, the woman's body unfolds as she exits the car and steps lightly onto the pavement. Her black *tarha* is studded with tiny gemstones and is wrapped multiple times around her head, giving the illusion of added height. The woman's manicured red fingernails expertly place a layer of veil across her face allowing only her dark khol-drawn eyes to peer back at my gaze. Though her body is swaddled within the folds of her black *abaya*, her waistline is highlighted by the tightly stitched seams and braided belt. She murmurs instructions to her driver and begins her ascension up the steps to the mall. As she walks past me, I notice that the extra length along the back of the robe gives added movement and lightness to the fabric. The musk-scented perfume of oud trails behind her long after she disappears from view.

I have recently arrived in Saudi Arabia and am teaching at the first private university for women in the kingdom. I know little about the students and even less about the country, culture, and customs. The image I have captured reflects my ignorance. I have just completed my doctoral dissertation on women, culture, and writing in academia (Kamanos, 2001). Issues of culture, ethnicity, gender, and the interplay of class, power, and identity have intersected with my own life. The decision to accept a position in Saudi Arabia seems sensible. The financial, physical, and psychological scaffolding that has propped up my life during the dissertation process collapses under the weight of part-time contractual work, limited opportunities, student loans, and a mid-life crisis of consciousness. I realise how the noose of poverty has unmoored my sense of security and regardless of the piercing social and cultural differences I decide to leave behind family, language, culture, and a part of my Self for a world that I know only through Western eyes.

Border Crossings

How does a discussion of gender and education in the context of a university classroom in Saudi Arabia shape our understanding of reflexive practice? Certainly, the political nature of reflective practice and its relation to "voice," critical pedagogy, and thinking are at the epicenter of democratic values and therefore exemplary of the tenuous border-crossings that the Saudi students manipulated daily.

Unlike their counterparts from more liberal and democratic societies, Saudi women have had much less time and opportunity to reflect on and respond to the impact of globalization and technology on their society and culture. Therefore the terms under which they accommodate change are in constant flux, changing and shifting while in the midst of constant reformulation. Their position on the fault lines of modernity and tradition, old and new paradigms of a post-9/11 world, suggests that their stories would have a strong de-stereotyping effect. However, the fundamental paradox here is that Saudi women, who are best suited to describe their lives, are dissuaded from doing so because the political, cultural, and social risks are too great. Hence, the need to participate in reflective practice becomes more urgent as it returns control of the mind to the mindful.

The Outsiders

> The reverse of mobility is not always immobility. Women who spend most of their lives in the same location may perceive that place quite differently in various periods of their lives. What makes the difference here is not the moving between places, but the outside world moving into their place. (Sizoo, 1997, p. 227)

My students and I size each other up...they've seen Western professors come and go. They're young, animated, and look at me with short but inquisitive stares. I see a blur of dark and light curls; brown, mocha, and white skins. I am immersed in the unfamiliar rumble of the ubiquitous "r" and the dry hum of the glottal "h." I am anchored to the floor by an overarching feeling of distance. Through the window, at the end of a palm-lined walkway, I see the entrance to the building that houses single female professors. Beyond that are the whitewashed 14-foot high walls that surround the campus grounds. Though already 10 minutes late, students continue to stroll in with the same "Sorry miss, my driver was late" chime. I write my name and course number on the board and turn to meet the students' gaze.

The memory of what actually happened that first day is hazy. However, the clarity of what the experience felt like is striking in its veracity. Many months later, students recalled their own initial feelings of ambivalence and discomfort as they recounted how the "flow," atmosphere, and openness of the classroom was so contrary to their past experience of schooling. As one student put it, "at first we couldn't trust you...thought you wanted to trick us...wanted to humiliate us...to change us. No one asked about our thoughts on something before...all of a sudden we felt like somebody and couldn't handle it...everything was turned upside down."

Curriculum of the Un-Conscious

Saudi Arabia's particularly paralysing school system for girls is predicated on Wahhabi religious principles and serves to prepare women for their role in the home as mothers and wives. In a Saudi student's unpublished Master's thesis, female participants describe their education in traditional Saudi schools as a time when they had "no voice." One respondent expresses her frustration:

> School in Saudi is all about how good you are in memorizing. How much you remember of the material when you are taking an exam. I cannot remember there ever being a question about your opinion or something that you needed to analyse. What a sham. I spent years being a follower.

Another woman asks:

> what did I learn from school? That women are valued only because they raise both men who will build futures with their good solid Islamic manners and Saudi traditions and women who will be future mothers. The only things we talked about was marriage, when we were going to be married and stop coming to school...

Duomoto & Posusney (2002) explains that the most effective medium used to re-inscribe "traditional" place for women has been the national education system (p. 243).

Living Contradictions

The paradox of my own life in Saudi Arabia meant I was a photographer, in a country that prohibits the use of a camera in public; a writer, in a country that condones the silencing of women; and a feminist in a kingdom that segregates women both actually and metaphorically. As an educator, I teach who I am. I therefore questioned how I would manage to live and teach a life of contradictions. My initial thoughts or concerns were not about my young female students as I had imagined them as "women" rather than "Saudi women." My response therefore was to create an environment, both in and out of the classroom, where common threads plucked from each of our lives could be re-woven into tales of possibilities.

My office became a gathering place to discuss "the world" and our place in it, now and in the future. Photographs of the home and family I left behind were displayed in a way that explained my world to the students. The young women read these images as an invitation to engage in sincere, meaningful discussion and critical questioning on topics as controversial as abortion and sexuality, religion and relationships. Though I was "advised" not to discuss religion, it was impossible to avoid as Islam was central to students' lives and identities.

Oftentimes these discussions captured the scope of the contradictions between the students' private and public lives. Many times the encounters were destabilizing, my momentary muteness a sign of the gaps in my "repertoire" (Schön 1983, p. 138). It was during these exchanges that Reema revealed her decision to leave her newly-wed husband on the grounds that he could not satisfy her sexually; that Dalal eloquently articulated the angst, pain, and shame she felt as a closeted homosexual; and that Luluwa revealed the sexual abuse she suffered while in the care of a family member.

I mention these here as a way to illustrate reflection-in-action and to provide a Polaroid-type image whose imperfections reveal the constraints of time, space, and clarity. To understand this requires looking to our experiences, attending to our feelings and to our theories in use. It also means building new understandings to inform our actions in the situation that is taking place. As Schön explains:

> The practitioner allows himself to experience surprise, puzzlement, or confusion in a situation which he finds uncertain or unique. He reflects on the phenomenon before him, and on the prior understandings which have been implicit in his behaviour. He carries out an experiment which serves to generate both a new understanding of the phenomenon and a change in the situation. (Schön 1983, p.68)

A crucial element of our encounters was to reflect on our discussions by engaging in reflective practice that was safe and integral in its authenticity. Though students were at first uneasy, journaling responded to and fulfilled our needs. Writing about the inner lives of private worlds required intention, attention, and a wilful trust in a writing process that sometimes brought the women to unexpected places. Surprise!

Educating Reema

> Even if I do not choose, that is still a choice. (Sartre)

The story told by many Saudi female students was of being torn between family's and culture's expectations for women and their own desire to pursue their education. And though education was a way to maintain femininity and added value to their position as a wife, a woman's personal transformation also meant that she had more self-value.

For many of the students, the experience of attending a university, where the diversity of faculty and exposure to diverse ideas was the norm, supported an "awakening" to their potential as powerful women in positions of authority. As Banaja writes: "The environment provided them with the (until that time) unheard of possibility to ask difficult questions about faith and tradition and challenge those many assumptions that were outlined by society" (2007, p. 45).

For some, their desire to pursue their education abroad was strengthened by the realization of their academic possibilities. However, as women make up only 5% (Duomato & Posusney, 2002, p. 241) of the work force in Saudi Arabia and are restricted to specific professions (teaching, nursing), the knowledge that they would probably not be employed after graduation served to motivate rather than dampen their resolve. In fact, the reason stated for pursuing an education was the desire to be an agent of change in Saudi society. In an autobiographical essay one student writes:

> Now I understand why they would treat me in such a way but it doesn't make it easier to cope with this situation. Knowledge gives me the tools to analyse and document my situation so that I can start to facilitate change in the culture. A change that will lead to the acceptance of women and support their contribution to society.

She explains that though some encouraged her to challenge Saudi social norms, others suggested graduate school for women was a waste of time and that her degree would end up hanging in the kitchen where she was cooking for her husband. The young woman also writes of her crushing disappointment when her "liberal-minded" father denied her the permission to study abroad. She describes his mode of thinking as a "…virus that infects everyone in society…and is something that people cannot recover from." She continues:

> Following my father's declaration I talked to my mother who actually reiterated that she wanted me to have the life of a traditional Saudi woman. For me there were other choices. I could delay marriage and focus on education or I could do both. For me empowerment was more important.

However, the authority of the Wahabbi Ulama (religious scholars) has particularly strong repercussions for women. For example, they dictate that a woman cannot go out unless accompanied by a male member of the family (mahram), that her face be covered, that she speak to no man other than her blood relatives, and that she be denied travel outside the Kingdom without the permission of a male member of her family. Such restrictions make it extremely difficult for women to pursue their studies.

Transformation

The transformative potential of education as a "maker and shaper of human lives" is powerful. Roland Martin (2007) explains that "throughout history and across cultures education, defined broadly, has changed the way we humans walk, talk, dress, behave, view the world and live our lives" (p. 1). At an individual level, what she has termed as "educational metamorphoses" has both "inner" and "outer" dimensions. She explains that "on the one hand they are personal transformations or identity changes; and on the other they are culture crossings" (p. 1). It's little wonder therefore that "world shaking" experiences of education would foster mistrust for the students, as the issue of a new way of being in the world that results from transformative experience signaled assimilation into a Western culture that the students at once envied and mistrusted, one that they both feared and resented. The importance of "reflecting" on their responses, voices, reactions is in the recognition of "fracture areas" (Foucault, 1988) that "open up the space of freedom...of possible transformation" (p. 36).

Re-Collections

> When we are interested in fashion, we are concerned with relations of power and their articulation at the level of the body.

The historical, traditional, and metaphorical purpose we attribute to shoes goes beyond their utilitarian functions. They are at once commodities and esthetic artifacts. For many, they symbolize the march from the homeland, the fleeing from violence, the move from poverty to middle-class, the trek across real and metaphorical mountains, and the triumphs across invisible finish lines. They both underscore and subvert class, gender, ethnic, and racial identities. They tell of tragedy and triumph. Shoes (or the lack thereof) have a narrative quality (Benstock & Harris, 2001).

By the time I left Saudi Arabia, I had accumulated 70 pairs of shoes. Most pairs were colorful, with some sort of beading, chain, strap, or sparkle. My compulsion to collect shoes had started long before I arrived in Saudi Arabia but could be qualified as moderate in comparison to my students' penchant for extravagant footwear. Gamman (2001, p. 4) maintains that women's passionate attachment to shoes, their particular pleasure in collecting and wearing them, is connected to our impulse for self-fashioning and self-presentation. The satisfaction in having purchased a pair that is "us" and represents us, reveals much about the constructedness of individual identity. Shoes serve as markers of gender, class, race, ethnicity, and even sexuality.

I began this chapter with a discussion of the misconceptions that the Western world harbors in regard to Islam in general and Muslim women in particular. The concept of patriarchy and its footprint on women's lives was evoked as the condition and context within which my students and I engaged in reflective practice. Narratives exemplifying reflective practice documented the "double loop" (Schön, 1983) of practice and transformation as more than just a simple process of thinking back on what has happened. Shifts in ways of thinking are rarely neutral activities. To understand the scope of this, reflective practice requires artistry. Indeed, the qualities and characteristics that identify artistic practice, such as attention to detail, interpretation, curiosity, exploration and discovery, patience and vision, are qualities identified with reflective practice. And like any creative act, reflective practice cannot be applied, it has to be enacted.

Finding Our Footing

The "commonality" or "ordinariness" of shoes underscores the extraordinary lengths my students must cover to "find their footing" in Saudi society. Literally, for women, the ordinary activity of walking with an *abaya* and *niqab* requires careful negotiation as it hinders mobility. As the only visible accessory, women in Saudi Arabia take their shoes seriously. Shoes symbolize status, independence, and liberation. They uphold values of modesty, detracting the gaze from the body; attracting it to the feet. Shoes never make you look fat. As one student told me, "there are no sensible women's shoes in Saudi."

The Perfect Fit

Clifford Geertz (1973) writes that:

> Looking at the ordinary in places where it takes unaccustomed forms brings out not, as has so often been claimed, the arbitrariness of human behavior…but the degree to which its meaning varies according to the pattern of life by which it is informed…understanding a people's culture exposes normalness without reducing their particularity….it renders them more accessible: setting them in the frame of their own banalities, it dissolves their opacity. (p. 14)

The shoe metaphor gives meaning to both my own and my students' transformation. The mutuality of our experience as we took our "first steps" together signaled a desire to enter and understand each other's worlds. For the teacher and learner, reflective practice promotes an ontological awareness. As mutually reinforcing concepts, reflective practice and transformative learning provided the perfect fit for the promotion of an emancipatory pedagogy based on principles of mutual compassion, empowerment, respect, and understanding.

References

Adcichie, C. The danger of a single story. Retrieved November. 2009 http://www.ted.com/talks/lang/eng/chimamanda_adichie_the_danger_of_a_single_story.html

Banaja, O. (2007). *Identity borders: The sociocultural identity of Saudi women.* Unpublished. MA thesis. University of London.

Benstock, S., & Harris, S. (Eds.). (2001). *Footnotes on shoes.* New Brunswick, NJ: Rutgers University Press.

Boud, D., Keogh, R., & Walker D. (1985). *Reflection: Turning experience into learning.* London: Kogan Page.

Caldwell, J. C. (1978). A theory of fertility: From high plateau to destabilization. *Population & Development Review.* 4(4),553–577.

Dewey, J. (1933). *How we think.* Lexington, MA: D.C. Heath & Co.

Duomoto, E. A., & Posusney, M. (Eds.). (2002). *Women and globalization in the Arab Middle East.* Boulder, CO: Lynne Rienner Publishers.

Foucault, M. (1988). Critical theory/intellectual history. In L. Kritzman (Ed. & Trans.), *Politics, philosophy, culture: Interviews and other writings 1977–1984.* New York: Routledge (pp. 17–46).

Gamman, L. (2001). Self-fashioning: gender display & sexy girl shoes. In S. Benstock. & S. Harris. (Eds.). *Footnotes on Shoes.* New Brunswick, NJ: Rutgers University Press (pp. 93–115).

Geertz, C. (1973). *The interpretation of cultures.* New York: Basic Book Publishers.

Kamanos, A. (2001). *Home & away: The female artist in academia.* (Unpublished doctoral thesis). McGill University, Montreal.

Kandiyoti, D. (1988). Bargaining with patriarchy. *Gender & Society,* 2(3), pp. 274–290.

Roland Martin, J. (2007). *Educational metamorphoses.* Lanham, MD: Rowman & Littlefield Publishing.

Schön. D. (1983). *The reflective practitioner.* London: Temple Smith.

Shaheed, F. (2006) Controlled or autonomous: Identity and the experience of the network, women living under Muslim laws. in Grewal, I., & Kaplan, C. (Eds.). *Gender in a transnational world.* New York: McGraw-Hill Publishers (pp. 245–260).

Sizoo, E. (Ed.). (1997). *Women's lifeworlds.* London: Routledge.

Smith, D. (1987). *The everyday world as problematic.* Toronto: University of Toronto Press.

Seventeen

A Frank Intercourse: Combating Islamophobia in Sex Education

Fida Sanjakdar

Fear or hatred of Islam, known as "Islamophobia," began long before the tragic events of September 11, 2001. The stereotypical assumptions and pronouncements regarding selected Islamic customs publicly announced in the mass media and in various literature have created a conundrum of misunderstandings and misconceptions about Islam and Muslims, which have subsequently translated into ideological and systemic forms of prejudice and discrimination. The image of Islam as a savage, intolerant religion, a monolithic creed that is socially retrogressive, fundamentalist in inclination and irredeemably backward not only exacerbates a sense of "otherness" but also demonstrates that many people do not have an informed understanding of Islam.

The constant barrage of media reports about alleged Muslim extremist activity around the world has created a social anxiety toward Islam and Muslim cultures. Intolerance toward Muslim individuals and communities continue to be translated in a variety of acts of racism and discriminations, creating what Dalal (2008) calls "thought paralysis" of Islam and Muslims. However, long before Islam appeared on the world stage, there was a war waging on issues regarding the treatment of women in Islam, modest Islamic dress, polygamy, and sexuality. The opportunity to insult and slander Islam on these issues has never ceased. Subjecting these Islamic principles and teachings to grotesque distortions has helped to widen the chasm between so-called Western "values" and Islamic ones which is deeply ingrained and enduring in the European mind. Modest Islamic dress is deemed inherently fanatical, and Islam has been viewed as a religion of sexual suppression and has been accused of widely divergent practices such as forbidding all foreplay or desiring only virgins. As a result, Muslim communities around the world have found themselves the focus of speculation, misinformation, fear, and derision regarding their beliefs and practices. Over the centuries, some of these perceptions have become powerful enough to reciprocally influence how Muslims perceive themselves.

In today's postmodern world, rapidly proliferating media disseminate cultural signifiers of global capital and although the meaning is subjected to multiple viewpoints, the antagonism toward Islam has assumed new significance and has become difficult to engage in let alone counter. Joe Kincheloe (2004, p. 10) attributes the "distorted, demonized view of the Islamic world" to a "new cultural pedagogy," the entertainment media: "a pedagogy much more powerful than tradition and academic scholarship" (ibid). Judging from the ongoing negative perception of and treatment toward Muslims, many receivers of the knowledge era appear "anesthetized" into believing the "new cultural pedagogy" as the truth (Kincheloe, 2004). Confronting and possibly combating these kinds of pervasive portrayals thus become a major part of the task Muslims face as they work to protect an image of Islam as peaceful and workable in Western societies. This was the case for a group of teachers at an Australian Islamic College who deliberated on how to develop an appropriate sex education curriculum for their Muslim students. Faced with the lack of appropriate resources in sex education for their students and the possibility of parental objection and community criticism, these teachers set out to address the problematic situation they had witnessed over many years at their school.

This chapter reports on some of my findings and creates space to present the voices of both Muslim teachers and students on a curriculum area in which they have for too long remained voiceless. In addition, the purpose of the chapter is to be frank and advance a major debate among and about Islamic school curricula in Australia. At its broadest, the debate is about how Islamophobia is not only an unfounded hostility against Islam and against the wider society but also at the grass roots level of curriculum planning and decision-making in Australian Islamic schools that choose to deliberately omit comprehensive sex education and thus create a null curriculum.[1] I argue that a null curriculum within these schools puts Muslim students in a difficult position. In these schools, students reside at the nexus of dual oppressions; confronting racism and Islamophobia in society at large and at the same time contending with religious oppression in their own "Islamic" education and cultural forms of knowledge. As demonstrated in this chapter, Muslim students' (mis)understandings of sex education are informed by cultural folklore and western misconceptions.

This chapter begins with a brief overview of the purpose of sex education in Islam and demonstrates how any deliberate omission of this curriculum is in violation to the principles of a holistic and democratic education in Islam. This is followed by a discussion on contemporary sex education in Australian schools and how fear, hatred, and misunderstandings of Islam are perpetuated within current content and forms of delivery of this curriculum. A brief description of the research is then presented before the necessary space is given to teacher and student conversations.

Unveiling the Islamic Position on Sex Education

It should be noted from the outset that Islam can mean many different things to different people. While some people use the word "Islam" to refer to the practice of religious rituals and/or to spirituality, others use the term to refer to cultural traditions or practices. In some circles, "Islam" is to talk about a political viewpoint, often referring to what is known as *Sharia*, Islamic law. The different use of the term is highly influenced by the body of rules, norms, and laws made up of several schools of thought and differing individual opinions of Muslim scholars. These differences are also testimony that "there is no essentialized, unified Islamic world about which we can make uncomplicated generalizations" (Kincheloe, 2004, p. 20). Although Islam is a universal religion, Muslims do not constitute a homogenous group.

The Muslim community reflects the secular, ethnic, and linguistic diversities found in other ethnic or religious groups. While some Muslims' views of education are strict, others can be quite liberal. Thus, when looking to serve the particular educational needs of Muslim students in an Australian school context, for example, teachers and schools would benefit from acknowledging the secular, pluralistic society in which Muslim students live and the culturally diverse nature of the Australian Muslim society. Thus, although at times it is more plausible to talk of "Muslim" rather than "Islamic" discourses and identities, Islam as a world religion transcends specific cultural transactions. In this chapter, the Islamic perspectives on sex education are derived from the teachings provided in the Qur'an, Hadith, and *Sharia*, the "absolute reference frame of Islam" (Sardar, 1979, p. 24) and what all Muslims have in common. The teachings of the Qur'an "provide a shared spiritual, ideological and moral framework for Muslims of different backgrounds" (Bennett, 2004, p. 1).

Rules concerning sexual health govern every facet of a Muslim's life and many Islamic practices such as prayer, (*salat* in Arabic), fasting *(sawm)*, bathing (*ghusl*), marriage (*ziwaj*), divorce (*talaaq*), performing the pilgrimage (*hajj*), as well as the entire spectrum of human behavior, including justice and equality (Mabud, 1998). Islamic teachings also show concern for matters regarding sexual etiquette between husband and wife. For instance, it is a religious requirement that married couples try to fulfill each other's sexual needs; "neither may deny the other right to satisfy these needs" (Noibi, 1998, p. 45), and explicit information is provided in the Qur'an on how a Muslim married couple should approach each other, including the importance of foreplay. While procreation is an aim for a Muslim couple, it is not an exclusive aim. Companionship and enjoyment of the spouse along with avoidance of unlawful or sinful relationships are also important. In Islam, sexual relations between husband and wife are blessed. Having lawful sexual relations earns its reward in the life to come, while celibacy and refusal to marry leads to depravity (Boudhiba, 1985). In a Hadith, it is narrated that *Allah* rewards a husband and wife for cohabiting despite the pleasure derived thereby (cited in Kazi, 1992). Similarly, fulfilling the sexual desire unlawfully (i.e., outside an Islamic marriage) is subject to *Allah's* punishment (Noibi, 1998). Since there is adequate provision for the lawful fulfillment of the sexual desire within the bonds of marriage, adultery and fornication are considered *haram* (forbidden) in Islam.

In light of this discussion, a comprehensive and Islamically appropriate sex education curriculum would therefore aim to develop in Muslim students an appreciation that Islam is relevant to their life. Sex education becomes an important part of the religious upbringing of a child strengthening *taqwa* (piety) and *eman* (faith), as well as becoming an avenue for Muslim students to explore Islamic ideology and consciousness (Ashraf, 1998; Noibi, 1998; Sarwar, 1996). Acknowledging the relevance and importance of this knowledge in the overall education of a Muslim student, Halstead (1995) suggests that knowledge be "Islamicized"; that is, centralize the teachings of the Qur'an and the Hadith and thus encourage an Islamic perspective to sex education.

Sexuality has a prominent place in the teachings from the Qur'an, the Hadith and the *sira* (life history) of Prophet Muhammad ﷺ.[2] Given the centrality of sexuality in human affairs, in both the public and private spheres, discussion, teaching, and learning about sex, sexuality, and sexual health, are not taboo or opposed in Islam; the teaching and learning of sex education are not only desirable in Islam but become obligatory and incumbent upon every Muslim. Despite this, my earlier research (Sanjakdar, 2000, 2006) found that many Australian Islamic schools are deliberately omitting this knowledge from the school curriculum, hence demarcating and delineating what constitutes appropriate, relevant, and important knowledge and violating the holistic aims of Islamic education, which many of the schools espouse. I was left asking myself: If Islamic principles advocate the seeking of all knowledge, then why is a comprehensive health education curriculum that includes studies in sex education, removed from Islamic schools' curricula which claim to be Islamic?

More poignantly, the deliberate omissions of a comprehensive sex education curriculum make these schools at risk of creating their own kind of Islamophobia. As discussed earlier in this chapter, Islamic teachings from the Qur'an and Hadith present no barriers to the teaching and learning of sex education. Both texts invite conversations on sex education, can be used to "formulate a workable curriculum with a unique philosophy and methodology" (Al-Afendi, 1980, p. 30) and "provide a framework within which a genuinely Islamic approach to education can be worked out" (Halstead, 1995, p. 27), suitable for young Australian Muslims. Furthermore, the absence of a religious framework gives way to legitimizing various Muslim cultural knowledge and tradition, which contradict the Islamic viewpoint, to take authority and consequently exert dominant control on the development of emerging sexual perspectives and subsequent behavior on young Muslim students (Sanjakdar, 2000, 2006). It is not uncommon for various traditions and practices within Muslim cultures to determine the boundaries for what is acceptable and unacceptable when it comes to sex and as demonstrated in this chapter, the absence of this curriculum is breeding fear and misunderstandings of sex education among many young Muslim students.

Where did the dilemma come from? And what can be done about this? As discussed in the following section, the absence of any Islamic representation in contemporary sex education curricula and discourse fails to acknowledge the Muslim perspectives on sex education and thus leaves the Muslim educational community with a scarcity of appropriate resources.

Islamophobia and Sex Education

Controversy surrounds the teaching of sexuality, with many people still most comfortable if "sex" remains invisible in the school curriculum. Many families still withdraw their children from participation in sex education programs at school. While many people in the Islamic community would agree that Muslim students need to understand the nature of their developing sexuality, how it should be taught and by whom is a source of contention among many Muslim parents. Like other parents, many Muslim parents still widely view sex as an intimate and private matter that is not appropriate for open discussion, thus provide very little or no sexual education to their children (Cok & Gray, 2007). The popular myth that providing adolescents with information about sex will only encourage them to start sexual experimentation is also prevalent amongst many Muslim cultures. Due to its cultural sensitivity, talking about sex, even in a positive manner, is a difficult task for many Muslims. As Khan (2006, p. 90) explains:

> Muslim people are still reserved when it comes to sex. It is still very much a taboo topic.... Sex is hushed and curtained off to the bedroom and speaking about it is considered a sin and accredits a loose character.... For today's Muslim parents, sex is a dirty word....

Although many parents would believe that they are shielding their children from potentially harmful education, no sex education is sex education and the absence of any Islamic underpinning to this knowledge is no doubt sending a strong message that learning about sex education is taboo in Islam. Further, the absence of any religious underpinning promotes "culture" as a heuristic tool to frame learning and understandings and as discussed earlier, this can be problematic when Muslim cultural viewpoints often oppose or contradict Islamic viewpoints. The dominant status of culture would also mean that cultural myths and beliefs will go unchallenged and the effects on students, unmodified.

Compounding parental fear and concerns is the absence of any significant identification of Muslim youth and Islamic perspectives and values in sex education research and popular school textbooks. For many years, Australia has achieved local and international respect for innovation in dealing with complex health issues such as drug education, HIV/AIDS, and sexual health. However, addressing the sexual health needs of Muslim students in the Australian school curriculum has been significantly marginalized (Sanjakdar, 2004). Despite the cultural and ethnic diversification of Australia's society and the growing Muslim student population in many Australian schools, present health education curriculum decision-making and practice exert a dominant Judeo-Christian values system and ideology (Sanjakdar, 2004). Australian schools have become agents incorporating and transmitting a "monocultural" (Halstead & Reiss, 2003) education ideology to a multicultural, multiethnic, multireligious, and multilingual society and the school curriculum has become a powerful method of legitimacy, conformity, and social control. As the number of Muslim student population grows in Australian schools, and the host societies fail to integrate them in the school curriculum, an increasing number of students become more and more marginalized and alienated.

Non-procreative sex, including masturbation, oral sex, and acceptance of homosexuality as morally valid (Epstein & Johnson, 1998; Lees, 1993; Sears, 1997) is a driving force shaping the nature and scope of sexual health education in Australia today (Dyson & Mitchell, 2005; Farrelly, O'Brien and Prain, 2007; Ollis & Mitchell, 2001). These perspectives can further contribute hostility toward a heterosexual/procreative Islamic perspective on sex education. As mentioned earlier in this chapter, many Islamic ideologies on sex education view procreative intercourse within a monogamous marital relationship as morally valid sexual behavior and look unfavourably upon masturbation, homosexuality and pre/extramarital sexual relations. Contemporary Australian sexual health education tends to present certain behaviors, which many Muslims believe are sinful (i.e., adultery, homosexuality) as normal or acceptable. Teaching the "etiquettes of dating," for example, as it is currently practised in much of the world, can not only violate some Islamic principles of decency and chastity but endorse terms and concepts such as "free sex," "boyfriend–girlfriend" relationships, which are viewed by many Islamic teachings as devoid of any responsibility and accountability and would be considered in direct violation of appropriate Islamic behavior and Islamic law. For example, according to the *Sharia*, Muslims are not permitted to touch, have intimate relationships or date members of the opposite sex outside of an Islamic marriage (Al-Qaradawi, 1960). The liberal and secular underpinning of sex education in Australian schools is often justified as forming an important part in the rhetoric concerning schools' responsibilities in education for citizenship. However, differences between human collectivities are based on the incompatibility to mainstream culture and religion. Therefore, the paucity of representation of many Islamic perspectives about this subject in mainstream social affairs such as the school curriculum not only excludes Muslim student populations but can create a view that Muslims lack social responsibility and cooperation, perpetuating intolerance toward Muslim communities and manifesting Islamophobia.

As discussed earlier, the main arguments surrounding sex education for Muslim students go beyond whether this subject should be taught in the schools, but essentially are concerned with conflicting and competing ideologies and between divergent moral visions for humanity. In analyzing the conflicts surrounding sexuality and sex education that permeate Western culture, McKay (1997) suggests these conflicts are, first and foremost, conflicts of ideology: "We are not talking about simple differences of opinion, but conflicts that represent a clash of opposing systems of belief about the nature of the world and human kind" (p. 286). Although the dominant permissive sexual ideology contravenes many Islamic principles of sex education, as Halstead and Reiss (2003, p. 57) suggest, this ideology "reflects the actual political, legal and economic circumstances that prevail in western societies generally." Acknowledging this rationale can present further significant implications for Muslim educators and Australian Islamic schools. Further, if a clash of ideologies appears to be impacting on the development of a sex education program, then a solution can present itself within the ideological. The next section presents a brief overview of my research which engaged in critiquing ideology to bring about reform to sex education for Australian Muslim youth. The potential for comprehensive sex education and the possibility of combating Islamophobia in sex education, within an outwardly secular and plural western society, is actualized by returning back to Islamic teachings within the Qur'an and Hadith. These religious texts became the pedagogical force necessary to challenge the Judaeo-Christian heritage of Australia sex education curricula.

This Research

My research asks if and how an appropriate sex education curriculum for Australian Muslim youth can be developed in an Islamic school context. My earlier research (Sanjakdar, 2000, 2004) indicates a curriculum paradox across Australian Islamic schools; health issues such as drugs, HIV/AIDS, and sexual health are deliberately omitted, and became a part of the schools' null curriculum, but school curricula claimed to reflect a holistic Islamic education. As stated earlier in this chapter, in deliberately omitting these health issues from the school curriculum and thus creating a null curriculum, these schools are taking it upon themselves to demarcate and delineate what constitutes appropriate, relevant, and important knowledge; something which is in strict violation to the holistic view of Islamic education, which these schools espouse to.

The development and implementation of a comprehensive sexual health education curriculum exclusive to the special educational needs of Australian Muslim students required a careful undertaking to discover new theory, knowledge, and pedagogy concerning a solution that was unknown. As a powerful tool for change and improvement at the local level, participatory action research (Kemmis & McTaggart, 2005) was employed. Developed in Australia by Stephen Kemmis and Robyn McTaggart during the 1980s and still being promoted widely, PAR involves a series of reflective spirals in which a general plan, action, observation of action, and reflection on action are developed and then moves to a new and revised plan with action, observation, and further reflection. The practical and collaborative nature of PAR presented the vehicle required to create spaces for teachers participating in this study to develop awareness of existing practices and organizational constraints that were preventing them from developing curricula relevant to the students' educational needs.

Wise College (pseudonym) is one of eight Islamic schools in Melbourne, Australia and was the case-study school in which this action research took place. First established in 1995, Wise College is a coeducational Preparatory to Year 12 College with a Muslim-only student population. Wise College prides itself in being a community school which caters to the educational needs of its students and thus was very keen in participating and contributing to this research. In preparing for critical conversations on sexual health at Wise College, a Professional Learning Team (PLT) of teachers was established. As noted by Johnson (2000), a PLT of teachers would enable for more structured conversations and team work in curriculum development and reform. Table 1 presents the teachers at Wise College who volunteered to be members of the PLT.

Table 1: The Professional Learning Team at Wise College (All names are pseudonyms)

Name	Position at the school
Emra	Deputy Principal and school board member.
Wafia	School board member, secondary coordinator, and science teacher.
Nadia	Science teacher.
Amy	Islamic Studies teacher.
Mu'min	Islamic Studies teacher.
Sahar	Health and Physical Education teacher (for female students).
Sulay	Health and Physical Education teacher (for male students).
Nemet	School nurse.

To generate conversations about this curriculum within the PLT, focus group interviews were conducted, tape-recorded, and later transcribed for review by the participants. Focus group interviews took place during the "planning" and "reflection on teaching" stages of the PAR. For the purpose of this chapter, the various conversations generated by the PLT as they tried to confront and dispel their students' misconceptions about sexual health and the Islamic perspective will be presented.

Combating Islamophobia in Sex Education: Using Difference to Make a Difference

The participants acknowledged that to remove sex education from Islamic principles and teachings is to cause oppressive education, for it is Islam that gives permission to discuss and learn about these matters. Thus, the dominant perspective put forward by the PLT concerned the participants' desire for their Muslim students to develop Islamic knowledge of sexual health issues and an appreciation that this subject is essential and valued learning, inextricably linked to their Islamic beliefs. To achieve this, the PLT engaged in discussion about an "Islamicized" curriculum (Halstead, 1995), where the teachings from the Qur'an and Hadith would be at the center of all curriculum decision-making, enriching, and building on all other knowledge. For Wafia, using the teachings from the Qur'an and Hadith is the logical first step in developing this curriculum:

> *The Qur'an and the life of Prophet Muhammad are open books for us. We've got all the answers to our questions in these books.*

Nemet, the school nurse, hoped that in using the Qur'an and Hadith the students would be encouraged to view these texts as their first source of information and answers to their questions:

> *I agree. These students need to know that they can get the information they want from the Qur'an and Hadith rather than* Cosmopolitan *or* Dolly *magazines!*

Amy suggested that centralizing the teachings from the Qur'an and Hadith might "lift the controversy" associated with some health issues and the "uneasy feelings amongst parents." Not only will the broad spectrum of knowledge offered in these texts enable Muslims to recognize and appreciate revelation as a valid source of knowledge (Mabud, 1998), but this way Islamic knowledge, principles, and beliefs will impact on the decisions made about the school philosophy and ethos, school policy guidelines, and classroom practice and pedagogy.

During the "action stage" of PAR, the PLT implemented its curriculum plan and met every fortnight across one school term, to reflect on their teaching. At each meeting, teachers produced samples of student work and several pages of handwritten notes in their reflective journals. At these meetings, teachers capitalized on "teachable moments": what worked well in their classes and the notable problems. They reported on their teaching practice and student reactions and made suggestions for change and improvement for the next cycle. Their conversations provided insight into their thinking, their interactions with their students, and this curriculum reform inquiry. A common theme at these meetings was the students' cultural understandings of sex education that presented real challenges to teaching the Islamic perspective of these issues. As presented in the following section, the PLT was concerned about the students' views of sexuality, intimacy, and related gender expectations and wanted to confront these.

Myth 1: It Is Taboo for Muslims to Talk about Sex

In recounting an incident with his grade 5 and 6 Islamic studies classes, on the rules of fasting during the month of Ramadan, Mu'min brought to the

PLT's attention the serious implications the "taboo" stigma attached, and perpetuated by the absence of sex education in the school curriculum, is having on the students' knowledge and development of appreciation for this subject:

> *In my grade 5/6 class this week I gave them a handout about things that break your fast [during Ramadan] and on the sheet was the word 'sex'. We hadn't even started to read and one of the students found the word. Then there was uproar in class. One student put his hand up and said, 'Sir sir, this is an Islamic school'. It took me nearly ten minutes to settle them down again.*

In handling this situation, Mu'min explained to his class that openly discussing sex and, in particular, intimate sexual relations between husband and wife to strangers is discouraged in Islam. However, learning about sex with the intention of seeking knowledge is not only encouraged in Islam but becomes obligatory learning for every Muslim:

> I said, if you go and open the Qur'an, you will see that Allah talks about this issue and Prophet Muhammad ﷺ talks about it. These are the facts. Of course we don't talk about these things openly, but we have to learn about it. I even said that it is not rude to discuss these issues if it means we are learning about it.

As mentioned earlier in this chapter, maintaining modesty in everything a practising Muslim does is central to developing his/her moral and ethical outlook on life. Thus, open, free discussions about sex will do little to uphold and preserve one's modesty. Mu'min's motivation to continue this conversation was to demonstrate how sexual issues govern many Islamic practices and thus becomes important and necessary knowledge.

Myth 2: Sex Is Evil and Dirty—Sex Is Zina

When reflecting on his discussion with his Year 10 boys, Sulay noted his concern that many of his students perceived sex as evil and equivalent to *zina* (fornication). Although he suggested that perhaps his students said "...sex was a dirty word because they were ashamed of saying it so instead he (the student) said *zina*," Sulay was concerned that his students' lack of understanding of the purposes of sex were developing into negative attitudes toward sex. Wafia supported Sulay's response by suggesting that Quranic terms for sex, such as *tamassa* (gentle touch) should be used to demonstrate to students the non-threatening nature and beauty of a sexual relationship between a married couple. Wafia continued to express the importance of teaching students that sex is an expression of love and not a dirty word or deed and not only for procreation purposes. "Sex is a sacred institution between husband and wife and apart from procreation, it is meant for the enjoyment of both man and woman."

Myth 3: Marital Rape Is Acceptable in Islam

Wafia promoted this line of conversation in a PLT meeting. She was concerned about how some of her students held the view that a Muslim woman's primary role in Islamic sexual relationships was utilitarian and instrumental; that is, she is to produce as many children as possible. Wafia continued to explain how many of her students believed that it is taboo for the wife to refuse sex with her husband when he demands it, thus believing that marital rape is common practice in Islamic marriages:

> *A lot of them [the students] think that when a husband comes to his wife, she just has to hurry up, or stop what she is doing and be with him, like be forced to. And a lot of them see that as rape and then think that Islam allows that.... Can we please make sure the students understand that if a man comes home to his wife and wants to be with her, you know, to have sexual intercourse with her, that she must not stop everything and just do it! That's NOT what happens. We have to let them know that if a woman is not emotionally up to it, that the man has to respect that and can't force it.*

Silencing both her female and male colleagues with her emotional plea, Wafia continued to discuss her personal disgust with Muslim male practices, which regulate women's sexuality and sexual pleasure and, thus, send the wrong message regarding marriage and intimacy from the Islamic perspective.

> *Sometimes I just think that they [the students] are...so confused, so desperate for this knowledge. I would love to go into class and tell all the girls that Islamically, you don't have to do ANYTHING for your husband. [At this point, all the male teachers faced Wafia in disbelief and shock]. Yes, if you don't want to breastfeed his children, you don't have to, Islamically, that's the woman's right. Islamically, a wife is not obliged to be her husband's slave. She is supposed to be honoured in Islam. The man has all the responsibility, to care for her, the children, to love her etc. But when she serves her husband, she does so out of love.*

In an attempt to confront her students' misunderstandings, Wafia wanted to make it clear to her students that although some Muslim cultures may practise customs that regulate women's sexuality, the teachings from the Qur'an and Hadith, clearly indicate that both husband and wife have equal right to sexual pleasure and time for each other. As a *Hafez*,[3] she presented the following verses from the Qur'an to feature in the curriculum:

- "They are as a garment for you and you are a garment for them" (chapter 2, verse 187). This verse describes men and women as "garments" fitting each other and emphasises how both husband and wife need to complement each other.
- "And among His signs is this: He creates for you mates out of your own kind, so that you might incline toward them and He engenders mutual love and compassion between you" (chapter 30, verse 21).

- "He has created you from a single soul and from that soul He created its mate" (chapter 4, verse 1). These two verses, speak about sexual duality in creation and once again how marriage and the sexual relationship unites two souls into one.

Wafia also suggested that teachings about sexual etiquette between husband and wife should also feature in this curriculum.

> *When there is etiquette between husband and wife the sexual relationship becomes an act of piety. In a Hadith, the Prophet Muhammad ﷺ said:*
>
> *Let none of you fall suddenly upon his wife like a lower animal. Let him send message before cohabitation. Someone asked the Prophet, "what is the message?" He replied, "kisses and words of love."*

Myth 4: It Is Taboo for Women in Menses to Engage in Daily Life Activities

At one of the PLT meetings, Nadia shared with her colleagues a class discussion she had with her students about menstruation. Of particular concern to Nadia were the misconceptions surrounding this topic that her students believed were true:

> *Many of my girls… have said that they can't pick a lemon from a lemon tree when they have their period. It would poison the tree. Their mother doesn't pick lemon from the lemon tree but would actually wait for the husband or son to come home to do that. Some suggested that you can't water the garden, can't take pickles from the pickle jar, otherwise you spoil the rest. They're not allowed to dye their hair, cut their hair or cut their fingernails. One of my students even told me "I don't know if you know Miss but you are not allowed to shower for five days because it stops your period."*

In contemplating ways to dispel this myth, Nadia wanted to introduce to her students the Quranic teachings available about this issue. As she explained, the Qur'an speaks of a woman's menstrual cycle as a time of "hurt" and a time in which she needs to rest. Islam does not consider a menstruating woman to be "unclean," "untouchable," or "cursed." A menstruating woman is encouraged to engage in her usual daily activities with only one restriction; a married couple is not allowed to have sexual intercourse during the period of menstruation (The Qur'an, chapter 2, verse 222).

Myth 5: Muslim Women Seeking Marriage Must Be Virgins; Muslim Men Not

Nemet wanted teachers to address this common cultural perspective surrounding virginity:

> When discussing virginity, can we please get rid of the idea that you have to bleed on the first night [of marriage]? That doesn't happen to all women. And the need to sleep on white sheets that have to then be shown to your mother-in-law! Please!

Amy agreed and added:

> Yes, even the idea that some people think that it's okay for the man not to be a virgin on their wedding night, but a woman has to. That's wrong and that's not Islamic. It has to be made clear that this is expected from both man and woman.

Conclusion

In this chapter, I have opened for debate that it is not only through the stereotyping of physical characteristics that Islamophobia spreads but also through the deliberate omission of Muslim ideological and philosophical representation in key discourses such as the school curriculum. Positioning sex education in the null curriculum within an Islamic school curriculum can leave young Muslim youth in search of their own sex education and can heighten the possibility of perpetuating common misconceptions and misrepresentations of the Muslim world.

Many schools, because of the ideological conflict surrounding sexuality, omit important sexual health information. This was the situation at Wise College, an Islamic college in Victoria, Australia. In the face of growing criticism of Islam and, consequently, growing concern about the emerging young Muslim identity, teachers at Wise College set out to challenge the school's status quo by removing sex education from the school's null curriculum and centering it in the Islamic education and ethos of the school. In their pursuit for a comprehensive sex education curriculum for their students, the PLT at Wise College was also motivated to dispel some of the popular myths and misconceptions about Islam as an attempt to counter Islamophobic attitudes toward sex and Islam. Hence, in their deliberations and action, the PLT was in fact, confronting institutional Islamophobia as well as confronting the attitudes and behavior of individual students and teachers about sex education.

Although the students' cultural and popular knowledge of sex education often proved stronger and more powerful than Islamic knowledge, the PLT's tenacity in this work was underpinned by their strong desire for the students to confront their own Islamophobic attitudes and appreciate Islam as relevant to their lives. Although at times, the PLT questioned whether its work was that of cultural reproducers or cultural reconstructors, there was common consensus that accommodating for cultural and religious pluralism in sex education curriculum will allow individuals to see themselves in discussions.

Endnotes

1. Elliot Eisner (2002) defines the null curriculum as "the options students are not afforded, the perspectives they may never know about, much less be able to use, the concepts and skills that are not part of their intellectual repertoire" (p. 107).
2. There are a number of well-known Hadith that are considered part of the common domain of Muslim thought, just as proverbs are in English. When quoting Hadith, Muslims always end it with a blessing for Prophet Muhammad saying "Peace be upon him" (pbuh). In Arabic, it is written like this ﷺ. This Arabic script will be used when Hadith is quoted or other reference is made to the Prophet throughout this chapter.
3. An Arabic term used to describe a person who has learned and memorized most and in some cases, all the verses from the Qur'an.

References

Al-Afendi, M. H. (1980). Towards Islamic curricula. In M. H. Al-Alfendi, & N. A. Baloch, (Eds.), *Curriculum and teacher education*. Jeddah: King Abdulaziz University/London: Hodder and Stoughton.

Al-Qaradawi, Y. (1960). *The lawful and prohibited in Islam*. Indianapolis, IN: American Trust Publications.

Ashraf, S. A. (1998). The concept of sex in Islam and sex education. *Muslim Education Quarterly*, 15(2), 37–43.

Bennett, L. R. (2004). Zina and the enigma of reproductive rights for single women: Providing reproductive education in Victorian Islamic secondary schools. Paper presented at *Islam, human rights and gender workshop*. University of Newcastle, UK, July 5–6. 1–19.

Boudhiba A. (1985). *Sexuality in Islam*. London: Routledge and Kegan Paul.

Cok, F., & Gray, L. A. (2007). Development of a sex education programme for 12-year-old to 14-year-old Turkish adolescents. *Sex Education*, 7(2), 127–141.

Dalal, F. (2008). Thought paralysis: Tolerance, and the fear of Islam, *Psychodynamic Practice*, 14(1, February), 77–95.

Dyson, S., & Mitchell, A. (2005). Sex education and unintended pregnancy: Are we seeing the results? *Australian Health Review*, 29(2), 135–139.

Eisner, E. W. (2002). *The educational imagination: On the design and evaluation of school programs*. Upper Saddle River, NJ.: Prentice Hall.

Epstein, D., & Johnson, R. (1998). *Schooling sexualities*. Buckingham, UK: Open University Press.

Farrelly, C., O'Brien, M., & Prain, V. (2007). The discourses of sexuality in curriculum documents on sexuality education: An Australian case study. *Sex Education: Sexuality, Society and Learning*, 7(1), 63–80.

Halstead, J. M. (1995). Towards a unified view of Islamic education. *Islam and Christian-Muslim Relations*, 6(1), 25–41.

Halstead, J. M., & Reiss, M. J. (2003). *Values in sex education: From principles to practice*. London: RoutledgeFalmer.

Johnson, N. (2000). *An implementation model based on professional action-learning teams*. Paper presented at the CSF II Conference, Melbourne.

Kazi, M. U. (1992). *A treasury of Ahadith*. Jeddah, Saudi Arabia: Abdul-Quasim Publishing House.

Khan, M. A. (2006). *Sex and sexuality in Islam*. Lahore: Nashriyat.

Kemmis, S., & McTaggart, R. (2005). Participatory action research. In N. K. Denzin & Y. S. Lincoln. (Eds.), *Handbook of qualitative research*. Thousand Oaks, CA: Sage Publications.

Kincheloe, J. L. (2004). Introduction. In J. L. Kincheloe and S. R. Steinberg. (Eds.), *The miseducation of the West: How schools and the media distort our understanding of the Islamic world*. Westport, CT: Praeger.

Lees, S. (1993). *Sugar and spice: Sexuality and adolescent girls*. London: Penguin.

Mabud, S. A. (1998). An Islamic view of sex education. *The Muslim Education Quarterly,* 15(2), 67–93.

McKay, A. (1997). Accommodating ideological pluralism in sexuality education. *Journal of Moral Education,* 26(3), 285–300.

Noibi, D. (1998). The Islamic concept of sex, sexuality and sex education: A theological perspective. *Muslim Education Quarterly,* 15(2), 44–67.

Ollis, D., & Mitchell, A. (2001). *Talking sexual health: National framework for education about HIV/AIDS, STDs and blood-borne viruses in secondary schools.* Canberra: Australian National Committee on AIDS and Related Diseases.

Sanjakdar, F. (2000). *A study of the hidden and core curriculum of an Islamic school.* M. Ed dissertation. The University of Melbourne, Australia.

Sanjakdar, F. (2004). Developing an appropriate sexual health education curriculum framework for Muslim students. In B. van Driel (Ed.), *Confronting Islamophobia in educational practice,* Stoke-on-Trent, UK: Trentham Books.

Sanjakdar, F. (2006). *Revelation versus tradition: Beginning "curriculum conversations" in health and sexual health education for young Australian Muslims.* PhD dissertation, The University of Melbourne, Australia.

Sardar, Z. (1979). *The future of Muslim civilization.* London: Croom Helm.

Sarwar, G. (1996). *Sex education: The Muslim perspective.* London: The Muslim Education Trust.

Sears, J. T. (1997). Centering culture: Teaching for critical sexual literacy using the sexual diversity wheel. *Journal of Moral Education,* 26(3), 273–283.

Eighteen

A *Bifocal* Lens on Islamophobia: Using Young Adult Fiction as a Teaching Tool

Krista Riley

Introduction

The novel *Bifocal*, co-written by Deborah Ellis and Eric Walters, was published in 2007. A fictional story based on the arrests of the "Toronto 18," a group of young Muslim men arrested in June 2006 on charges related to terrorism, *Bifocal* examines the racist backlash at a high school after a student is arrested. Described by one reviewer as a "powerful and important book" that will "raise [questions] that are topical and urgently need to be addressed in our world today" (Doucet, 2007, para. 5), *Bifocal* has drawn attention as a novel that provokes necessary and pertinent discussions about racism and Islamophobia. The timeliness of its topic and the wide praise that it has received mean that it is important to analyze further the kinds of messages that it presents and conversations that it creates.

Moreover, as a white Muslim Canadian woman, my motivation for this project comes from personal connections and not only from academic or political interest. My relationship to the novel is informed by my whiteness, which means that I can identify with many of the themes of privilege and complicity that I read from the novel, and by my Muslim faith and my connection to various Canadian Muslim communities, which have directed me toward examining and responding to representations of Muslims, particularly in Canadian media and popular culture. As a graduate student in Sociology and Equity Studies in Education, and as someone who, even in my mid-twenties, often reads young adult literature, I find it important to consider the ways that such literature can be used to address themes of oppression and to promote critical reflection and social justice activism.

This research represents an attempt to better understand both the positive and negative impacts that *Bifocal* can have as a novel that claims to address themes of racism and intolerance, and, by extension, to consider what would be needed for readers of a young adult novel to engage with themes of Islamophobia (and/or other forms of oppression) in more effective, realistic, and responsible ways. Specifically, it looks at how these themes can be, and are being, addressed by white, non-Muslim teachers in predominantly white, non-Muslim classrooms, and the effects of the novel in provoking conversations about Muslims and Islamophobia in contexts where the readers have little contact with, or knowledge about, Muslims. The majority of this chapter will look in particular at the novel's handling of two major issues: the racial profiling of Muslims by the police and the decision of one character to wear *niqab*. In my conclusion, I ask how it might be taken up in ways that do challenge Islamophobia, even despite the areas where the book itself might fall short, and propose additional strategies for reading *Bifocal* in order for it to be used as an effective tool for teaching against Islamophobia.

Introducing *Bifocal*

Loosely based on the arrests of the Toronto 18, a group of young Muslim men arrested on terrorism charges in June 2006, *Bifocal* is a fictional account of a high school in suburban Canada where a student is arrested as part of a raid on a suspected terrorist group. The novel's narration alternates between Jay, a white Christian Canadian of European background, and Haroon, a Muslim Canadian of Afghan descent. The characters are written, respectively, by Eric Walters and Deborah Ellis, both well-known Canadian children's authors.

The story begins with a school lockdown, as Jay witnesses the arrest of a fellow student. We later find out that Haroon had also been initially (and mistakenly) taken by the police and that his friend Azeem has been arrested as part of a mass operation against a suspected terrorist group. As the narrative progresses, the tensions in the school and broader community rise. Muslims are talked about in the media as terrorists; the police are continuously questioning Haroon and implying that he must bear some guilt or hold some information; and the area of the school where Muslim students often congregate is vandalized. Jay witnesses increasing expressions of racism from the captain of his football team, although he remains silent. Haroon's twin sister, Zana, begins wearing clothing that covers her head and face, a decision that confuses and angers her family.

The climax of the story occurs on Halloween night, when Jay joins other members of his football team in a night of vandalism that culminates in an especially intense attack on Haroon and Zana's house. Jay participates—at times reluctantly, and at times even enthusiastically—in the attacks but comes to regret it the following morning and eventually apologizes to Haroon. The story finishes with Jay deciding to defy the entrenched divisions of his school environment and to choose to sit with Haroon in the cafeteria as an act of resistance against the social (and largely racial) segregation of the student body.

After it was first published, *Bifocal* found high praise in Canadian media and literary journals. Reviews praised it as "perhaps the bravest, most important, engaging and enraging, most satisfying work of fiction for young Canadians in a long while" (Curtis, 2007, para. 1); highlighting its "examination of the dangers of racism and the redeeming value of tolerance" (Mills, 2007, para. 4) as well as its depictions of "other cultures, the schisms within cultures and how easy it is for intolerance to fester" (Curtis, 2007, para. 18). *Bifocal's* value as a pedagogical text is particularly emphasized. *Bifocal* is recommended "in the English, social studies, religion or civics classroom" (Mackey, 2008, p. 30), and for use in both junior high and senior high school classrooms (Rosser, 2007) and touted as "an excellent choice for class, or group, discussion" (Doucet, 2007, para. 6). The emphasis on this novel as a vehicle for conversations on and explorations of themes of racism (and the suggestion, in all of these reviews, that *Bifocal* is, in fact, contributing something useful to such conversations) should be cause for us to look closely at what the book is actually doing toward these goals of discussing and addressing racism and Islamophobia.

Introduction to the Research Participants

Although I am investigating a work of children's literature in a classroom context, I locate this research less within the frameworks of pedagogy, within formal educational institutions, and more within broader frameworks of understanding the effects of popular and literary cultural products that claim to be promoting an anti-racist and anti-Islamophobic point of view. The writing that follows reflects a combination of my own analysis of *Bifocal* and of the themes that it covers and of interviews conducted with two teachers who have used *Bifocal* in their English classrooms. While this project could certainly be enhanced by discussions with a greater number of teachers (and, in particular, teachers working in more racially or religiously diverse classrooms than either of the two that I interviewed) or by interviewing students who are part of the youth demographic to which the novel is targeted, my research gives some sense of the possible impact of *Bifocal* on students in predominantly white, non-Muslim environments, and the potential that the novel has to raise questions about issues of Islamophobia and racism within such spaces.

Both of the teachers I interviewed are white women of middle-class, Christian background, and both grew up in small to mid-sized, predominantly white, Canadian cities. Both of their classes were also almost entirely white, and neither had any Muslims in their classes. It is worth noting, therefore, that my focus here is on the use of *Bifocal* as a way of talking about racism and Islamophobia among white, non-Muslim readers; teaching this novel in a classroom that was primarily composed of Muslims and/or of people of colour would likely bring about very different reactions and discussions.

The first interview I conducted was with Jennifer,[1] a grade 6 teacher who teaches in a public school an hour outside of Toronto. Her class this year had 25 students, 23 of whom were white. The second interview was with Hannah, a Canadian teacher at an international boarding school in Europe. Each of the 10 students in her high school English class was from a different country, mostly from across Europe, and all but one were white. Both teachers used *Bifocal* as part of a strategy for creating space for discussion and reflection on social justice-related topics throughout the school year. The interviews with Jennifer and Hannah are used here, not to evaluate their successes as teachers, but rather to uncover some of the possibilities and the limitations that *Bifocal* may provide as an anti-racist teaching tool, through considering, among other things, some of the issues that arose, and some of the questions that went unasked or unanswered. In order to understand some of the issues presented in *Bifocal* in a more concrete way, I will be looking in some detail at two of the book's major themes and events, and the reactions that arose to these in each of the two classrooms.

Institutional Racism and Racial Profiling

One of the major issues that surfaces throughout *Bifocal* is that of racial profiling. The topic is visible in many arenas; for example, in media reports that paint all Muslims as threats to Canada (Ellis & Walters, 2007, p. 155) or in the no-fly list, on which members of Haroon's family are erroneously placed (Ellis & Walters, 2007, p. 170). It is also clearly one of the reasons that the police repeatedly harass Haroon throughout the story. After being mistaken for a fellow student, who is later arrested and charged with terrorism, Haroon is repeatedly confronted by police officers who attempt to intimidate him and to suggest, based only on his background and religion, that he is also part of the alleged terror plot. Police officers even violate Haroon's legal rights by questioning him without a parent present (Ellis & Walters, 2007, p. 55), and by threatening to assume he is guilty if he does not talk to them (Ellis & Walters, 2007, p. 263).

Both Jennifer and Hannah mentioned this as a topic that provoked especially strong reactions for their students. Hannah told me that it "really got them," and Jennifer said that "they felt frustration with the injustice that […] Haroon was being questioned just because of the colour of his skin." From Jennifer's perspective, the salient message was that of the fear that the police provoked in Haroon, which was reflected in several images in the collective art project that the class later produced. The strong reactions that the scene elicited in each classroom reflect the potential that this issue has to reach students and to prompt discussion and reflection. The existing power structures are exposed and depicted as highly problematic and unjust, particularly threatening to Muslims. On the other hand, the focus on fear as the primary response means that the specificity of Haroon's situation is elided; although they can imagine that the scene would be scary, the majority of Jennifer's students, who are almost exclusively white, and entirely non-Muslim, would likely never actually have to face this kind of fear. The privilege of not being the one vulnerable to being wrongfully arrested in this way should be more deeply examined in order to more fully understand the effects of Islamophobia, and to maintain a focus on the systems of power and oppression that exist.

The specific depictions of racism drew strong reactions in both classrooms, with Jennifer emphasizing how "shocked" her students were, and Hannah relating her students' "indignation" and their angry questions about the police officers' actions and clear racism:

> There's this one part where the police officer says, um, something really racist, like, "he's brown, so I just took them both" […] and my students were like, did he actually say that? Did that really happen? That's shocking! I was like, that probably didn't happen [in real life], but at the same time, the reality is that there *is* a lot of racism in policemen and -women as well as other people.

Despite some successes of the presentation of this facet of Islamophobia, there are also some troubling elements to the way that this issue is depicted, such as the moment when Haroon eventually seems to free himself from the psychological hold that the police have on him, simply by deciding not to let it affect him anymore. Toward the end of the book, Haroon finally stands up to the police officers by challenging them to either arrest and charge him or to leave him alone (Ellis & Walters, 2007, pp. 263–264). There are, certainly, many significant positive aspects to this moment, as Haroon is shown to be standing up for himself and asserting his rights—an action that might be used to encourage readers to be aware of their own legal rights. My concern, however, comes in the implication that this small moment of triumph has solved the greater problem of racial profiling and police intimidation. Haroon's request for due process is one that is not always honored, particularly for Muslims, as recent histories of detentions based on security certificates and deportations based on dubious evidence, have demonstrated. Ultimately, this exchange, which occurs in the penultimate chapter of the novel, might suggest that, although police racism and abuse of power exist, they can be overcome if their targets simply decide not to be affected. The absurdity of this assumption should be obvious; in addition, it places the onus on the oppressed group to not let the dominant group's racism bother them and not on the more powerful groups (in this case, the police) to reform themselves or to stop what they are doing. This perspective ignores the very real abuses of power that occur within police forces and that oppress and marginalize many racialized groups, and the particular context in which Muslims are specifically vulnerable. An anti-Islamophobia reading of this text needs to remain attentive to the power dynamics at play and the ways that the novel reflects the existence of racial profiling as one of the manifestations of Islamophobia in Canadian society (a phenomenon that plays out in US and European societies as well).

Examining Narratives of Veiling and Resistance

A second element of the novel that I want to discuss here is the decision of Haroon's twin sister, Zana, to begin dressing in *abaya* (a long garment that covers the body) and *niqab* (clothing covering her head and face, leaving her eyes visible.) While Haroon spends most of the story trying to stay as far as possible away from controversy, Zana, in contrast, deliberately chooses to become *more* involved, explaining her decision to begin wearing this clothing as an act of resistance against a social structure that she views as hostile toward Muslims (Ellis & Walters, 2007, p. 168).

In many ways, Zana's active decision to dress in this way (despite, even, the wishes of her family) challenges stereotypes that paint Muslim women as oppressed or passive and Muslim women's clothing as restrictive and imposed by patriarchal structures. Zana's strong feminist personality—she explicitly states that "we can wear the *abaya* and still be feminists" (Ellis & Walters, 2007, p. 125)—further complicates this picture. By clearly stating that her culture is under threat and that this threat requires a response that actively resists the racism that her community faces, Zana's character deliberately works to claim a space that is safe for Muslims in Canada and refuses to accept a project of quiet racial harmony that would ultimately entrench inequalities. Although she is not a main character, she comes across as a strong character, with a level of personal agency that goes beyond the usual "oppressed veiled woman" stereotype.

Zana's friends, however, do not fare so well. Those who also wear similar clothing are repeatedly referred to by Jay, Haroon, and others as faceless and indistinguishable from one another (Ellis & Walters, 2007, p. 119), even "eerie to watch" (Ellis & Walters, 2007, p. 187). Furthermore, none of Zana's friends (or any Muslim women aside from Zana and her mother) ever speaks, and none is ever individually named. Against this silent backdrop, Zana is seen as perhaps an anomaly, with the suggestion that her agency is a rare exception to a much more passive norm, which limits the potential for Zana's character to challenge stereotypes or to present alternative possibilities of how Muslim women may act and make decisions.

This tension between seeing Zana as a strong and independent character while remaining sceptical about the potential for other Muslim women to reach the same level was reflected in the interviews with both teachers. Zana was the subject of great controversy and debate in each of the classrooms, with students struggling to reconcile their admiration for her confidence and assertiveness with their stock mental images of the clothing she wears as oppressive and imposed. A quote from Jennifer's interview reflects the back-and-forth that occurred as her class attempted to understand Zana's character:

> the students felt that, number one it was her right if she wanted to wear it, but they were also very torn with what her mom says, which was, "women for centuries in our family have been fighting to get this off, and here you are going against all of that." [...] The final thought was that it was her right if she wanted to wear it, but she shouldn't be made to wear it.

Although the students ultimately sided with Zana against those who might object to her decision, the emphasis that she "shouldn't be made to wear it" still demonstrates a level of doubt that this truly is her choice, or that other Muslim women who wear similar clothing have much agency in doing so. After all, there is no evidence at all in the novel of anyone making Zana wear *niqab*; on the contrary, her family tries to dissuade her from that decision (Ellis & Walters, 2007, p. 125), and her brother expresses that it would be impossible to force Zana to wear anything (Ellis & Walters, 2007, p. 158). Why, then, would the students be so concerned about voicing their opposition to the hypothetical imposition of *niqab* or *abaya*? Perhaps this is simply reflective of the power of the anti-veiling sentiment, which can hardly be expected to be overcome as a result of one book alone; however, it may also reflect an insufficient addressing of the theme within the novel itself, a portrayal that positions Zana, to some degree, as an anomaly within a practice that is still normally oppressive. Still, Jennifer's students were powerfully drawn to

Zana's character. The tension created between this feeling of discomfort and uncertainty about Zana's clothing choices and their support for her in other areas might be one way to open opportunities for building solidarity across difference, rather than expecting Zana to conform with the students' perspectives on what she should be wearing in order for them to be able to relate to her. This element of the story could be used as a significant challenge to the kinds of gendered Islamophobia that paint Muslim women, especially veiled ones, as inherently oppressed and irredeemably Other.

At an international school in Europe, with students a few years older than Jennifer's, Hannah's class saw a wider range of opinions regarding Zana and her clothing. Although Hannah also noticed a strong level of support for Zana as a character, especially among the girls in her class, who admired the way Zana stood up for herself, the students were divided on their reactions to her decision to wear *niqab*. Some felt that she should wear it if she so chooses, while others argued that it should be banned. As with Jennifer's class, it seems that Hannah's students were unwilling to let go of the idea that this clothing is most often imposed, and that even if it might be possible to see it as more or other than a tool or oppression, the default assumption was that it was something forced on women and girls.

As the discussions continued, Hannah was able to convey some alternate meanings and experiences to the students:

> The whole class [wondered] why would you want to do that, like you wouldn't be able to move, that would be horrible. And then, I'd say, but she chose it, she chose it in the book, some people do choose it, they choose it knowing full well what it means, and they choose it because for her, it was important to show an outward sign of her religion and her solidarity, and to be visibly part of this, whatever the cost was to her. And, you know, she knew that she would get picked on and talked about at school. [...] So that—that also kind of made them think a bit.

Hannah's emphasis on the "cost" of Zana's actions being experienced not as gendered oppression but as marginalization based on race and religion adds important nuances and challenges to the ways that Zana's experiences may be understood. She also reminded her students that the only clothing-related physical violence that Zana faces in the novel comes from the non-Muslim football team captain. Through these discussions, oppression against Muslim women can be understood as coming not only from Muslim men but as racist and sexist violence from the outside community as well, and the gendered dimensions of Islamophobia can be complicated and challenged.

Using *Bifocal* in a Critical Way

There are many other issues for which *Bifocal* can be celebrated (e.g., its portrayal of a strong diversity of Muslim characters) or questioned (such as its possible reinforcement of "bad Muslim" stereotypes through the character of Hadi, another student, or the suggestion from its ending that interpersonal friendships are a sufficient solution to racism). The intent of this research is not to determine whether or not *Bifocal* should be read by children or taught in classes. The book *is* being widely read, and it has already made its way into a number of classrooms. The teachers that I interviewed both spoke enthusiastically about their students' (and their own) love for the book, and recommended it as a novel that immediately engaged its readers, who in turn recommended it to their families and friends. Both teachers also spoke about the deep impact that *Bifocal* had on their students; Jennifer mentioned aspects that "haunted" her students "in a way that stayed with them," while Hannah talked repeatedly about her need to constantly remind her students that they were reading a work of fiction, in reaction to their passionate responses of indignation and anger with some of the scenes of the book. The studies of *Bifocal* raised connections with themes of racism and violence in other arenas as well; both classes, for example, looked at the particular role of the media in contributing to racism and to support for wars. The high praise for the book among both teachers and students, and the popularity of its authors in the field of children's literature, mean that, even with its significant problems, *Bifocal* has had, and will likely continue to have, an impact on young readers. Given this context, we should look at what the advantages may be of reading or teaching a book such as this one, and how *Bifocal* could be used to further anti-racist thought even despite its problems.

The interviews with both Jennifer and Hannah reflected an encouragement of the students' visceral reactions of anger and indignation to many of *Bifocal's* themes, which is certainly a useful approach. Jennifer's encouragement to students to become emotionally engaged with their reading formed part of her overall teaching practice as well:

> I always tell my students [...] they need to have a conversation with the text as a reader. [...] that's always what I've advocated that good readers do, they have a conversation with the text, and they question, and they—you know, they get angry at certain parts, and, you know, want to throw the book down.

This invitation to become an active part of the process of their reading, and even to get angry with the text, can demonstrate to students that it is not necessary to simply accept a text's message at face value. It is important, of course, to remain aware that readers have their own agency, and that they are able to look critically at the text; the problematic aspects of the book are not the only factors that determine its effects. Readers should be encouraged to look critically and actively at the messages that *Bifocal* conveys and even to see the novel not only as a portrayal of racism but also as a *product* of the systems of racism that it seeks to criticize. This can be helpful in responding to Islamophobic images and stereotypes that students may encounter.

Another important pedagogical strategy is to look critically at the meaning of difference. Although Jennifer was drawn to the ways that Jay and Haroon both "felt the exact same thing" in terms of pressures, fears, and confusion about what was happening in their school, this claim is dangerous in that it erases power, and more importantly, erases the responsibility to think about how and why the two boys are *different*. After all, it is not exactly a coincidence that Haroon is the one being repeatedly questioned by the police. The racial privilege that Jay experiences—and any possibilities for considering his own responsibility and accountability—should not go unacknowledged nor should the Islamophobia that Haroon and his family face. An attempt at building empathy that ignores difference can be also problematic in that it often constitutes a projection of the self rather than a deeper understanding of the one to whom the empathy is supposedly being extended (Boler, 1999, pp. 159–160). In this context, Islamophobia can become depoliticized and the importance of its effects is reduced, which is surely a counterproductive way of reading the novel. In contrast to this "passive empathy," we might strive instead for a practice of "testimonial reading" in which empathy exists alongside an acknowledgment that the reader does not truly know the "other"; this form of reading "recognizes its own limits, obstacles, ignorances, and zones of numbness" (Boler, 1999, p. 170). Similarly, Kumashiro (2000) advocates a "'pedagogy of positionality' that engages both students and teacher in recognizing and critiquing how one is positioned and how one positions others in social structures" (p. 37). Applied to *Bifocal*, such practices can allow students to feel themselves drawn into the story in an ethical way, one that provokes them to maintain a critical eye toward both themselves and the text, to remain aware of their own privilege in relation to the story, and of their own responsibility to act on what they have read. The role of Islamophobia and other systems of oppression in creating these inequalities thus becomes a much more integral part of the reading.

Educators should also encourage readings that "denaturalize the spaces and identities that appear to come about organically" (Shujah, 2008, p. 152) and involve "a meticulous historicization of the access, selection and reception of texts" (Taylor, 2007, p. 311). This can be done even for elements of the story that may be easily overlooked. What kind of power relations have to exist, for example, in order for Haroon to be repeatedly questioned by police despite having done nothing wrong, while the football captain, who actually *does* break the law while speeding, can express confidence that the police are "not interested in [him]" (Ellis & Walters, 2007, p. 28)? When Jay says that he knows few South Asian or Middle Eastern students because few of them "ever tried out for school teams," a fact that he attributes to those students being "[t]oo busy studying" (Ellis & Walters, 2007, p. 32), might it be possible to ask whether there might be other systemic factors dissuading these students from joining teams, especially given that we already know that Zana is a skilled basketball player (Ellis & Walters, 2007, p. 21)? Why is it that the predominantly Muslim area of the school has been "stuck" with the name "Brown Town," when this name was first given to it by the "white" (non-Muslim) students, and is something that Haroon and his peers find "insulting" (Ellis & Walters, 2007, p. 53)? Asking questions that problematize the ways that social relationships in *Bifocal* come to appear natural is one way to expose the existing systems of power that inform the social relationships in the story.

Sensoy (2007) suggests two main strategies for encouraging readings that disrupt stereotypes and entrenchment of inequalities within the text. Her first principle is that of "self-focus," which encourages the readers to look critically at themselves and their own reactions, asking what it is that has led them to expect certain representations and to be surprised by others, rather than assuming that the representations that surprise are anomalies (pp. 362–363). Second, Sensoy proposes acting as "perspectives detectives," asking "what *else* is going on? How else might we conceptualize 'the problem'? And *where* and with whom is the problem located?" (Sensoy, 2007, p. 363; emphasis in original). Sensoy's focus is on "disrupting gendered Orientalism" (Sensoy, 2007, p. 361), and indeed her recommended approaches might be helpful for understanding Zana's character, both as a way of questioning whether Zana's agency should be seen as so exceptional, and as a way of seeing diversity among Zana's female Muslim peers, even while they may be portrayed as a homogenous collective.

Although far from perfect, *Bifocal* presents significant possibilities for discussing the many manifestations and effects of Islamophobia; on its own, however, the novel may not push readers far enough in their understanding of the ways that Islamophobia operates, and additional effort is needed in order to use the novel as a truly effective educational resource against Islamophobia. Readers—and particularly educators who use the book as a teaching tool—need to remain self-reflexive about their own relationship to the text, and critical of the text's own presentation of the issues that it raises. They must also work to integrate a systemic analysis into their readings, so that stereotypes continue to be questioned, and systems of power and privilege are not overlooked.

Endnote

1. Both "Jennifer" and "Hannah" are pseudonyms.

References

Boler, M. (1999). *Feeling Power: Emotions and Education.* New York: Routledge.
Curtis, G. (2007, November 24). *Bifocal* is a timely teen must-read. *The Hamilton Spectator.* Retrieved August 7, 2009, from http://www.thespec.com/printArticle/286610
Doucet, L. (2007). *Bifocal* (Book review). *CM,* 14(7). Retrieved August 7, 2009 from http://umanitoba.ca/outreach/cm/vol14/no7/bifocal.html
Ellis, D., & Walters, E. (2007). *Bifocal.* Markham, ON: Fitzhenry & Whiteside.
Kumashiro, K. K. (2000). Toward a theory of anti-oppressive education. *Review of Educational Research,* 70(1), 25–53.
Mackey, M. (2008). *Bifocal* (Book review). *Resource Links,* 13(3), 30.
Mills, J. (2007). *Bifocal* (Book review). *Quill and Quire.* Retrieved August 7, 2009 from http://www.quillandquire.com/reviews/review.cfm?review_id=5843
Rosser, C. (2007). *Bifocal* (Book review). *Kliatt,* 41(6), 10.
Sensoy, Ö. (2007). Pedagogical strategies for disrupting gendered Orientalism: Mining the binary gap in teacher education. *Intercultural Education,* 18(4), 361–365.
Shujah, S. (2008). Personal but not political: A critical analysis of the movie *Crash's* educational potential. In G. J. S. Dei & P. S. S. Howard (Eds.), *Crash politics and antiracism: Interrogations of liberal race discourse* (pp. 147–159). New York: Peter Lang.
Taylor, L. K. (2007). Reading desire: From empathy to estrangement, from enlightenment to implication. *Intercultural Education,* 18(4), 297–316.

Nineteen

Teaching Islamic Themes at the College Level

Sevak Manjikian

Following the Oil Crisis of 1973 and the Iranian Revolution of 1979, pundits and politicians in Western countries have increasingly paid a great deal of attention to the Muslim world. It goes without saying that Muslim societies in North Africa, the Middle East, South Asia, and Indonesia have strategic geo-political interests as well as resources in which the West is very interested. As a result, American, Australian, Canadian, and European governments are pursuing more and more foreign policy objectives in Muslim countries. Moreover, these same countries have attracted millions of Muslim immigrants who, along with their children, have made the West their home during the course of the past 30 years. Despite numerous interconnections with the Muslim World, few Western educational institutions offer their student bodies an in-depth study of Islam, its history, its peoples, or its traditions.

My interest in Islamic Studies stems from my experiences living in an American oil compound in Saudi Arabia for the first 17 years of my life. The close proximity to Muslim societies in the region fed my lifelong fascination with Islamic cultures and societies. My mother and father, both Christian Armenians from Lebanon and Syria, respectively, regularly took my family off the compound for weekly shopping excursions where I witnessed first hand the dynamics of a Muslim society. In Saudi Arabia this included the mandatory closing of shops during prayer time, patrons being escorted out of the stores for 20 minutes while prayers were called out from the various mosques dotting the landscape. Growing up, it never occurred to me that this was novel in any way. Rather, it was simply a part of the urban landscape we happened to inhabit at the time. Although I am not a Muslim, I have grown to appreciate the vibrancy of the religion. Perhaps my most vivid memories of growing up in Arabia are the streams of heavily decorated cars, buses, and trucks from Jordan, Syria, Iran, Iraq, India, and Pakistan ferrying pilgrims to Mecca during the annual *Hajj* pilgrimage. Seeing the trains of heavily decorated vehicles teeming with sacks, mattresses, and people from countries I had only know as locations on maps somehow brought me to the realization of the enormity of Islam. It was this vast subject that I would later choose to earn two graduate degrees in Islamic Studies.

College-level teaching, in the Canadian Province of Quebec, offers a unique avenue for the teaching of Islamic themes in a post-secondary setting. The two-year academic or three-year technical program for high school graduates is designed to prepare them for either university studies or the job market. All students enrolled in the province's five English-language colleges are required to take a number of general education courses, which include English, French, Physical Fitness, and Humanities. The Humanities component of the curriculum is comprised of general interest courses that cover a vast array of topics taught by instructors who have a graduate degree in a relevant field. This chapter will discuss how one course that I teach, offered through the Vanier College Humanities Department, provides students with a perspective on Islam that seeks to demonstrate the vibrancy and diversity of the faith, while at the same time debunking a number of stereotypes.

I first taught my Islamic World Views class in the fall of 2001. Prior to that time, the college had not offered a class specifically on the Muslim world; although one professor did offer Religious Studies and Humanities classes where Islamic themes were prevalent. Moreover, a number of current faculty members teaching in various academic disciplines cover topics related to the Muslim world in their respective courses. The decision to offer a course focused exclusively on the Muslim world was not one taken at the college's administrative level. Rather, as in all Humanities classes offered across the provincial curriculum, it is the responsibility of the individual instructor to choose the actual course content and make it fit within the competency-based learning approach administered by Quebec's Ministry of Education.

Because Islam is often poorly understood by North American audiences, one of the primary goals of my course is to introduce some of the basics of the tradition to a non-Muslim audience. However, because a large number of students who register for this particular class are themselves Muslim, a secondary goal is to offer these particular students an approach to their religion that is academic in orientation as opposed to one that is experienced from a believer's point of view. The course itself is broken down into various sections, each one dealing with specific components of Islamic society and culture. What follows is a brief description of some of the components of the class and the pedagogical motivations for teaching these particular themes.

The Particular Challenges Involved

Vanier College is located in a district of Montreal that is richly populated by recent immigrants as well as second-generation immigrant communities. As a result, many of the students who register for my class are Muslim. This fact makes teaching my Islamic World Views class particularly challenging and rewarding. Unlike other courses where the subject matter may be unfamiliar to those enrolled, a number of students in this particular class are fully engaged in the religious tradition we are studying. These students regularly contribute to the class discussions, making for a healthy pedagogical experience for students and instructor alike. Moreover, owing to the multicultural nature of Montreal, many of the non-Muslim students have Muslim friends and are thus naturally curious about the tradition, adding another layer of inquiry and commentary to the class.

Student contributions are more than welcome in my classroom. As a non-Muslim instructor, I insist that the Muslim students feel comfortable to correct me if I make a mistake or express something in a way that they find offensive or problematic. For instance, one semester, during a discussion on the concept of God, I kept pointing to the ceiling whenever I mentioned the word "God." Toward the end of the class, one student intervened and informed the class that he found this particular action on my part troublesome. His main concern centered on my pointing toward the ceiling and by extension the sky. By pointing toward the sky, he felt that I was limiting God's presence to that one particular locality. The student wanted the class to understand that God was everywhere and not just above us in the heavens.

During the time I have taught this class, I regularly have Muslim students offer fascinating details that would not otherwise be part of my official lectures. This information may pertain to things as curious as the physical makeup of angels, or the games the Prophet Muhammad used to play with his children. Although this kind of material may strike the non-Muslim as novel, to the initiated Muslim, these facts are important and significant in the understanding of their faith. Creating a learning environment where students feel welcome to discuss these kinds of notions is crucial in enhancing the learning experience within my Islamic World Views course.

When a student offers this kind of commentary, I welcome the intervention and integrate the new idea into the content of the course. I do this by asking the students to take note of the remarks made by their colleagues and announcing that these student contributions may be referred to in the tests and essays assigned during the term. By opening up the floor to this kind of participation, it allows the intervening students to feel empowered, while also demonstrating to the other students how valuable such contributions are to the overall class dynamic. In my mind, this is the best kind of learning that can take place in a classroom.

One of the greatest challenges of extensive classroom participation lies in scenarios where a student misrepresents facts about Islamic culture that defy historical, textual, or theological fact. For instance, during a class on the reforms the Prophet Muhammad made in Arabian society during the 7th century, I informed the students that the religion beseeches individuals to treat slaves with dignity and free them whenever possible. One student took exception to this remark as she assumed that Islam outlawed slavery altogether. In reality, Muslim societies throughout the historical Near East, Europe, Asia, and Africa used slaves in various capacities following the death of the Prophet. Conveying this kind of information, where the facts may interfere with an individual student's personal perceptions, requires considerable delicacy and tact.

I certainly want and demand student participation, but when the student's comments are inaccurate, I am required to not only correct the false assertions, but to do so in a manner so as to not offend the student who raised the inaccurate point. Here, the tone I adopt in my response is crucial, as is my body language. If I come across too harshly, briskly, or condescendingly, I run the risk of quashing the student's enthusiasm and silencing their future commentary. Moreover, such a reaction could send a message to other students that I am not open to student challenges and arguments. Moreover, my status as a non-Muslim correcting the assertions of a Muslim student does not go unnoticed during these exchanges. In these situations, rather than adopt a defensive posture, I will often walk toward the student, smile and welcome the contribution verbally. Following these gestures of openness, I will offer a response with some kind of textual or historical support.

In this particular instance, where the student was adamant that slavery was abolished by Muhammad and the Qur'an, I simply referred to the Mamluk and Ottoman Empires and their regular use of slave soldiers (Pipes, 1981). These medieval Islamic empires purchased young boys as slaves, trained them in the arts of war, converted them to Islam and eventually promoted them into various government positions where they gained not only prestige, but in some cases a great deal of wealth and political power. At the end of the day, the class became aware of something that was not necessarily part of the official curriculum, but something that furthered their knowledge of the

Muslim world. Moreover, and most importantly, when I am able to successfully harness student challenges, I create an atmosphere where members of the class feel comfortable to debate interesting points with me. This will often blossom into interesting discussions for the entire class.

Owing to the nature of the topic, I find that there are a number of expectations on the part of the students long before they arrive for the first day of class. Some Muslim students have expressed to me their initial suspicion at having a non-Muslim teach them ideas about their own religion. Meanwhile non-Muslim students may harbor certain misunderstandings of the Islamic faith. Because of the various pre-conceived ideas that students may have before the course begins, I feel that the first day of class is the most important day in teaching this class. From the start, students are told that the course is not one where I will be promoting the religion or looking at the religion from a believer's perspective. Rather, the course they have enrolled in is a college survey course where students are asked to consider various Islamic themes. The course content is to be approached with the objective of learning *not* judging. Meanwhile, I explain to the Muslim students that although I am not a Muslim, I have over 10 years of graduate training in Islamic history, religion, and law. However, I also make it very clear to the Muslim students that my degrees do not qualify me to speak for Muslims, emphasizing that my role in the class is that of a moderator and instructor.

Course Content and Pedagogical Objectives

I often begin my survey course on Islam with an analysis of the pre-Islamic Arabian society that flourished during the life of the Prophet Muhammad (Zeitlin, 2007). By contrasting the religious, economic, and social systems of 7th century Arabia with the revelations that appeared in the Qur'an, students can begin to appreciate how revolutionary Muhammad's message and mission was. One of the first challenges some of my Muslim students encounter during this section of the course is divesting themselves, at least for the duration of the course, of negative value judgments they have of the pre-existing Arabian polytheism in Mecca and the rest of Arabia. Prior to the revelation of the Qur'an, Meccan society paid tribute to various gods while the city itself hosted a yearly pilgrimage where over 300 deities were worshiped at the Ka'ba, the cubed structure at the heart of the city (Hoyland, 2001). This form of worship is in stark contrast to the principle of *tawhid* (oneness of God), which is the central credo of the Muslim faith. Worshiping more than one deity is a form of polytheism, which Muslims will refer to as *shirk*. In adopting an academic perspective, I do not discount the polytheistic idolatry that existed in Arabia during the time of the Prophet. Rather, I point out that this particular religious phenomenon is a long-standing part of the human condition and is found throughout the world. It is essential to establish this academic and impartial tone early in the class in order to not offend students who may come from religious traditions that are in fact polytheistic.

Another pedagogical goal of the course is to demonstrate to students that an academic approach to religion does not assume that individual faiths are distinct entities. Rather, different religions are frequently fusions of pre-existing spiritual and cultural traditions. Thus, I point out that a number of pre-Islamic tribal institutions remained following the appearance of the Qur'an and were altered to fit the newly emerging religious movement introduced by Muhammad. For instance, I describe how the pre-Islamic pilgrimage ritual would later become the *Hajj*, and that rather than commemorate the 300-plus gods housed in the Ka'ba, the Arabs of Arabia would now pay homage to one god (Peters, 1994). Over the years, I have discovered that this kind of thinking is perhaps the greatest challenge certain Muslim students face while enrolled in my course. My goal is to never offend or challenge their particular beliefs; rather I seek to introduce to them how academics view Islam within a post-secondary learning environment.

Meanwhile, some of the challenges non-Muslim students have during this introductory section of the course is letting go of some of the negative stereotypes they may have. For instance, it is often taken as fact throughout the West that men in Muslim societies regularly abuse women and that this abuse is sanctioned in the Qur'an. Approaching this topic head on, I begin by stressing the ethical and social reforms Muhammad introduced, such as the legal status granted to Arabian women, which significantly improved their rights as members of that society (Hekmat, 1997). It is important to point out that the rights in question, namely, the right to contract their own marriages, the right to an inheritance (albeit half that of their brothers') were revolutionary for 7th century Arabia despite the fact that certain inequalities between men and women persisted. By demonstrating these points, I try to impress upon the students the notion that Islam is a reformative religion seeking to improve the human condition. For students whose knowledge of Islam has been shaped by a post-9/11 discourse, these realizations are the first steps toward a deeper and more nuanced understanding of Muslim societies.

Following the introductory component of the class, the course then delves into the text of the Qur'an. When presenting the Qur'an to non-Arabic speaking students, it is crucial that one not overwhelms them with the complexity of the text (Cook, 2000). Though poetically and linguistically beautiful, the Qur'an is a very difficult read for the non-initiate. Its non-chronological presentation as well as its frequent repetition and non-contextualized verses can pose many complications. I begin my section on the

Qur'an by reading some of my favorite verses in the original Arabic (an act that regularly surprises my Muslim students). Frequently, I will pick verses that deal with charity in order to highlight principles of social justice found throughout the text, furthering the theme that Islam is a reformative movement (Quran, 2:261). Thereafter, we usually delve into passages that re-tell some of the Biblical stories students may already be familiar with. These include the stories of Creation as well as the struggles faced by Abraham, Noah, Moses, and Jesus (Quran, 2:136). This serves to demonstrate to non-Muslim students how Islam fits into the Western Religious Tradition through Prophets and a similar belief in God.

After our discussion of the Qur'an and the life of the Prophet Muhammad, students will have gathered a reasonable understanding of the main themes of the religion. From this point, I delve into issues of social history with a discussion of the early Islamic conquests as well as the cosmopolitan societies that emerged throughout the Middle East, North Africa and Spain following the Arab expansion out of Arabia after Muhammad's death in 632 CE. One of the first things we discuss is why the Arabs were so successful in conquering significant amounts of territory out of the existing Byzantine and Sassanid Empires during the 7th and 8th centuries (Kennedy, 2007). This section can pose some difficulties and has to be approached with a great deal of care.

Muslims frequently declare that their religion is one that represents and promotes peace. In fact the word Islam is a derivative of the Arabic word for peace (*salam*). Yet, along with the declarations of peace, Islamic societies throughout history have regularly excelled at military pursuits. A large reason why the Arabs were so successful at their military conquests, derives from the fact that the religion unified previously disparate tribes throughout Arabia, fusing them into a cohesive fighting force with clear motivations based on the principle of *jihad* (struggle for God) and martyrdom (Cook, 2005). Principles of cohesion, diplomacy, and sheer force would serve Muslim armies well as they would later conquer territories in Asia, Africa, and Europe. It would be tempting to skip over the astounding success of the military conquests in order to avoid linking the religion with violence, a link that is so frequently emphasized in the popular media. But a discussion of the subject on the conquests allows for a more complete and mature analysis of Islamic societies from which college students will benefit. Thus it is important not to shy away from such opportunities.

Following our discussion of the conquests, I emphasize to the students that the first Muslim empires that appeared in the Middle East represented a flowering of human achievement in intellectual, architectural, and scientific pursuits. Moreover, empires such as the Umayyads of Damascus (661–750

CE) and the Abbasids of Baghdad (750–1258 CE) made frequent use of pre-existing knowledge in order to administer and run their respective empires. For instance, although new coins were struck with the Caliph's image and inscribed with Islamic invocations, the actual monetary and taxation systems employed by the Umayyads were derived from the Byzantine Empire (Broome, 1985). Similarly, manuals of political governance used by the Abbasid Empire were in fact translations of pre-existing Persian manuals of state (Rizvi, 1978). Exposing students to this kind of cross-cultural syncretism is paramount in helping them realize that societies rarely stand alone, but regularly borrow from previous social systems. Islamic societies, like so many other world civilizations, incorporated existing social practices, all the while improving upon them.

The greatest benefit of this particular component of the course is that it demonstrates some of the major intellectual and social achievements of Muslim societies during the Middle Ages. For instance, many non-Muslim students are not aware that Spain was home to one of the most vibrant Islamic societies to have emerged during the medieval period. Islamic Spain or Andalusia is a fascinating stepping stone from which to discuss the cosmopolitan nature of Muslim societies (Glick, 1979). For instance, I focus on the use of the Arabic language and demonstrate that individuals speaking and writing Arabic in Spain were able to communicate with like-minded scholars of various faiths, cultures, and ethnicities in cities such as Damascus, Cairo, and Baghdad. This represented an early form of globalization whereby religious, scholarly, economic, and scientific data were regularly exchanged throughout the Muslim world. Although not as immediate as today's techniques of telecommunication, I often describe the hand-written manuscripts transported across the countryside on caravans as a form of medieval Internet.

One of my favorite sections in the course is the one devoted to Islamic Law. As an expert in this particular subject, I would like to spend a great deal of time on this theme, but, owing to the time restrictions of a survey course, I must limit myself to the basic structure of Islamic law (*Sharia*). In this section of the course, I attempt to correct some of the most striking misrepresentations Western audiences have regarding the *Sharia*. Frequently, it is assumed that Islamic law is "God's Law" and thus entails very little human involvement in the formulation and interpretation of the law (Hallaq, 2009). In correcting this misperception, I begin by explaining that the Qur'an has roughly 80 specific rules that Muslims must follow. I impress upon my students the shear impossibility of running a small family let alone an entire society with only 80 laws. We then begin to unpack how Muslims have traditionally formulated their laws. In doing so, I explain that Islamic law derives from four primary sources that include the Qur'an, the Prophet Muhammad's sayings and actions (*Hadith* and *Sunna*), the principle of analogy (*qiyas*), and, finally, legal consensus (*ijma*).

What becomes evident is how much human intervention is actually involved in the formulation of the *Sharia*. Keeping in mind the age and interests of some of the students, I find that a discussion on issues related to drinking alcohol and the use of narcotics is always of interest. We begin our discussion by pointing out the prohibition against the consumption of wine that is stipulated in the text of the Qur'an. Although the Qur'an does specifically address the consumption of wine (Quran, 5:90), it does not mention mind-altering substances more generally nor does it address whether or not it is permissible to produce, sell, and profit from the sale of alcohol or other such substances. Here, I direct the students to various *Hadith*, which provide Muhammad's verbal directives banning the avails of the alcohol trade for Muslims. Meanwhile, various jurists such as the ultra-conservative Ibn Taymiyyah (1328 CE) have used analogy (*qiyas*) to apply the ban against alcohol to other intoxicants, such as hashish, which purportedly produce similar effects. Finally, I point out that if an enterprising Muslim scholar seeks to argue for the acceptability of a specific intoxicant not mentioned in the Qur'an or the Hadith, for example whiskey, other scholars would undoubtedly cancel out his erroneous judgment by way of consensus (*ijma*) since the majority of scholars ultimately hold court in determining God's Will. The effects of these two sources of Islamic law (*qiyas* and *ijma*), clearly demonstrate to students how human intervention regularly shapes the substance of the *Sharia*.

Perhaps the most anticipated section I teach in my class is the one that deals with Muslim women. This particular subject regularly inspires interesting class discussions that require careful moderation to ensure that no one leaves the class offended or misinformed. For instance, in a typical class at Vanier, some of the Muslim students will wear the *hijab*, while other Muslim women in class will choose not to wear the headscarf. As previously mentioned, one of my goals in the course is to demonstrate the diversity within the tradition; this issue serves a visual reminder of that goal (Bullock, 2007). This section of the class usually falls during the mid-way point in the term, and by that time a classroom dynamic has been established whereby students feel comfortable expressing their views openly. Students who don't wear the headscarf will describe their motivations for not doing so, while those who wear the *hijab* will offer their perspectives. As the moderator, I will explore this divergence of practice by discussing the textual basis for the wearing of the *hijab* and highlighting the cultural pressures and influences that also come into play. What becomes clear is that the Qur'an's text is actually ambiguous on this point. Although Muhammad's wives were required to speak to the public from behind veils, there is no specific mention that all Muslim women should adopt this practice. Rather, the Qur'an requires that women dress modestly by covering their breasts. Meanwhile, the Hadith offers the more specific instruction that all women should cover their hair as well as their bodies. On a cultural, familial, and individual level, many additional factors will influence a woman's decision to wear or not wear the *hijab*.

If asked whether or not it is incumbent on Muslim women to wear the *hijab*, I never provide a definitive answer, as this is not my role. However, I do add an academic twist that often surprises the students. In particular, I inform them of a theory proposed by a number of Western academics as to the origins of the Muslim headscarf. These scholars have theorized that the *hijab* is in fact a cultural artifact borrowed from the pre-existing Byzantine culture that once flourished in Middle Eastern cities such as Damascus. According to this particular theory, elite Greek women wore headscarves so as to visually demarcate themselves from the urban population, thereby garnering themselves a certain measure of respect. When the Arabs conquered Byzantine territories, elite Arab women took on this practice which then trickled down to other Muslim women. I don't insist that the students accept this hypothesis; I simply present it to them in order to demonstrate how scholarly research can uncover interesting ideas that may provide additional insight.

Another section of my course focuses on Sufism, or the mystical tradition within the Muslim world. Sufism is a major form of Islamic religious expression popularized during the medieval period of Islamic history (Chittick, 2000). Although characterizing Sufism in a singular light is difficult, the movement can be described as one in which adherents seek to establish a direct relationship with their Creator. The relationship can range from the ecstatic to the sublime and can be expressed in ways as diverse as quiet meditation to energetic chanting and dancing. For some of my Muslim students, the Sufi movement falls outside the scope of their conception of Islam. For instance, when we discuss groups such as the Mehlevi Dervishes of Turkey (the so-called Whirling Dervishes), many students are at a loss as to how to explain this group's position within the overall perspective of Islamic culture and tradition. For these students, as well as for my non-Muslim students, our analysis of Sufism regularly uncovers some interesting themes that once again demonstrate the vibrancy and diversity of Islam.

Sufism first appeared in the Muslim world in cities such as Damascus and Baghdad during 7th and 8th centuries. The movement became prevalent when piously inclined individuals sought to complement the legal and theological formalities that were beginning to emerge within Islamic civilization. The Sufis wished to insert a more experiential form of religious expression into the religion. Thus, early Sufis stressed the importance of striking a personal relationship with God using various techniques of worship and meditation. Our discussion of mysticism begins with a number of early Sufis such as Rabia al-Adawiyya (801 CE), a woman whose love for God was so great that she turned down suitors in order to devote herself to God. Rabia frequently expressed this love through her poetry, which I read aloud in class in order to illustrate how women most certainly participated in the intellectual and literary realms of the Muslim world (El Sakkakini, 1982). Western scholars have labeled Rabia a "sober" Sufi owing to the fact that she did not reject the standard forms of religious and legal expression of Islam that were being practiced during her lifetime.

Alongside our discussion of figures such as Rabia, no study of Sufism would be complete without delving into the interesting realm of the so-called "drunk" Sufis as they have been dubbed by Western scholars. Although these individuals regularly exceeded the boundaries of faith as practiced by most Muslim societies, they nevertheless represent a dynamic component of Islam. Our analysis of this particular segment of Islamic mysticism regularly raises eyebrows among the conservative students in the class who bristle upon hearing of the practices of the ecstatic Sufis who lived in cities such as Baghdad during the 10th century. Individuals such as Al-Hallaj (922 CE) who declared himself to be the Truth (he saw himself as the reflection of God), remind the class of the different perspectives that exist within the Muslim tradition (Massignon, 1982). Interestingly, studying these less mainstream perspectives also serves to reveal some biases that some of the more conservative Muslim students have against Sufism. Because of the heterodox status of these extreme Sufis, many modern students simply discount the entire movement altogether without first realizing the prevalence of mysticism within the Islamic tradition during the medieval period.

Teaching a survey course on the Muslim world offers various challenges, least of which is deciding what to include in the curriculum. Time ultimately dictates that a great deal of information is left out of the curriculum. However, by focusing on the early development of the faith along with some of the key passages from the Qur'an, students can garner an understanding of some of the major themes and goals of the religion. Moreover, analyzing some of the cultural, legal, and social achievements spearheaded by Muslim leaders, scholars and mystics will provide students with a deeper understanding of Islamic civilization. This type of knowledge is crucial in an ever-shrinking world. Moreover, as Western societies turn toward immigrants to sustain their population base, there will be a heightened need to understand the nuances of the various new immigrant communities that lay down roots in the West. Toward this end, my course plays a miniscule role in helping uncover some of the complexities of Islamic civilization.

References

Broome, M. (1985). *A handbook of Islamic coins.* London: Seaby Press.
Bullock, K. (2007). *Rethinking Muslim women and the veil.* London: International Institute of Islamic Thought.
Chittick, W. (2000). *Sufism: A short introduction.* Oxford: Oxford University Press.
Cook, D. (2005). *Understanding Jihad.* Berkeley, CA: University of California Press.
Cook, M. (2000). *The Koran: A very short introduction.* New York: Oxford University Press.
El Sakkakini, W. (1982). *First among Sufis: The life and thought of Rabia al-Adawiyya, the woman saint of Basra.* N. Safwat (Trans.), London: Octagon Press.
Glick, T. F. (1979). *Islamic and Christian Spain in the early Middle Ages.* Princeton: Princeton University Press.
Hallaq, W. (2009). *An introduction to Islamic law.* Cambridge: Cambridge University Press.
Hekmat, A. (1997). *Women and the Koran: The status of women in Islam.* New York: Prometheus Books.
Hoyland R. G. (2001). *Arabia and the Arabs: From the Bronze Age to the coming of Islam.* London: Routledge.
Kennedy, H. (2007). *The great Arab conquests: How the spread of Islam changed the world we live in.* London: Weidenfeld and Nicolson.
Koran. (1998). M.A.S. Abdel Haleem (Trans.). New York: Oxford University Press.
Massignon, L. (1982). *The passion of al-Hallaj, mystic and martyr of Islam.* H. Mason (Trans.), Princeton, NJ: Princeton University Press.
Peters, F. E. (1994). *The Hajj: The Muslim pilgrimage to Mecca and the holy places.* Princeton, NJ: Princeton University Press.
Pipes, D. (1981). *Slave soldiers and Islam: The genesis of a military system.* New Haven, CT: Yale University Press.
Rizvi, Rizwan Ali S. (1978). *Nizam al-Mulk: His contribution to statecraft, political theory and the art of government.* Lahore: Muhammad Ashraf.
Zeitlin, Irving M. (2007). *The historical Muhammad.* Cambridge: Malden Press.

Twenty

"How Do You Expect Me to Teach This without Any Resources?"

Melanie Stonebanks

> Alone, now you are free
> You pick a sky and name it
> a sky to live in
> a sky to refuse
> But to know that you are free
> and to remain free
> you must steady yourself on a foothold of earth
> so that the earth may rise
> so that you may give wings to all
> the children of the earth.
> Saadi Youssef

I suppose the word to best describe what I was feeling at that moment was shock. Yes, shock which was instantaneously followed by surprise, disbelief, and then uncertainty. I scanned the room, my eyes searching for a glimmer of acknowledgment—a connection, a possibility, a window through which the conversation could begin. My smile remained perfectly in place, never once giving away the overwhelming confusion brought on by the lack of response to what I truly believed to be a simple question. What was my query that appeared to stump my colleagues, seasoned teachers, and respected leaders in the field of education?

> What resources and lessons have you been applying in your classrooms in order to teach against Islamophobia?

Quickly my mind raced, searching for a reason as to why the anticipated chorus of book titles, critical questions, and conversation starters for young minds were not forthcoming. I settled on the possibility that maybe the concept of Islamophobia was new to them. Maybe due to the fact they were somewhat removed from the current trends and language of the academic world, they had simply not heard the term before and therefore couldn't make direct connections to all the wonderful teaching and learning that had taken place in their classrooms.

Now, I must be honest at this point. I myself didn't have much to add to the conversation either. I had been in the field of education for over 15 years and could hardly think of a single lesson that I had taught where the notion of "Teaching against Islamophobia" had either been a part of the overt or covert curriculum that I was providing for my students. There was one unit on poetry that I had done with my grade six class that investigated the work of Hafez and some other Sufi poets as well as sharing our home spring celebration of Noruz (my children are part Iranian on their father's side) and a fund-raising campaign spearheaded by my students to help raise money after the Bam, Iran earthquake in 2003, but other than that my contribution in this area was quite lacking. My question to my colleagues was a genuine one, in hopes of gaining some new insight, some direction, and ultimately some brilliant children's books and resources that I could use and recommend to others.

As a mother of three children ranging in ages from four to fourteen, I have had plenty of experience trying to engage their teachers into professional pedagogical dialog around such topics as selected book choice, concept, and thematic curriculum development as well as direction for student critical thinking and questioning. A few would make the attempt to talk around the issues and then politely excuse themselves from the conversation, while others simply wouldn't even respond to my enquiry. I recall the time my eldest was in grade 2 and she came home talking about the book *The Lion, the Witch and the Wardrobe* by C.S. Lewis, which her teacher was reading to the class. I had read the Narnia series myself as a child and coming from a white, middle-class Protestant upbringing had failed to notice any of the subtle and not so subtle anti-Islam/Muslim undertones (or should I say overtones). Through discussions with my husband, followed by some research into the author and his work, it became quite clear that this was an opportunity for the teacher, if she so wanted, to approach the book with a critical literacy lens. We then sent a letter to school explaining our daughter's heritage (highlighting the European Iranian mix), my own experiences with the book, and some recent research on the author's religious leanings as well as some possible ideas on how to assist young children develop into critical readers. I would like to say that this was the beginning of our conversation but it was not. This is where the dialog began and ended. The teacher, for whatever reason, did not respond, complete silence, and another potential window to "teach against Islamophobia" was closed.

There is the distinct possibility that the concept of critical literacy was foreign to her, as it may be to others reading this chapter. In order for us all to be on the same page, let me offer a brief definition of the term and how it can be applied in the elementary school setting. Following this I will present three potential resources for the classroom paired with a critical analysis of each text to illustrate how one might facilitate young students in the process of "reading between the lines" and developing critical thinking and questioning skills.

Critical Literacy

Luke (1997) describes critical literacy as a "commitment to reshape literacy education in the interests of marginalized groups of learners, who on the basis of gender, cultural and socioeconomic background have been excluded from access to the discourses and texts of dominant economics and cultures" (p. 143). Critical literacy can be more simply defined as "the ability to read texts in an active, reflective manner in order to better understand power, inequality, and injustice in human relationships" (Coffey, 2008). For the purposes of critical literacy, *text* is defined as a "vehicle through which individuals communicate with one another using the codes and conventions of society" (Robinson & Robinson, 2003, p. 3). Therefore, in the elementary classroom setting, illustrated picture books, novels, conversations, songs, pictures, movies, and the like are all considered texts. One must at all times remember that central to this is the notion of dialog, or in Freire's terms, "reading the word" and "reading the world" (Freire & Macedo, 1987).

The development of critical literacy skills enables people to interpret messages in the modern world through a critical lens and challenge the power relations within those messages. Teachers who facilitate the development of critical literacy encourage students to interrogate societal issues and institutions like family, poverty, education, equity, and equality in order to critique the structures that serve as norms as well as to demonstrate how these norms are not experienced by all members of society (Coffey, 2008).

Critical literacy is a way to use texts to help children better understand themselves, others, and the world around them. Using children's literature, teachers can help their class through difficult situations, enable individual students to transcend their own challenges, and teach students to consider all viewpoints, respect differences, and become more self-aware.

There are many activities that are already going on in our classrooms that build critical literacy. Reading novels written from the point of view of a child, from another culture or set in another country; sharing stories about families and their religious traditions or considering the lives of young people like them who lived through war, persecution, or poverty; as well, when we ask our students to write from the point of view of someone else—all of these classroom experiences are ways of developing critical literacy. As Melissa Thibault (2004) reminds us, these activities all serve the same purpose: they help the student to see the world through someone else's eyes, to learn to understand other people's circumstances and perspectives, and to empathize with them.

A Critical Conversation

I need to preface the upcoming book selections by stating that I am in no way forwarding them as exemplary works that must be used in every classroom nor am I stating that they should be censored. As I have learned, each of us comes to literacy with our own perspective, our own history and experience, and our own knowledge and understanding. What I am proposing is a detailed analysis of three eminent illustrated picture books with Muslim main characters. At the end of the chapter is a list of children's books with Muslim and related cultural themes that could easily be used as a springboard into critical literacy conversations with colleagues and students alike. What I hope to offer is a point of entry into what has been and remains in most North American classrooms a curriculum that is for the most part neglected, misunderstood, or feared.

One Green Apple (2006) by Eve Bunting is the story of a Muslim girl, Farah, on her 2nd day in a new school and in a new country. She is joining her class on a field trip to an apple orchard and one cannot help but experience along with her the isolation she feels as she is set apart from her classmates in her inability to speak English and the reactions she receives by wearing a *dupatta* (headscarf). At the cider press, Farah adds a single green apple to her classmates' red apples, and although they protest at first, they happily drink up the sweet juice from the mixed apples and Farah begins to see some common threads between this culture and her own.

This story can heighten youngsters' awareness of and empathy for the immigrant experience as well as what it must be like to feel different and alone. However, the cider-making activity along with Farah's statement "I will blend with others the way my apple blended with the cider" presents a very unidirectional assimilationist view as Farah's ultimate satisfaction arises from her "blending" in with her classmates. As Muzzillo (2008) reminds us "The other children do not learn her language; she adopts theirs. They do not wear the *dupatta*; she wears the jeans and tee shirt they all sport. When Farah's apple is chewed up unrecognizably in the cider press, Bunting speaks through the girl; the girl imagines an effect on the overall product, but we are given no confirmation from other perspectives that her presence makes a difference at all" (p. 2).

I can easily think of myself doing an activity like this one at the beginning of the school year and not giving it a second thought. However, as a Canadian teacher, the idea of promoting a lesson steeped in an American "melting pot" vision as opposed to a Canadian mosaic model is somewhat problematic. But, isn't it curious that I can imagine myself doing it?

Children's author, Rukhsana Khan (2006), boldly adds a strong voice to the conversation in stating "A community trying to express itself often starts with such didactic and issue-driven stories. These books serve a purpose and make good starting points for discussion, but I'd like to see the trend move away from these 'Muslim as victim' scenarios. In these stories, being Muslim is part of the conflict. I'd like to see a character's Islamic identity be like wallpaper, part of the setting—providing flavor but definitely not part of the problem" (p. 20).

Khan (2006) continues to forward another issue prevalent in today's literature in that many authors "use a simplistic approach and take Western-styled heroes and heroines and plunk them into Muslim-styled settings with plots based on timely political issues from abusive fathers to horrible theocratic regimes. By dealing in such shallow stereotypes these books do little to create genuine understanding. In fact, their appeal seems to involve indirectly preaching that Western culture is superior" (pp. 11–12).

A book that seems to be heading in the anticipated direction is *Sami and the Time of the Troubles* (1992) by Florence Parry Heide and Judith Heide Gilliland. In this story, 10-year-old Sami lives in Beirut, Lebanon. He and his family spend most of their time in the basement of his uncle's home as bombing and gunfire fill the streets. Memories abound of a time "before the time of the troubles" and "the day of the children." They sit listening to the radio and venture outside when the fighting subsides for the moment. There Sami goes to the beach, makes a fort with his friend and plays at war. This time outdoors is short lived, and as the story closes we are back in the basement with Sami listening to the "noises of the night."

Children as victims of war even when not directly in the line of battle are not unusual figures in children's literature. This text though makes clear that war threatens not only physical survival but affects the human spirit as well. It is not done in a "let's feel sorry for Sami" sort of way but instead gives us a thoughtful, understated narrative which forces us to think about current warfare and its effects on the innocent. We leave the story understanding how children and others try to carry on a normal life during a period of war and uncertainty.

One book that will bring about much dialog and discussion not only with young students but with teachers and educational leaders as well is Jeanette Winter's *The Librarian of Basra: A True Story from Iraq* (2005). In brief, the story is about the courageous exploits of Alia Muhammad Baker, chief librarian of Basra's Central Library, who was responsible for saving 70% of her library's book collection. In April 2003, the invasion of Iraq reaches Basra. With the government refusing to help, she, along with friends and community members, transfers some 30, 000 volumes first to a nearby restaurant and then to various homes only days before the library is burned to the ground.

Without a doubt, this story illustrates the impact one person can have in order to bring people together to work for a common cause. As well, it emphasizes the influence and value libraries and books have on cultures and communities all around the world. At this point, what also needs to be mentioned is this was one of the very first books where the main character was from the Middle East to find its way into elementary classrooms post-9/11. A great many children saw themselves in print and illustration for the very first time. Here their culture and their heritage were highlighted in a heroic and powerful manner. Thanks to this text, strength, bravery, and selflessness were now depicted as qualities and characteristics synonymous with Islam.

In our home, my husband (see Chapter Two) and I have had countless discussions over curriculum, classrooms, and how to put theory into practice always with the principal intention of developing strategies that encourage teachers to use their classrooms as locations for social transformation, student empowerment, and social justice. Recently, one of our exchanges centered on this very book. What follows is part of his thinking about what is missing from many of the lesson and unit plans that have been developed on *The Librarian of Basra* for elementary classroom use.

> When I first read it, one aspect about it I found troubling is that it "whitewashes" US/British (the whole coalition of the willing) culpability in the act. The only time we see a flag is the large Iraqi flag that is above the unsympathetic governor. The bomber planes, the tanks, the soldiers, none of them carries the symbols of the US or mentions the US. I've read it with our children and we've talked about it. None of them see it as being a story that relates to the West. It is framed in a "war is always happening in that part of the world." Even the jacket of the book mentions that Iraq is "… a war stricken country where civilians—especially women—have little power …" overlooking the significant outrage (by people like Iraqi artist Haifa Zangana) that women had greater power in Iraq before the US invasion. "War" in this book, has simply "come to this country." (Christopher Darius Stonebanks, personal correspondence)

He is not alone in his critical deconstruction. Khan (2006) joins in the dialog by admitting that as she was compiling a list of children's books that promoted positive Muslim storylines she "felt conflicted when it came to including two picture-book stories about the now well-known efforts of Alia Muhammad Baker, the 'Librarian of Basra'." She qualifies her feelings by acknowledging "I found it condescending that Jeanette Winter would focus on saving books when there were so many human victims. It would be like writing a book about a New York librarian fretting over the damage to her collection on Sept. 11th" (p. 28). Powerful words, indeed, that many would not put out in print for the world to see. Not being one to simply end the conversation there, Khan corresponded with a mother in Syria who presented a different perspective and helped change her position. The anonymous mother contended that "She viewed the books quite differently. She liked them because they were about a woman in horrendous circumstances who couldn't do much about the carnage around her but she could do this one thing. She could save these books for when peace would return. And her efforts showed how very much knowledge was valued in her culture." (p. 28). Powerful words, yet again!

As a resource for my own or any classroom, I know reading and sharing this book can help to make a difference in the lives of so many students; and even though it does not discuss the war and political issues in detail, simply being aware of what has been left out from this author's story would be an appropriate conversation starter for children of all ages and their teachers.

A Place to Start

In order to properly prepare our students to be literate in this ever-changing technological and multimodal world, we teachers need to reflect upon and challenge our own beliefs and understanding of literacy. Harwood (2008) advocates that "educators need to challenge children and provide balanced literacy opportunities that value the social-cultural construction of knowledge while reflecting the diversity of children's lives" (p. 25). She strongly supports the notion that classroom "opportunities to collaborate, discuss, critique, deconstruct, and reconstruct a multitude of *meaningful* and *radical* texts (Kohl, 1995) are equally important in literacy development as learning to identify phonemes of sound" (p. 25).

For the sake of brevity, the definition of "radical texts" has been borrowed from Leland, Harste, Ociepka, Lewison, and Vazquez's (1999) suggestions for choosing critical texts. Radical texts chosen for elementary aged children should meet the following criteria:

- Texts don't make difference invisible but rather explore what differences *make a difference*;
- Texts enrich children's understanding of history and life by giving voice to those who have been traditionally silenced or marginalized;

- Texts show how people can begin to take action on important social issues;
- Texts should explore dominant systems of meaning that operate in our society to position people and groups of people;
- Texts should not provide "happily ever after" endings for complex social problems. (p. 70)

Children can be encouraged to think critically and answer critical questions that will enable them to examine their own insights as well as those presented in texts. Teachers need to encourage children to challenge the status quo of what is represented within texts, asking questions such as:

- Whose voice is heard and whose voice is left out?"
- Who is the intended reader? (For example, asking, is the text intended for specific groups of people and if so how is that group portrayed?)
- What was the world like when the text was created?
- What does the author want you to feel or think?
- What does the author expect you to know or value?
- What does the text say about boys (about girls)?
- Is it important that the main character is beautiful (powerful/wealthy)? (Harwood, 2008)

This list is not exhaustive, and the critical questions that arise will often depend on the children and the issue involved. There is no single "recipe" of how to incorporate critical literacy within an elementary school curriculum, so teachers need to work against the "commodification" (Luke & Freebody, 1999, p. 6) of critical literacy, as they begin to recognize the important benefits of fostering children's critical viewing of texts. Harwood (2008) does well to remind us that children's interests and questions should also be incorporated into the literacy curriculum and form an important addition to the critical questions that arise. By honoring children's own natural curiosity and using their inquisitiveness as a starting point, greater depth and engagement with texts is possible.

Conclusion

As an eternal optimist, I have to admit that I tend to prefer stories that have happy endings. If you don't have the same affinity for "warm fuzzies" then you are free to skim over what I offer up as a "happy beginning" rather than a "happy ending." A short while back, I walked into a room where a couple of my colleagues were sitting hard at work, deep in the throes of curriculum development. As I approached to see what they were doing, one dear friend looked up at me, her face bursting with excitement, "Oh! I'm so glad you're here! I have found a wonderful book that I know you're going to love!" As I watched her sift through the pile of children's books that lay strewn across the table, I wondered what marvellous gem she was about to share with me. *The Golden Sandal: A Middle Eastern Cinderella Story* by Rebecca Hickox was the title she eagerly placed in my hands. Shock, surprise, and disbelief again washed over me, but this time confusion did not follow. Instead, what came next was a lengthy conversation about the book, the storyline, and all the possibilities that could come from sharing this piece of literature with our students. We are not living happily ever after yet, but I do believe with exchanges of ideas such as this one, we are one step closer than we were before.

> Everybody said it was useless
> Everybody said, "you're trying to lean on sun dust"
> that the beloved before whose tree I stand
> can't be reached
>
> Everybody said, "you're crazy to throw yourself
> headlong into a volcano and sing"
> Everybody said that salty mountains
> won't even yield one glass of wine
> Everybody said, "You can't dance on one foot"
> Everybody said there won't be any lights at the party
> That's what they all said
> but everybody came to the party anyway
> Qasim Haddad

References

Coffey, H. (2008). *Critical literacy. LEARN North Carolina.* Retrieved November 22, 2009 http://www.learnnc.org/articles/article?id=maples0601

Freire, P. & Macedo. D. (1987). *Literacy: Reading the world and the word.* Westport, CT: Heinemann.

Harwood, D. (2008). "Deconstructing and reconstructing Cinderella: Theoretical defense of critical literacy for young children. *Language and Literacy,* 10(2, Fall). Retrieved December 1, 2009 from http://www.langandlit.ualberta.ca/Fall2008/Harwood.htm

Khan, R. (2006). Muslims in children's books: An author looks back at the ongoing publishing challenges. *School Library Journal.* Retrieved November 22, 2009 from http://www.schoollibraryjournal.com/article/CA6367083.html

Kohl, H. (1995). *Should we burn Babar? Essays on children's literature and the power of stories.* New York: The New Press.

Leland, C., Harste, J., Ociepka, A., Lewison, M., & Vazquez, V. (1999). Exploring critical literacy: You can hear a pin drop. *Language Arts,* 77(1), 70–77.

Luke, A. (1997). Critical approaches to literacy. In V. Edwards & D. Corson (Eds.), *Encyclopedia of language and education, Vol. 2: Literacy* (pp. 143–151). Dordrecht, The Netherlands: Kluwer Academic Publishers.

Luke, A., & Freebody, P. (1999). A map of possible practices: Further notes on the four resources model. *Practically Primary,* 4(2), 3–8.

Muzzillo, J. (2008) *A first opinion: Learning about difference*. Retrieved November 22, 2009 from http://docs.lib.purdue.edu/cgi/viewcontent.cgi?article=1026&context=fosr

Robinson, E., & Robinson, S. (2003). *What does it mean? Discourse, text, culture: An introduction*. Sydney: McGraw-Hill.

Thibault, M. (2004). *Children's literature promotes understanding*. LEARN, North Carolina. Retrieved November 22, 2009 from http://www.learnnc.org/articles/article?id=maples0601

Further Resources

Bunting, E. (2006). *One green apple*. New York: Clarion Books.

Habbas, C. (2008). *The runaway scarf*. Tempe, AZ: Muslim Writers Publishing.

Heide, F. P., & Gilliland, J. H. (1990). *The day of Ahmed's secret*. New York: Mulberry Books.

Heide, F. P., & Gilliland, J. H. (1992). *Sami and the time of the troubles*. New York: Clarion Books.

Hickox, R. (1999). *The golden sandal: A Middle Eastern Cinderella story*. New York: Holiday House.

Khan, R. (1988). *The roses in my carpets*. Markham, ON: Fitzhenry & Whiteside.

Mobin-Uddin, A. (2005). *My name is Bilal*. Honesdale, PA: Boyds Mills Press.

Mortenson, G., & Roth, S. L. (2009). *Listen to the wind: The story of Dr. Greg & three cups of tea*. New York: Dial Books.

O'Brien, T. & Sullivan, M. (2008). *Afghan dreams: Young voices of Afghanistan*. New York: Bloomsbury.

Oppenheim, S. L. (1995). *The hundredth name*. Honesdale, PA: Boyds Mills Press.

Robert, N. B. (2002). *The swirling Hijaab*. London: Mantra Lingua.

Rumford, J. (2008). *Silent music*. New York: Roaring Brook Press.

Shihab Nye, N. (1994). *19 varieties of Gazelle: Poems of the Middle East*. New York: Harper Collins.

Shihab Nye, N. (1994). *Sitti's secrets*. New York: Aladdin Paperbacks.

Shihab Nye, N. (1998). *The flag of childhood: Poems from the Middle East*. New York: Aladdin Paperbacks.

Williams, K. L. & Mohammed, K. (2007). *Four feet, two sandals*. Grand Rapids, MI: Wm. B. Eerdmans Publishing Co.

Winter, J. (2005). *The librarian of Basra: A true story from Iraq*. Orlando: Harcourt.

Contributors

SAMAA ABDURRAQIB is completing her dissertation (U Wisconsin-Madison) on the contested overlap between the concepts of home and nation in diasporic women's writing. Her research focuses on the intersection and conflict between discourses of diaspora and homes that are rendered unsafe by factors such as domestic violence and political turmoil. Her interests include women's writing, multiethnic and immigrant literature, and violence against women. Her work has been published in MELUS and a new anthology entitled *Arab Voices in Diaspora*. Samaa is also hilarious.

CAROLYNE ALI-KHAN is a high school teacher who specializes in alternative high school settings, and is completing her doctorate in the Urban Education Program at the CUNY Graduate Center. She has worked with youth on conflict resolution, HIV peer education, political theatre projects, international cooperative educational projects, art-based education, and Restorative Practices. She graduated from the International School of Islamabad, Pakistan, received her BA in Anthropology from the American University in Cairo, Egypt and her Masters degree in Education from the University of Bath, England. She travels to Pakistan frequently and in addition has lived/worked/studied in Germany, Ghana, Jordan, Japan and Canada. Her publications include works in the journals *Qualitative Inquiry* and *Cultural Studies of*

Science Education, and in *Muslim Voices in School* edited by Özlem Sensoy and Christopher Darius Stonebanks.

YASSIN ALSALMAN, AKA The Narcicyst, Narcel X, is a Media Studies graduate and a multi-media multi-tasker. A journalist, MC, producer, novelist and actor, Yassin is an Iraqi-Canadian that delved his identity issues into the magazine of life, making music and film about the hyphenated Arab experience. Starting off as the lead MC of Euphrates, Arab Hip-Hop's underground heroes, he flowed his way through post-9/11 media inundation and bombarded stereotypes engendered by a post-war world. His albums have taken him on tours through North America, the Middle East and Europe, whereas his writing has brought him attention worldwide. After graduating with a Masters in Media Studies, Yassin became one of the first people in North America to tackle Arab identity formation and Hip-Hop through his thesis study and album *Fear of an Arab Planet.* On the verge of releasing it as a book, as well as writing a to-be-titled fiction novel; Yassin is anti-public enemy number 1. Catch him on the silver screen in his acting debut as Khalfan in Dubai's *City of Life*. His newest video can be viewed at http://www.youtube.com/watch?v=TtoHCUMpNMY.

NAVED BAKALI is a Mathematics and Ethics & Religious Culture teacher at Heritage Regional High School in St. Hubert, Quebec. He is currently pursuing graduate studies at McGill University in the Department of Integrated Studies in Education and resides in Montreal with his wife.

JEHANZEB DAR IS a Pakistani Muslim-American writer, blogger, and independent filmmaker. His articles have been published on Muslim feminist websites such as "AltMuslimah" and "Muslimah Media Watch," and on anti-racist outlets like "Racialicious." He won the 2008 Brass Crescent Award for "Best Series" on his two-part essay on Muslim women in comic books. Also in 2008, he won the Wellness Connection's "College Competition" for directing the best anti-smoking commercial, which played on MTV in the Philadelphia region.

MICHAEL D. GIARDINA is a visiting assistant professor of advertising and cultural studies at the University of Illinois, Urbana-Champaign. He is the author or editor of several books, including *Sporting Pedagogies: Performing Culture & Identity in the Global Arena* (Peter Lang, 2005) and *Contesting Empire/Globalizing Dissent: Cultural Studies after 9/11* (2006, with Norman K. Denzin). He is the Associate Editor of *Sociology of Sport Journal,* and a member of the editorial board of *Cultural Studies<>Critical Methodologies.*

AWAD IBRAHIM is an Associate Professor at the Faculty of Education, University of Ottawa, Canada. He is a curriculum theorist and teaches and publishes in the areas of cultural studies, critical theory and applied linguistics. He is the editor (with Samy Alim and Alastair Pennycook) of *Global Linguistic Flows: Hip-Hop Cultures, Youth Identities and the Politics of Language*.

ANASTASIA KAMANOS GAMELIN'S research and development activities have focused on women in higher education, diversity, teacher training, language and literacy; and qualitative methodologies, including narrative, visual, feminist, arts-based and autobiographical inquiry. She was awarded a postdoctoral research fellowship from GREAPE (research in ethnicity and pluralism in education) at the University of Montreal's Center for Ethnic Studies and is a member of the Image and Identity Research Collective (www.iirc.mcgill.ca). The collaborators of IIRC share an interest in developing interdisciplinary, image-based research methodologies and artistic forms of representation for the Humanities and the Social Sciences. Dr. Kamanos has taught at universities in Canada, the United States and has been involved in establishing the first private universities for women in Saudi Arabia and Bahrain.

JOE L. KINCHELOE (1950–2008) was the quintessential scholar and humanitarian. The author of over 55 books, and hundreds of articles, Joe traveled extensively with Shirley Steinberg, giving tag-team presentations to schools, political organizations, and community groups. He was the co-creator of the Urban Education Doctorate at the CUNY Graduate Center and has scores of students now teaching in higher education all over the world. His last book was *Knowledge and Critical Pedagogy* (Springer, 2008), and he left six unfinished manuscripts and many songs, poems, and a novel. His research/teaching involved devising and engaging students in new, more intellectually rigorous, socially just ways of analyzing and researching education. He developed an evolving notion of criticality that constructed innovative ways to cultivate the intellect as it worked in anti-oppressive and affectively engaging ways. Joe founded the Paulo and Nita Freire International Project for Critical Pedagogy which aims to improve the contribution that education makes to social justice and the democratic quality of people's lives. His most recent work and rage centered around the nature of racism and anti-Islamic/Arab issues which pervade North American society. Joe is the father of Ian and Christine, Meghann and Ryan, Chaim and Marissa, and Bronwyn, and the *zaydeh* of Maci, Luna, Cohen, Hava, Tobias, Seth, and Milo Joe. He is eternally loved and missed.

DANIEL LUNA (cover artist) was born and raised in Colorado, and now lives in Denver with his wife, Paula and his son, Lucas. He tries to paint and have fun every day.

SEVAK JOSEPH MANJIKIAN teaches Religious Studies and Humanities at Vanier College. His area of specialty is multiculturalism in general and the use of Islamic law in non-Muslim societies in particular. He holds a doctorate from McGill University's Institute of Islamic Studies.

HASSAN AHMAD MIAN is in his final year of studies to obtain his teacher certification, having previously successfully studied exegesis, grammar, scholastic theology, logic, jurisprudence, legalistic methodology and Sufism under traditional Islamic authorities. He has taught courses on Islamic jurisprudence and spirituality at the university level.

KHURRUM MIRZA teaches Social Sciences at a high school in the greater Montreal area and is pursuing his Master's degree in Educational Administration.

PREACHER MOSS, founder of the internationally acclaimed "Allah Made Me Funny" comedy tour and is a lecturer, writer, and activists on the concept of Muslim Imaging, and diversity issues. Recognized as the Best Diversity Artist for the last two years on college campuses, Moss is a leading social commentator on the scene today.

YOUNES MOURCHID has been an Associate Professor of International Studies and Director of Degrees at a Distance Programs at Cogswell College. Initially trained as a journalist and a linguist, Younes published over 25 editorials in the Moroccan newspaper *L'Opinion*, served as editor of *Newsweek* in Arabic between 2002 and 2005. Younes has focused his academic research on issues of higher education reform and globalization in the Arab world and on issues of identity formation among Muslim immigrants in the West. Younes authored a number of chapters addressing a variety of issues in identity formation and peace education in peer-reviewed journals. Younes' current teaching and research interests revolve around co-relational topics in Middle Eastern Studies and Identity Education. His goal has been to create teaching and textual nuggets deriving directly from the perspective of peoples and native scholars of the Middle East.

KRISTA RILEY'S chapter in this book is drawn from her thesis, "Reading Racism: Race and Privilege in Young Adult Fiction." Krista writes regularly for

Muslimah Media Watch (www.muslimahmediawatch.org), a blog that examines representations of Muslim women in media and popular culture.

FIDA SANJAKDAR is a Lecturer in Curriculum and Pedagogy in the Faculty of Education at Monash University, Melbourne, Australia. She is a scholar of critical pedagogy, curriculum reform and sexuality education. She has written widely about Muslim youth and sexual identities.

ÖZLEM SENSOY is an assistant professor in the Faculty of Education at Simon Fraser University. A frequent international speaker and writer, she often addresses issues of anti-Muslim activity and oppression. She is the co-editor (with Christopher Stonebanks) of *Muslim Voices in School: Narratives of Identity and Pluralism*.

SHIRLEY R. STEINBERG is the co-founder and director of The Paulo and Nita Freire International Project for Critical Pedagogy. She is a distinguished scholar at The University of Barcelona, and teaches at McGill University. She is the author and editor of many books in critical pedagogy, urban and youth culture, and cultural studies. Her most recent books include: *19 Urban Questions: Teaching in the City* (2010); *Christotainment: Selling Jesus Through Popular Culture* (with Joe Kincheloe, 2009); *Diversity and Multiculturalism: A Reader* (2009); *Media Literacy: A Reader* (2007); the award-winning *Contemporary Youth Culture: An International Encyclopedia*; *Kinderculture: The Corporate Construction of Childhood* (2010); and *The Miseducation of the West: How Schools and Media Distort Our Understanding of the Islam World* (with Joe Kincheloe, 2004). She is currently finishing two books: *Writing and Publishing* (Fall 2010) and *The Bricolage and Qualitative Research* (Fall 2010). A regular contributor to CBC Radio One, CTV, *The Toronto Globe and Mail*, *The Montreal Gazette*, and Canadian Press, she is an internationally known speaker and teacher. She is also the founding editor of *Taboo: The Journal of Culture and Education*, and the managing editor of *The International Journal of Critical Pedagogy*. The organizer of The Baeza Congress, she is committed to a global community of transformative educators and community workers engaged in radical love, social justice, and the situating of power within social and cultural contexts.

H.G. SIAM is tall, big headed, big eared but mostly big footed. Not abnormally, but definitely head and shoulders above average. Born on Christmas Day, a stone's throw away from Bethlehem, he is closer to Jesus Christ than blond, blue-eyed renditions in European and North American churches. He self-describes as an Arab man whose ego speaks a foreign tongue, sometimes French, but mostly English. H.G. has lived in 6 countries and 9 different cities in his under-30 years. He belongs both nowhere and everywhere—a state of being that is both a gift and a curse. He is currently completing a doctorate in education and media studies, taking life one day at a time, trying not to choke someone in the process. His love of Hip Hop has helped him remain level-headed.

CHRISTOPHER DARIUS STONEBANKS is an Associate Professor of Education and currently the Chair of the Research Ethics Board at Bishop's University. Raised in North America of mixed Iranian-European descent, he often brings the experience of living the life as the Other to his teaching, research and writing. Recent publications, such as "Spartan Superhunks and Persian Monsters: Responding to Truth and Identity as Determined by Hollywood" (*Journal of Symbolic Interactionism*, 2008) and "If Nancy Drew Wouldn't Wear a Hijab, Would the Hardy Boys Wear a Kufi?" (*Muslim Voices in Schools: Narratives of Identity and Pluralism*, 2009) explore the failings of mainstream multiculturalism to recognize the continued prejudice in the media and education settings regarding Muslims and people commonly associated with Islam.

MELANIE STONEBANKS has been an elementary teacher for the past 15 years. She is presently a lecturer at McGill University and is a consultant for Quebec's Ministère de l'Éducation, du Loisir et du Sport, focusing on English Language Arts and the newly developed Ethics and Religious Culture program. Recent publications include "Religious Identity in Schools and the Looking Glass Self" (2009) and "Religion and Diversity in our Classrooms" (2008) both co-authored with her husband, Christopher Darius Stonebanks. Being the mother of three children of mixed ethnic and religious heritage, she has become increasingly interested in the manner in which schools create curriculum to foster the development of respect and positive self-image.